Also in the Variorum Collected Studies Series:

T.D. BARNES
Early Christianity and the Roman Empire

BRIAN CROKE
Christian Chronicles and Byzantine History, 5th-6th Centuries

LESLIE S.B. MACCOULL
Coptic Perspectives on late Antiquity

C.R. WHITTAKER
Land, City and Trade in the Roman Empire

FRANK M. CLOVER
The Late Roman West and the Vandals

JOSEPH MÉLÈZE-MODRZEJEWSKI
Statut personnel et liens de famille dans les droits de l'Antiquité

R.A. MARKUS
From Augustine to Gregory the Great
History and Christianity in Late Antiquity

SEBASTIAN BROCK
Studies in Syriac Christianity: History, Literature, Theology

LUISE ABRAMOWSKI
Formula and Context: Studies in Early Christian Thought

W.H.C. FREND
Archaeology and History in the Study of Early Christianity

CHARLES KANNENGIESSER
Arius and Athanasius: Two Alexandrian Theologians

CHARLES MUNIER
Autorité épiscopale et sollicitude pastorale (IIe-VIe siècles)

HENRY CHADWICK
Heresy and Orthodoxy in the Early Church

HENRY CHADWICK
History and Thought of the Early Church

VARIORUM COLLECTED STUDIES SERIES

From Eusebius to Augustine

Professor T.D. Barnes

T. D. Barnes

From Eusebius to Augustine

Selected Papers 1982–1993

ASHGATE
VARIORUM

This edition copyright © 1994 T. D. Barnes

Published in the Variorum Collected Studies Series by

Ashgate Publishing Limited
Gower House, Croft Road,
Aldershot, Hampshire GU11 3HR
Great Britain

Ashgate Publishing Company
Suite 420, 101 Cherry Street
Burlington, Vermont 05401–4405
USA

Ashgate website: http://www.ashgate.com

Reprinted 2004

ISBN 0-86078-397-9

British Library CIP Data
    Barnes, Timothy D.
    From Eusebius to Augustine: Selected Papers, 1982-93
    (Variorum Collected Studies Series; CS 438)
    I. Title II. Series
    270

U.S. Library of Congress CIP Data
    Barnes, Timothy David.
    From Eusebius to Augustine: Selected Papers, 1982-93 / T.D. Barnes
    p. cm. -- (Collected Studies Series: CS438)
    Includes bibliographical references (p. xxx-xxx).
    ISBN 0-86078-397-9 (alk. paper)
    1. Church history--4th century. 2. Constantine I, Emperor of
    Rome, d. 337--Religion.
    I. Title. II. Series: Collected Studies Series:CS438.
    BR205.B38 1994
    270.2--dc20

The paper used in this publication meets the minimum requirements of the
American National Standard for Information Sciences – Permanence
of Paper for Printed Library Materials, ANSI Z39.48-1984. ∞ ™

Printed in Great Britain by Biddles Limited, King's Lynn

VARIORUM COLLECTED STUDIES SERIES CS438

CONTENTS

Preface   ix–xi

PART ONE: INTRODUCTORY

I   Pagan perceptions of Christianity   231–243
Early Christianity. Origins and Evolution to A.D. 600.
In honour of W.H.C. Frend, ed. I. Hazlett London:
S.P.C.K., 1991

II   Some inconsistencies in Eusebius   470–475
Journal of Theological Studies N.S. 35. Oxford:
Oxford University Press, 1984

PART TWO: CONSTANTINE

III   The conversion of Constantine   371–391
Échos du Monde Classique/Classical Views, N.S. 4.
Calgary, Alta.: University of Calgary Press, 1985

IV   Constantine's prohibition of pagan sacrifice   69–72
American Journal of Philology 105. Baltimore, Md.:
John Hopkins University Press, 1984

V   The Constantinian reformation   39–57
The Crake Lectures 1984. Sackville, New Brunswick:
The Crake Memorial Foundation, 1986

VI   Constantine and the Christians of Persia   126–136
Journal of Roman Studies 75. London: Society for the
Promotion of Roman Studies, 1985

VII   The religious affiliation of consuls and prefects, 317–361   1–11
First publication

VIII   Pagans and Christians in the reign of Constantius   322–337
Entretiens sur l'Antiquité Classique 34.
Vandoeuvres–Genève: Foundation Hardt, 1989

IX   The Constantinian settlement   635–657
            Eusebius, Christianity, and Judaism, ed. H.W. Attridge
            and G. Hata Detroit, Mich.: Wayne State University
            Press, 1992

X   The consecration of Ulfila   541–545
            Journal of Theological Studies N.S. 41. Oxford:
            Oxford University Press, 1990

XI   Panegyric, history and hagiography in Eusebius'
            Life of Constantine   94–123
            The Making of Orthodoxy. Essays in Honour of
            Henry Chadwick, ed. R. Williams. Cambridge:
            Cambridge University Press, 1989

XII   The two drafts of Eusebius' *Life of Constantine*   1–11
            First publication

PART THREE: THE REIGN OF CONSTANTIUS

XIII   Praetorian prefects, 337–361   249–260
            Zeitschrift für Papyrologie und Epigraphik 94. Bonn:
            Dr. Rudolf Habelt GmbH, 1992

XIV   Two victory-titles of Constantius   229–235
            Zeitschrift für Papyrologie und Epigraphik 52. Bonn:
            Dr. Rudolf Habelt GmbH, 1983

XV   The career of Abinnaeus   368–374
            Phoenix 39. Toronto, Ontario: University of Toronto
            Press, 1985

XVI   Himerius and the fourth century   206–225
            Classical Philology 82. Chicago, Ill.: University of
            Chicago Press, 1987

XVII   Hilary of Poitiers on his exile   129–140
            Vigiliae Christianae 46. Leiden: E.J. Brill, 1986

XVIII   The capitulation of Liberius and Hilary of
            Poitiers   256–265
            Phoenix 46. Toronto, Ontario: University of Toronto
            Press, 1992

XIX   The date of the Council of Gangra   121–124
        Journal of Theological Studies N.S. 40. Oxford:
        Oxford University Press, 1989

XX   Angel of light or mystic initiate? The problem of
        the *Life of Antony*   353–368
        Journal of Theological Studies N.S. 37. Oxford:
        Oxford University Press, 1986

PART FOUR: THEODOSIUS AND AFTER

XXI   Religion and society in the reign of Theodosius   157–175
        Grace, Politics and Desire. Essays on Augustine,
        ed. H. Meynell. Calgary, Alta.: University of Calgary
        Press, 1990

XXII   Augustine, Symmachus and Ambrose   7–13
        Augustine: From Rhetor to Theologian, ed. J. McWilliam
        in collaboration with T. Barnes, M. Fahey and P. Slater.
        Waterloo, Ontario: Wilfrid Laurier University Press, 1992

XXIII   The Conversion of the Roman aristocracy in
        Prudentius' *Contra Symmachum*   50–61

        (Co-authored with R.W. Westall)

        Phoenix 45. Toronto, Ontario: University of Toronto
        Press, 1991

XXIV   Aspects of the Background of the *City of God*   64–80
        Revue de l'Université d'Ottawa/University of Ottawa
        Quarterly 52. Ottawa, Ontario: University of Ottawa
        Press, 1982

Addenda   1–4

Index   1–10

This volume contains xii + 334 pages

PUBLISHER'S NOTE

The articles in this volume, as in all others in the Collected Studies Series, have not been given a new, continuous pagination. In order to avoid confusion, and to facilitate their use where these same studies have been referred to elsewhere, the original pagination has been maintained wherever possible.

Each article has been given a Roman number in order of appearance, as listed in the Contents. This number is repeated on each page and quoted in the index entries.

It has not been possible to reproduce all the illustrations originally included in these articles; in some cases new illustrations have been substituted.

PREFACE

It has been a pleasure to put together a second volume of articles for the Variorum Series of Collected Studies at the invitation of John Smedley. I have included the full text of twenty one papers published in scholarly journals and special volumes between 1982 and 1993. One published paper is reproduced only in part (VIII) because I have composed a new and more systematic exposition of the main argument of its first part (VII), while a second previously unpublished paper (XII) rounds out the argument of the published one which it follows (XI). Misprints have been corrected, but I have neither standardised the spelling and stylistic requirements of different publishers nor removed my own inconsistency in the rendering of certain proper names. I have corrected minor factual mistakes only where correction does not affect the argument in any way. The addenda are deliberately brief and selective: they note obvious errors which are embedded in the argument and some (though not all) important issues on which I have changed my mind since the original publication.

For permission to reproduce published work I am deeply grateful to the following: The Society for Promoting Christian Knowledge (I); Oxford University Press (II, X, XIX, XX); the editors of *Échos du Monde Classique/Classical Views* (III); the Johns Hopkins University Press (V); the Crake Foundation and the Department of Classics, Mount Allison University (VI); the Society for the Promotion of Roman Studies (VI); M. Olivier Reverdin and the Fondation Hardt, Geneva (VIII); Gohei Hata and Wayne State University Press (IX); Cambridge University Press (XI); Werner Eck on behalf of the editors of the *Zeitschrift für Papyrologie und Epigraphik* (XIII, XIV); Catherine Rubincam as editor of *Phoenix* and the Classical Association of Canada (XV, XVIII, XXIII); the University of Chicago Press (XVI); E. J. Brill and the editors of *Vigiliae Christianae* (XVII); the University of Calgary Press (XXI); Wilfid Laurier University Press (XXII); and the University of Ottawa Press (XXIV). I must also thank Richard Westall for consenting to allow the reproduction of the article of which he is a joint author (XXIII).

One general issue of wider significance than the present volume requires brief discussion here. My unqualified use of the words 'pagan' and 'paganism' requires justification or at least explanation. When I presented an earlier version of the tables printed in VII at a colloquium in Toronto some years ago, the commentator on my presentation did not, as I had hoped, attempt to assess the significance of my results for the overall interpretation of the religious history of the fourth century, but instead concentrated on questioning the propriety of using the term 'pagan' at all as a category for historical analysis. Moreover, Garth Fowden has recently scolded classical and Christian scholars for continuing to use the term 'paganism' and thereby exhibiting 'one more sign of their isolation from other disciplines, particularly anthropology, where "polytheism" is the norm': 'paganism', he holds, may legitimately be used only to refer to 'Christian representation of polytheism', since 'it is inappropriate to use a term derived from Christian apologetic to denote a religious culture whose study is struggling to emerge from Christian stereotypes'.[1]

Prejudicial vocabulary should of course be avoided. But it is not clear to me that substituting 'polytheist' and 'polytheism' for 'pagan' and 'paganism' brings any benefits when discussing religious change in the Roman Empire in the fourth century. The Greek word *polytheismos* was originally coined by Philo for apologetic or polemical purposes to designate under one heading all the incorrect alternatives to the true religion of Judaism, while its modern equivalents have more often than not been employed in a derogatory sense. It thus requires to be demonstrated, not merely proclaimed, that 'polytheism' is a significantly less tainted word than 'paganism'. Moreover, when discussing the period between the birth of Eusebius c. 260 and the death of Augustine in 430, we need a collective noun which conveniently and unambiguously designates the traditional polytheistic religions of the Mediterranean world and a word for the people who wished to preserve the ancient religious cults, rites and ceremonies whose survival was now imperilled. The main disadvantage of the word 'polytheist' is that it has a far wider field of reference than 'pagan', and includes, for example, most modern Hindus. Hence, whatever the general or theoretical drawbacks may be, Fergus Millar has recently justified use of the term 'pagan' with an argument relating specifically to the period which the present volume seeks to illuminate: 'by the fourth century the challenge of Christianity had long since forced those who observed the cults of the gods into explicit philosophical

---

[1]G. Fowden, 'Constantine's Porphyry Column: The Earliest Literary Allusion', *JRS* 81 (1991), 119–131, at 119 n. *. He appeals to the recent collection of essays edited by F. Schmidt, *L'Impensable Polythéisme. Études d'historiographie religieuse* (Montreux/Paris, 1988), which was published in English as *The Inconceivable Polytheism. Studies in Religious Historiography (History and Anthropology* 3, 1987).

reflection on their system of belief and practice—which we therefore may appropriately call paganism'.[2]

T.D. BARNES

Toronto
June, 1993

---

[2] F. Millar, 'The Jews of the Graeco-Roman Diaspora between Paganism and Christianity, AD 312–438', *The Jews among Pagans and Christians in the Roman Empire*, ed. J. Lieu, J. North and T. Rajak (London and New York, 1992), 97–123, at 105. Another essay in the same volume argues that paganism should be regarded 'as a religion invented in the course of the second to third centuries AD' (J. North, 'The Development of Religious Pluralism', ib. 174–193, at 188).

A study is an advance if it is more incisive—whatever that may mean—than those that preceded it; but it less stands on their shoulders than, challenged and challenging, runs by their side.

Clifford Geertz, *The Interpretation of Cultures* (New York, 1973), 25

I

Pagan Perceptions of Christianity

'Blessed are ye when men shall revile you, and persecute you and shall say all manner of evil against you falsely, for my sake.'[1] Whether or not Jesus actually uttered these words, they accurately reflect what his followers in the second half of the first century believed to be their fate. When Nero needed to deflect blame from himself for the great fire of Rome in AD 64, he was able to find a scapegoat in the Christians of the city, because the general populace detested them as immoral enemies of the whole human race, so that the official story of Christian arson gained ready acceptance.[2] Three centuries later, one of the leading pagan aristocrats of Rome who died as consul-designate in December 384 was in the habit of saying to bishop Damasus: 'Make me Bishop of Rome and I will become a Christian at once'.[3]

The present chapter surveys pagan perceptions of Christianity between these two points. It has a different emphasis from Pierre de Labriolle's classic study *La réaction païenne*,[4] whose emphasis is reflected in its subtitle 'A Study of anti-Christian polemic from the first to the sixth century'. I have concentrated on social attitudes rather than explicit statements by members of the intellectual élite, and I have attempted, following the example of John Gager's *The Origins of Anti-Semitism*,[5] to capture the diversity of Graeco-Roman attitudes towards early Christianity as well as their development over the course of time. Perhaps the main novelty of my treatment is that it refrains from using the *Historia Augusta* (for example, for the private chapel of the emperor Severus Alexander), since I believe that all the references to Christianity in that work are inventions of the author, who was writing c. 395. My survey begins with the attitude of the ruling classes of the Roman Empire in the second century, then documents Christianity's gain of social status and intellectual respectability, and finally discusses anti-Christian polemics.

IGNORANCE, HOSTILITY AND CONTEMPT[6]

Most inhabitants of the Roman Empire in AD 100 were either unaware of or uninterested in the Christians in their midst. Even in Rome, where there had certainly been Christians since the reign of Claudius, the varied epigrams of Martial and the satires of Juvenal make no identifiable allusion to the new religion, though both authors deride Jews and Judaism. There is equally no hint of Christianity in the numerous speeches that Dio Chrysostom delivered in various cities throughout the East between c. 70 and c. 110, or in the voluminous and variegated ethical and theological writings of Plutarch of Chaeronea (c. 50–c. 120). Plutarch's silence is all the more significant since his work contains so many coincidences of thought and diction with early Christian literature.[7] Similarly, the guide to dreams which Artemidorus of Daldis composed in the middle decades of the second century has no Christians in its everyday world. Moreover, as late as the 230s Cassius Dio could complete a history of Rome down to 229 in eighty books without ever mentioning Christians. Dio's silence, however, betrays itself as both deliberate and forced when he makes Maecenas recommend the persecution of religious innovators[8] – a covert but undeniable allusion to the newly won respectability of the Church in the early third century.

Educated pagan attitudes at Rome can first be documented in three authors of the early second century. A letter of the younger Pliny, a successful orator and senator, whose correspondence reveals him as a man of relatively enlightened but conventional views, is devoted entirely to the Christians. The emperor Trajan sent Pliny as a specially appointed governor to the province of Bithynia–Pontus. There, probably in the autumn of 111, Pliny found himself sitting in judgement on people accused of being Christians. Although he had never been present at the trial of Christians, Pliny had no hesitation in punishing those who admitted that they were Christians, reasoning that their pertinacity and inflexible obstinacy deserved to be punished: the Roman citizens among them he sent to Rome, the rest he executed forthwith. Those who denied that they were Christians or ever had been, Pliny acquitted and released after they had performed a symbolic cult act and cursed Christ. But Pliny was puzzled by a third category of defendant – those who admitted that they had once been Christians but asserted that they now were no longer. He questioned them, using torture on those of servile status as was normal, and discovered only what he describes as 'a depraved and immodest superstition'. Pliny, therefore, held these apostates in prison while he consulted Trajan. The polished phrases in his letter to the emperor, with their subtle argument for clemency, mask an urgent practical question: were the prisoners still in custody to be executed or set free? In reply, Trajan laid down (or reaffirmed) the legal principle that Christianity was a capital crime, but of a unique type, in that anyone accused of Christianity would be acquitted if he performed an offering or libation to the pagan gods in court.[9]

Shortly after Pliny, his friends Tacitus and Suetonius expressed very similar opinions when describing Nero's burning of Christians in 64. Tacitus clearly believed that the Christians were innocent of the charge of setting fire to Rome: he informs his readers that, after Christ was executed by Pontius Pilate, the 'deadly superstition' spread from Judaea, 'the origin of that evil', to Rome where all the shameful excesses of the world flow together and are welcomed.[10] Suetonius for his part includes it among the neutral or praiseworthy actions of Nero that 'the Christians were punished with execution, a race of men belonging to a new and criminal superstition'.[11]

The stereotype of Christian immorality reappears in two Latin writers during the reign of Marcus Aurelius. Apuleius wrote in Carthage, but set his novel *The Golden Ass* (*Metamorphoses*), in contemporary Greece. One of its villains is unambiguously and unmistakeably depicted as a Christian. The wife of the baker who purchased the hero was the wickedest of women: she tortured her husband, she practised every vice, she was cruel, avaricious, a spendthrift and a nymphomaniac, she despised the gods in order to worship her own unique deity, and she used her devotions to deceive her husband, begin drinking at dawn and spend the whole day in an unbroken sexual orgy.[12] Fronto (100–66), the greatest Latin orator of the day and Marcus Aurelius' former tutor, is often credited with a formal 'speech against the Christians'. It seems more probable that he attacked Christianity in his lost forensic masterpiece *Against Pelops*, and that it was the mythological associations of his adversary's name that led him to associate Pelops with Christian ritual murder, the cannibalism of infants and incestuous banqueting.[13] Christians had long been regarded as immoral as well as impious, but Fronto's charges of Thyestean feasts and Oedipodean intercourse added precision to the general distrust. The first Christian apologist to answer these specific charges is Athenagoras, who probably presented his *Plea on behalf of the Christians* to Marcus Aurelius in Athens in 176.[14] Moreover, Fronto's allegations appear to have been believed, at least for a time: in the pogrom at Lyon conventionally dated to 177, not only confessing Christians but also Christians who apostatized were executed.[15] This is the only known occasion when Christians who denied being Christians or performed a pagan cult act were executed: they were executed, therefore, not for being Christians, but for what Pliny called 'offences attached to the name'.[16]

A much more sympathetic attitude is exhibited by the satirist Lucian of Samosata, who mentions Christians in two works. In neither case are the Christians accused of any serious offence. On the contrary, they appear respectively as enemies and as dupes of Lucian's two main targets. Alexander of Abonuteichos, the 'false prophet', complained that Pontus was full of atheists and Christians who uttered terrible blasphemies against him and he ordered them to be driven away with stones. The festival of Alexander's new god began with the proclamation, 'If any atheist or Christian or Epicurean has come to spy on the rites, let him depart': Alexander led the expulsion of undesirables with the cry, 'Out with Christians'; to which the crowd replied, 'Out with Epicureans'.[17] This appears to be a factual report. Christians play a much larger role in Lucian's earlier account of Peregrinus who immolated himself at the Olympic Games of 165.

On Lucian's presentation, after adultery in Armenia, pederasty in Asia and rumoured parricide in his native Parium, Peregrinus went to Palestine and learned 'the wonderful wisdom of the Christians'. He soon excelled his teachers so that the Christians revered him as a god, treated him as a lawgiver and enrolled him as their official patron, all in due subordination to 'the man crucified in Palestine' whom they still worship. When Peregrinus was imprisoned for his beliefs, his co-religionists visited him, maintained him in luxury, and spent nights in prison with their 'new Socrates'. Christians even came from Asia with contributions, and Peregrinus rapidly amassed great wealth in prison. Lucian comments that Christians accept all the injunctions of 'that crucified sophist' without rational demonstration, including his command that they all be brothers and share everything: as a result any sharp operator can quickly make himself rich from them. In the sequel, Peregrinus was released by the governor of Syria, a friend of philosophy (conceivably to be identified with Bruttius Praesens, a friend of Pliny and probably an Epicurean, like Lucian himself), who saw that he sought only notoriety. Peregrinus returned to Parium, still a Christian but also now a Cynic philosopher, and publicly donated his estates to the city. He then left Parium again, supported in luxury by his fellow-Christians – until they expelled him for eating forbidden food.[18]

Lucian's picture reflects many facets of the reality described by Christian writers, but he consistently interprets what he knows only from a distance in terms of his own, Greek concepts. On an absolute scale, Lucian can hardly be characterized as favourable to Christianity, yet he avoids the customary wild allegations and presents Christians as nothing worse than credulous simpletons. An attitude intermediate between Lucian and Apuleius appears to surface in one passage in the vast output of the sophist Aelius Aristides (117–c. 185), who compares Cynic philosophers whom he is denouncing to 'those impious men of Palestine' who 'do not believe in the higher powers', and suggests that they resemble them because they too 'have defected from the Greek race, or rather from all that is higher'.[19]

The philosophers of the second century who mention Christianity do so with a mixture of intellectual contempt and moral admiration. The Stoic Epictetus, whose discourses are recorded by Arrian, who had studied with him at Nicopolis in the reign of Trajan, asked why philosophical reflection cannot remove men's fear of a tyrant when an individual can become fearless through madness and 'the Galileans from habit'.[20] Similarly, the emperor Marcus Aurelius approved of readiness for death, but recommended that it come from one's own dignified and unmelodramatic ratiocination, 'not from sheer contrariness like the Christians'.[21] Galen (c. 133–c. 200), who grew up in Asia Minor, criticized both Jews and Christians for appealing to divine authority and accepting everything on faith instead of using proper scientific methods, but he also expressed admiration for the Christians' steadfastness when facing death, for their sexual restraint, for their moderation in eating and drinking, and for their sense of justice – qualities which raised them to the level of genuine philosophers.[22]

SOCIAL AND INTELLECTUAL ACCEPTANCE

When Galen praised the Christians, probably c. 180, the general attitudes of society towards the Christians were already beginning to change. From the reign of Hadrian onwards a series of Greek apologists had attempted to disprove pagan calumnies. It is unlikely that many pagans ever listened to them. Yet a more confident tone can be detected in the *Apology* which Tertullian composed in Carthage in 197: he presents the Christian Church as a respectable corporation which conducts business as any Roman *curia* would, and he seeks throughout to make common cause with the cultured and educated classes of Carthage against the ignorant urban mob. Indeed, Tertullian claims that Christians already fill every stratum of Roman society, even the imperial palace and Senate.[23] In 197 he gave that boast no specific content, but fifteen years later his open letter to the proconsul Scapula reels off a list of senators, governors and imperial freedmen who are either Christians or sympathetic to Christianity, and warns the governor that if he continues to execute Christians he will decimate his own entourage.[24]

With Tertullian in Carthage, Clement and Origen in Alexandria, it became obvious to provincial pagans in the reign of Septimius Severus (193–211) that Christians could not any more be dismissed as uncultured simpletons. Hence Christian apologetic in the second century manner was no longer needed, though it finds an echo in the *Octavius* of Minucius Felix (probably composed c. 240), which documents the conversion to Christianity of leading citizens of the African colony of Cirta, the home town of Fronto. On the contrary, Christian intellectuals were now treated with respect. Origen was invited to an interview by a governor of Arabia; later, the empress Julia Mammaea summoned him to expound Christianity to her in Antioch; and later still, he corresponded with Otacilia Severa, wife of the emperor Philip (244–249), who had attended a Christian Easter service while a private citizen.[25]

After the first quarter of the third century, Christians were in practice rarely persecuted for their religion. Popular hostility towards them, however, may have continued to be widespread for a little longer. The attitudes of the inarticulate strata of any society are usually hard to measure, but the authentic *Acts* of the early martyrs provide an index of changing popular attitudes. In the second century, the crowd in the amphitheatre at Smyrna demanded the arrest of Polycarp, asked the Asiarch Philippus to set a lion on him, settled for burning the bishop and finally constructed a pyre themselves, while popular agitation was behind the executions at Lyon.[26] In this period it was plausible for Tertullian to claim that whenever disaster struck, the common people always reacted in the same way, by demanding 'the Christians to the lion'.[27] But the last attested outbreaks of popular fury against the Christians occurred in Cappadocia and Pontus in 235 and at Alexandria in 249.[28] It is true that the *Passion of Marianus and Jacobus* and the *Passion of Montanus and Lucius*, which appear to be contemporary accounts of the executions of Christians under Valerian in Africa in 257–9 still show the crowd jeering at Christians. But the *Acts of Fructuosus* present the bishop of Tarraco, who was martyred in January 259, as a figure loved by Christians and pagans alike, and the biographer of Cyprian claims that his hero was respected throughout Carthage and that the prospect of his execution in September 258 caused grief to pagans.[29] Fifty years later, neither the authentic *Acts* of the martyrs from the Diocletianic persecution nor Eusebius' contemporary memoir of the persecution in Palestine between 303 and 311 in his *Martyrs of Palestine* records any acts of pagan hostility towards the Christians; on the contrary, much of the local population was openly sympathetic to them and local magistrates often enforced the imperial edicts of persecution with great reluctance.

By the late third century, it is clear that the Christian church and its bishop were accepted as a normal part of the community in most cities of the Greek East and Roman Africa. The stages of this acceptance cannot be reconstructed in detail, but popular attitudes were decisively affected by the attempts of Decius in 250 and Valerian in 257/8 to compel all the inhabitants of the Roman Empire (except Jews) to sacrifice to the traditional gods for the welfare of the state. Since Christians and pagans shared a pragmatic or talismanic view of religion, the death of Decius on campaign against the Goths in 251 and the capture of Valerian by the Persians in 260 were widely interpreted as proof that the Christian God was more powerful than the traditional gods. Origen and Eusebius were typical of their age in their readiness to deduce the truth of Christianity from its observable worldly success.

ANTI-CHRISTIAN POLEMIC

The known literary polemics against Christianity share some common characteristics, but each was composed by an individual who had a specific motivation which can in principle be discovered. The first known large-scale polemic was Celsus' *True Word*, composed probably in the 160s and certainly in the East, possibly in Alexandria.[30] The greater part of the text survives as quotations in Origen's *Against Celsus*, but it cannot be assumed (as it often has been) that these quotations give an accurate overall impression of Celsus' work. On the contrary, Carl Andresen showed in 1955 that Origen largely omitted the non-philosophical parts of Celsus' work in which he had no great interest, but which were important for Celsus' general thesis. Andresen also explained in detail why Celsus wrote at all: he set out as a philosopher to refute Justin's claim that Platonism and Christianity were compatible.

Celsus presented the Church as an unpatriotic secret society whose typical members were 'wool-workers, cobblers, laundry-workers and bucolic yokels', who were able to convert 'the foolish, dishonourable and stupid, and only slaves, women and little children': Christianity was 'successful only among the uneducated because of its vulgarity and utter illiteracy'.[31] Celsus argued at length that the ancient 'true doctrine (*logos*)' had been perverted by the Jews and by the Christians, who were themselves no more than apostates from Judaism: in sum, what was intellectually acceptable in Christianity had been proved rationally by Greek thinkers, especially Plato, while what was new was irrational and usually also absurd.

More than a century after Celsus, the philosopher Porphyry composed fifteen books *Against the Christians*, the largest, most learned and most dangerous of all the ancient literary attacks on Christianity. Porphyry was dangerous because he wrote with a precise and detailed knowledge of the Bible (using a 'western text' for the New Testament), so that he could expose contradictions in the Scriptures and thus cause Christians to question their divine inspiration. He also deployed a vast scholarly knowledge of Greek literature and philosophy to criticize the Old Testament; for example, he quoted Philo of Byblos to show that Hebrew religion derived from Phoenician, and he used his knowledge of Hellenistic history to construct a proof that the book of Daniel was written in the 160s BC, not in the sixth century to which it purports to belong. Porphyry attacked Origen, whom he had met in his youth, as an apostate from Greek culture, and he systematically substituted historical inter-pretations for Origen's allegorical exegesis of Scripture. It seems likely, therefore, that Porphyry's main target was Origen – just as that of Celsus had been Justin. Unlike Celsus, however, Porphyry could not be laughed off as an ignorant and ill-informed critic. His attack on Christianity dominated philosophical disputes between pagans and Christians until the focus of debate shifted to 'the fall of Rome' in the early fifth century.

Unfortunately, much is problematical about Porphyry's *Against the Christians*.[32] The standard edition of the fragments, by Adolf Harnack in 1916, needs complete revision. The fifty-three 'frag-ments' which Harnack included from the work by Macarius of Magnesia whose title is probably to be translated '*Answer-book, or the Only-begotten to the Pagans*' are not verbatim quotations of Porphyry, but Macarius' rewriting of him in the light of conditions in his own day a century later. On the other hand, new fragments have been discovered, and much more can probably be extracted from Eusebius' *Chronicle* and from his *Preparation for the Gospel* (*Praeparatio Evangelica*) and *Proof of the Gospel* (*Demonstratio Evangelica*), which together constitute a vast anonymous polemic against Porphyry; for Eusebius was writing before possession of Porphyry's work became a capital crime under Constantine. Mod-ern estimates of the date of *Against the Christians* have ranged from 270 to *c*. 303, and it has been regarded on the one hand as a purely academic exercise and on the other as a politically motivated jus-tification for the Diocletianic persecution. The arguments advanced in favour of a date as late as *c*. 300 lose their force if, as has recently been demonstrated, Porphyry never composed a *Chronicle* – a work which appears in all modern lists of his writings and in the standard collection of the fragments of the Greek historians. For, if Porphyry never wrote a *Chronicle*, then it follows that *Against the Christians* was used by Eusebius in the first edition of his *Chronicle*, which he probably completed before 300. However, Eusebius does not, as has universally been assumed, assert that Porphyry composed *Against the Christians* in Sicily.[33] All in all, it now seems more probable to me

that Porphyry was writing in Rome between *c. 275* and *c. 290.*
Finally, the relationship of *Against the Christians* to Porphyry's
fragmentary *Philosophy from Oracles* is also disputed: whereas most
scholars regard the latter as an early work of Porphyry, composed
before he went to Rome in 263 and hence before he met Plotinus,
it has recently been argued that Porphyry wrote it in 303 'at the
request of the emperor' to defend traditional religion against
Christianity.

Lactantius describes two pamphleteers who attacked Christianity
in Nicomedia in 303 when Diocletian initiated the 'Great
Persecution'.[34] One was the magistrate Sossianus Hierocles, the
other a philosopher who often dined with the emperor – and who has
been identified with Porphyry himself. Hierocles ridiculed Jesus'
low-class disciples and treated Jesus himself as a brigand who
performed miracles inferior to those of Apollonius of Tyana, while
the philosopher urged Christians to return to worship of the gods.

These two polemics had an obvious political motivation. So too
did the savage attack on Christianity which the emperor Julian
composed during the winter of 362/3 as he prepared to invade
Persia. The content of the work, which bore the title *Against the
Galileans*, is known only through quotations in the refutation which
Cyril of Alexandria composed in the 430s, and of which only half
survives. Hence the overall scope of Julian's work must be uncertain.
However, three main themes can be disentangled: first, Julian
ridiculed the notion of revelation as unnecessary and objectionable
in itself; second, he attacked the Jewish concept of God and the
biblical presentation of God as the protector of the Jews as crude and
exclusive; and third, he criticized the 'Galileans' as Jewish apostates,
and attempted to discredit the New Testament as a basis for
Christian beliefs.

Julian composed *Against the Galileans* as part of a wholesale
attempt to undo Constantine's establishment of Christianity as
the official religion of the Roman Empire and to replace the
Christian Church with what was in effect a pagan church.[35] He drew
material and arguments from Celsus and Porphyry (whose work he
doubtless put into circulation again): the unique feature of his
attitude to Christianity was his visceral detestation of Constantine,
Constantius and all that they represented in his mind. Brought up a
Christian, losing his mother in infancy and most of his relatives in
dynastic murders as a child, Julian came to regard Christianity as

inherently evil. His most effective statement of this thesis, however, was not the open attack in *Against the Galileans*, but the covert one in his *Caesars*, also written in Antioch in the winter of 362/3. In this political satire, Constantine can find no model for his career among the gods, but when he sees Luxury and runs to her, she introduces him to Incontinence – next to whom is standing Jesus, who promises to purify seducers and murderers, the sacrilegious and unclean.[36]

After the disastrous defeat at Adrianople in 378, Julian's hints were taken up and developed into an interpretation of recent Roman history which blamed Constantine for destroying the Empire. This pagan historical apologetic, which we can see in the fragments of Eunapius, in Ammianus Marcellinus and most fully in Zosimus, equated Christianity with corruption, decadence and barbarism. Augustine answered the pagan case in his *City of God* by denying the traditional belief, common to pagans, Christians and Jews, that God rewards devotion with success in this life. But the pagan historical thesis was revived in a modified form during the sixteenth century, and it lies behind Edward Gibbon's presentation of the 'decline and fall of the Roman Empire' as the triumph of Christianity and barbarism. As a consequence, the continuing controversy over the 'conversion' of Constantine is to a large extent heir to ancient pagan perceptions of Christianity, and in particular of the first Christian emperor.

NOTES

1 Matt. 5.11 (AV), cf. Luke 6.22.
2 Tacitus, *Annals*, 15.44.
3 Jerome, *Against John of Jerusalem*, 8. PL 23.377.
4 Paris, L'Artisan du Livre, 1948[2].
5 Oxford and New York, Oxford University Press, 1983.
6 Translations of all the passages discussed in this section (and of some others too) are conveniently reproduced in S Benko, 'Pagan Criticism of Christianity during the first two centuries A.D.', *Aufstieg und Niedergang der römischen Welt* II.23.2 (Berlin and New York, De Gruyter, 1980), 1055–1118.
7 See H D Betz, ed., *Plutarch's Theological Writings and Early Christian Literature*. Studia ad Corpus Hellenisticum Novi Testamenti 3. Leiden, Brill, 1975; *Plutarch's Ethical Writings and Early Christian Literature*. Studia ad Corpus Hellenisticum Novi Testamenti 4. Leiden, Brill, 1978.

I

8   Dio, 52.36.
9   Pliny, *Letters*, 10.96, 97.
10 *Annals*, 15.44.
11 *Life of Nero*, 16.2, cf. 19.3.
12 *Metamorphoses*, 9.14.
13 Minucius Felix, *Octavius* 8.3–9.6; 30.2–31.2; cf. E Champlin, *Fronto and Antonine Rome* (Cambridge, Mass. and London, Harvard University Press, 1980), pp. 64–6.
14 *Plea*, 3.1, 31–32.
15 Eusebius, *Ecclesiastical History*, 5.1.14, 33.
16 *Letters*, 10.96.2.
17 *Alexander*, 25, 38: written after 180.
18 *Peregrinus*, 11–16. For discussion, see H D Betz, 'Lucian von Samosata and das Christentum', *Novum Testamentum* 3 (1959), 226–37; C P Jones, *Culture and Society in Lucian* (Cambridge, Mass. and London, Harvard University Press, 1986), esp. pp. 121–3.
19 *Oration*, 3.671, Lenz-Behr: tr. from C A Behr, *P. Aelius Aristides: The Complete Works* 1 (Leiden, Brill, 1986), p. 275. Although some discussions quote much more of this passage as referring to the Christians, Aristides' use of the demonstrative pronoun 'these' after a 'those' referring to the people in Palestine seems to mark an immediate return to his main target, the Cynics.
20 *Discourses*, 4.7.6.
21 *Meditations*, 11.3. The last three words are rejected as an interpolation by P A Brunt, 'Marcus Aurelius and the Christians', *Studies in Latin Literature and Roman History* 1. *Collection Latomus* 164 (Brussels 1979), pp. 483–520.
22 R Walzer, *Galen on Jews and Christians* (London, Oxford University Press, 1949), esp. pp. 14–16.
23 *Apology*, 37.4.
24 *To Scapula*, 4.1–4; 5.1–3.
25 Eusebius, *Ecclesiastical History*, 6.19.15; 21.3–4; 36.3; 34.
26 *Martyrdom of Polycarp*, 3.2; 12–13; Eusebius, *Ecclesiastical History*, 5.1.7 ff.
27 *Apology*, 40.1–2.
28 Cyprian, *Letters*, 75.10; Eusebius, *Ecclesiastical History*, 6.41.1–9.
29 See, respectively, H Musurillo, *The Acts of the Christian Martyrs* (Oxford, Clarendon Press, 1972), nos. 14, 15, 12; Pontius, *Life of Cyprian*, 15.
30 For translations and recent studies of Celsus, see C Andresen, *Logos und Nomos. Die Polemik des Kelsos wider das Christentum* (Berlin, De Gruyter, 1955); H Chadwick, *Origen: Contra Celsum* (Cambridge, University Press, 1965[2]); R Wilken, *Christians* (1984), pp. 94–125; R J Hoffman, *Celsus: On the True Doctrine* (New York and Oxford, Oxford University Press, 1987).
31 Origen, *Against Celsus*, 1.1; 3.55, 44; 1.27.

32 Among relevant recent studies, note R M Grant, 'The Stromateis of Origen', *Epektasis. Mélanges patristiques offerts à Cardinal Jean Daniélou* (Paris, Beauchesne, 1972), pp. 285–92; T D Barnes, 'Porphyry *Against the Christians*: Date and the Attribution of Fragments', *Journal of Theological Studies* N.S. 24 (1973), pp. 424–42; R Goulet, 'Porphyre et la datation de Moïse', *Revue de l'histoire des religions* 184 (1977), pp. 137–64; A Meredith, 'Porphyry and Julian Against the Christians', *Aufstieg und Niedergang der römischen Welt* II.23.2 (Berlin and New York, De Gruyter, 1980), pp. 1119–49; B Croke, 'Porphyry's Anti-Christian Chronology', *Journal of Theological Studies* N.S. 34 (1983), pp. 168–85; R Wilken, *Christians* (1984), pp. 126–63; R Goulet, 'Porphyre et Macaire de Magnèse', *Studia Patristica* 15. *Texte und Untersuchungen* 128 (1984), pp. 448–52; B Croke, 'The Era of Porphyry's Anti-Christian Polemic', *Journal of Religious History* 13 (1984/5), pp. 1–14.

33 *Ecclesiastical History*, 6.19.2.

34 *Divine Institutes*, 5.2.3.–4.1.

35 On the historical context of the work, see G W Bowersock, *Julian the Apostate* (London, Duckworth, and Cambridge, Mass, Harvard University Press, 1978), pp. 94–105; R Wilken, *Christians* (1984), pp. 164–96. The fullest study is by W J Malley, *Hellenism and Christianity. The Conflict between Hellenic and Christian Wisdom in the* Contra Galilaeos *of Julian the Apostate and the* Contra Julianum *of St. Cyril of Alexandria*. Analecta Gregoriana 210 (Rome, Università Gregoriana, 1978).

36 *Caesars*, 336 A–B.

BIBLIOGRAPHY

Barnes, T D, *Constantine and Eusebius*. Cambridge, Mass., and London, Harvard University Press, 1981.

——, *Tertullian. A Historical and Literary Study*. Oxford, Clarendon Press, 1985².

Frend, W H C, 'Prelude to the Great Persecution: The Propaganda War', *Journal of Ecclesiastical History* 38 (1987), pp. 1–18.

Lane Fox, R, *Pagans and Christians*. Harmondsworth, Penguin, 1986; New York, Knopf, 1987.

Momigliano, A, ed., *The Conflict between Paganism and Christianity in the Fourth Century*. Oxford, Clarendon Press, 1963.

Wilken, R L, *The Christians as the Romans saw them*. New Haven and London, Yale University Press, 1984.

II

SOME INCONSISTENCIES IN EUSEBIUS

EUSEBIUS of Caesarea composed several editions of his *Ecclesiastical History*—that is both obvious and universally acknowledged. But precisely how many editions were there? and what was the date and compass of the first edition? To these questions, very different answers have been given. Moreover, it must also be asked: why did Eusebius write two versions of his *Martyrs of Palestine*? and what relationship do the two versions of the *Martyrs* have to the *History*?

A single, if complicated, hypothesis has recently been propounded to explain both the existence of the two extant recensions of the *Martyrs of Palestine* and the textual evidence for revision in Books viii, ix, and x of the *History*.[1] It postulates the following sequence of composition and revision. First, before Diocletian ordained persecution in February 303, Eusebius wrote an *Ecclesiastical History* in seven books, which probably concluded its narrative c.280. Some years later, in the summer or autumn of 311, immediately after Galerius declared an end to the persecution begun in 303, Eusebius wrote the long recension of the *Martyrs of Palestine* as a separate work entirely independent of the *Ecclesiastical History*. But the emperor Maximinus unexpectedly renewed the persecution of the Christian church in the East in November 311, thus rendering Eusebius' coverage of contemporary persecution incomplete. Accordingly, after Maximinus was defeated by Licinius in the spring of 313, and the persecution begun in 303 finally ceased, Eusebius abbreviated and rewrote his *Martyrs of Palestine* to serve as an integral part of his *History*. Hence the second edition of the *History*, completed in 313/14, comprised (*a*) the original seven books superficially revised, (*b*) the short recension of the *Martyrs of Palestine*, preceded by a preface and conclusion which now stand in Book viii of the *History* (viz. *H.E.* viii. 1.1–2.3; 17.3–10; App.), and (*c*) the present Book ix, which describes the persecuting policies of Maximinus from 311 to 313. Next, probably c.315, Eusebius replaced the short recension of the *Martyrs* with the present Book viii of the *History*, and added a tenth book comprising (*a*) an introduction, (*b*) his own sermon at the dedication of a new basilica at Tyre, and (*c*) six imperial enactments of 313 and 314 in favour of the Christian church. The fourth edition, a decade later, after the defeat and deposition of Licinius in 324, was identical to the third in scope and content, except that Eusebius changed all the passages in the last three books in which he had earlier praised Licinius as a benefactor of Christianity, and he replaced the six documents of 313

---

[1] *Greek, Roman and Byzantine Studies*, xxi (1980), pp. 191 ff.

and 314 (*H.E.* x. 5–7) with a brief account of the regime of Licinius after 313 and of his defeat by Constantine (*H.E.* x. 8–9). Finally, the absence of the name of Crispus from the fourth-century Syriac translation of the *Ecclesiastical History* implies that Eusebius retouched the last two chapters of Book x *c*.325 when he learned of Crispus' execution in the spring of 326.

Such an analysis implies not only that the long recension of the *Martyrs of Palestine* (fully extant only in Syriac) and Book ix of the *Ecclesiastical History* deserve primacy as witnesses to the course of persecution in the East between 303 and 313, but also that the first seven books of the *History*, apart from a few added or rewritten passages, represent a history of the Christian church which Eusebius wrote before 303. Hence these seven books, and their underlying assumptions, become contemporary evidence for the standing of the Christian church in Roman society in the late third century.[2]

To treat Books i–vii thus, however, is to assume that they survive substantially as Eusebius originally wrote them, and that Eusebius has not revised and rewritten them in a fundamental way. R. M. Grant's recent study of Eusebius as a historian of the church challenges this assumption and argues that Eusebius changed his mind on six important issues between the first and subsequent editions of the *History*.[3] At first sight, that contention might be welcomed as confirmation of the view that the first edition of the *History* ought to be dated as early as possible.[4] On deeper reflection, it is evident that the thesis of substantial revision implicitly disallows the use made of the extant Books i–vii as essentially a work written before 303. For, if Eusebius changed his mind on six important issues between the first and second editions, then the mere subtraction of obvious additions and revisions from the extant Books i–vii will not necessarily produce an approximation to the first edition of these books. Moreover, if a change of mind on six issues can be detected by literary and historiographical analysis, then it must be suspected that there were other changes too between editions which Eusebius has successfully concealed. An important question has been raised. The evidence and the arguments which Grant adduces to prove that Eusebius changed his mind deserve close examination.

Eusebius (Grant argues) changed his mind between the first and second editions of the *History* about 'the death of the apostle James,

---

[2] *Constantine and Eusebius* (Cambridge, Mass., 1981), pp. 148 ff., 126 ff.

[3] R. M. Grant, *Eusebius as Church Historian* (Oxford, 1980), esp. pp. 10 ff. The page numbers in the text all refer to this book.

[4] *Constantine* (1981), p. 346.

the nature of the book of Revelation, the reliability of Papias of Hierapolis, the date of Hegesippus, the date of the Gallican martyrs, and the circumstances of the death of Origen' (p. 15). In several cases the initial argument assumes that the first edition of the *History* must have repeated the *Chronicle*: hence a discrepancy between the *Chronicle* and the *History* as extant is adduced to prove that Eusebius modified his views between the first two editions of the *History* (pp. 15–16). That inference must be disallowed. It is more plausible to suppose that Eusebius changed his mind while working on the *History*, that the Christian writers whom he studied closely for the later work convinced him that his *Chronicle* contained some errors and misjudgements, and that, even though the *History* is professedly based on the *Chronicle* (*H.E.* i. 1.6), Eusebius felt free tacitly to correct the earlier work. Furthermore, Hegesippus is so embedded in the structure and logic of Books i–iv that it seems implausible to suppose that 'Eusebius found Hegesippus' work' only after the first edition of the *History* had been written (pp. 67–8).[5] There remain individual arguments relevant to each of the six issues.

First, the death of James. Grant detects a contradiction (p. 15) between the explicit dating of the death of James early in the reign of Nero (*H.E.* ii. 22.7–8), before the emperor's eighth year, i.e. 61/2 (ii. 24), and the statements elsewhere, both in quotation of and based on Hegesippus, that Jerusalem was besieged immediately after his death (ii. 23.18–19; iii. 7.8; 11). The contradiction does not exist. Eusebius knew perfectly well that Titus captured Jerusalem in the second year of Vespasian (iii. 7.3, from Josephus, *A.J.* xx. 435): he simply uses temporal phrases such as 'immediately' with some elasticity.[6]

Second, the book of Revelation. Grant argues (p. 126) that a sentence near the beginning of Book iii (*H.E.* iii. 3.3) originally stood in the preface to the whole work (i. 1.1–2). That could be true—if such alterations had been demonstrated on other grounds. But the sentence seems natural enough in its present context: Eusebius realized that he was already treating the canon of scripture as a seventh main theme of the *History*, and decided to draw the reader's attention to the fact.[7] Grant further argues (pp. 126–7) that

[5] Grant earlier argued that Eusebius 'knew Hegesippus when he composed the *Chronicle*' (*Paganisme, Judaïsme, Christianisme. Mélanges offerts à Marcel Simon* [1978], p. 201).

[6] Compare the phrase 'a little while later' in *Mart. Pal.* 5. 3—which led some papyrologists to misread a consular date in *P. Cairo Isid.* 69 in order to make Sossianus Hierocles prefect of Egypt in 307 instead of 310–11, at which date he is now indubitably attested by *P.Oxy.* 3120; *P. Coll. Youtie* 75.

[7] *Constantine* (1981), p. 129.

Eusebius' views on Revelation went through three stages: first, acceptance of Revelation as the work of John the apostle and evangelist (iii. 23.6; iv. 18.8; 24; 26.2; v. 8.5–6; 18.4; vi. 25.9–10); second, rejection as 'a heretical forgery' which was 'completely wicked and impious' (iii. 25.7; 28.1–6); and finally a qualified acceptance 'as canonical but by an author different from the evangelist' (vii. 24–5). Unfortunately for this argument, the work which Eusebius denounces as 'a heretical forgery' is not Revelation, but *Acts of John*, along with *Acts of Andrew* and other apostles (iii. 25.7). Eusebius' attitude to Revelation is consistent, though not quite straightforward:[8] he disliked its millenarianism, and the authority of Dionysius of Alexandria led him to claim that 'the opinion of the majority is still to this day divided' (iii. 24.18); yet he conscientiously chronicled early testimony to its apostolic authorship, and he describes the work as 'the Apocalypse of John' without any equivocation, even when about to quote Dionysius' rejection of its Johannine authorship (iii. 29.1; vii. 25.1).

Third, the reliability of Papias. Grant discerns two strata in the chapter which the *History* devotes to Papias (p. 136), viz. a favourable presentation (iii. 39.1–10, 14–17) and a later addition which denounces Papias as 'a stupid millenarian enthusiast' (iii. 39.11–13). Again, it is not clear that any real inconsistency exists. Eusebius quotes Irenaeus on Papias (iii. 39.1), then quotes and discusses Papias on the elders of the church (2–10); next, he blames Papias for the influence of millenarianism (11–13), but he concludes the chapter by quoting Papias on the gospels of Mark and Matthew, to which he adds further remarks on Papias' preservation of very early Christian traditions (14–17). It is not inconsistent for Eusebius to use a writer 'of exceedingly small intelligence' (13) as historical evidence.

Fourth, the date of Hegesippus. Grant detects a contradiction (p. 67) between Eusebius' statement that Hegesippus 'belonged to the first succession from the apostles' (ii. 23.3) and a later recognition that Hegesippus referred to the death of Antinous in 130 (iv. 8.2) and was in Rome while Anicetus and then Eleutherus were bishops, i.e. into the reign of Marcus Aurelius (iv. 11.7). The contradiction disappears when allowance is made for hyperbole. When introducing him, Eusebius emphasizes how close Hegesippus was to the apostles: he belonged to a generation born within the lifetime of the longest-living apostles.

Fifth, the martyrs of Lyon, where 'the date under Marcus Aurelius alone must be taken from the second edition, that under Lucius Verus (who died in 169) from the first' (p. 16). Eusebius

[8] Ibid., p. 140.

474

does indeed get into a muddle over emperors in the early chapters of Book v. But is the hypothesis of successive drafts the correct explanation? It is perhaps more plausible to invoke anachronism. The *History* dates the martyrdoms at Lyon to the seventeenth year of the emperor 'Antoninus Verus', i.e. Marcus Aurelius (v, pr. 1), who sanctioned the executions (v. 1. 44, 47). (Fortunately, the correctness or otherwise of this date is not here relevant.) Eusebius subsequently distinguishes this Antoninus from 'his brother Marcus Aurelius Caesar', who benefited from the miracle of the Thundering Legion (v. 5.1). By the latter Eusebius must mean the emperor normally known as Lucius Verus, even though the events to which he alludes occurred after 169 and when Marcus Aurelius was on campaign north of the Danube.[9] The evidence available to Eusebius spoke of the emperor Marcus both as ordering Christians to be executed (the letter of the Gallic churches) and as their protector (Apollinaris and Tertullian, as quoted in *H.E.* v. 5. 4ff.). Eusebius (it may be suggested) removed this apparent contradiction by interpreting the evidence in terms more appropriate to the Diocletianic college of emperors: he supposed that Verus (whom we call Marcus Aurelius) was a persecutor of Christians, whereas his brother and subordinate, the Caesar Marcus Aurelius (whom we call Lucius Verus), protected Christians.[10]

Sixth, the death of Origen. Again, the facts do not establish that Eusebius changed his mind between editions of the *History*. Origen was tortured under Decius (vi. 39.5), but died in the reign of Gallus (vii. 1). When Pamphilus and Eusebius defended Origen against the charge of heresy in 309, they represented him as a martyr of the Decian persecution, presumably arguing that his death c.252 was the direct result of his earlier torture. It is a mistake to assume that the *Defence of Origen and his Opinions* gave an account identical to that in the first edition of the *Ecclesiastical History* (p. 16); it surely enhanced and embellished the facts recorded there for apologetic purposes.[11]

The conclusion that Eusebius changed his mind on important issues between the first and second editions of the *Ecclesiastical History* has not been proven from the evidence and arguments adduced. It remains legitimate, therefore, to treat the extant

---

[9] On the date, see recently W. Jobst, *11. Juni 172 n. Chr. Der Tag des Blitz- und Regenwunders im Quadenland* (*Sb. Wien*, Phil.-hist. Kl. cccxxxv, 1978), pp. 16ff.

[10] *Constantine* (1981), p. 137. For a somewhat similar analysis, see R. M. Grant, *Studia Patristica*, xii (*T.U.* cxv, 1975), p. 416. It is not necessary, however, to accept Grant's accusation that 'Eusebius has sacrificed historical fact on the altar of his moralistic political narrative'.

[11] *Constantine* (1981), p. 200.

first seven books (apart from obvious additions) as a work completed before Diocletian issued the first persecuting edict on 23 February 303.

III

THE CONVERSION OF CONSTANTINE

The conversion of Constantine (or, with inverted commas, the "conversion" of Constantine) has bulked large in modern debates about the first Christian emperor of Rome and his place in history.[1] Often, indeed, the reality or sincerity of this conversion has been presented as the central issue in the history of the age of Constantine – and, supreme accolade, the conversion of Constantine has a volume to itself in a series of European Problem Studies produced for college students, by the side of such topics as the Reformation, the French Revolution, and British Imperialism.[2] In contrast, Constantine and Eusebius briskly dismisses the conversion as unproblematical, and declines to give this chestnut of Constantinian studies the fresh roasting which some reviewers (and doubtless many readers) had expected.[3] Why? The reason is simple and fundamental. I believe that Constantine was sympathetic to Christianity long before he was "converted" (whatever that word may

---

[1]"The one event that needs signalizing," according to R. MacMullen, Christianizing the Roman Empire (A.D. 100-400) (New Haven and London 1984) vii. The text printed here is a revised version of a lecture given on several occasions in England during the winter of 1983/84 and in Western Canada in October 1984. I am most grateful to the editors of Classical Views for their willingness to publish it in its present form – as a lecture designed to introduce the innocent to a fatally difficult topic.

[2]The Conversion of Constantine, edited by J.W. Eadie (New York 1971). The notes which the editor adds to the articles and extracts reprinted regrettably contain a large number of minor factual errors.

[3]T.D. Barnes, Constantine and Eusebius (Cambridge, Mass. 1981) 43. References will not usually be given for statements which can be verified through that book or its companion-volume The New Empire of Diocletian and Constantine (Cambridge, Mass. 1982).

mean) in 312. The view that Constantine in 312 underwent a psychological process which can legitimately be called conversion is neither original nor even adventurous, since the majority of scholars who have recently written about Constantine accept that he was in some sense converted before the Battle of the Milvian Bridge. Where I dissent from the scholarly tradition as a whole is in asserting that this conversion was not a sudden, unexpected, and unpredictable event, but the culmination of a process of rapprochement which had begun long before 312.

Almost all those who have written about the conversion of Constantine fall into two categories: first, those who doubt or deny that Constantine can have been converted to Christianity in 312 because they believe that his actions after 312 were non-Christian, un-Christian, or anti-Christian; and second, those who argue that his actions and public pronouncements after 312 are only explicable on the hypothesis that he was converted in that year. I accept the main arguments of this second group of scholars, but believe that they do not go far enough. For I hold that both groups share several fundamental misconceptions. In particular, virtually everyone who has written about Constantine seems to me to go astray in rejecting or dismissing, explicitly or implicitly, two crucial propositions which are central to my interpretation of Constantine. These are:

(1) that Constantine's conversion was in his political interest, not contrary to it;
(2) that Constantine was a reasonably well-educated man with an interest in philosophy and a sympathy for Christianity which long antedated his conversion, not an ignorant, uneducated, or semi-illiterate soldier.

I shall proceed by discussing, first, the political context of Constantine's conversion; second, Constantine's dealings with Christians before 312; and third, the central issue of what actually happened in 312. In conclusion, something will be said about the Speech to the Assembly of the Saints, which is the main, though by no means the only, evidence for Constantine's intellectual attainments and for his interest in philosophy and theology.

* * *

Constantine was born at Naissus in 272 or 273, the son of a young and promising officer in the army of Aurelian. Twenty years later, Constantius was appointed to the imperial college which began to rule the Roman Empire jointly on 1 March 293: Diocletian and Galerius as Augustus and Caesar in the East, Maximian and Constantius as Augustus and Caesar in the West. This "tetrarchy" has sometimes been treated as a radical innovation which substituted appointment by merit for hereditary succession.[4] That picture is grossly misleading. Diocletian did indeed devise a radically new form of imperial rule, reforming the administration, systematizing court ceremonial, and seeking to establish a permanent college of four emperors, two senior and two junior. But he did not intend to exclude normal dynastic considerations when deciding who should fill a vacancy in the imperial college. Diocletian knew that such an attempt would be futile. Accordingly, he tried to enlist dynastic loyalties in support of his tetrarchic system.

Diocletian was proclaimed emperor in 284 and gained control of the whole Roman Empire in 285. At once he chose an old comrade, Maximian, to rule the West, briefly as his subordinate, then as his colleague, though it was clear that Diocletian was in charge. In 293, two Caesars were appointed: Constantius was both the son-in-law and praetorian prefect of Maximian, and Galerius (I believe) stood in the same double relationship to Diocletian. What of the succession? By 300 only two of the tetrarchs had sons who were old enough to be considered candidates for the purple, viz. Constantine and Maxentius, the son of Maximian, and these two princes were being groomed as the next emperors. In 300, and in 304, any well-informed observer who was told that Diocletian and Maximian were about to retire could have supplied the names of their successors: Constantius and Galerius would automatically be promoted to Augusti, with Maxentius as the new Caesar in the West and Constantine as the new Caesar in the East.

---

[4]W. Seston, Dioclétien et la Tétrarchie 1 (Paris 1946) 193ff.

Yet something happened to divert the expected course of events. That something was the Persian War of 296-299, in which Galerius won a smashing victory - and won it alone, while Diocletian was taking many months to smother a minor rebellion in Egypt. As a result of his victory, Galerius, who was in rank the most junior emperor, became the most powerful politically. The immediate consequence, in 299, was a purge of Christians from the eastern armies. More important, Galerius attempted to halt the rapid Christianisation of the Roman Empire before it was too late. In 303 and 304 he enforced on Diocletian a policy of persecution which, significantly, he was able to extend to most of the western provinces only very briefly and ineffectively. And, in the dynastic sphere, Galerius persuaded or compelled Diocletian to set aside the obvious heirs and, on 1 May 305, when he abdicated, to appoint instead as Caesars Galerius' henchman Severus and his young nephew Maximinus.

The new tetrarchy was unstable, and in 306 Galerius made the disastrous mistake of introducing a tax reform, ordering the landless city-dwellers to be registered on the census-rolls for the first time, including the inhabitants of Rome and peninsular Italy. Constantius died of natural causes in Britain on 25 July 306, and Constantine, who had prudently joined his father in 305, was proclaimed emperor in his place. On 28 October in Rome, the rebellious populace and praetorian guard proclaimed Maxentius ruler. The status of Constantine and Maxentius, however, was very different: Constantine sought and obtained recognition from Galerius as the legitimate ruler of Britain, Gaul, and Spain, but Maxentius was never able to secure a similar recognition. Hence an enormous difference in the security of their rule and their political durability. Constantine was not the young usurper who fills so many of the pages written about the early years of his reign: from September 306 he was acknowledged throughout the Roman Empire as a member of the imperial college and as the lawful ruler of his father's territories. Maxentius, in contrast, was never able to remove the stigma of usurpation. Admittedly, there were some temporary uncertainties. Constantine recognised Maxentius for a period of 307/8, and Maximinus did so in 311/2, while Galerius gave Constantine the cold shoulder in 307/8. Moreover, the politics and warfare of the years 306 to 308 are immensely complicated. But by the end of 308, the political configuration of the post-Diocletianic empire became clear to all.

The Conference of Carnuntum in November 308 reinstituted a tetrarchy which resolved any uncertainty about Constantine's legitimacy, even though he and Maximinus disputed their standing within the imperial college. The composition of this revamped tetrarchy provides the vital background for understanding Constantine's invasion of Italy in 312. The new imperial college constituted at Carnuntum comprised Galerius and Licinius as Augusti, Maximinus and Constantine as Caesars, then as filii Augustorum, and finally (from 310) as Augusti. The territorial implications ought to be obvious. Constantine had ruled Britain, Gaul, and Spain since 306, while since 305 Galerius had ruled the whole of the Balkans and Asia Minor, Maximinus the Levant and Egypt. What about the new emperor Licinius? Whether he was formally assigned a geographical sphere or not,[5] he was expected soon to establish his control over the territories then ruled by Maxentius, viz. Italy and Africa. An early and normally well-informed source states that Galerius made Licinius emperor specifically to wage war on Maxentius,[6] and there is numismatic and epigraphic evidence that he tried to invade Italy shortly after the Conference of Carnuntum, or at least that there was fighting on the north-eastern borders of Italy.[7]

Let us turn now from historical reality to the fictitious setting which writers about Constantine have imagined for their hero's

---

[5]A. Arnaldi, "Osservazioni sul convegno di Carnuntum," Rendiconti dell' Istituto Lombardo, Classe di Lettere, Scienze Morali e Storiche 35 (1975) 217-238, argues that Licinius was appointed Augustus of the West.

[6]Origo Constantini Imperatoris 5.13: "a Galerio factus imperator velut adversum Maxentium pugnaturus." Similarly, Zosimus 2.11.

[7]V. Picozzi, "Una campagna di Licinio contro Massenzio nel 310 non attestata dalle fonti literarie," Numismatica e antichità classiche 5 (1976) 267-275.

conversion. If I quote Norman Baynes, it is because he puts most eloquently a point of view which is very widely shared, being adopted, for example, without question in Alistair Kee's recent book Constantine versus Christ, where the emperor appears to win by a technical knockout in the fourth round. Kee compares Constantine at the Battle of the Milvian Bridge to "some Old Testament leader whose army was outnumbered two to one, but whose trust was in the Lord."[8] In a more leisurely fashion, Baynes wrote to much the same effect:

> It was a moment of crisis for Constantine: his forces were outnumbered by those of Maxentius;...the newly-built walls of Aurelian made the western capital impregnable; two armies which had previously marched into Italy against Maxentius had perished miserably. In Rome Maxentius was supported by pagan prophets and augurs who promised victory, and in an age when it was really believed that victory or defeat was in the gift of Heaven, the sure promise of victory meant much.... The gods of Rome, then, had declared for Maxentius; whence in this crisis should Constantine seek aid?... Against the advice of his generals, against the counsel of the augurs, with amazing daring Constantine invaded Italy, and having defeated in the north of the peninsula the troops of Maxentius, took the still more surprising step of marching directly against the fortifications of the western capital.... This is more explicable if Constantine was convinced that the Christian God had assured him victory.[9]

To my mind, that sounds more like a boys' adventure story or a gushing biography of Alexander the Great than critical history. Like so many others, Baynes fails to ask why, when Constantine invaded Italy, the main army of Maxentius was stationed near Verona, far to the east. Why were Maxentius' troops not guarding the Alpine passes from Gaul? The Conference of Carnuntum provides the answer: Maxentius' troops were defending Italy against the threat of invasion from the Balkans, i.e. by Licinius.

---

[8] A. Kee, Constantine versus Christ. The Triumph of Ideology (London 1982) 17.

[9] N.H. Baynes, Constantine the Great and the Christian Church (London 1931) 8-9, partly paraphrasing Pan. Lat. 12 (9).2.4.

The year 312 was indeed in a sense "a moment of crisis for Constantine." But the crisis was not one in which he confronted overwhelming odds or faced the prospect of imminent defeat. The psychological crisis was subtler, and deeper. What Constantine faced in the spring of 312 was the prospect that his ambition to rule the whole of the Roman Empire would be forever frustrated by Licinius' conquest of Italy. Galerius had died in the spring of 311, whereupon Maximinus seized Asia Minor. Galerius was not replaced in the imperial college, and Licinius rapidly arranged a truce with Maximinus. In 312, it is clear, he intended finally to suppress the usurpation of Maxentius and to become master of Italy and Africa himself. But Constantine forestalled Licinius: he invaded Italy from Gaul while Maxentius was unprepared to meet him, and defeated Maxentius' armies in north Italy. These battles (I assume) took place early in the year. Constantine then accepted the surrender of all the cities of northern Italy, and began a slow and deliberate march south towards Rome.

If we want to understand Constantine's advance on Rome, we should not seek an analogy from the biblical narrative, but from earlier Roman history. The strategic situation in 312 shows striking similarities to that in the autumn of the year 69. In both cases, the civil war was won in the north Italian plain, and after desperate battles there, resistance to the invader began to crumble. In 69, however, Antonius Primus was in a hurry and marched on Rome too quickly. The strategy which Constantine adopted in 312 corresponds exactly to what Mucianus urged on Primus in 69: he advanced on Rome slowly and cautiously, not reaching the vicinity of the city until late October. And when he arrived before the walls of Rome, he discovered that Maxentius was unable to sustain the siege for which he had carefully prepared.

Maxentius had gathered huge supplies of grain from Africa and had severed the Milvian Bridge. His initial strategy was to stand a siege. Opposition inside Rome, however, was so strong that, when Constantine's army arrived, Maxentius judged it politically impossible to do so. He therefore changed his plans, constructed a bridge of boats over the River Tiber, marched out and offered battle. But his army fled at the first charge, and Maxentius himself was drowned in the ensuing stampede over the temporary bridge, which collapsed under the weight of his defeated army.

In several important respects, the Battle of the Milvian Bridge resembles an earlier battle, equally famous in Roman history - the Battle of Actium. By the time the actual fighting took place, neither Octavian nor Constantine could have lost, except through enormous incompetence. Yet both battles rapidly acquired partly mythical characteristics as heroic victories from which a new political order was born. Both victories became legendary, and yet, from a military point of view, the Battle of the Milvian Bridge, like the Battle of Actium, was "a shabby affair."[10] The political and military context in which Constantine publicly proclaimed allegiance to the Christian God was not when he faced defeat, but before a battle which he knew he would win.

* * *

In 303 Maximian had promulgated in the West the first persecuting edict of Diocletian, ordering the surrender of the scriptures and other church property, the demolition of churches, and the cessation of Christian worship. Moreover, some of his governors, such as the proconsul of Africa and the governor of Numidia, enforced the edict with a zeal which led them to exceed its strict provisions. The Caesar Constantius contented himself with a formal application of the edict, taking care that no Christian in his territories was executed or imprisoned, as non-compliers were in Spain, Italy, and Africa. But even Maximian declined to promulgate any of the subsequent persecuting edicts, and persecution had probably in practice ceased in much of the West before the abdication of Diocletian and Maximian on 1 May 305. So far as we can tell, when Constantius became senior emperor in 305, he issued no imperial edict or constitution to alter the legal status of Christians or Christianity. Constantine, however, did.

---

[10]R. Syme, Roman Revolution (Oxford 1939) 294ff., esp.297.

Lactantius states categorically, both in the pamphlet On the Deaths of the Persecutors and in the second edition of the Divine Institutes, that Constantine's first action as emperor was to restore the Christian religion to the position which it had enjoyed before the persecution.[11] There is no compelling reason to reject or even to doubt Lactantius' testimony. For he was not, as has so often been assumed, a propagandist of Constantine disseminating a pro-Constantinian version of recent history from the imperial court at Trier from about 318 to 320.[12] He wrote both the passages in question in Nicomedia, as a subject of Licinius, not of Constantine, one about 314, the other in 324. Furthermore, Lactantius had probably been in Gaul before the Battle of the Milvian Bridge: if that is so, then he was in a position to know what the legal status of Christians in Gaul was between 306 and 312. Lactantius asserts (and we should accept) that in 306 the Christians of Gaul, Britain, and Spain received both toleration and restitution of what they had lost under the first persecuting edict of 23 February 303. That is to say, the Christians of Constantine's territories began, from the moment of his accession in 306, to enjoy the legal protection and privileges which most writers about Constantine have asserted that they received in the winter of 312/3.[13] The importance of Lactantius' testimony cannot be emphasised too strongly, nor its relevance to the conversion of Constantine. The Christians who lived under Constantine had enjoyed religious freedom and unfettered rights of assembly, with full restitution of confiscated property, for six years before Constantine proclaimed himself an adherent of their faith.

If we accept Lactantius' picture of Constantine as basically truthful (as I believe we should), then Constantine's political support

---

[11] Lactant. Mort. Pers. 24.9; Div. Inst. 1.1.13.

[12] So J. Moreau, Lactance: De la Mort des Persécuteurs (Sources chrétiennes 39, 1954) 34ff., 51ff. In disproof, JRS 63 (1973) 41ff.

[13] The document traditionally styled "the Edict of Milan" is in fact a letter of Licinius to provincial governors in Asia Minor and the East (Lactant. Mort. Pers. 48.2-12; Eus. Hist. Eccl. 10.5.2-14).

for Christianity was obvious from 306. I should trace his sympathy back at least a decade, to the time when Constantine was in Nicomedia while Lactantius and the biblical scholar Lucian of Antioch were also there. Moreover, it may be significant that, when Constantine took part in Galerius' capture of Ctesiphon in 298, he went to see the ruins of Babylon:[14] that could be mere tourism, but a desire to visit Babylon perhaps indicates that the young Constantine was already interested in biblical history. Whatever its motivation, however, Constantine's religious attitude in the early years of his reign is clear and consistent. Between 306 and 312 he advertised himself as a champion of religious freedom. In 311 he wrote to Maximinus protesting against the latter's persecution of eastern Christians.[15] Again Lactantius provided the evidence; again his testimony has received short shrift from modern scholarship; and again there is no compelling reason for disbelief.

Maxentius, who came to power three months after Constantine, put a formal end to persecution of Christians in Italy and Africa. He granted what is described as pax or indulgentia, i.e. toleration and permission for Christians to resume their normal forms of worship.[16] But Maxentius did not at the outset, in 306/7, restore Christian property. He only took that step in 311, precisely at the time when he declared war on Constantine. The synchronism surely implies that Maxentius was unwilling to commence hostilities with an emperor who was more obviously pro-Christian than he was. And it may be that Constantine was impelled towards conversion by a subconscious or semi-conscious desire to outdo Maxentius. His conversion certainly made Constantine more attractive as a potential ruler to the large and influential Christian community inside Rome.

* * *

---

[14]Constantine, Oratio ad sanctorum coetum 16.4.

[15]Lactant. Mort. Pers. 37.1.

[16]Optatus 1.18; App.1, p.194.12 Ziwsa.

The conversion of Constantine (I have so far argued) was not "an erratic block which has diverted the stream of history" (to use the phrase which Baynes applied to Constantine's life and achievement as a whole),[17] nor was it politically disadvantageous. We must now tackle the difficult question of what the conversion comprised, in what sense it is legitimate to use the term, whether in fact it occurred.

The most helpful modern discussion of this question is, in many ways, that of Heinrich Schrörs, professor of Catholic theology at the University of Bonn early in the present century. In 1913 Schrörs published a monograph with the title Konstantins des Grossen Kreuzerscheinung. Eine kritische Untersuchung (Bonn 1913), and three years later he restated his views against reviewers in a long article in the Zeitschrift für Katholische Theologie (40 [1916] 485-523). Neither the monograph nor the article has had the influence which they deserve, for the monograph is rare (no copy, for example, in either the Bodleian Library in Oxford or the British Library in London) and the article has had fewer readers than might have been expected (in October 1983 I needed to cut the pages of the Bodleian copy). However, I have no desire to repeat, expound, or criticise Schrörs' arguments, merely to acknowledge that the formulation of the argument which follows owes much to his monograph and article. The argument has three stages:

(1) we must distinguish between direct and indirect evidence for Constantine's conversion;
(2) the only independent direct witnesses are Lactantius and Eusebius;
(3) it is Eusebius, not Lactantius, whose testimony is the more reliable, even though it is later.

The distinction between direct and indirect evidence is fundamental and has been widely employed. The indirect evidence settles the question whether conversion or something akin to a conversion occurred. Scholars such as Baynes and A.H.M. Jones, Andreas Alföldi and Jean Gaudement, S. Calderone and, recently,

---

[17]Baynes (above, n.9) 3.

Fergus Millar have assembled a large amount of evidence to show that from the winter of 312/3 Constantine began to proclaim his adherence to the Christian faith, to give the church a privileged position in Roman society, and to reshape Roman law in a Christian direction.[18] And some of this evidence explicitly refers to a change of belief. For example, Constantine wrote in 314:

> The eternal and religious incomprehensible piety of our God by no means permits the state of man to stray too long in darkness, nor does it allow the hostile wills of certain men to be so strong that it does not grant an opportunity of conversion to the rule of righteousness (iustitia) by opening anew with its own most glorious lights a path to salvation. I know this from many examples; I extrapolate the same conclusion from my own case. For there were in me at first things which seemed alien to righteousness, and I did not think that a power on high saw any of the things which I carried inside the secret places of my heart. What fortune ought these things to have earned me? Surely one overflowing with every evil. But almighty God, sitting in the watch-tower of heaven, bestowed on me what I did not deserve: assuredly, what he has granted to me his servant by his heavenly benevolence cannot at present be described or enumerated. Most holy bishops of Christ the saviour, dearest brothers![19]

Most of the evidence is of course less explicit than that, but it is abundant, and some of it is earlier than the letter which I have quoted: for example, an official panegyric of 313 which avoids overt paganism.[20] Hence there can be no real doubt that Constantine began to present himself as a worshipper of the Christian God from about the time of the Battle of the Milvian Bridge.

---

[18] Baynes (above, n.9) 10ff.; J. Gaudement, "La legislation religieuse de Constantin," Revue de l'histoire de l'église en France (1947) 25-61; A. Alföldi, The Conversion of Constantine and Pagan Rome (Oxford 1948) 36ff.; A.H.M. Jones, Constantine and the Conversion of Europe (London 1949) 79ff.; S. Calderone, Costantino e il Cattolicesimo 1 (Florence 1962); F. Millar, The Emperor in the Roman World (31 BC-AD 337) (London 1977) 577ff. See also now L. de Giovanni, Costantino e il mondo pagano³ (KOINΩNIA 2, 1983).

[19] Optatus, App.5, p.208.19-31 Ziwsa.

[20] Pan. Lat. 12 (9), cf. J.H.W.G. Liebeschuetz, Continuity and Change in Roman Religion (Oxford 1979) 285ff.

Such indirect evidence, however, reveals nothing about why and how Constantine ceased to worship the traditional pagan gods of Rome. For that we need direct evidence, and the direct evidence is meagre, for writers subsequent to Eusebius do not deserve to rank as independent witnesses.[21] When they present versions of Constantine's conversion different from his, the changes and additional details do not come from genuine tradition, but are legendary accretions or else the results of a double process of fictionalisation and rationalisation: for example, when Rufinus has Constantine hear angels chanting the words "By this conquer," rather than seeing them in the sky,[22] the change is clearly motivated by the desire to avoid a prima facie implausibility.

Lactantius and Eusebius alone, therefore, need to be considered. It was the great merit of Schrörs to see that Lactantius' account, though much earlier, is the less reliable and informative.[23] Moreover, the vital passage contains a serious textual difficulty. The sole manuscript of On the Deaths of the Persecutors is badly corrupt in many passages, which include the description of the Christian sign which Constantine put on his soldier's shields. I agree with the French scholar Jean Rougé that the description should be deleted as a gloss (ms.: transversa X littera, summo capite circumflexo), and that the passage which describes Constantine's conversion should be read as follows:

> Constantine was instructed in a dream (commonitus est in quiete) to mark the heavenly sign of God on the shields (of his army) and thus to join battle. He did as he was

---

[21] For the principal texts, see J.B. Aufhauser, Konstantins Kreuzesvision (Kleine Texte 108, 1912); J. Bidez and P. Heseler, "Fragments nouveaux de Philostorge sur la vie de Constantin," Byzantion 10 (1935) 403-442, reprinted in Philostorgius Kirchengeschichte³, ed. J. Bidez and F. Winkelmann (CCS, 1981) 363-392.

[22] Rufinus HE 9.9, p.829 Mommsen.

[23] Schrörs, Kreuzerscheinung (1913) 14ff.

ordered, and marked Christ on the shields. Armed with this sign, the army seized its swords.[24]

With Rougé's text, the sign described is the chi-rho monogram, and that brings Lactantius into line with all the other evidence. But what is the status, the source of Lactantius' account? He knows that Constantine put a Christian emblem on his army's shields, yet what he offers as explanation and motivation is the merest literary common-place. Lactantius need have had no evidence better than rumour for the psychological experiences of the emperor: he assimilates the conversion of Constantine to one of the most familiar of ancient religious stereotypes – action in response to a dream.[25]

Eusebius gives a very different account, which he attributes to the emperor himself. When he wrote Book Nine of the Ecclesiastical History, Eusebius knew of Constantine's conversion and alluded to the statue comemorating its role in the liberation of Rome, which stood in the basilica of Maxentius – the statue from which comes the famous gigantic head now in the Palazzo dei Conservatori on the Campidoglio.[26] By the time Eusebius wrote the Life of Constantine, he had heard the emperor's own version of his conversion. But before I analyse it, I must make a crucial preliminary point. Eusebius neither states nor to my mind implies that Constantine told him alone or in secret. I totally reject the view, perhaps put most succinctly by A.H.M. Jones, but very widely held, that "Constantine had never given any publicity to his experience: it was only when they had got on to terms of intimacy that the emperor revealed to [Eusebius] his proud secret."[27] Eusebius was never an intimate of Constantine,

---

[24]Lactant. Mort. Pers. 44.5-6, cf. J. Rougé, "A propos du manuscrit du 'De Mortibus Persecutorum'," Lactance et son temps (Théologie Historique 48, 1978) 13-22.

[25]For some examples, A.D. Nock, Essays on Religion and the Ancient World (Oxford 1972) 46.

[26]Eus. Hist. Eccl. 9.9.9-11.

[27]Jones (above, n.18) xiv, 96.

whom he only ever met on four occasions: the account which he reproduces is not a secret confession, but a public or semi-public pronouncement, which Constantine most probably delivered to the bishops at Nicaea in 325 when he entertained them to dinner after the Council.

Eusebius sets the scene in measured prose. Constantine realised that he needed divine aid in his war against Maxentius: he therefore implored assistance from the god who had given his father prosperity and success. Eusebius continues:

> As the emperor was making these requests incessantly, a most remarkable sign from God appeared to him, which it would perhaps not be easy to accept on anyone else's authority; but since the victorious emperor himself reported it to us the writer of this account many years later, when we were deemed worthy of his acquaintance and society, and confirmed his story with oaths, who could hesitate to credit the narration? Especially when the subsequent period provided reliable corroboration of the story. The emperor said that about the noon-hour, when the day was already beginning to wane (ἀμφὶ μεσημβρινὰς ἡλίου ὥρας, ἤδη τῆς ἡμέρας ἀποκλινούσης), he saw with his own eyes in the sky above the sun a cross composed of light, and that there was attached to it an inscription saying "By this conquer." At the sight, he said, astonishment seized him and all the troops who were accompanying him on the journey and observers of the miracle.

Constantine next told Eusebius how, during the following night, Christ appeared to him in a dream with the celestial phenomenon which he had seen and ordered him to make a replica of it to use as a standard and talisman in battle. Accordingly, the emperor supervised the manufacture of the labarum, which Eusebius describes in the form in which he saw it many years later. Marking the anachronism, Eusebius returns to 312 and continues his narrative: Constantine summoned expounders of God's word to explain to him the full significance of what he had seen, began to read the Bible, made priests of God his constant companions, and thus prosecuted the campaign against Maxentius with total confidence.[28]

---

[28]Eus. Vit. Const. 1.27-32.

I have already indicated that this account should be treated as a public pronouncement, a declaration which Constantine made to eastern bishops to explain how he became a Christian. We must, therefore, take seriously Constantine's claim that both he and his army (either the whole of his expeditionary force against Maxentius or a large detachment of it) saw something in the sky. What was it? Fortunately, there is no need to invoke miracle, or to pose a stark choice between miracle and hallucination.

Two plausible scientific explanations have been propounded by astronomers. E.N. da C. Andrade suggested to A.H.M. Jones that Constantine and his troops saw a rare, but well-attested form of solar "halo phenomenon," on this occasion in the shape of a cross.[29] Quite independently, F. Heiland identified that crosslike phenomenon as the conjunction of Saturn, Mars, and Jupiter close to the sun, while J. Gagé, accepting and refining his theory, was able to deduce the date and place as central Italy between 10 and 15 October 312.[30]

One specific detail in Constantine's account, as repeated by Eusebius, tells heavily against the latter theory. The army saw the phenomenon which they interpreted as a cross slightly after mid-day, not "above the setting sun" towards evening.[31] If Eusebius' temporal setting is correct and correctly reported, then the planets Saturn, Mars, and Jupiter would not have been visible in the sky because of the brightness of the sun.

To sum up. Constantine and his army saw a real or objective phenomenon, probably a solar halo, but they saw it with the eyes of faith as well as of reason, and their imagination supplied the words "by this conquer." The location and the precise date of the episode are unclear. Constantine perhaps did not give the bishops at dinner

---

[29]Jones (above, n.18) xiv, 96.

[30]F. Heiland, Die astronomische Deutung der Vision Konstantins (Jena: Zeiss Planetarium, 1948); J. Gagé, Revue d'histoire et de philosophie religieuses 31 (1951) 190ff. (unfortunately, with no reference to the alternative theory advanced by Andrade and Jones).

[31]Alföldi (above, n.18) 16.

too much pedantic detail. We have a choice. Solar halos are produced by ice crystals: presumably, therefore, Constantine and his army saw their solar halo either while crossing the Alps into Italy in the spring of 312 or in the Appennines while advancing on Rome in the autumn. Eusebius' placing of the episode might favour the earlier date, but we should probably allow more weight to Lactantius' clear statement that the Battle of the Milvian Bridge was the first battle which Constantine's army fought under the Christian banner.

One extremely important fact confirms the origin of the labarum which Eusebius describes. The word first occurs, in extant texts, in the chapter-headings to the Life of Constantine which the posthumous editor added when publishing the Life immediately after Eusebius' death in 339.[32] All attempts to find a Greek or a Latin etymology have failed. Not surprisingly. For the word is Celtic, meaning "eloquent, resonant, roaring, powerful" or something similar: Silius Italicus, a north Italian, had used Labarus as an invented name for a Gallic warrior in his epic on the Punic Wars.[33] Hence the name, and the labarum itself, must go back to 312, when Constantine invaded Italy with a largely Gallic army.

* * *

In conclusion, I wish to say something about Constantine's Speech to the Assembly of the Saints. This is an immensely difficult text, since what we possess, appended to Eusebius' Life of Constantine, is a corrupt version of an official but often defective Greek translation of an often obscurely expressed Latin original. Moreover, its authenticity, or at least Constantine's authorship of the Speech in its transmitted form, has often been denied. In addition, by a peculiar quirk of fortune, some important passages are omitted

---

[32] Eus. Vit. Const. 1.31, heading.

[33] Sil. Pun. 4.232, cf. R. Egger, "Das Labarum, die Kaiser-standarte der Spätantike," Römische Antike und frühes Christentum 2 (Klagenfurt 1963) 325-344.

from the manuscripts used by editors before Ivar Heikel in 1902,[34] so that there is at present no English translation which can give Greekless readers a full and accurate idea of what the Speech contains.

I believe in the integral authenticity of the Speech to the Assembly of the Saints. To justify that belief, I use three main arguments. First, I draw a distinction between taking advice and textual interpolation. If Constantine is considered incapable of the philosophizing which the Speech contains (and even that seems to me a dubious and a priori premise, but let us assume, for the sake of argument, that the Speech may contain philosophical passages beyond Constantine's abilities), then I submit that the emperor was capable of employing a good speechwriter in advance. It is improbable and implausible to suppose that the Speech has been systematically interpolated after its delivery by philosophically-minded translators who rendered it from Latin into Greek. The significant fact is that Constantine delivered the Speech publicly and endorsed its sentiments. There is a perfect contemporary analogy. The President of the United States normally has his speeches on policy written for him, and most of us might doubt whether the present President is capable of writing his own speeches (except of course for the jokes). Yet these speeches, even when mouthed from a teleprompter, clearly express the President's policy and his ideology. Let us not, however, degrade Constantine to that level! I merely wish to stress that arguments of the form that Constantine cannot have composed the contents of the Speech to the Assembly of the Saints would not suffice to prove that he did not deliver it.

My second argument is the positive side of the negative argument which I have just rejected. If we examine the contents of

---

[34]Principally Oratio 11.1, p.165.23-116.13 Heikel; 13, p.172.14-173.10 Heikel; 25.5, p.191.27-192.1 Heikel. The English translation by E.C. Richardson in A Select Library of Nicene and Post-Nicene Fathers, Second Series 1 (Oxford and New York 1890) 561-580, is a revision of the anonymous translation published by S. Bagster (London 1845).

the Speech, we can see large areas of resemblance to other writings of the early fourth century. The philosophy of the Speech shows a marked similarity to Calcidius' commentary on Plato's Timaeus, which John Dillon and John Rist have recently proved to belong to the early fourth century[35] - at which date the Osius to whom it is dedicated must surely be Osius of Corduba. Moreover, several passages of the Speech not only resemble Lactantius' Divine Institutes in thought and diction, but also appear to betray direct intellectual indebtedness, and it was probably Lactantius who inspired the use which the Speech makes of Virgil and the Sibylline Oracles.[36] Such features of the Speech, which in any event belongs intellectually to the early fourth century, locate it in Constantine's milieu.

My third argument is that the historical allusions in the Speech, when properly identified and interpreted, fit delivery by Constantine on a Good Friday in a year close to 320. Unfortunately, it is hard to be certain of the exact place and year: in 1976 I argued for Serdica in 317, while in 1981 I preferred Serdica in 321; on the other hand, André Piganiol in 1932 proposed Thessalonica in 323 or 324, while an Oxford ancient historian wishes to propose Antioch in 325.[37] It may never be possible to attain certainty: my view entails emending the name Maximinus in a chapter-heading of the Speech to Maximianus

---

[35] J. Dillon, The Middle Platonists (London 1977) 401ff.; J.M. Rist, Basil of Caesarea: Christian, Humanist, Ascetic, edited by P. Fedwick (Toronto 1981) 151ff.

[36] D. de Decker, "Le 'Discours à l'Assemblée des Saints' attribué à Constantin et l'oeuvre de Lactance," Lactance et son temps (Théologie Historique 48, 1978) 75-87. The same scholar also argues for Constantinian authorship in "Evocation de la Bible dans le 'Discours à l'Assemblée des Saints' prêté à l'empereur Constantin," Studia Biblica 1978 (Journal for the Study of the Old Testament, Supplement Series II, 1979), I, 133-144.

[37] Delivery on Good Friday 325 in the newly founded Constantinople is argued by S. Mazzarino, "La data dell' Oratio ad Sanctorum Coetum, il ius Italicum et la fondazione di Constantinopoli: note sui 'Discorsi' di Constantino," Antico, tardoantico ed èra costantiniana 1 (Rome 1974) 99-150.

(i.e. Galerius),[38] whereas a date of Easter 325 seems hard to reconcile with what else we know about Constantine's movements and events preceding the Council of Nicaea. But the uncertainty is a very minor one, since the range of possible dates has been narrowed to a very few years before the Council of Nicaea.

The contents of the Speech to the Assembly of the Saints are thus entirely appropriate for Constantine. Hence the Speech can be treated as valid evidence of how Constantine envisaged, or at least advertised, his role in history. It falls into three sections. In the first, Constantine expounds the philosophical basis of Christianity, drawing heavily (it seems) on Numenius of Apamea. The importance of this lies in the fact that Constantine equates the second person of the Christian Trinity with the Second God of the Timaeus and Numenius.[39] That brings him close to the theology of Eusebius of Caesarea, whom his opponents consistently regarded as an Arian. The second section of the Speech presents a theology of history, with emphasis on the Incarnation, arguing both that idolatry always leads to disaster and that Virgil foretold the coming of the Messiah. And the third section of the Speech explains how God has intervened in recent history to punish the persecutors and make Constantine prosper.

In the course of the Speech the emperor states his imperial mission to evangelise the empire:

> We strive to the best of our ability to fill with good hope those who are uninitiated in such doctrines, summoning God as our helper in the undertaking. For it is no ordinary task to turn the minds of our subjects to piety if they happen to be virtuous, and to reform them if they are evil and unbelieving, making them useful instead of useless. So, rejoicing in these undertakings, and believing it the task of a good man to praise the Saviour, I reject everything which the inferior state of fortune irrationally imposed by the mischance of ignorance, deeming repentance the greatest (step towards) salvation. I should have wished that this revelation had been vouchsafed to me long

---

[38] Oratio 22, heading.

[39] Rist (above, n.35) 155ff.

ago, since blessed is the man who from his earliest days
has been steadfast and has rejoiced in the knowledge of
things divine and the beauty of virtue.[40]

That is the imperial convert telling an audience of bishops that he
wishes he had been born a Christian. The conversion of Constantine
in 312 does not at all resemble the conversion of Paul on the road
Damascus, with which it has often been compared. Constantine did
not change from hostility towards or ignorance of Christianity to
sudden adherence. The step which he took in October 312 resembles
rather the conversion of Augustine. It marks a far more subtle
change: since his accession, Constantine had given the Christian
church political support; from the Battle of the Milvian Bridge
onwards, he publicly proclaimed himself God's servant and the
church's champion.

---

[40]Oratio 11.1 - a passage not to be found in published English
translations of the speech.

IV

CONSTANTINE'S PROHIBITION OF PAGAN SACRIFICE

When he died on May 30, 339, Eusebius of Caesarea had not yet put the finishing touches to his *Life of Constantine:* another hand gave it to the world as Eusebius left it, with many obvious doublets, inelegancies, and other signs which reveal that its author had not completed his final revision.[1] The *Life of Constantine*, as it survives, represents a conflation of two literary genres, two conceptions, two drafts. The earlier was a conventional panegyric of the dead emperor; the other, which resembles Eusebius' *Ecclesiastical History* in presentation and technique, is an account of Constantine as a Christian emperor, with an almost exclusive emphasis on his actions and policies in the religious sphere and with relevant documents quoted entire.

The central section of Book Two, between the defeat of Licinius (narrated in II.1-19) and the origins of the Arian controversy (described allusively and tendentiously in II.61-62), begins with a relic of the earlier draft. Eusebius summarizes legislation in favor of the Christians which Constantine enacted immediately after he defeated Licinius in 324 (II.20-22). There immediately supervenes, however, a long and homogeneous stretch of the *Life* which quotes the full text of the law just summarized, and summarizes other documents which Eusebius does not quote. It may be analyzed schematically as follows:

II.24-42 Letter of Constantine to the provincials of Palestine. Constantine expounds his view of his imperial mission to convert the Roman Empire to Christianity (24-29), orders the restitution of status and property to Christians who lost them under Licinius' anti-Christian legislation, or to relatives or the church in the case of martyrs (30-36), and ordains that all present owners of confiscated Christian property, including the imperial *fiscus*, shall surrender it with all speed (37-42).

II.43-46 43 Constantine's will was obeyed.

44 Constantine appointed mainly Christians to be provincial governors and forbade pagan magistrates the long-

[1] G. Pasquali, *Hermes* 46 (1910) 369 ff.; F. Winkelmann, *Eusebius Werke* 1.1 (Berlin GCS, 1975) liii ff.

established custom of preceding official business with a sacrifice.

45 Next Constantine issued two laws: one forbade "the disgusting idolatry performed of old in cities and countryside," specifically the erection of cult-statues, consultation of oracles, and sacrifice (ὡς . . . μήτε μὴν θύειν καθόλου μηδένα), while the other ordered the building of new churches and enlarging of existing ones to receive converts to Christianity.

46 Letter of Constantine to Eusebius instructing him to enlarge existing churches or build new ones and to apply to imperial officials for funds.

II.47–60 Introduction to (47) and text of (48–60) a letter of Constantine to the eastern provincials.

The significance, even the meaning, of the last letter depends on its date and context. Eusebius expressly sets it later than the prohibition of sacrifice (47.1): hence its guarantee to the eastern provincials that they may retain possession of their "shrines of falsehood" should be less important than its total silence about their right or ability to perform ritual acts of sacrifice in pagan temples. On the assumption that Eusebius' report is reliable and accurate, it may be argued that in 324 Constantine established Christianity as the official religion of the Roman Empire, and that he carried through a systematic and coherent reformation, at least in the eastern provinces which he conquered in 324 as a professed Christian in a Christian crusade against the last of the persecutors.[2]

*   *   *

Such was one of the main theses of a recent study of Constantine and Eusebius, whose interpretation of Constantine proceeded from the prohibition of sacrifice which Eusebius attests. A long and careful review by Dr. H. A. Drake contests both the overall interpretation of Constantine there advanced and the very existence of a prohibition of sacrifice, which is twice characterized as a "posited law."[3] A protest must be entered. In the normal meaning of words, a "posited law" is a law whose existence is posited, postulated, or assumed as a hypothesis

[2] *Constantine and Eusebius* (Cambridge, Mass. 1981) 210 ff., 245 ff.
[3] *AJP* 103 (1982) 462–66.

to explain either other evidence or a historical situation which otherwise seems inexplicable. A "posited law" is by no means an apt description of a law whose existence Eusebius asserts in categorical and explicit terms. However, something more serious is at issue than Dr. Drake's use of words: did Constantine issue a prohibition of pagan sacrifice or not?

Eusebius, fortunately, does not stand alone. The Theodosian Code preserves a brief extract from an imperial constitution addressed in 341 to Crepereius Madalianus, the *vicarius* of Italy, which prescribes quick and appropriate punishment for anyone who "contra legem divi principis parentis nostri et hanc nostrae mansuetudinis iussionem ausus fuerit sacrificia celebrare" (*CTh* XVI.10.2). That might seem confirmation enough: not only Eusebius writing between 337 and 339 in Palestine, but also the emperor Constans in 341 affirm that Constantine forbade pagan sacrifice. In an earlier publication, Dr. Drake addressed himself to the law of 341: he seized on the fact that Constantine's law is not extant, construed it as "a curious lack of documentation," and argued that "it is permitted to wonder whether it is not another example of the method of tardy attribution that Constantine's sons engaged in rather freely."[4] In his review, Dr. Drake brings into play Libanius' claim, made in 386 or thereabouts, that Constantine "made absolutely no alteration in the traditional forms of worship" (*Orat.* XXX.6, trans. A. F. Norman), and he puts Libanius on the same level as Eusebius, since "neither statement is documented." He contends, moreover, that Eusebius cannot be believed: "his tendency to see everything through a pro-Christian filter is too well known for a statement this broad and general to be taken at face value."[5]

Such thoroughgoing skepticism about Eusebius is hard to refute. It should perhaps be left to defeat itself. However, two considerations deprive the skeptical arguments of almost all their force. First, the loss of Constantine's law prohibiting sacrifice is not in itself suspicious. There is a perfect parallel in Constantine's legislation on another subject. The lawyer and ecclesiastical historian Sozomenus had read three laws issued by Constantine on the manumission of slaves *in ecclesia* (*HE* I.9.6). But the Theodosian Code and the Justinianic Code preserve only two of Constantine's laws on the subject (*CJ* I.13.1; *CTh* IV.7.1 = *CJ* I.13.2), and it is the innovatory law first establishing *manumissio in*

[4] H. A. Drake, *In Praise of Constantine: A Historical Study and New Translation of Eusebius' Tricennial Orations* (Berkeley 1976) 150, n. 17.

[5] *AJP* 103 (1982) 465.

ecclesia as a valid legal form which has perished, even though it is clearly presupposed in the two extant laws.[6]

Second, Eusebius' failure to quote the law prohibiting sacrifice can readily be explained. Like the law prohibiting provincial governors, *vicarii* of dioceses, and praetorian prefects from sacrificing before they commenced official business (II.44), the prohibition of the erection of cult-statues, the consultation of oracles, and sacrifice on any occasion was probably enacted by letters addressed to imperial officials. Eusebius, therefore, had probably never seen a copy of the original law. He knew the law through the regulations which the praetorian prefect residing at Antioch or the governor of Palestine issued on receipt of Constantine's instructions in order to put them into effect. Eusebius could normally quote only those imperial documents whose text he possessed: his failure to quote a letter of Constantine to praetorian prefects or provincial governors is neither surprising nor suspicious, and it lay beyond the scope of the *Life of Constantine* to quote proclamations which prefects or governors issued in compliance with the emperor's orders.

It is hardly legitimate, moreover, to prefer Libanius to Eusebius, or even to regard his testimony as being of equal weight. Not only was Libanius writing nearly five decades after the death of Constantine and in an apologia addressed "to the emperor Theodosius on behalf of the temples," but he does manifestly exaggerate. Libanius does not claim merely that Constantine did not prohibit pagan sacrifice; he claims that he "made absolutely no alteration in the traditional forms of worship" apart from confiscating temple treasures. Even Dr. Drake concedes that Constantine forcibly suppressed some pagan cults, as Eusebius attests (*Panegyric to Constantine* 8.4 ff.).[7]

*   *   *

The point at issue is no trivial one. It concerns more than the validity of a modern interpretation of Constantine. It concerns the accuracy and probity of Eusebius of Caesarea, the most voluminous and most important surviving witness to the "Constantinian revolution."

---

[6] *Constantine and Eusebius* (1981) 50 f. *CTh* IV.7.1 is unambiguously and unproblematically dated April 18, 321, while the correct date of *CJ* I.13.1 appears to be December 8, 316; cf. *The New Empire of Diocletian and Constantine* (Cambridge, Mass. 1982) 73.

[7] H. A. Drake, *In Praise of Constantine* (1976) 65 ff.

V

The Constantinian Reformation

It is difficult for a speaker to produce a satisfactory lecture on a topic about which he has produced two large books — and there is the fatal danger of lapsing into that most unfortunate genre, "an answer to my critics," which seems somewhat distasteful even when set to music by the genius of a Richard Strauss. As I pondered this problem of presentation, a remark of Norman Baynes came into my mind. Baynes advised his readers to study Eduard Schwartz's interpretation of Constantine in his book *Kaiser Constantin und die christliche Kirche* (originally published at Leipzig in 1913) rather than in Schwartz's later article on Constantine in the volume *Meister der Politik* (published in 1922). Baynes explained that "the latter is brilliantly written, but it carries to yet further lengths the views expressed in the book. This harsher restatement reads as a gage of challenge flung down before the critics."[1] That seemed to me an example worthy of emulation, at least in a lecture, and especially one in honour of a teacher and benefactor of scholarship who numbered Christianity in the Roman Empire among his academic interests.[2] My purpose in this lecture is to restate, to buttress and in part to amplify the thesis advanced in *Constantine and Eusebius* that Constantine carried through changes in the structure of religion in the Roman Empire which resemble those brought about in England in the reign of Henry VIII.[3] I shall try to take account of the criticisms of reviewers and others, but I do not intend to let criticisms dictate either the form or the content of the restatement.[4]

The *Oxford English Dictionary* defines "Reformation," when used as a proper noun, as

the great religious movement of the sixteenth century having for its object the reformation of the doctrines and practices of the church of Rome, and ending in the establishment of the various Reformed Protestant churches of central and north-western Europe.[5]

The great religious movement of the third and fourth centuries was

Christianity itself, which aimed to reform Roman society, or at least Roman religious customs. I wish to claim that Constantine carried through a reformation which had three interlocking aspects. He disestablished the pagan cults of the eastern provinces of the Roman Empire; he established Christianity as the official religion of the Empire and its emperor; and he created a new privileged class which had a strong vested interest in preserving and perpetuating this changed state of affairs.

* * *

The title of my lecture is provocative. It is deliberately provocative. The emperor Constantine is and always has been a controversial subject. In the fourth century, the instant panegyric of Eusebius was answered in the next generation by the clever denigration of Julian the Apostate and the hostile portrait painted by Eunapius of Sardis. More recently, the two poles of interpretation represented by Eusebius and by Zosimus, the follower of Eunapius, have continued to reassert themselves, from the controversy between Cardinal Baronius and the German humanist Löwenklau in the sixteenth century down to the present decade. One recent book pronounces Constantine "a sincere Christian, a truly great Christian emperor and a genuine Apostle of the Christian church,"[6] while another argues that Constantine was not a Christian at all, but merely enlisted Christianity "in his own personal crusade to gain control of the Empire," and that, upon close analysis, the religion of Constantine turns out to be "not simply non-Christian but positively anti-Christian."[7]

Such continuing divergence of views is no accident, since the subject is inherently controversial, and most of the problems are of such a nature that they cannot be resolved by steering a judicious middle course between extremes. An example, perhaps trivial in itself, but with far-reaching implications, concerns Constantine's date of birth. The day is undisputed, being clearly and unambiguously attested by good evidence (27 February),[8] but for the year modern opinions range between 272 and 288.[9] Hence the apparently safe and prudent *communis opinio* that Constantine was born c. 280.[10] Yet close scrutiny reveals not only that almost all the precise evidence for Constantine's age at his death in 337 presents him as aged between sixty-two and sixty-five,[11] but also that the imprecise evidence which speaks of his youthfulness at or close to the time of his accession in 306 appears to reflect Constantine's own propaganda.[12] The choice, therefore, is not between discrepant testimony from witnesses of equal standing, but between an approximation to the truth and systematic misrepresentation.[13] If that analysis of the evidence is correct, then it should be the precise, though later, evidence which deserves preference over the early, but apparently tainted evidence of Constantine's panegyrists and admirers. Constantine (it follows) was probably born in 272 or 273. Hence, when he became emperor in 306, he was a mature adult of thirty-three or thirty-four, not a young man of twenty-five or so, still less a callow youth of eighteen. Moreover, if he was born in 272 or 273, then the years which he spent at the eastern court of Diocletian embraced the years of his intellectual maturity, and it becomes both reasonable and necessary to ask how he spent his time in Nicomedia before his abrupt departure in 305. There is a possibility (to put it no higher) that he discussed philosophy and religion with Christian intellectuals: both Lucian of Antioch and Lactantius are known to have been in the city at the beginning of the fourth century.[14]

* * *

Many obstacles hinder a proper understanding of Constantine. Perhaps the most serious is the existence of Jakob Burckhardt's classic study of Constantine and his age, first published in 1853, which embodies not only nineteenth century assumptions, but also a seriously flawed assessment of the main literary evidence. For more than a century, Burckhardt has dictated the terms in which "the Constantinian problem" has been debated, and his influence has perhaps percolated more widely than ever in the last three decades, with the publication of translations into English in 1949 and Italian in 1957.[15] The intellectual, historical and literary merits of *Die Zeit Constantin's des Grossen* are undeniable, and there is no point in essaying another historiographical survey of Burckhardt's influence on subsequent writers about Constantine.[16] It may be helpful, however, to illustrate how Burckhardt has determined the approach to Constantine even of those scholars who disagree most profoundly with his overall interpretation.

Burckhardt voices his deepest historical assumptions with refreshing honesty and clarity:

In a genius driven without surcease by ambition and lust for power there can be no question of Christianity and paganism, of conscious religiosity or irreligiosity; such a man is essentially unreligious. . . . All of his energies, spiritual as well as physical, are devoted to the great goal of domination, and if he ever pauses to think of his convictions, he finds they are pure fatalism.

He also dismisses the two main literary sources for Constantine as habitual liars: Lactantius' *On the Deaths of the Persecutors* "begins straightway with a demonstrable untruth" and continues in the same vein, while Eusebius "has been proven guilty of so many distortions, dissimulations, and inventions that he has forfeited all claim to figure as a decisive source." Hence the way is open for Burckhardt to propound his interpretation of Constantine as a fourth century Napoleon, whose religion was nothing more than "the dreary deism of a conqueror who requires a god in order to justify his acts of violence by an appeal to something outside himself."[17]

Completely different is the Constantine of Norman Baynes and A.H.M. Jones: this Constantine has "definitely identified himself with Christianity, with the Christian Church and the Christian creed," he rules in the genuine conviction that the Christian God "had entrusted to him, His servant, the governance of all earthly things."[18] Baynes and Jones thus completely and explicitly reject Burckhardt's picture of Constantine. Yet they both accept his implicit dilemma between religious belief and political acumen. Both Baynes and Jones set out to prove that Constantine was a convinced Christian, not a ruler who merely adopted Christianity as a device to secure political power. Both argue that Constantine's conversion in 312 was genuine, not feigned, because it was contrary to his political interest. They imagine Constantine in 312 as fighting against overwhelming odds, as facing defeat before the walls of Rome, as exhibiting a confidence which is hardly explicable except on the hypothesis that Constantine felt God had promised him victory.[19] The premiss of the argument is deeply flawed. When Constantine marched on Rome in the autumn of 312, the war against Maxentius had already been won in North Italy.[20] Moreover, the accounts of the North Italian campaign in panegyrics of Constantine delivered in 313 and 321 make it clear that Maxentius' main army was not guarding the Alpine passes from Gaul, but awaiting an invasion of Italy from the east, i.e. by Licinius.[21] When Constantine invaded Italy in the spring of 312, he acted swiftly in order to forestall his imperial colleague Licinius: Maxentius was doomed, but it was an open question whether Licinius or Constantine would replace him as ruler of Italy.[22] Maxentius' main army was destroyed near Verona: after that, only enormous incompetence could have lost Constantine the Battle of the Milvian Bridge. That is to say, Constantine put Christian symbols on the shields of his army and made the Christian *labarum* his standard, not at a moment of crisis when defeat and death threatened, but before a battle which he knew he would win — and which he did win at the first charge.[23]

The conversion of Constantine (whatever we mean by that term) was not contrary to his political interest. Quite the opposite — as the changing policy of Maxentius towards the Christians in his domains makes clear. When Constantine came to power in Britain in July 306, he immediately decreed religious toleration and restored to the Christians of Britain, Gaul and Spain the churches and property which had been confiscated under Diocletian's persecuting edict of 23 February 303.[24]

When Maxentius came to power in Rome in October 306, he very soon granted toleration to the Christians of Italy and Africa.[25] But the restitution of confiscated Christian property in these areas was delayed until 311, when the ruler of Italy became embroiled in war with Constantine.[26] The synchronism, which is not likely to be coincidental, implies that the Christians were a political force of some importance in Maxentius' domains. The conversion of Constantine made him attractive as a potential ruler to the Christian subjects of Maxentius in Rome, who constituted a large and powerful political group in the city.

Modern attempts to decide what proportion of the population of the Roman Empire was Christian before Constantine tend (I believe) to underestimate the importance of Christians.[27] The reason is not so much that no precise figures are obtainable, as that concentration on proportions and percentages draws attention away from significant indications that long before 300 Christians had achieved acceptance, even prominence, in those echelons of Roman provincial society which set the tone for the rest.[28] The evidence that Christianity was regarded as socially respectable begins around 200. In Severan Carthage, the leading literary figure was undoubtedly Tertullian, who resembles contemporary Greek sophists in many respects.[29] Tertullian speaks confidently of Christians at the court of Septimius Severus, in the Roman Senate and among the entourage of a proconsul of Africa.[30] In Alexandria at the same date, Clement was writing moral and exhortatory essays for an audience which clearly included many rich Christians,[31] while Origen not only gave Christian instruction openly, but also gained fame outside the church: a governor of Arabia and, later, the empress Julia Mamaea summoned him to come to speak before them.[32] Two generations later, in the late third century, the Christian church and its bishop were prominent in the life of many eastern cities: an episode such as the appeal of the church of Antioch to Aurelian for aid in ejecting the deposed bishop Paul of Samosata illustrates how the Christian church had, by 270, become a normal part of the institutional fabric of Roman provincial society.[33]

A fine vignette of the church as a functioning institution in the third century is given by the so-called *Didascalia Apostolorum*, of which there survive a full Syriac translation and long fragments of a Latin version, both of the fourth century.[34] The original *Didascalia* was written in Greek, probably in Northern Syria, and at a time when ordinary Christians were in constant danger of arrest, but when no state-directed persecution was in progess: that is to say, before 250, perhaps many years before.[35] One of the main purposes of composition of the *Didascalia* may have been to introduce and commend a six-day fast before Easter. The pretence of apostolic authorship enables the writer to claim first-hand evidence for a most peculiar chronology of Holy

Week, which flatly contradicts the New Testament: according to the *Didascalia*, Jesus ate the Passover with the authors, his disciples, on the third day of the week, and spent the whole of the fourth day in the High Priest's house, the fifth day and the following night in custody with Pilate.[36] From this aberrant chronology, the writer deduces that Christians have an obligation to fast from the second day of Holy Week until Easter Day.[37] Since Dionysius of Alexandria c. 260 refers to such a six-day fast before Easter as a normal practice, the fantastic justification which the *Didascalia* advances implies that such a fast was an innovation, or at least controversial, in Syria at the time of writing — which accordingly ought to be the early third century.[38]

The content of the *Didascalia Apostolorum* is very varied: it begins with general moral exhortations (e.g., "abstain from all avarice and evildoing") and concludes with discussion of problems which confront Christians in dealing with the world (the adoption of orphans and upbringing of children; martyrdom and the prospect of resurrection; the Paschal fast; heresies and schisms; and the relationship of Christianity to the Old Testament). The central section, however, comprises a lengthy treatise on the episcopal office, followed by regulations on divine worship, on church attendance, on the order of widows and on deacons and deaconesses. Much of these chapters is predictable (e.g., prohibition of drunkenness), but there are exhortations about bishops which reveal a great deal about the nature of the ecclesiastical organisation which the *Didascalia* envisages.[39]

Bishops (the *Didascalia* ordains) must be aged fifty, unless "the congregation be a small one" containing no one suitably qualified. When elected, he must not defer to the rich or favour them unduly, nor dispense forgiveness of sins for money. The bishop is the steward of the revenues of the church, which suffice both to clothe and feed him and to support orphans, widows, the distressed and strangers: he must not live in luxury himself, but share the revenues with the needy. The laity, in turn, have an obligation to contribute tithes and offerings to the bishop, their chief and leader, their mighty king. Christians ought not to seek legal redress from heathen courts: if they have a suit against a pagan, they should be prepared to suffer some loss; if there is a quarrel between Christians, the bishop should act as judge, with priests and deacons in attendance. The *Didascalia Apostolorum* thus assumes something more than small conventicles of Christians. It presupposes local churches of some size, incorporating all levels of society, wealthy and able to support a full-time clergy and engage in large-scale charitable activities. A standard of comparison comes from Rome: there, in 251, the Christian community supported more than fifteen hundred widows and beggars.[40]

There is nothing quite like the *Didascalia Apostolorum* for Christianity in the West in the third century, although the evidence of Minucius Felix and Cyprian documents its steadily increasing role in African provincial life.[41] From around 300, moreover, survive the eighty-one canons of the Council of Elvira, which deal with a wide variety of penitential and disciplinary problems in the church of southern Spain.[42] Many of the canons concern universal and entirely predictable topics, such as adultery, or questions which have always troubled the church, such as clerical celibacy or which professions are permissible, which impermissible for a Christian. A few canons, however, address the unique problems of a church emerging into social prominence in a pagan society. In Baetica, Christians were holding local magistracies and priesthoods, and there were even Christian *flamines*, i.e., men who held the provincial high-priesthood of the imperial cult while catechumens or after baptism. The Canons of Elvira lay down regulations which permit such men to be readmitted to the church: they treat the performance of sacrifice as apostasy and hence entailing permanent excommunication, but allow Christian magistrates and *flamines* who have avoided the act of sacrifice to resume communion after appropriate penance. Most striking of all, the canons deny the title of martyr to those who are killed while smashing pagan idols — which implies that some Christians were already using violence against pagan shrines.[43]

The significance of the Canons of Elvira depends in large part on their date. The majority of scholars have opted for a date immediately after the cessation of the Great Persecution in Spain (usually 306 or 309).[44] That is not plausible, since the canons show no trace of the problems posed elsewhere by persecution: they never mention *traditio* (the surrender of the scriptures in accordance with the edict of 23 February 303), and their only allusion to confessors speaks of those who bring letters from a confessor, who could be far removed from Baetica.[45] The choice, therefore, must lie between a date before 303 and one long after 305. On the later dating, of course, the Canons of Elvira would become evidence for the effect in Spain of Constantine's conversion in 312. But such a late date has found few recent advocates and seems quite impossible. The canon relating to local magistrates specifies that the *duumvir* of a city shall stay away from church during his year of office:[46] can we believe in such an exclusion after 312? Surely not: Constantine's policy was to make it easier for Christians to play a full role in Roman public life. Moreover, the list of bishops who subscribed the canons includes Ossius of Corduba in second place: after 312, he would surely have presided at such a council of nineteen bishops.[47] By elimination, therefore, the Council of Elvira should be dated before 303, as Louis Duchesne saw long ago.[48] The Canons of Elvira reflect the standing of the Christian church in southern Spain before Constantine became emperor.

Constantine did not suddenly proclaim himself the champion of a sect which was small and insignificant, even in the West. As early as 306, he saw that no Roman emperor could rule securely without the acquiescence of his Christian subjects. Neither his toleration of Christianity in 306 nor his conversion in 312 involved any serious political risk. On the contrary, both actions brought him immediate political benefits. Burckhardt's dilemma can be abolished or transcended: Constantine was both a consummate politician and, from 312, a convinced Christian.

* * *

Modern historical method rightly requires that the historian utilise all available types of evidence, and that he employ a wide variety of techniques in its interpretation. In ancient history, however, there are many periods and subjects where the framework or basic picture depends upon the assessment of long-familiar literary works. The historian of Constantine and his age finds himself (and is likely, I fear, always to find himself) in this predicament. Whatever it may be, his interpretation rests, in the final analysis, upon the value he puts upon Lactantius and Eusebius, who provide not only most of our basic political narrative for the Diocletianic persecution from 303 to 313, but also much of our evidence for the religious policies of Constantine. It has been traditional to discount their testimony, either in general (as Burckhardt did) or specifically in regard to crucial aspects of Constantine's religious policies. I believe that the conventional estimates of both Lactantius and Eusebius are seriously misleading, and that once their relationship to Constantine is correctly defined, then their testimony can be accepted as weighty and accurate.

The career of Lactantius is disputed. It is certain that Lactantius was an African, that he came to Nicomedia in the reign of Diocletian, that he forfeited his offical chair of Latin rhetoric there in 303, and that at some subsequent date he taught Constantine's son Crispus in Gaul.[49] But it is not immediately obvious when Lactantius left Bithynia, where he then went, or at what date he was Crispus' tutor.[50] On the most widely accepted reconstruction of his career, he remained in Asia Minor until 311, then repaired to the court of Constantine in Gaul and stayed there: hence he wrote *On the Deaths of the Persecutors* in Trier c. 320 as a journalistic hack penning political propaganda on behalf of Constantine.[51] That reconstruction (I firmly believe) is unsound. Various passages in works other than *On the Deaths of the Persecutors* imply that Lactantius was alive and active in Nicomedia in 324, and that he had returned there some years earlier.[52] Now, under the terms of Licinius' legislation of 313, Lactantius became entitled to resume his chair of rhetoric — and I believe that he did so. Further, I think that I can detect hints in the *Divine Institutes* that Lactantius completed that work in Africa in 308/9. Consequently, I reconstruct the career of Lactantius between 305 and 315 as follows. He left Asia Minor in May 305, when it passed under the control of Galerius, the instigator of the persecution which began in 303.[53] Lactantius then returned home to Africa, but was obliged to flee Africa in 309 when Maxentius suppressed the rebel Domitius Alexander. He fled to Gaul, to the court of Constantine, who had also left Nicomedia in May 305, and Constantine gave him employment teaching his son Crispus. In 313, Lactantius returned to Nicomedia, where he soon wrote *On the Deaths of the Persecutors* as a subject of Licinius, not of Constantine.[54]

On this reconstruction of Lactantius' career, which I believe to be supported throughout by both evidence and probability, he cannot have written *On the Deaths of the Persecutors* primarily as a work of Constantinian propaganda. The Constantinian propaganda which the work contains appears, on internal grounds, to come from the period before the Battle of the Milvian Bridge.[55] Moreover, Lactantius makes mistakes in describing the battle which imply that he did not accompany Constantine's march on Rome.[56] It follows that Lactantius probably took his leave of the emperor before Constantine first proclaimed himself a Christian. Consequently, since Lactantius was writing in Nicomedia c. 314, it becomes reasonable to believe two crucial assertions which *On the Deaths of the Persecutors* makes about Constantine, viz.

(1) that in 305, when Diocletian abdicated, everyone expected him to proclaim Constantine the new Caesar of the East;
(2) that in 306 his first action as emperor was to restore the Christian church to the position which it had enjoyed before 303.[57]

These statements sharply contradict the conventional view of Constantine as a young usurper who suddenly, in 312, proclaimed adherence to a small and persecuted sect. Lactantius presents a Constantine who showed political sympathy for the Christians from the moment of his accession, six years before his conversion.

A similar revaluation is needed for Eusebius of Caesarea too. It has been the almost universal view of modern scholarship that Eusebius was a good courtier who stood close to Constantine, that he served the emperor as a constant adviser on ecclesiastical matters, and that as a writer he put his pen at the emperor's service.[58] Basic facts of geography and chronology contradict. Eusebius, born c. 260 and bishop of Caesarea in Palestine from c. 314 to 339, was a provincial and an academic, by instinct and training primarily a biblical scholar. He wrote the whole of the *Ecclesiastical History*, except the last two chapters, long before he became a subject of Constantine, and I believe that he completed the first edition of the *History* in seven books several years before Constantine's accession in Britain. Even after 324, Eusebius remained primarily a scholar, remote from the imperial court, which he visited only four times, on each occasion on ecclesiastical business in the company of other bishops. Eusebius of Caesarea enjoyed no special relationship with Constantine: he was a distant admirer, not a court propagandist. His historical views were formed before Constantine became emperor, and he deserves to be regarded as a basically honest writer — prejudiced and with a limited vision, to be sure, but intent on portraying the truth as he saw it.[59]

This general estimate of Eusebius is very relevant to the *Life of Constantine*, which has seemed to many scholars to be an extremely problematical work.[60] Their puzzlement largely derives from a failure to distinguish carefully between the literary and the historical problems which the *Life* poses. The literary problems were solved in 1910 by Giorgio Pasquali in a lucid article whose conclusions were totally misreported by Jules Maurice and by Baynes.[61] Pasquali observed that the *Life* exhibits some obvious doublets and inconsistencies, yet that each half of each pair of doublets is equally Eusebian in style and diction. He concluded, therefore, that Eusebius died before he finished revising the text:

> Then someone came and published the work at once, as he found it: perhaps Acacius, Eusebius' successor in the see of Caesarea, was the editor; but the name does not matter. The work was published with the same piety and the same lack of understanding as Plato's *Laws* were by Philip of Opus. With the *Life*, political considerations too affected the publication.[62]

That analysis is entirely apposite: many other features of the *Life* and its appended speeches besides those noted by Pasquali are most readily explicable on the hypothesis that someone else published the *Life* in a state which its author, had he lived longer, would greatly have transformed.[63] Hence the *Life of Constantine*, though wholly Eusebian in style, contains inconsistencies which are the result of its unfinished condition. That fact alone disarms all the internal arguments ever advanced against Eusebius' authorship or in favour of interpolation. The external arguments are equally lacking in cogency: unless I am mistaken, they are all variants of the basic argument that Eusebius cannot have written a particular passage because it contains factual errors which he cannot have made, or because it attributes to Constantine actions which he did not take.[64] A papyrus has ruined that line of argument and caused it to be completely discredited and abandoned. One of the documents in the *Life* to which critics had always taken the greatest exception, and had most confidently denounced as a forgery,[65] is partly preserved on a London papyrus dated palaeographically to the second quarter of the fourth century. Since A.H.M. Jones, following a suggestion of C.E. Stevens, identified the previously published papyrus fragment in 1951,[66] both Eusebius' authorship of the *Life of Constantine* and the authenticity of all the documents which he quotes have been generally (though not universally) conceded.[67]

It is otherwise, however, with enactments of Constantine which Eusebius reports or summarises, but does not quote, either because he could not do so or because he chose not to do so. Scholars who unquestioningly accept the documents quoted still dismiss or ignore those which Eusebius only reports: hence they become evidence for Eusebius' picture of Constantine more than for historical reality.[68] One is of particular importance. Eusebius reports a law which prohibited the erection of cult-statues, the consultation of pagan oracles, divination and sacrifice to the pagan gods on any occasion whatever. He reports it in a carefully constructed section of the *Life* which describes Constantine's actions immediately after the defeat of Licinius.[69] First, Eusebius quotes a long imperial letter to the provincials of Palestine undoing the effects of Licinius' anti-Christian legislation. The next step (he observes) was to appoint Christians to most high offices and to forbid governors, *vicarii* and praetorian prefects to perform sacrifice before conducting official business, even if they were pagans. Two laws followed: one totally prohibited sacrifice and other forms of pagan cult, the other ordained the building of new churches and the enlarging of existing ones, and to illustrate the latter law Eusebius quotes Constantine's letter to him. Finally, Eusebius quotes a long and fiery imperial letter to the eastern provincials, which has commonly been styled "an edict of toleration."[70] The document has quite a different meaning if read in the light of an antecedent prohibition of sacrifice. Constantine allows the eastern provincials to have their shrines of falsehood if they must, but he makes no mention of sacrifice: by implication, therefore, he reiterates the existing prohibition.

Eusebius' report has usually been dismissed as panegyric or exaggeration, as invention or wishful thinking, or simply ignored and omitted.[71] But such a dismissal ignores the context of Eusebius' assertion and assumes a degree of conscious dishonesty or misrepresentation which cannot be found elsewhere in his work. And it is wrong to posit a sharp distinction between quoted and reported documents. If Eusebius does not quote the law prohibiting sacrifice, that probably means that the imperial enactment itself was not published, but took the form of a letter to officals who then issued regulations on their own authority to enforce it in their jurisdictions.[72] Of set purpose, the *Life* quotes only documents written or dictated by Constantine himself.

The point at issue is (I believe) in many ways the central *crux interpretationis* for understanding Constantine. For it involves both the credibility of Eusebius and Constantine's attitude towards paganism. The law prohibiting pagan sacrifice is the lynch-pin of the thesis that Constantine carried through a religious Reformation.

*   *   *

In the development of Constantine's religious policies, there are three quite separate stages, and to understand and distinguish them we must appreciate two crucial facts. The first is that Constantine gained control of different parts of the Roman Empire at different dates: in 306, he succceeded his father Constantius as ruler of Britain, Gaul and Spain; in 312, the war against Maxentius added Italy, Africa and the islands of the western Mediterranean; in 316/7, Constantine acquired most of the Balkans, including Greece and the islands of the Aegean in his war against Licinius; and in 324 the second war against Licinius, waged as a Christian crusade, made him ruler of the whole Empire. The second crucial fact is that Constantine was able to adopt different policies in different parts of the Empire. This resolves the familiar dispute over whether Constantine prohibited pagan sacrifices and despoiled pagan shrines of their treasures. The best evidence that he did so comes from Eusebius, and therefore, given Eusebius' perspective, applies primarily to the territories which Constantine conquered in 324, viz. Asia Minor and the East.[73] The early evidence that Constantine tolerated paganism until the end of his reign comes from Firmicus Maternus, who in 343 denounced the continuation of sacrifice and urged Constantius and Constans to seize temple treasures.[74] But Maternus lived and wrote in Italy, and his evidence is valid primarily for those territories over which Constantine began to rule in 306 and 312, at a time when he still presented himself as a champion of religious toleration.

Constantine was proclaimed emperor at York on 25 July 306. He immediately went beyond his father's passive policy of declining to enforce the persecuting edicts against the Christians: he restored them to their worship and their God.[75] Clearly, this "first sanctioning of the restored holy religion" (as Lactantius calls it) included the reparation of Christian losses in the persecution. Constantine himself, however, continued to perform the traditional religious role of a Roman emperor, and in 310, at a time of dynastic crisis, he sought supernatural legitimation of his rule by proclaiming Sol Invictus as his personal protector.[76]

In 312, Constantine went beyond political support for Christians and proclaimed himself a convert to their religion, a worshipper of the one true God. Whatever the nature of Constantine's personal experience (and I do not think that that is an important question), the effects of his conversion were immediately apparent. The court and its ceremonial began to reflect the emperor's new religion, and Constantine began to remould Roman society and Roman law in a Christian direction. He endowed vast churches in Rome and granted tax-exemptions to the Christian clergy; he gave Christian bishops the power to manumit slaves in church; he defined the relationship between *episcopalis audientia* and the secular courts — and much more.[77] Fortunately, in the present context, I do not need to insist on the often controversial details, since historians such as Baynes and Jones, Andreas Alföldi and Jean Gaudemet, S. Calderone and Fergus Millar have shown beyond doubt that the Christian trend in Constantine's legislation begins very shortly after the Battle of the Milvian Bridge.[78]

In 324, his victory over Licinius gave Constantine an opportunity to go much further, at least in Asia Minor and the East, where the Christians formed a larger proportion of the population than in the West or the Balkans. For in 324, as in 313, the Christians of the East, on hearing of the defeat of their pagan ruler, rose and took revenge on their persecutors. "All the advocates of attacking God paid the appropriate penalty and were destroyed": Eusebius' coy allusion masks the fact that dozens, perhaps even hundreds, of prominent pagans were killed.[79] We must picture (I think) a situation not unlike Iran after the fall of the Shah. In such circumstances, Constantine could (and did) move decisively to disestablish the traditional cults of the East and to replace them with Christianity as the official and established religion.

Constantine had a coherent and comprehensive policy. Pagan ceremonial was purged from public life. Pagan rites such as sacrifice and divination were prohibited. If pagans kept their temples, they were expected to worship there in a Christian fashion, with prayer but without sacrificial smoke to carry their prayers aloft to the gods. And the temples soon lost the treasures accumulated over centuries: Constantine sent special *comites* to inspect the shrines of both town and country in each eastern province, and to confiscate everything of value which they contained.[80] The proceeds of this massive seizure were then used to build churches and to provide funds for supporting the poor — in both cases, of course, channelled through the local bishop, who thereby became a dispenser of imperial patronage in a way familiar to any Canadian audience. Eusebius aptly sums up the new situation of the church after 324 in his exegesis of Isaiah 49:23, which reads, in the version of the New English Bible: "kings shall be your foster-fathers, and their princesses shall be your nurses." He comments:

With our eyes we have seen this very thing being literally fulfilled, as those who hold the highest office sustain the church of
God like foster-fathers, while their princesses, that is, the rulers
and powers in each race and in each province who serve the
highest monarchy will minister to the needy of the church like
nurses, giving supplies of grain to them by imperial command.[81]

Constantine had created a new privileged class, the Christian clergy
and especially the Christian bishops. Yet the political power of the
church was not Constantine's creation, for it antedated his reign. The
church, therefore, expected to be independent of, not subservient to,
its new imperial patrons. But that is another story.

* * *

The phrase "the Constantinian revolution" has gained a certain currency; indeed, I have written as if "the Constantinian revolution" and
"the Constantinian reformation" were equally valid descriptions of
Constantine's achievement.[82] Yet I have come to doubt whether we
can legitimately speak of a Constantinian "revolution," for it is difficult to see what Constantine changed fundamentally outside the
religious sphere — except as a consequence of his religious innovations.
Most of the military, administrative and fiscal reforms with which he
has been credited, or for which he has been blamed, have been shown
by modern research (or can be shown) to be the work of others, and
they all form part of a gradual process of radical transformation which
began long before 306 and continued long after 337.[83] In contrast, the
notion of a "Constantinian reformation" seems to me both illuminating
and true to the facts. The Roman Empire had two halves. The western
half underwent a long, slow and usually peaceful process of Christianisation: the eastern half became officially Christian in war and
violence, when a Christian emperor defeated "the last of the persecutors"
and the Christians of the East slaughtered their oppressors. We should
not be misled by our adoption of a predominantly western perspective in assessing the fourth century as a whole. In Asia Minor and the
East, Constantine carried through a reformation which was sudden,
complete and irreversible.

NOTES

The text printed here represents a revision of the lecture delivered at Mount Allison University on 28 September 1984 made in the light of the discusssions which followed its delivery both there and on subsequent occasions during a lecture tour of Western Canada organised by the Classical Association of Canada. I am grateful to all those who offered comments and suggestions: for obvious reasons I cannot thank them by name.

1.   N.H. Baynes, *Constantine the Great and the Christian Church* (London 1931) 37. The article is reprinted in E. Schwartz, *Charakterköpfe aus der Antike*[2] (Leipzig 1943) 223-280.

2.   J.E.A. Crake, "Early Christians and Roman Law," *Phoenix* 19 (1965) 61-70. It deserved (but did not receive) mention in the long paper "Legislation against the Christians," *JRS* 58 (1968) 32-50.

3.   T.D. Barnes, *Constantine and Eusebius* (Cambridge, Mass. 1981) 210 ff.; 245 ff.

4.   For some objections to the thesis in reviews, see H.A. Drake, *AJP* 102 (1982) 462 ff.; Averil Cameron, *JRS* 73 (1983) 184 ff.; B.H. Warmington, *CR*, N.S. 33 (1983) 283. The most sustained critique to appear so far can be found in R. MacMullen, *Christianizing the Roman Empire A.D. 100-400* (New Haven 1984) 43 ff.

5.   *Oxford English Dictionary* 8 (Oxford 1933) s.v. 3b.

6.   P. Keresztes, *Constantine. A Great Christian Monarch and Apostle* (Amsterdam 1981) 8.

7.   A. Kee, *Constantine versus Christ. The Triumph of Ideology* (London: S.C.M. 1982) esp. 174, 50. Among the abundant and varied evidence for Constantine's religious beliefs, Kee gives primacy of place (23 ff.) to the panegyric which Euesbius delivered in Constantinople in July 336, as translated by H.A. Drake, *In Praise of Constantine. A Historical Study and New Translation of Euesbius' Tricennial Orations* (Berkeley 1976) 83 ff. Further, he advances the paradoxical claim that Eusebius' *Life* "does not present Constantine as a Christian" (65). The book clearly aims higher than historical accuracy: Kee vows that he is writing "political theology" in order to expose "the betrayal of Christ" under Constantine when "Christianity sold its birthright for a pension and became the state religion" (117 ff., esp. 159, 175).

8.   *CIL* 1,[2] pp. 255,258,259.

9.   For the extremes, see *The Prosopography of the Later Roman Empire* 1(Cambridge 1971) 223 (272); O. Seeck, *Geschichte des Unterganges der antiken Welt* 1[3] (Berlin 1910) 434 ff. (288); J.F. Matthews, *Encyclopedia Britannica*15: Macropaedia 5 (1974) 71 ('probably in the later A.D. 280's').

10. E.g., A. Piganiol, *L'empereur Constantin*(Paris 1932) 37; N.H. Baynes, *Cambridge Ancient History* 12 (Cambridge 1939) 678; R. MacMullen, *Constantine* (New York 1969) 21; R. Syme, *Historia Augusta Papers* (Oxford 1983) 63.

11. Victor, *Caes.* 41.16 (62); *Epitome de Caesaribus* 41.15 (63); Sozomenus, *HE* 2. 34. 3; Zonaras 13.4 (c. 64); Eutropius, *Brev.*. 10. 8. 2; Jerome, *Chronicle* 234[b] Helm; Socrates, *HE* 1. 39. 1; 40. 3; Photius, *Biblotheca* 234 (65). The late writer Malalas, p. 324. 10/11 Bonn has sixty, but Eusebius' comparisons of the emperor to Alexander assume that Constantine was born c.273 (*VC* 1. 8; 4. 53).

12. *Panegyrici Latini* 7(6). 5. 3 (307); 6(7). 17. 1 (310); Lactantius, *Mort. Pers.* 18. 10; 24. 4; 29. 5 (c.314); *Panegyrici Latini* 4(10). 16. 4 (321); Lactantius, *Div. Inst.* 1. 1.14 (324); Constantine, quoted by Eusebius, *VC* 2.51 (c.325); Firmicus Maternus, *Math.* 1.10.12 (337); Eusebius, *VC* 1. 19 (c.338).

13. *The New Empire of Diocletian and Constantine* (Cambridge, Mass. 1982) 39 ff.

14. *Constantine and Eusebius* (1981) 74; 194.

15. Viz. by M. Hadas as *The Age of Constantine the Great* (New York 1949), and by E. Dupré Theseider as *L'età di Costantino il Grande* (Florence 1957). Both translate the second, revised edition of *Die Zeit Constantin's des Grossen* (Leipzig 1880).

16. On Burckhardt's influence, see esp. S. Mazzarino, *Antico, tardoantico ed èra Costantiniana* 1 (Rome 1974) 11 ff. ; 32 ff. (a revised version of an article originally

published in German in *Saeculum* 22 (1971) 25 ff.).

17.　Quotations from J. Burckhart, *The Age of Constantine the Great*, trans. M. Hadas (1949) 292, 246, 293, 297.

18.　Quotations from N.H. Baynes, *Constantine* (1931) 29; A.H.M. Jones, *Constantine* (1949) 252.

19.　N.H. Baynes, *Constantine* (1931) 8 ff.; A.H.M. Jones, *Constantine* (1949) 95 ff.

20.　M.A. Levi, "La campagna di Costantino nell' Italia settentrionale (A.312)," *Bolletino storico-bibliografico subalpino* 36 (1934) 1-10.

21.　*Panegyrici Latini* 12(9). 8.1 ff.; 4(10).25. 1 ff. Compare the summary of the north Italian campaign in the normally well-informed *Origo Constantini Imperatoris*: "interea Constantinus apud Veronam victis ducibus tyranni Roman petiit" (J. Moreau, *Excerpta Valesiana*[2] (Leipzig; Teubner 1968) 4). Zosimus 2.14.1 alleges that Maxentius' armies were going to advance into Raetia.

22.　V. Picozzi, "Una campagna di Licinio contra Massenzio nel 310 non attestata dalle fonti letterarie," *Numismatica e antichità classiche* 5 (1976) 267-275; A. Arnaldi, "Osservazioni sul convegno di Carnuntum," *Memorie dell' Istituto Lombardo*, Classe di Lettere, Scienze Morali e Storiche 35 (1975) 217-238.

23.　*Constantine and Eusebius* (1981) 41 ff.

24.　Lactantius, *Mort. Pers.* 24.9.

25.　Optatus 1.18; App. 1, p.194.12 Ziwsa, cf. Eusebius, *Mart. Pal.* (S) 13.12; *HE* 8.14.1 ff.

26.　Augustine, *Brev. Coll.* 3.18.34; *Contra Partem Donati post Gesta* 13.17 (*CSEL* 53.84; 113/4), cf. *Constantine and Eusebius* (1981) 38 f.

27.　The classic attempt is by A. Harnack, *Die Mission und Ausbreitung des Christentums*[4] (Leipzig 1924) 946 ff., cf. K. Baus, *From the Apostolic Community to Constantine (Handbook of Church History*, ed. H. Jedin and J. Dolan, 1 (Freiburg and London 1965)) 367 ff.

28.　See, e.g., R.A. Markus, "The Problem of Self-Definition: From Sect to Church," *Jewish and Christian Self-Definition* 1, ed. E.P. Sanders (Philadelphia 1980) 1-15; R.M. Grant, "The Social Setting of Second-Century Christianity," ibid. 16-29.

29.　*Tertullian. A Historical and Literary Study* (Oxford 1971) esp. 212 ff., 228 ff.

30.　Tertullian, *Scap.* 4.5/6; 5.2/3, cf. H.U. Instinsky, *Marcus Aurelius Prosenes — Freigelassener und Christ am Kaiserhof (Abhandlungen Mainz*, Geistes- und Sozialwissenschaftliche Klasse 1963, Nr. 3); W. Eck, "Das Eindringen des Christentums in den Senatorenstand bis zu Konstantin d. Gr.," *Chiron* 1 (1971) 381-406.

31.　W.H.C. Frend, *Martyrdom and Persecution in the Early Church* (Oxford 1965) 351 ff.

32.　Eusebius, *HE* 6.3.8.ff.; 19.15; 21.3 f., cf. *Constantine and Eusebius* (1981) 82 ff.

33.　On Paul, Eusebius, *HE* 7.30.6 ff., cf. F. Millar, *The Emperor in the Roman World (31 B.C. - A.D. 337)* (London 1977) 566 ff.

34　The Syriac text has recently been re-edited by A. Vööbus, *The Didascalia Apostolorum in Syriac (CSCO* 406, 407 = Scriptores Syri 178, 179: Louvain 1979), with an English translation (*CSCO* 402, 408 = Scriptores Syri 176, 180: Louvain 1979). The Latin fragments were edited by E. Hauler, *Didascaliae Apostolorum fragmenta Veronensia Latina* (Leipzig 1900): on their language and date, E. Tidner, *Sprachlicher Kommentar zur lateinischen Didascalia Apostolorum* (Stockholm 1938). Exiguous fragments of the original Greek were published by J.V. Bartlett, *JTS* 18 (1916/7) 301 ff., but most of the work was incorporated in the *Apostolic Constitutions* composed in the late fourth century: the Greek text of this work was edited *en face* with the Latin fragments of the *Didascalia* and (where they are lacking) a Latin translation of the Syriac by F.X. Funk, *Didascalia et Constitutiones Apostolicae* 1 (Paderborn 1905). For a clear exposition of the textual problems and the historical significance of the document, see the preface to the English translation by R.H. Connolly, *Didascalia Apostolorum* (Oxford 1929) xi-xci.

35.　R.H. Connolly, ibid. lxxxvi ff.; P. Galtier, "La date de la Didascalie des apôtres," *Rev. d'hist. eccl.* 42 (1947) 315-351. The tone and assumptions of Chapter 19, on the Christian's duty to be prepared for martyrdom, show striking resemblances to Tertullian.

36. Chap. 21, p. 191 Vööbus: "When we had eaten the Passover on the third day of the week in the evening, we went out to the Mount of Olives," etc.
37. Chap. 21, p. 191 Vööbus: "Fast thus from the second day of the week, six days entirely, until the night after the Sabbath, and it shall be reckoned to you as a week."
38. Dionysius of Alexandria, *Letter to Basilides*, pp. 101/2 Feltoe, cf. R. Arbesmann, *Reallexicon für Antike und Christentum* 7 (1969) 514.
39. Chaps. 4-16, cf. H. Achelis and J. Flemming, *Die syrische Didascalia (Texte und Untersuchungen* 25.2, 1904) 266 ff.
40. Eusebius, *HE* 6.43.11 (quoting a letter of Bishop Cornelius).
41. M.M. Sage, *Cyprian* (Cambridge, Mass. 1975) 47 ff. (arguing that the *Octavius* was composed in Africa rather than at Rome); G.W. Clarke, *The Letters of St. Cyprian of Carthage* (Ancient Christian Writers 43, 44, 1984) 1. 12 ff.; 2. 13 ff.
42. M.J. Routh, *Reliquiae sacrae*[2] 4 (Oxford 1846) 258 ff.; *PL* 84.301 ff.; J. Vives, *Concilios Visigóticos e Hispano-Romanos (España Cristiana*, Textos 1, 1963) 1 ff. (text); S. Laeuchli, *Power and Sexuality: The Emergence of Canon Law at the Synod of Elvira* (Philadelphia 1972) 126 ff. (English translation).
43. Canons 56, 2-4, 60. The present argument assumes the unity of the eighty-one transmitted canons — a premiss denied by M. Meigne, "Concile ou Collection d'Elvire?" *Rev. d'hist. eccl.* 70 (1975) 361-387. Meigne distinguishes three groups of canons of disparate origin, viz. (A) 1-21, which belongs to a Council of Elvira c.300; (B) 63-75, which probably come from the period 314-325; and (C) 22-62 and 76-81, a miscellaneous collection, partly of much later date.
44. H. Koch, "Die Zeit des Konzils von Elvira," *Zeitschrift für die neutestamentliche Wissenschaft* 17 (1916) 61-67 (306); S. Laeuchli, *Power and Sexuality* (1972) 86 f. (309).
45. Canon 25. It follows a canon dealing with "all who have been baptised abroad" (24).
46. Canon 56.
47. Despite A. Lippold, "Bischof Ossius von Cordova und Konstantin der Grosse," *Zeitschrift für Kirchengeschichte* 92 (1981) 1-15. Lippold's denial of Osius' importance rests upon denying that he is the Hosius in the letter of Constantine written in the winter of 312/3 and quoted in Greek by Eusebius, *HE* 10.6.
48. L. Duchesne, "Le concile d'Elvire et les flamines chrétiens," *Mélanges Renier* (Paris 1877) 159-174.
49. Jerome, *De viris illustribus* 80.
50. Neither Jerome's entry of Lactantius under the eleventh year of Constantine (*Chronicle* 230e Helm) nor his statement that he taught Cripus "in extreme old age" (*De viris illustribus* 80) should be allowed much weight, cf. *Tertullian* (1971) 3 ff.
51. J. Moreau, *Lactance: De la Mort des Persécuteurs* (Paris 1954) 34 ff., 44 ff.
52. J. Stevenson, "The Life and Literary Activity of Lactantius," *Studia Patristica* 1 (*Texte und Unersuchungen* 63, 1957) 661-677; E. Heck, *Die dualistischen Zusätze und die Kaiseranreden bei Lactantius (Sitzungsberichte Heidelberg*, Philosophisch-historische Klasse 1972, Abh. 2).
53. Gregory of Nazianzus, *Orat* 4. 96 (*PG* 35.629), notes that Galerius persecuted the Christians more harshly than Diocletian, in a context which must refer to Asia Minor.
54. *Constantine and Eusebius* (1981) 13 f. 291.
55. See "Lactantius and Constantine," *JRS* 63 (1973) 29-46.
56. For example, he imagines Maxentius as marching out to battle over the Milvian Bridge, then severing it (*Mort. Pers.* 44.9), whereas it had in fact been severed well before 28 October 312, cf. *Constantine and Eusebius* (1981) 305 f.
57. Lactantius, *Mort. Pers.* 18. 1 ff.; 24.9.
58. For some examples, see K. Setton, *Christian Attitude towards the Emperor in the Fourth Century* (New York 1941) 40 ff.; A. Momigliano, *The Conflict between*

Paganism and Christianity in the Fourth Century (Oxford 1963) 79 ff.; P. Brown, *The World of Late Antiquity* (London 1971) 82 ff. G. Chesnut, *The First Christian Histories (Théologie Historique* 46, 1977) 34, speaks of Christian political theory being "given official form in the writings of Eusebius."

59. For the full delineation of this picture, see *Constantine and Eusebius* (1981) esp. 94 ff.; 265 ff.

60. See the superb survey by F. Winkelmann, "Zur Geschichte des authentizitätsproblems der Vita Constantini,"*Klio* 40 (1962) 187-243.

61. G. Pasquali, "Die Composition der *Vita Constantini* des Eusebius," *Hermes* 46 (1910) 369-386, cf. J. Maurice, *Bulletin de la Société Nationale des Antiquaires de France* 1913. 387 f.; N.H. Baynes, *Constantine* (1931) 42: "Dr. Pasquali contended that the original text of the *Vita* had suffered very considerable additions and alterations." Baynes then proceeded to argue Pasquali's conclusion against him, concluding that "Dr. Pasquali has failed to prove his case" (ibid. 45, cf. 49). The false report deceived several subsequent scholars until F. Winkelmann exposed the misrepresentation as such (*Klio* 40 (1962) 208 ff.)

62. *Hermes* 46 (1910) 386 (my translation).

63. F. Winkelmann, *Eusebius' Werke* 1.1 (*GCS*, 1975) liii ff.; T.D. Barnes, "Two Speeches by Eusebius," *GRBS* 18 (1977) 341-345; *Constantine and Eusebius* (1981) 267 ff.

64. For particularly clear statements of this line of argument (based in part, as it happens, on a misdating of the War of Cibalae to 314 instead of 316), see H. Grégoire, "Eusèbe n'est pas l'auteur de la 'Vita Constantini' dans sa forme actuelle et Constantin ne s'est pas 'converti' en 312," *Byzantion* 13 (1938) 561-583; P. Orgels, "A propos des erreurs historiques de la *Vita Constantini* attribuée à Eusèbe, "*Mélanges H. Grégoire* 4 (*Annuaire de l'Institut de Philologie et d'Histoire Orientales* 12, 1953) 575-611.

65. Viz. *VC* 2. 24-42, cf. A. Crivellucci, *Della fede storica di Eusebio nella Vita di Costantino* (Livorno 1888) 50 ff.; "Gli editti di Costantino ai provinciali di Palestina e agli orientali (Eus. V.C. II, 24-42, 48-60)," *Studi Storici* 3 (1894) 369-384; 415-422; V. Schultze, "Quellenuntersuchungen zur Vita Constantini des Eusebius," *Zeitschrift für Kirchengeschichte* 14 (1894) 503-555; A. Mancini, "Osservazioni sulla Vita di Costantino di Eusebio,"*Rivista di filologia* 33 (1905) 309-360; P. Batiffol, "Les documents de la Vita Constantini," *Bulletin d'ancienne littérature et d'archéologie chrétienne* 4 (1914) 80-95.

66. A.H.M. Jones, "Notes on the Genuineness of the Constantinian Documents in Eusebius's Life of Constantine," *Journal of Ecclesiastical History* 5 (1954) 196-200, with a revised text of *P. Lond.* 878 by T.C. Skeat.

67. When Jones presented his discovery to the society "Théonoé" in Brussels on 8 April 1952, H. Grégoire argued that the quotation of genuine documents failed to prove Eusebius' authorship of the *Life* (*La Nouvelle Clio* 5 (1953) 215), which he continued to deny: see "L'authenticité et l'historicité de la Vita Constantini attribuée à Eusèbe de Césarée,"*Bulletin de l'Academie royale de Belgique*, Classe des Lettres[5] 39 (1953) 462-479. For a subsequent argument that the *Life* projects actions of Theodosius back to the time of Constantine, see M.R. Cataudella, "La 'persecuzione' di Licino e l'authenticità della 'Vita Constantini'," *Athenaeum*, N.S. 48 (1970) 48-83; 229-250.

68. R. Farina, *L'impero e l'imperatore cristiano in Eusebio di Cesarea. La prima teologia politica del Cristianesimo* (Zürich 1966) 252 ff.

69. *VC* 2. 24-60. The following chapter introduces the Arian controversy and the Council of Nicaea (*VC* 2. 61. 1).

70. H. Dörries, *Das Selbstzeugnis Kaiser Konstantins (Abhandlungen Göttingen*, Philologisch-historische Klasse[3] 34 (1954) 51 ff.; 329 ff.; *Constantine and Religious Liberty*, trans. R.H. Bainton (New Haven 1960) 25 ff.

71. No mention whatever, for example, in G. Bonner, "The Extinction of Paganism and the Church Historian," *Journal of Ecclesiastical History* 35 (1984) 339-357.

72. As argued in "Constantine's Prohibition of Pagan Sacrifice," *AJP* 105 (1984) 69-72.

73. Eusebius, *Triac.* 7 1 ff.; *VC* 2.45; 3.54 ff.

74. Firmicus Maternus, *De Err. Prof. Rel.* 16.4; 28.1 f.

75. Lactantius, *Mort. Pers.* 24.9; *Div. Inst.* 1.1.13f.

76. J. Maurice, *Numismatique Constantinienne* 2 (Paris 1911) xx ff. On the significance of this action, see esp. K. Aland, *Studia Patristica* 1 (*Texte und Untersuchengen* 63, 1957) 580 ff.; J.H.W.G. Liebeschuetz, *Continuity and Change in Roman Religion* (Oxford 1979) 281 f.

77. *Constantine and Eusebius* (1981) 48 f.

78. N.H. Baynes, *Constantine* (1931) 10 ff.; J. Gaudemet, "La législation religieuse de Constantin," *Revue de l'histoire de l'église en France* 33 (1947) 25-61; A. Alföldi, *The Conversion of Constantine and Pagan Rome* (Oxford 1948) 36 ff.; A.H.M. Jones, *Constantine* (1949) 79 ff.; S. Calderone, *Costantino e il Cattolicesimo* 1 (Florence 1962); F. Millar, *Emperor* (1977) 577 ff.

79. Eusebius, *VC* 2.18. For the purge of 313, Eusebius, *HE* 9.11.1 ff.; *PE* 4.2.10 f. The bloodletting and denunciations led Licinius to issue the edict *de accusationibus* which survives both on stone and in the law codes, cf. *New Empire* (1982) 128.

80. Eusebius, *Triac.* 7.1ff.

81. Eusebius, *In Isaiam* p. 316.9 ff. Zeigler.

82. *Constantine and Eusebius* (1981) 245; *AJP* 105 (1984) 72.

83. On which, see now A. Chastagnol, *L'evolution politique, sociale et économique du monde romain de Dioclétien à Julien* (Paris 1982). I do not, however, accept Chastagnol's view of Constantine's role in this evolution — nor does he accept mine (*CP* 79 (1984) 258 f.).

CONSTANTINE AND THE CHRISTIANS OF PERSIA*

The twenty-three *Demonstrations* of Aphrahat are not likely to be familiar to most students of Roman history or of Constantine. Aphrahat was head of the monastery of Mar Mattai, near modern Mosul, with the rank of bishop and, apparently, the episcopal name Jacob:[1] as a consequence, he was soon confused with the better known Jacob of Nisibis, and independent knowledge of his life and career virtually disappeared.[2] Fortunately, however, twenty-three treatises survived, whose attribution to 'Aphrahat the Persian sage' seems beyond doubt.[3] Aphrahat wrote in Syriac and composed works of edification and polemic for a Mesopotamian audience outside the Roman Empire.[4] Nevertheless, he provides crucial evidence not only for the attitude of Persian Christians towards Rome,[5] but also for the military situation on Rome's eastern frontier at the end of the reign of Constantine.[6] It is worth the effort, therefore, to set Aphrahat's fifth *Demonstration*, which bears the title 'On wars' or 'On battles', in its precise historical context.[7] The present paper begins by considering the place of this *Demonstration* in Aphrahat's *oeuvre* and its exact date (I–III); it then argues that in 337 Constantine was preparing to invade Persia as the self-appointed liberator of the Christians of Persia (IV, VI), that Aphrahat expected him to be successful (V), and that Constantine's actions and the hopes which he excited caused the Persian king to regard his Christian subjects as potential traitors—and hence to embark on a policy of persecution (VII).

I

The twenty-three *Demonstrations* of Aphrahat fall into three groups composed at different times:
(1) I–X are addressed to an unnamed enquirer who is frequently addressed as 'my dear friend'.[8] The addressee (whose letter survives complete only in the Armenian version), wrote to Aphrahat and received from him ten treatises arranged alphabetically by their

* Earlier versions of the present paper were delivered in Toronto and New York, in Oxford and Cambridge, and in Marburg, to audiences whose varied questions and comments have greatly clarified and improved the over-all argument. I am especially grateful to Sebastian Brock for his advice on textual matters. The final version was largely written during my tenure of a Guggenheim Fellowship in 1983/4.

[1] See the notice in BL, Orient. 1017, fol. 160a (dated A.D. 1364), printed by W. Wright, *Catalogue of the Syriac Manuscripts in the British Museum acquired since the year 1838* II (1871), 401; 896. Episcopal rank is presupposed by Aphrahat's composition of the synodical letter which comprises *Demonstration* XIV, cf. J. Forget, *De Vita et Scriptis Aphraatis, Sapientis Persae* (Diss. Louvain, 1882), 82 ff.

[2] Within a hundred and fifty years of Aphrahat's death, Gennadius can summarize the content of the *Demonstrations* (albeit not quite accurately), but ascribe them to 'Jacobus cognomento Sapiens Nizebenae nobilis Persarum modo civitatis episcopus' (*De viris illustribus* 1). BL, Orient. 1017, fol. 159a confuses Aphrahat with Jacob of Tagrit.

[3] Edited by W. Wright, *The Homilies of Aphraates* I (1869); R. Parisot, *Patrologia Syriaca* I, 1 (1894); 1, 2 (1907) (with Latin translation).

[4] On the literary context of Aphrahat, see R. Murray, 'The Characteristics of the Earliest Syriac Christianity', *East of Byzantium: Syria and Armenia in the Formative Period* (Dumbarton Oaks Symposium 1980, publ. 1982), 3–16.

[5] See, recently, G. G. Blum, *Zeitschrift für Kirchengeschichte* XCI (1980), 27 ff.

[6] See *ZPE* I.II (1983), 234.

[7] Translated into English by A. E. Johnston in *A Select Library of Nicene and Post-Nicene Fathers*, Second Series XIII, 2 (1898), 352–62. (For the identity of the translator, sometimes mis-stated as J. Gwynn, see ibid. 116.) The translations offered here are my own: references are to the paragraphs in Parisot's edition.
The fifth *Demonstration* survives in Armenian and Ethiopic as well as in the original Syriac: for the former, see G. Lafontaine, *CSCO* CCCLXXXII = *Scriptores Armeniaci* VII (1977), 88–114 (text); *CSCO* CCCLXXXIII = *Scriptores Armeniaci* VIII (1977), 46–60 (translation); for the latter, F. M. E. Pereira, 'Jacobi, episcopi Nisibeni, Homilia de adventu regis Persarum adversus urbem Nisibin', *Orientalische Studien Th. Nöldeke zum siebzigsten Geburtstag gewidmet* II (1906), 877–92 (based on only one of the two extant manuscripts, and with no translation). The Ethiopic is throughout a paraphrase rather than a translation: see F. Thureau-Dangin, reported by R. Parisot, *Patrologia Syriaca* I, 1 (1894), xl. The Armenian translation appears to belong to the fifth century, even though none of the numerous manuscripts which preserve it antedates the seventeenth: see G. Lafontaine, 'Pour une nouvelle édition de la version arménienne des "Démonstrations" d'Aphraate', *Bazmavep, Revue des études arméniennes* CXXXIII (1975), 365–75. To judge from the Latin translation provided by Lafontaine, the Armenian translator tried to stay close to the Syriac, but resorted to paraphrase where he found Aphrahat obscure: he is also guilty of some careless lapses (e.g., confusing Roman emperors with Seleucid kings).

[8] *Dem.* I, 1, etc. The address is combined with a claim to be systematic in *Dem.* II, 11.

initial letters. The closing paragraph of the tenth *Demonstration* makes it clear that Aphrahat was doing more than responding to a private request for advice:

These ten tiny books which I have written for you receive from one another and build on one another: do not separate them from one another! I have written for you from aleph to yodh, letter following letter. Read and learn, you and the brothers, the sons of the covenant and adherents of our faith, from whom mockery is far removed, as I wrote to you above (VI, 20). Remember that I told you that I have not brought these words as far as the end, but short of the end (V, 25). These words are not sufficient. But listen to these words from me without disputing and examine our brothers, who can be persuaded, about them: everything you hear which is truly edifying, accept, everything which establishes other teachings, refute and destroy utterly. For a dispute cannot build. But I, my friend, like one who quarries, have brought stones for the building: skilled masons will cut them and put them in place in the building, and all the workmen who labour on the building shall receive payment from the Lord of the house (X, 9).[9]

(2) XI–XXII complete the alphabetic series and were written six years after I–X. Towards the end of *Demonstration* XXII, Aphrahat describes the whole corpus of twenty-two treatises and dates the two stages of composition:

These twenty-two treatises I have written according to the twenty-two letters. I wrote the first ten in the year 648 of the rule of Alexander the son of Philip the Macedonian, as is written at the end of them;[10] these other twelve I have written in the year of 655 of the rule of the Greeks and Romans, that is of the rule of Alexander, and in year 35 of the Persian king (XXII, 25).

That the remaining *Demonstrations* were in fact written some time later than I–X is confirmed by their differing content. Whereas the first ten *Demonstrations* comprise a systematic exposition of doctrinal and disciplinary matters for a monastic community (with titles such as 'On faith' (I), 'On Christian love' (II), 'On fasting' (III), 'On prayer' (IV)), the next twelve are less systematic and more controversial, concerned with practical problems in the world, above all with the rival claims of Christianity and Judaism at a time when Christians, but not Jews, were being persecuted.[11]

(3) XXIII stands by itself and begins a second alphabetic series. Its concluding paragraph states that Aphrahat wrote it in the month Ab of the year 656 of Alexander and 36 of Shapur (XXIII, 69).

In addition, three individual *Demonstrations* carry dates which correspond: the fifth and the twenty-first refer to the time of writing as years 648 and 655 of the Seleucid era respectively (V, 5; XXI, 4), while the fourteenth concludes with a colophon, not written by Aphrahat, stating that 'this letter was written in the month of Shebat in the year 655 of the rule of Alexander the son of Philip the Macedonian and in year 35 of Shapur, king of Persia' (XIV, 50).

The chronology of Aphrahat's *Demonstrations* thus seems both clear and consistent. J.-M. Fiey, however, has impugned the whole chronological structure by arguing that the synodical letter which stands as *Demonstration* XIV was not written in 344, and perhaps not even written by Aphrahat, but belongs to a council of bishops, priests and deacons which met at Seleucia long before 344 to consider the conduct of the *catholicos* Papa, who died in 329. Moreover, Fiey contends, the present twenty-third *Demonstration* is the original fourteenth.[12] These are disturbing conclusions. As Fiey expressly concedes, they entail not merely that someone removed the original fourteenth *Demonstration* and replaced it by something which Aphrahat may not have written: the postulated interpolator must also

[9] *Dem.* X, 7, taken with III, 1; VI, 6–10, implies that the addressee is to use the *Demonstrations* for instructing a monastic community. Note also I, 20: 'so that you may learn and teach, believe and be believed'.

[10] No such statement in fact stands at the end of X in either of the extant manuscripts of that treatise.

[11] J. Neusner, *Aphrahat and Judaism. The Christian–Jewish Argument in Fourth-Century Iran* (*Studia Post-*

Biblica XIX, 1971), 4 ff.

[12] J.-M. Fiey, 'Notule de littérature syriaque. La Démonstration XIV d'Aphraate', *Muséon* LXXXI (1968), 449–54. Two centuries ago, when publishing the Armenian version, N. Antonelli, *Sancti Patris nostri Jacobi episcopi Nisibeni Sermones* (1756), 401 ff., segregated the synodical letter and denied that it could be from the same hand as the other *Demonstrations*.

128

have tampered with the opening words of both *Demonstrations* XIV and XXIII (to preserve alphabetical order) and with Aphrahat's description of the corpus of twenty-two *Demonstrations* (XXII, 25), and must himself have written the last paragraph of XXIII (69). If that were indeed so, then it would be unwise to trust the remaining passages which provide dates—and the whole chronology of Aphrahat would be cast adrift from its apparently secure mooring.

Fortunately, Fiey's conclusions need not be accepted. His arguments have been subjected to a searching scrutiny by G. Nedungatt and R. J. Owens, who have shown that *Demonstration* XIV can be exactly what it claims to be, viz. a letter written by Aphrahat in 344 in the name of 'bishops, priests, deacons and the whole church of God, with all its offspring in different places who are with us' (XIV, 1).[13] Moreover, Nedungatt stresses two passages which appear to allude to persecution:

> What we have done has happened to us. We have been plundered, persecuted and scattered. Those who did not show any propensity to give, ask us to give to them more than is proper. Because we hated one another, those who hate us gratuitously have been multiplied (cf. Psalm LXIX (LXVII) 5); because we mocked, we have been mocked; because we despised, we have been despised, because we lied cheated, because we exalted ourselves humiliated, because we oppressed oppressed ourselves, because we did wrong wronged. In the midst of this, dear friends, some have abandoned us, not judging correctly and not seeking out justice: no one has recalled the prophet who said 'Seek out judgement, and do good to the oppressed' (Isaiah 1, 17). (XIV, 4)

> These things, dear friends, it was necessary for us to write, in order to remind ourselves and you that all these things have happened to us at this time because we neglected the service of the holy one. Because we did not honour him, he has exposed us to derision before our enemies and has made us despised, as he said: 'Those who despise me shall suffer dishonour' (I Samuel 11, 30). (XIV, 21)

These allusions to persecution are important, not only as telling heavily against Fiey's early date for *Demonstration* XIV, but also because they contradict the argument that, since the synodical letter presupposes 'a church living in the open', it was written before Shapur began to persecute the Christians of Persia—and hence that persecution began in the summer or autumn of 344, not in 340 as the surviving passions of Persian martyrs assert.[14]

II

A serious textual problem is relevant to the chronology of the persecution under Shapur and requires explicit discussion.[15] Aphrahat refers to a great massacre of martyrs which occurred either in year 656 of the Seleucid era or in the fifth year before that (XXIII, 69). Both W. Wright's *editio princeps* and J. Parisot's edition print the relevant passage as follows:

> I have written you this letter, dear friend, in the month of Ab of the year 656 of the rule of Alexander the son of Philip the Macedonian, and in the year 36 of Shapur, the Persian king, who caused persecution, in the fifth year after the churches were destroyed, in the year in which occurred a great massacre of martyrs in the eastern region, after I wrote those former twenty-two chapters arranged in alphabetical order.

---

[13] G. Nedungatt, 'The Authenticity of Aphrahat's Synodal Letter', *Orientalia Christiana Periodica* XLVI (1980), 62–88; R. J. Owens, *The Genesis and Exodus Citations of Aphrahat the Persian Sage* (Monographs of the Peshitta Institute, Leiden III, 1983), 2 ff. Observe, however, that not all of Nedungatt's arguments are valid, in particular his claim that 'In epistolary language, the Syriac *kethbeth*, like its Latin equivalent "scripsi", can mean "I wrote or I dispatched", or "I am writing/dispatching" . . . When *kethbeth* is taken in the sense of dispatching or sending, the actual time of the

composition of the letter or letters is left out of consideration' (65–6).

[14] The thesis of M. J. Higgins, *BZ* XLIV (1951), 265 ff.; *Traditio* IX (1953), 48 ff.; *Traditio* XI (1955), 1 ff., cf. G. Kmosko, *Patrologia Syriaca* I, 2 (1907), 690 ff.

[15] G. Nedungatt, op. cit. (n. 13), 69 n. 11, draws attention to the problem, ignored to the detriment of their arguments by P. Peeters, *Anal. Boll.* LVI (1938), 131 ff.; P. Devos, *Anal. Boll.* LXXXIV (1966), 246 ff.

This is the text offered in the earlier of the two manuscripts which preserve the passage (BL, Add. 17182, fol. 174^r = B) and quoted by George the Arab in the seventh century (BL, Add. 12154, fol. 247^r).[16] It implies that, whereas the great massacre occurred in the very year in which Aphrahat was writing, i.e. during 344/5, the churches had been destroyed four or five years earlier. Hagiographical evidence contradicts this chronology.

Persian *acta martyrum* record two massacres during the early years of Shapur's persecution of the Christians.[17] One occurred in the fifth year of persecution and in Adiabene[18]—which Aphrahat, writing in nearby Mar Mattai, could never have called 'the eastern region'. The other, however, corresponds exactly to Aphrahat's allusion. Persecution began with the arrest of Simeon, the bishop of Seleucia-Ctesiphon, in the thirty-first year of Shapur, year 651 of the Seleucid era. Simeon was executed on 14 Nisan of that year, and with him no less than a hundred martyrs, including bishops of Susiana and Mesene, all at Karkâ d^e Ledan (Susa).[19]

Aphrahat's allusion is precise and pointed, for the 'great massacre of martyrs in the eastern region' marked the start of the persecution which he could see continuing around him.[20] It is relevant, therefore, that the other manuscript of *Demonstration* XXIII, which is also of venerable antiquity and belongs to the sixth century, offers a significantly different text in the clauses relating to persecution:

... Shapur, the Persian king, who has caused persecution with the destruction of our churches, in the fifth year, in the year in which occurred the great massacre ... (BL, Add. 14169, fol. 173^v = A)

Long ago, reviewing Wright's edition, T. Nöldeke suggested that there might be interpolation in the passage.[21] Both sense and consistency with other evidence can be restored by deleting the word which means 'in the year' (*b^{e}sanṭâ*): with this deletion, Aphrahat states that he wrote the passage in the fifth year after that in which the persecution began with a large massacre in Susiana/Huzistan—'in the fifth year after the great massacre of martyrs in the eastern region'.

III

An important question has so far been avoided. Granted that the 'years of Alexander' represent the Seleucid era, by which of the Seleucid eras then in use did Aphrahat reckon? There are three possibilities:[22]

(A) the official Seleucid era in use in the eastern provinces of the Roman Empire, reckoned from a starting date of 1 Dios (October) 312 B.C.;

(B) the official Seleucid era of the Sassanid kingdom with the new year adjusted to coincide with the Persian New Year on 1 Fravartin, which fell on 29 August from 336 to 339, on 27 August from 340 to 343, on 26 August from 344 to 347;[23]

(C) the Seleucid era normally employed in Babylonia in the Hellenistic and Parthian periods, with the new year in the spring and reckoned from a starting date of 1 Nisan 311 B.C. (= 3 April 311 B.C.).

The obvious method of deciding which computation Aphrahat employed would be to tabulate the Julian equivalents of the Seleucid dates and Persian regnal years which appear in the *Demonstrations* according to each of the three computations, and then to show that

---

[16] P. de Lagarde, *Analecta Syriaca* (1858), 111; W. Wright, *Homilies* (1869), xxii. For translations of the whole letter, B. H. Cowper, *Syriac Miscellanies* (1861), 61 ff.; V. Ryssel, *Georgs des Araberbischofs Gedichte und Briefe* (1891), 44 ff.

[17] The only systematic published collections of these *acta* are by S. E. Assemani, *Acta Sanctorum Martyrum Orientalium et Occidentalium* I (1748), 10 ff.; P. Bedjan, *Acta martyrum et sanctorum* II (1891), 131 ff.

[18] *BHO* 718 (Assemani, *Acta* 105 ff.; Bedjan, *Acta* II, 292 ff.).

[19] There is a critical edition of the two versions of the passion of Simeon (*BHO* 1117, 1119) by M. Kmosko,

Patrologia Syriaca I, 2 (1907), 715 ff.

[20] The connection was seen by J. Forget, *De Vita et Scriptis Aphraatis* (1882), 19.

[21] The relevant part of the relative clause in A reads:

ܕܘܪܒܐ ܗܘܐ ܬܡܢ . ܐܝܟܐ ܕܒܫܢܬܐ ܗܝ ܗܝ ܐܘܡܗ

ܒܫܘܪܝܐ ܕܪܕܘܦܝܐ ܗܘܐ ܘܡܚܪܒ ܥܕܬܢ.

[22] V. Grumel, *Traité d'Études byzantines* I. *La Chronologie* (1958), 209 f.

[23] T. Nöldeke, *Geschichte der Perser und Araber zur Zeit der Sassaniden* (1879), 436.

130

one or two of the three entail impossible or improbable corollaries. Unfortunately, however, there seems to be no reliable independent evidence for the precise date of Shapur's birth or accession, and the correspondences stated by Aphrahat comprise the best evidence for the Seleucid and Julian equivalents of the regnal years of Shapur.[24] Nevertheless, Aphrahat ought to be using either computation (A) or computation (B). First, *Demonstration* xiv was written in the month of Shebat, which is the eleventh month in computation (C): since *Demonstrations* xi–xxii were all written in year 655 of the Seleucid era and composed consecutively, use of computation (C) would imply that Aphrahat wrote the whole of *Demonstrations* xiv–xxii in somewhat less than two months. Secondly, computation (C) produces a potentially awkward discrepancy between Aphrahat's chronology and the official regnal years familiar to his audience.

On a priori grounds, therefore, Aphrahat should have written *Demonstration* v some time before September or October 337. The text confirms that he was in fact writing in the spring or early summer of that Julian year. The opening sentence states clearly that fighting between Rome and Persia has not yet commenced:

This thought has come to me at this time about the disturbance which is about to take place (v, 1).

Aphrahat deliberately uses words which stress that the event of which he speaks lies in the future (da'tidh l'mehwâ). And later on Aphrahat warns Shapur of the futility of attacking the Romans:

You who are raised up and exalted, do not be deceived by the proudness of your heart, and do not say: 'I will go up into a fertile land and against the strong beast.' For the beast will not be killed by the ram, since the horns of the latter are broken (v, 10).

It is important to put such utterances in their correct context. G. Bert provided what remains the fullest and most explicit discussion of the date of *Demonstration* v, and his conclusions seem not to have been challenged in the century since he propounded them: he dated the work to June or July 337, when he supposed that Shapur was using the opportunity afforded by the death of Constantine (22 May) to mobilize in order to seize Mesopotamia.[25] That is seriously misleading. The war whose coming Aphrahat heralds was not an ordinary frontier campaign initiated by the Persian king, and Aphrahat was not writing in the knowledge that Constantine was already dead. He wrote about a war in which he expected Constantine to invade Persia and to conquer the area in which he lived.

IV

When Constantine defeated Licinius, he established Christianity as the official religion of the Roman Empire.[26] Since defeating Maxentius in 312, he had been remoulding Roman law and the attitudes of society in a Christian direction. In 324, his defeat of Licinius, 'the last of the persecutors', offered the opportunity to make decisive changes, at least in the newly acquired territories of Asia Minor and the East. There was a purge of prominent pagans.[27] Then Constantine forbade officials, whatever their rank, to perform the customary act of sacrifice before commencing official business, even if they were pagans. He instructed governors and financial officials to co-operate with bishops in providing churches for the numerous converts which he expected. He prohibited the erection of cult statues, the consultation of pagan oracles, divination, and sacrifice to the pagan gods on any occasion whatsoever—and he reiterated the prohibition when pagans protested.[28] He sent out commissioners to survey and confiscate the treasures and

[24] T. Nöldeke, op. cit., 410 ff.; H. Lewy, *Orientalia*, N.S. x (1941), 45. No Sassanian coins earlier than Peroz bear the kings' regnal years, cf. R. Göbl, *Sasanian Numismatics* (1971), 23.
[25] G. Bert, *Aphrahat's des persischen Weisen Homilien* (*Texte und Untersuchungen* iii, 3/4 (1888), 1–431), xvi,

69–70, cf. recently R. N. Frye, *History of Ancient Iran* (1984), 310.
[26] T. D. Barnes, *Constantine and Eusebius* (1981), 208 ff.; 245 ff.
[27] Eusebius, *VC* ii, 18.
[28] Eusebius, *VC* ii, 44 ff., cf. *AJP* cv (1984), 69 ff.

valuables of every sort to be found in pagan temples and shrines throughout the East, and he forcibly suppressed some famous cult-centres which Christians found offensive on moral as well as religious grounds.[29]

This establishment of Christianity as the official religion of the Roman Empire and of the emperor soon began to affect foreign policy too. When Constantine concluded a treaty with the Goths in 332, and again when he concluded a treaty with the Sarmatians in 334, he insisted on including religious stipulations, which enabled him (and his panegyrist Eusebius) to claim that he had converted the northern barbarians.[30] Constantine regarded himself as a divinely ordained protector of Christians everywhere, with a duty to convert pagans to the truth, and this fundamental assumption about his mission in life inevitably shaped his policy towards Persia, where a large number of Christians lived under a Zoroastrian monarch.

Constantine's dealings with Persia are incompletely documented. Nevertheless, it is clear that the eastern frontier was inherently unstable. The victories of Galerius had brought Rome great gains in Mesopotamia, but Persia was unlikely to continue to acquiesce in the terms of the dictated peace of 299, which annexed territory and created a Roman protectorate to the east of the Tigris, unless Rome applied constant diplomatic and military pressure.[31] Licinius (it seems) campaigned in Mesopotamia in 313 and 314, and the official conversion of Armenia to Christianity in 314 cannot be totally unconnected with these campaigns.[32] Moreover, although Persian envoys had visited Constantine around 320, the poet Publilius Optatianus Porfyrius wrote in 324/5 as if Constantine were on the point of mounting an expedition against Persia.[33] It was probably on this occasion that Shapur sent to Constantine an embassy, recorded by Eusebius, which brought gifts and tokens of friendship and obtained a treaty.[34]

⁻While offering peace, however, Constantine was determined to assert himself, at least implicitly, as the protector of Shapur's Christian subjects. He wrote a personal letter to Shapur, in his own hand, not dictated as official correspondence normally was—though the fact that Eusebius possessed a text suggests that Constantine must at some time have had copies made for wide distribution.[35] The letter is polite, tactful, allusive, and indirect—so indirect indeed that one scholar has recently identified its recipient as the Christian king of Armenia.[36] That is to misunderstand both the political situation and the content of the letter.

The letter falls into three sections.[37] Constantine begins by affirming his devotion to God—the God whose sign Constantine's army, dedicated to God, bears on its shoulders, the God who protects Constantine, who sent Constantine from the far shores of the Ocean to rescue the whole world from oppression and misery. God has made clear how he wishes men to behave: he prizes virtue, piety, reasonableness, humanity, belief, humility and toleration, but punishes disbelief, arrogance and pride: 'he honours highly and strengthens with assistance from himself a just kingdom, and preserves a wise monarch in the tranquillity of peace.'

With an invocation of Shapur as 'my brother', Constantine appeals to recent history for proof of his general propositions: those Roman rulers who denied God have all encountered disaster, especially the one whom the wrath of God 'expelled from here and transferred to your territory' to exhibit his shame as a captive in war. Constantine refers of course to Valerian. He then reminds Shapur of the fate of the emperors who attacked

---

²⁹ Eusebius, *Triac.* 8, 1 ff.; *VC* III, 54, 4 ff.
³⁰ Constantine, quoted by Athanasius, *Apol. c. Ar.* 86, 10/11; Gelasius, *HE* III, 10, 10; Eusebius, *VC* IV, 5/6.
³¹ *Constantine* (1981), 18.
³² ibid. 65.
³³ *Pan. Lat.* IV (X), 38, 3; Porfyrius, *Carm.* XVIII, 4: 'et Medi praestas in censum sceptra redire'. The Persian prince Hormizd, a brother of Shapur, had recently fled from Persia and arrived at the imperial court (Zosimus II, 27, cf. John of Antioch, frag. 178).
³⁴ Eusebius, *VC* IV, 8. This section of the *Life* is arranged thematically, not chronologically.
³⁵ Eusebius, *VC* IV, 8.
³⁶ D. de Decker, 'Sur le destinataire de la lettre au roi

des Perses (Eusèbe de Césarée, *Vit. Const.*, IV, 9-13) et la conversion de l'Arménie à la religion chrétienne', *Persica* VIII (1979), 99-116.
³⁷ viz. Eusebius, *VC* IV, 9-10 (Winkelmann's first paragraph), 11-12 (Winkelmann's second and third paragraphs) and 13. Eusebius writes as if he translated the letter from Latin into Greek himself: on his competence as a translator, see E. Fisher, *YCS* XXVII (1982), 200 ff. Eusebius may slightly have distorted Constantine's undoubtedly often obscure Latin, but it is unlikely that he rewrote the letter entirely, as argued by P. A. Barceló, *Roms auswärtige Beziehungen unter der Constantinischen Dynastie (306-363)* (Eichstätter *Beiträge*, Abteilung Geschichte III, 1981), 77.

God's people in his own day: they were overthrown, and God is now, with the worship of his people, gathering all men to himself.

In his last paragraph, Constantine becomes more explicit. He has throughout been talking about the Christians, whom he here names for the first time: he was delighted to discover that the most important districts of Persia are full of them. But he closes with a felicitation and an exhortation which seem to conceal a veiled warning:

> Thus you will have the Lord of all kind, favourable and merciful. These then (i.e. the Christians of Persia) I commend to you because you are so great, committing the very same to you because you are eminent for piety. Cherish them in accordance with your usual humanity: for by this gesture of faith you will confer an immeasurable benefit on both yourself and us.

The letter should probably be dated very shortly after October 324.[38] Shapur's response is unknown, but he cannot have viewed with pleasure the conversion of the Caucasian kingdom of Iberia to Christianity, which appears to belong to the period around 330.[39] He may also have been apprehensive of Constantine's ultimate intentions. In campaigns north of the Danube, Constantine was comporting himself like a new Trajan.[40] In his youth, Constantine had fought under Galerius, had served in the Roman army which advanced to Ctesiphon, and had visited the ruins of Babylon:[41] might he not, like Trajan, embark upon an eastern war? And did Constantine not allude, even in his letter to Shapur, to a career of conquest which began in the far west and proceeded eastward?[42] Where would Constantine cease his conquests?

Shapur had good reason to suspect that the Roman emperor was planning to make war against him. He decided, therefore, to strike first. While Constantine was still occupied on the Danube, border raids began, and the Caesar Constantius was sent to reside in Antioch and guard the frontier.[43] In 336 a Persian army invaded Armenia and installed a Persian nominee as ruler.[44] Constantine seized the opportunity with enthusiasm, and may have attempted to put Shapur even more in the wrong by supporting the claims of Metrodorus, that Persians had stolen the royal presents which he was bringing from India to Constantine.[45] More significantly, Constantine proposed to conduct his Persian expedition as a religious crusade. Bishops were to accompany the army, a Christian version of the Old Testament tabernacle was prepared to accompany him, and he proclaimed his intention to be baptized in the River Jordan before he invaded Mesopotamia.[46] Persian ambassadors arrived in Constantinople, but were repulsed.[47] Further, Constantine proclaimed his half-nephew, Hannibalianus, not merely king, but *rex regum*;[48] coins which associate an obverse of Hannibalianus as *rex* with a reverse depicting the personified Euphrates and bearing the legend *Securitas publica* imply a deep and sinister significance in this proclamation, viz. that Hannibalianus was to replace Shapur as king of Persia, or at least as ruler in Ctesiphon, when Constantine had defeated him in war.[49] Death, however, overtook Constantine before the expedition set out: he fell ill in April 337 and died on 22 May near Nicomedia.[50]

[38] *Constantine* (1981), 258 f.
[39] On which, see now F. Thélamon, *Païens et chrétiens au IV⁴ siècle. L'apport de l'"Histoire ecclésiastique' de Rufin d'Aquilée* (1981), 85 ff.
[40] *RIC* VII, 331, Rome 298; Victor, *Caes.* 41, 18; *Chr. min.* I, 233 (rebuilding of Trajan's bridge on the Danube); *AE* 1934, 158 (title of *Dacicus maximus*).
[41] Constantine, *Oratio* 16, 4, cf. *Phoenix* XXX (1976), 186 ff.
[42] Eusebius, *VC* IV, 9.
[43] For Persian aggression, Libanius, *Orat.* LIX, 62 ff.; Eutropius, *Brev.* X, 8, 2; Festus, *Brev.* 26. It is significant that Libanius in 344 presents the Persians as plotting to renew warfare for the whole of the four decades since their defeat in the 290s (*Orat.* LIX, 65). On the other hand, both the date and the significance of the capture of Amida alleged by Theophanes, p. 20, 20 ff. de Boor, remain uncertain: Theophanes puts the

capture in 324, but couples it with the death of Narses—which occurred nearly twenty years later.
[44] Faustus III, 21, cf. W. Ensslin, *Klio* XXIX (1936), 102 ff.
[45] Ammianus XXV, 4, 23; Cedrenus I, 516 Bonn. However, the whole story is argued to be an invention of Eunapius, without any factual basis at all, by B. H. Warmington, 'Ammianus Marcellinus and the Lies of Metrodorus', *CQ* XXXI (1981), 464-8.
[46] Eusebius, *VC* IV, 56; 62, 2.
[47] Eusebius, *VC* IV, 57, chapter-heading (the text is lost); Libanius, *Orat.* LIX, 71 f.; Festus, *Brev.* 26.
[48] Eusebius, *VC* IV, 56, 3; *Epitome* 41, 20.
[49] *RIC* VII, 584; 589 f., cf. O. Seeck, *Geschichte des Untergangs der antiken Welt* IV (1911), 25.
[50] Eusebius, *VC* IV, 60 ff.; Festal Index 10; *Chr. min.* I, 235; Socrates, *HE* I, 39, 2; 40, 3.

The Caesar Constantius left Antioch as soon as he heard that his father was dying, and was not able to return to Syria until very late in the year.[51] Shapur took immediate advantage of this unexpected change in the political and military situation: he ravaged Mesopotamia and besieged Nisibis for sixty-three days.[52] The exact date of the siege is not directly attested, but Jerome's *Chronicle* puts it before the death of Dalmatius Caesar, which belongs to August 337,[53] and if Shapur had already prepared an army to resist Constantine, there was no reason to delay. The siege of Nisibis may have begun as early as May 337; at all events it belongs to the summer of 337 (not 338),[54] so that there was no long interval between the arrival of news that Constantine was dead and Shapur's invasion of Roman territory. Aphrahat wrote *Demonstration* v, not merely before Shapur invaded Roman Mesopotamia, but while he still believed that Constantine was alive and about to lead a crusade to establish a Christian on the Persian throne.

v

The main argument of *Demonstration* v is threefold, interlocking and largely scriptural. Aphrahat argues that God always casts down the arrogant and impious; that God has ordained the defeat of Persia, and has revealed his intention to do so in the book of Daniel, which predicts the outcome of the impending war; and that the now Christian Roman Empire will exist till the end of time, when it will surrender its power to Christ at his second coming.[55] At the outset, Aphrahat protests that because the times are evil, he must speak in symbols (v, 2). Yet it needs little percipience to see that his arguments imply that Shapur will be defeated, and that Constantine will soon rule over Persia in his stead.[56]

Aphrahat identifies the fourth kingdom of Daniel's vision (VII, 23) with the Roman Empire, but in an ambiguous fashion. The fourth beast in Daniel's vision, he maintains, following established conventions of exegesis, is the kingdom of the sons of Esau, i.e. the Roman Empire. But Aphrahat also equates the Roman Empire, which is the fourth kingdom, with the third kingdom of the Greeks. After he has identified the third beast as Alexander the Great (v, 18), he continues:

After Alexander the Macedonian ruled, there was the kingdom of the Greeks, Alexander being a Greek. But with him the vision of the third beast is completed, since the third and fourth are one. Alexander ruled for twelve years, and after Alexander there were seventeen Greek kings, whose years total two hundred and sixty-nine, from Seleucus Nicator to Ptolemy, and there were Caesars from Augustus to Philippus Caesar, twenty-seven kings, whose years total two hundred and ninety-three. But the years of Severus are eighteen (v, 19).

Beneath the confusions of this bizarre computation, there seems to hover an assumption that the central fact of Roman imperial history is the conversion of the empire to Christianity. Aphrahat himself reckoned by the Seleucid era, which he called 'the years of the rule (or kingdom) of Alexander', and which he believed to commence with Alexander's defeat of the Persian king (v, 5). Hence it was natural for Aphrahat to identify the third and fourth kingdoms, which belonged to an unbroken chronological continuum. Now 269 years take one from the inception of the Seleucid era in 312/11 B.C. to 44/3, when Octavian entered political life, and it was a common view in antiquity that that event marked the beginning of the Roman Empire.[57] Another 293 years from 44/3 B.C. bring one to A.D.

[51] Julian, *Orat.* I, 16 ff.; Socrates *HE* II, 2 ff., cf. *Phoenix* XXXIV (1980), 162.
[52] Jerome, *Chronicle* 234ᵈ Helm; *Chron. Pasch.* 533 Bonn, cf. *ZPE* LII (1983), 229 ff.
[53] *Constantine* (1981), 261 f.
[54] Jacob of Nisibis died in the Seleucid year 649 after taking an active part in the defence against Shapur's first siege: see P. Peeters, 'La légende de Saint Jacques de Nisibe', *Anal. Boll.* XXXVIII (1920), 285-373.
[55] F. Gavin, *Journal of the Society of Oriental*

Research VII (1923), 98 ff.; R. Murray, *Symbols of Church and Kingdom. A Study in Early Syriac Tradition* (1975), 241 ff.
[56] That Aphrahat's argument is not allegorical was rightly stressed by C. J. F. Sasse, *Prolegomena in Aphraatis Sapientis Persae sermones homileticos* (Diss. Leipzig, 1878).
[57] The *Chronicle of Edessa* notes that Augustus began to rule in year 266, i.e. 47/6 B.C. (*CSCO, Scr. Syri* III, 4 (1903), 3, 17-18).

250/1, only a year after the death of Philip, and a total of twenty-seven emperors can easily be obtained by judicious inclusion and exclusion of short-lived rulers. The significance of Aphrahat's calculation lies in the fact that many in the fourth century believed that Philip was the first Christian emperor.[58] And what of Severus? It may be suggested that Aphrahat, whose knowledge of Roman history is abysmally confused, has mixed up Septimius Severus and Galerius. Both Severus and Galerius reigned eighteen years (respectively, 193–211 and 293–311), and both invaded Mesopotamia successfully. But Galerius was also the moving force behind the Diocletianic persecution[59]—and hence relevant in the context.

What is the purpose of Aphrahat's laborious calculation? It seems to imply that he identifies the fourth kingdom with the pagan Roman Empire rather than with the Roman Empire which used to be pagan and is now Christian.[60] What then of the present in which Aphrahat is writing? If the fourth kingdom were already past, then the present would be the interim period, just before the end of the world, and the second coming of the Messiah and the Last Judgement would be very close at hand. On that assumption, Aphrahat's opening chapter acquires a pointed relevance:

> This thought has come to me at this time about the disturbance which is now about to take place, and (about) the forces which have gathered themselves for slaughter: The times were fixed beforehand by God. The times of peace are fulfilled in the days of the good and just; and the times of many evils are fulfilled in the days of the evil and wrong-doers. For thus it is written 'good must happen, and blessed is he through whom it shall come; and evil must happen, but woe to him through whom it shall come'.[61] Good has come to the people of God, and blessedness awaits the man through whom good came. Evil has been aroused because of the forces collected by the evil and arrogant one who has pride in himself, and misery is reserved later for him through whom the evil has been stirred up. Nevertheless, my friend, do not complain (openly) of the evil one who has roused evil against many, because the times were fixed beforehand and the time of their fulfilment is at hand (v, 1).

In the context of early 337, the good man and the evil man are instantly recognizable as Constantine and Shapur. Constantine is the benefactor of 'the people of God.' The blessedness which awaits him presumably includes both success in this world and felicity in the hereafter. Shapur, on the other hand, is the evil man who has gathered together an army. But there is no point in complaining or obstructing his actions, because what he is doing is in accordance with God's plan—and Aphrahat devotes the bulk of his treatise to an intricate argument from scripture that Shapur will be defeated in the imminent war.

Elsewhere, Aphrahat had voiced a firm conviction that the world would come to an end after six thousand years (II, 14), and the fifth *Demonstration* employs as its predominant assumption the belief that the Romans hold the fourth kingdom in trust for Christ, who aids them in war, and that the fourth kingdom will endure until Christ's second coming (v, 6; 14; 23–4). From this assumption it equally follows that God will not allow their enemies to overcome the Romans. Nevertheless, Aphrahat's confidence is not unbounded. At the very end, he anxiously contemplates the possibility against which he has argued so vigorously and consistently:

> Even if the forces go up and are victorious, know that it is a punishment from God; if they are victorious, they will be condemned (later) by a just decision. Yet be certain of this, that the beast will be killed at its (destined) time. You, my brother, at this time be earnest in imploring mercy that there may be peace for the people of God (v, 25).

Perhaps Aphrahat added this sombre conclusion when he heard fresh news of the progress of the war, possibly when he heard that Constantine was dead. For the death of

[58] Jerome, *Chronicle* 217ᶜ Helm: 'primusque omnium ex Romanis imperatoribus Christianus fuit'.
[59] Lactantius, *Mort. Pers.* 10, 6 ff.; 31, 1; Eusebius, *HE* VIII, App. 1; 3.
[60] Daniel VII, 23 stresses the difference between the third and fourth kingdoms which Aphrahat equates.
[61] A saying of Jesus quoted in the Pseudo-Clementine *Homilies* XII, 29 (*PG* II, 324) and *Epitome* 96 (A. Resch, *Agrapha. Aussercanonische Schriftfragmente*² (*Texte und Untersuchungen*, N.F. XV, 3/4, 1906), 106 f.

Constantine shattered his hopes of a Roman victory. Already mobilized for war, Shapur took the initiative in the summer of 337 and besieged Nisibis.

VI

A Latin text not adequately exploited by recent historians of the fourth century A.D. shows that, at least in some quarters, the hopes which Constantine aroused and which Aphrahat expressed survived the emperor's death and the changed fortunes of war.[62] One manuscript of Julius Valerius continues with the text known as the *Itinerarium Alexandri*—a title which disguises its true nature.[63] For the work originally comprised accounts of the exploits not only of Alexander, but also of Trajan, and it is only through an accident of transmission that the text breaks off just after the death of Alexander from overdrinking. The author confesses that the work is a *breviarium* rather than an *itinerarium*: he dedicated it to the emperor Constantius when he had begun his reign successfully and was about to embark on a Persian expedition (p. 1, 1–5 Volkmann). The choice of Alexander and Trajan as examples for the young emperor to emulate can only have one significance: the writer believed that Constantius too was about to invade Persia in an attempt at conquest. He declares his conviction that Constantius will surpass the achievements of the most famous emperors:

> hau scio an maiora longe felicioraque profecta sint vobis exempla de maximis Constantinis patre vel fratre: certe quae priora sunt tempore etiamsi meritis secunda tu feceris, ipsos illos, si quis functis est sensus, voto accessuros existimo; tibique in Persas hereditarium munus est, ut, qui Romana tamdiu arma tremuerunt, per te tandem ad nostratium nomen recepti interque provincias nostras civitate Romana donati, discant esse beneficio iubentium liberi, qui omnes illic fastibus regiis milites bello, servi pace censentur.[64]

The date must be close to 340, since the writer goes on to assert that Constantius is the same age as Alexander was when he invaded Asia. But he is clearly not a man close to the court or attentive to imperial etiquette and propaganda. For after the younger Constantinus invaded Italy and was killed in 340, his memory was damned. The dead emperor's name was erased on inscriptions, and panegyrists of Constantius pretended that he had only ever had one brother.[65] When the alert Athanasius addressed Constantius he studiously refrained from direct mention of Constantinus.[66]

The language of the unknown writer is confident and unambiguous. The Persians have long stood in fear of Roman arms, but now at last Constantius will make them Romans, incorporate them among the Roman provinces and give them Roman citizenship, that they may learn to be free. None of these steps is possible without a prior military conquest. In 338, Constantius supervised the installing of a Roman nominee on the throne of Armenia.[67] The *Itinerarium Alexandri* alludes to that and speaks of an aggressive expedition already undertaken. The date should probably be 340 precisely. For as time passed, such pipe-dreams must have seemed ever more unreal. The nature of the fighting

---

[61] Neither Aphrahat nor the *Itinerarium Alexandri* receives any mention in B. H. Warmington, 'Objectives and Strategy in the Persian War of Constantius II', *Limes. Akten des XI Internationalen Limeskongresses* (1977), 509–20, who argues that Constantius' strategy was from the start 'strictly defensive'.

[63] The sole manuscript appears to be Milan, Ambros. P 49 sup., fols. 54'–64', the most recent edition that by D. Volkmann (Prog. Pforta, publ. Naumburg, 1871). I am grateful to the Medieval Institute of the University of Notre Dame, Indiana for providing me with a microfilm.

The *Itinerarium Alexandri* is duly noted and discussed in standard handbooks: Schanz-Hosius, *Gesch. d. lat. Litt.* IV, 1¹ (1914), 115 f.; W. Kubitschek, *RE* IX (1916), 2363 ff.; A. Piganiol, *L'empire chrétien* (1947), 76 (missing the relevance of Trajan). Also, in her

survey of the myth of Alexander in late antiquity, by L. Cracco Ruggini, *Athenaeum*, N.S. XLIII (1965), 5.

[64] I print Volkmann's text (p. 2, 5–10). The only serious textual difficulty is in the first line, where the MS has 'iussio maiora longe felicioraque quae profecto sint'.

[65] Libanius, *Orat.* LIX, 43 ff.; 72 ff., cf. E. Ferrero, *Diz. Ep.* II, 657.

[66] e.g. Athanasius, *Apol. ad Const.* 4, where 'any others (ἄλλους τινάς)' means precisely Constantinus.

[67] P. Peeters, 'L'intervention politique de Constance II dans la Grande Arménie, en 338', *Bull. Acad. roy. de Belgique*, Classe des Lettres⁵ XVII (1931), 10–47, reprinted in his *Recherches d'histoire et de philologie orientales* I (*Subsidia Hagiographica* XXVII, 1951), 222–50.

in Mesopotamia soon made it clear to all that, whatever his initial aims, Constantius was waging a defensive war for the preservation of Roman territory, not one which might result in conquests, still less the subjugation of any part of Persia proper.

VII

Constantine's legacy to the Christians of Persia was a bitter one. Before 337, they had enjoyed toleration except for a brief period of about fifteen years in the late third century, when the Zoroastrian clergy induced king Vahran to execute Mani and then to persecute Christians.[68] On general grounds, it might be argued that persecution in Persia was a natural and inevitable corollary of Constantine's establishment of Christianity as the official religion of the Roman Empire.[69] Nevertheless, it was Constantine, not Shapur, who brought Christianity into play as a political factor in relations between Rome and Persia. The Persian frontier raids of the 330s and even the Persian invasion of Armenia in 336 were ordinary invasions in the traditional manner. It was Constantine who injected a religious dimension into the normal frontier dispute, by seeking to appeal to Shapur's Christian subjects in the same sort of way in which he had appealed to the Christian subjects of Maxentius in 312 and of Licinius in 324. Aphrahat's fifth *Demonstration* illustrates what response he found. If Aphrahat may be presumed typical, then the 'homily is a clear proof of how the Christians of Persia stood completely on Rome's side with their sympathies'.[70] Shapur, therefore, may be forgiven for regarding his Christian subjects as a potential fifth column in league with his Roman enemies. Two extremely important developments flowed from this suspicion. Shapur and his successors persecuted the Christians of Persia violently, if intermittently.[71] The Christians of Persia, for their part, tried to belie governmental suspicions of their loyalty by distancing themselves from the dominant orthodoxy of the eastern Roman Empire.[72]

[68] S. Brock, 'A Martyr at the Sasanid Court under Vahran II: Candida', *Anal. Boll.* XCVI· (1978), 167–81.
[69] J.-M. Fiey, *Jalons pour une histoire de l'Église en Iraq* (*CSCO* CCCX: Subsidia XXXVI, 1970), 87 f.
[70] T. Nöldeke, *Geschichte* (1879), 501; *Aufsätze zur persischen Geschichte* (1887), 97 ff.; G. Bert. op. cit. (n. 25), 69 n. 1.

[71] J. Labourt, *Le Christianisme dans l'empire perse sous la dynastie sassanide* (1904), 43 ff.; 104 ff.; J.-M. Fiey, *Jalons* (1970), 85 ff.
[72] S. P. Brock, 'Christians in the Sasanian Empire: A Case of Divided Loyalties', *Studies in Church History* XVIII (1982), 1–19.

VII

THE RELIGIOUS AFFILIATION
OF CONSULS AND PREFECTS, 317–361

THE PRESENT PAPER is a revised and systematic presentation of the argument of the first part of the paper "Christians and Pagans in the Reign of Constantius" which I composed in the summer of 1987, presented at the Entretiens Hardt in September 1987, and revised only superficially for publication; the concluding part is reproduced in the present volume (VIII 322–337). It sets out to show that the proportion of Christians among the consuls, praetorian prefects and *praefecti urbis Romae* appointed by Constantine and his sons is significantly higher than is usually suspected, and it reaches that conclusion by explicitly rejecting the tacit assumption so often made that holders of the highest offices in the fourth century whose religious affiliation is unattested may legitimately be presumed to be overwhelmingly pagan. It provides briefly annotated lists of the consuls and prefects between 317 and 361 which note what is known about their religious affiliation.[1]

The lists of consuls and prefects are taken from the following modern discussions:

(1) R. S. Bagnall, Alan Cameron, S. R. Schwartz and K. A. Worp, *Consuls of the Later Roman Empire* (Atlanta, 1987);

(2) T. D. Barnes, *The New Empire of Diocletian and Constantine* (Cambridge, Mass., 1982) 131–139; "Praetorian Prefects 337–361," *ZPE* 94 (1992) 249–260;

(3) A. Chastagnol, *Les Fastes de la Préfecture de Rome au Bas-Empire* (Paris, 1962) 68–153.

The annotation draws gratefully throughout on the large and helpful volume by R. von Haehling, *Die Religionszugehörigkeit der hohen Amtsträger des Römischen Reiches seit Constantins I. Alleinherrschaft bis zum Ende der Theodosianischen Dynastie* (Bonn, 1978). My conclusions differ, however, substantially from von Haehling's for two main reasons. First, von Haehling

---

[1]Petronius Probus (cos. 371) is erroneously claimed as the first Christian convert among the Roman aristocracy by Peter Brown, "Aspects of the Christianization of the Roman Aristocracy," *JRS* 51 (1961) 1–11, reprinted in *Religion and Society in the Age of Saint Augustine* (London 1972) 161–182, at 9 = 177. Nor do the facts support even the less emphatic claim that Probus was "a Christian when most of his peers were still pagan" advanced by Alan Cameron, "Polynomy in the Late Roman Aristocracy: The Case Of Petronius Probus," *JRS* 75 (1985) 164–182, at 164.

2   RELIGIOUS AFFILIATION OF CONSULS AND PREFECTS

counts offices rather than office-holders:[2] hence pagans are over-represented because of the relative abundance of evidence that survives for the careers of Roman aristocrats and the pupils and friends of Libanius. Second, all the *comites* of Constantius who wrote to Athanasius in 345/6 (*Hist. Ar.* 21.1) and all the witnesses who certified the accuracy of the stenographic record of the interrogation of Photinus in 351 (Epiphanius, *Pan.* 71.1.5) are certainly Christians—as André Chastagnol realised more than thirty years ago.[3]

The lists start with the year in which the first Christian ordinary consul is attested with certainty and end with the last year whose consuls were appointed by the last surviving son of Constantine. The evidence for the religious affiliation of each consul and prefect is presented as succinctly as possible, and where there is no relevant evidence, none is cited. For the consuls appointed by Constantius and Constans between 341 and 350 the letters E and W after the consular date denote whether the man held office under Constantius (E) or Constans (W). The lists are followed by tables which summarise the results obtained.

The consulates of emperors and their sons are excluded from consideration, as are consuls, praetorian prefects and the *praefecti urbis* of 350–352 appointed by Magnentius. Also, for obvious reasons, the starting point for praetorian prefects is the reunification of the empire in 324.

CONSULES ORDINARII

(1) Consuls attested as Christians

Ovinius Gallicanus, cos. 317
> *Liber Pontificalis* 34.29 (p. 184 Duchesne), cf. E. J. Champlin, "Saint Gallicanus," *Phoenix* 36 (1982) 70–76.

Amnius Anicius Julianus, cos. 322
> Prudentius, *Contra Symmachum* 1.552/3, implies that the family converted to Christianity before 303, cf. T. D. Barnes and R. W. Westall, "The Conversion of the Roman Aristocracy in Prudentius" *Contra Symmachum*," *Phoenix* 45 (1991) 50–61.

Severus, cos. 323
> Presumably identical with the Acilius Severus attested as *praefectus urbi* from 4 January 325 to 13 November 326, to whom Lactantius wrote

---

[2] As pointed out gently in the review in *Phoenix* 32 (1978) 364/5. Nevertheless, von Haehling's statistics continue to be accepted and made the basis for historical inferences and analysis: see, for example, M. R. Salzmann, *On Roman Time. The Calendar-Codex of 354 and the Rhythms of Urban Life in Late Antiquity* (Berkeley, 1990), esp. 195; K. Cooper, "Insinuations of Womanly Influence: An Aspect of the Christianization of the Roman Aristocracy," *JRS* 82 (1992) 150–164. The latter scholar asserts that von Haehling's "evidence undermines the triumphalist accounts of Eusebius and Theodoret" (150 n. 4).

[3] A. Chastagnol, *Fastes* (1962) 137, 149.

two books of letters: Jerome, *De viris illustribus* 111, cf. *PLRE* 1.834; J. F. Matthews, *Western Aristocracies and Imperial Court AD 364-425* (Oxford, 1975) 147.

Sex. Anicius Paulinus, cos. 325
Praised as *benignus, sanctus* in *CIL* 6.1651: for the inference that these epithets imply a Christian, see *PLRE* 1.680; D. M. Novak, "Constantine and the Senate: An Early Phase in the Christianization of the Roman Aristocracy," *Ancient Society* 10 (1979) 271–310, at 293.

Junius Bassus, cos. 331
Identified as the Christian consul depicted on a Roman sarcophagus by M. Fuhrmann, "Studien zu den Consulardiptychen verwandten Denkmälern I," *Röm. Mitt.* 54 (1939) 161–175; W. N. Schumacher, "Zum Sarkophag eines christlichen Konsuls," *Röm. Mitt.* 65 (1958) 100–120.

Flavius Ablabius, cos. 331
Const. Sirmond. 1; Athanasius, *Festal Letter* 4.5

Amnius Manius Caesonius Nicomachus Anicius Paulinus, cos. 334
Anicius Paulinus appears to have held no pagan priesthood: *ILS* 1220, 1221 (Rome)

Flavius Felicianus, cos. 337
Johannes Malalas pp. 318/9 Dindorf

Flavius Polemius, cos. 338
Athanasius, *Hist. Ar.* 22.1

Septimius Acindynus, cos. 340
Augustine, *De sermone domini in monte* 1.50 (*PL* 34.1254)

Flavius Philippus, cos. 348E
Athanasius, *Fug.* 3.6; Theodoretus, *HE* 2.5.4

Flavius Salia, cos. 348W
Theodoretus, *HE* 2.8.54

Censorius Datianus, cos. 358
Libanius, *Ep.* 81.5; Epiphanius, *Pan.* 71.1.5

Naeratius Cerealis, cos. 358
Epiphanius, *Pan.* 71.1.5

Flavius Taurus, cos. 361
Athanasius, *Hist. Ar.* 22.1; Epiphanius, *Pan.* 71.1.5; Sulpicius Severus, *Chronica* 2.41.1, 43.3–44.1

Flavius Florentius, cos. 361
Athanasius, *Hist. Ar.* 22.1

(2) Consuls who were probably Christians

Petronius Probianus, cos. 322
Possibly identical with the Probinus to whom Lactantius dedicated a lost work (*CSEL* 27.155/6) as proposed in "More Missing Names (A.D. 260–395)," *Phoenix* 27 (1973) 135–155, at 149.

Flavius Constantius, cos. 327 ⎫
Valerius Maximus, cos. 327 ⎬
    Eusebius, *VC* 2.44: on the identity of Maximus, see *New Empire* (1982) 103, 117/8, 132; "Himerius and the Fourth Century," *CP* 82 (1987) 206–225, at 217/8.

Flavius Januarinus, cos. 328
    Commissioned and dedicated a Christian sarcophagus for his wife Marcia Romania Celsa: J.-M. Rouquette, "Trois nouveaux sarcophages chrétiens de Trinquetaille (Arles)," *CRAI* 1974.254–273, at 257–263, whence *AE* 1974.418.

Flavius Dalmatius, cos. 333
    Half-brother of Constantine.

Domitius Zenophilus, cos. 333
    Optatus, App. 1. The dedication which Zenophilus made as governor of Numidia *diis salutaribus Escolapio et Hygiae quorum ope adversae valetudines depelluntur* as a *sacrum religionis suae iuxta eos indicium* (*AE* 1915.30: Lambaesis) is held to prove him a pagan by D. M. Novak, *Ancient Society* 10 (1979) 309. However, his spectacular career and his conduct of the official enquiry in 320 into the alleged *traditio* of the Donatist bishop of Cirta ought to imply that he was at least a nominal Christian, cf. A. Piganiol, *L'Empereur Constantin* (Paris, 1932) 111. The dedication shows that Zenophilus himself or a close relative was seriously ill while he was *consularis* of Numidia: the prayers of a sick or despairing man to the traditional gods of healing do not necessarily reflect his normal comportment while healthy and cheerful.

Flavius Optatus, cos. 334
    Apparently an imperial relative: *New Empire* (1982) 107.

Julius Constantius, cos. 335
    Half-brother of Constantine.

Virius Nepotianus, cos. 336
    Apparently husband of Eutropia, the half-sister of Constantine: *PLRE* 1.625; *New Empire* (1982) 108.

Petronius Probinus, cos. 341W
    Son of the consul of 322.

Flavius Domitius Leontius, cos. 344E

Flavius Eusebius, cos. 359 ⎫
Flavius Hypatius, cos. 359 ⎬
    Brothers of the Christian Eusebia, whom Constantius married c. 352.

(3) Consuls whose religious sympathies are unknown

Caesonius Bassus, cos. 317
Vettius Rufinus, cos. 323

Vettius Justus, cos. 328
Flavius Gallicanus, cos. 330
L. Papius Pacatianus, cos. 332 }
Maecilius Hilarianus, cos. 332 }
Tettius Facundus, cos. 336
Flavius Ursus, cos. 338
Antonius Marcellinus, cos. 341W
Flavius Romulus, cos. 343W
    Romulus himself is no more than a consular date, but Flavius Pisidius
    Romulus, who was *praefectus urbi* under Stilico and a westerner, is pre-
    sumed to be his descendant (*PLRE* 1.771/2).
Flavius Bonosus, cos. 344W }
Flavius Julius Sallustius, cos. 344 }
    On the mysterious and badly attested consulate of Bonosus, who is
    clearly a western consul, see *Consuls* (1987) 222, correcting *PLRE* 1.164.
    He was replaced as consul in the West c. April: there is no strictly con-
    temporary evidence for the form of the consular date in the East before
    August, and it is not certain whether Sallustius was the nominee of Con-
    stantius or Constans (*Consuls* [1987] 22/3).
Flavius Amantius, cos. 345E }
M. Nummius Albinus, cos. 345W }
    Amantius is otherwise totally unknown, but it seems a *priori* improbable
    that Constantius would have accepted a pair of Constans' nominees at
    a time of political tension between the two halves of the empire.[4]
Flavius Eusebius, cos. 347E
    Probably father of the Christian Eusebia, whom Constantius married
    c. 352.
Flavius Sergius, cos. 350 }
Flavius Nigrinianus, cos. 350E }
    Nothing whatever is known about Sergius, but Nigrinianus probably came
    from Antioch (*PLRE* 1.631: he was the father of Florentius, consul in
    361); on the "Fl. Anicius" given as Nigrinianus' colleague by *CIL* 6.498
    (ms. report only), see *Consuls* (1987) 234.
Flavius Arbitio, cos. 355

(4) Consuls who were probably pagan

V[alerius] Proculus, cos. 325
    Presumably a relative of the consul of 340, an attested pagan, Proculus
    was apparently deposed and disgraced in April 325: *New Empire* (1982)
    102, 234–237.

---

[4]On the political context in 344/5, see *Athanasius and Constantius. Theology and
Politics in the Constantinian Empire* (Cambridge, Mass., 1993) Chapters 9, 10.

Julianus, cos. 325

Three papyri state the consul's name as Ionius Julianus, which is accepted in *Consuls* (1987) 184/5, 629. The name is emended to "Julius Julianus" and the consul is identified with the former praetorian prefect of Licinius in *New Empire* (1982) 102/3.

(5) Consuls attested as pagans

Aurelius Valerius Tullianus Symmachus, cos. 330

Firmicus Maternus, *Math.* 8.15.4

Rufius Albinus, cos. 335

Firmicus Maternus, *Math.* 2.29. cf. "Two Senators under Constantine," *JRS* 65 (1975) 40–49.

Fabius Titianus, cos. 337

Attested as *quindecimvir sacris faciundis* (*ILS* 8983: Cumae)

L. Aradius Valerius Proculus, cos. 340

Proculus was *augur, pontifex maior, quindecimvir sacris faciundis, pontifex Flavialis* (*CIL* 6.1690 = *ILS* 1240).[5]

M. Maecius Furius Baburius Caecilianus Placidus, cos. 343W

Attested as *pontifex maior, augur publicus p. R. Quiritium, quindecimvir sacris faciundis* (*ILS* 1231: Puteoli).

Vulcacius Rufinus, cos. 347W

Attested as *pontifex maior* (*ILS* 1237: Rome). As a non-Christian, Rufinus was not present at the interrogation of Photinus at Sirmium in 351, but one of the short-hand writers who transcribed the proceedings was an "*exceptor* of the prefect Rufinus" (Epiphanius, *Pan.* 71.1.5, 8).

Aconius Catullinus, cos. 349W

As governor of Gallaecia, Catullinus made a dedication to Iuppiter Optimus Maximus (*CIL* 2.2635: Astorga, cf. *CTh* 16.10.3 [342]).

Ulpius Limenius, cos. 349W

Libanius, *Orat.* 1.46, cf. A. Chastagnol, *Fastes* (1962) 128–130; R. von Haehling, *Religionszugehörigkeit* (1978) 292.

Q. Flavius Maesius Egnatius Lollianus Mavortius, cos. 355

Lollianus' religious sympathies are unusually well documented: Firmicus Maternus, *Math.* 8.33.4; *ILS* 1223 (Suessa), 1224a-c (Puteoli, showing

---

[5]The consul of 340 was tentatively identified as the pagan aristocrat who built a spectacular villa in central Sicily by L. Cracco Ruggini, "La Sicilia fra Roma e Bizanzio," *Storia della Sicilia* 3 (Naples, 1980) 1–96, at 67–68 n. 57—a suggestion treated as demonstrated fact in A. Carandini, A. Ricci and M. de Vos, *Filosofiana. The Villa of Piazza Armerina. The Image of a Roman Aristocrat in the Time of Constantine* (Palermo, 1982), where the consul is also presumed identical with the "Balerius comes" whose wife was buried in a Christian sarcophagus at Syracuse (*ILCV* 174). The first identification is no worse than many a completely unsupported speculation, but the second is totally impossible: see Alan Cameron, *JRS* 75 (1985) 175/6.

that he was an augur), 1225, 1232, 3245 (Rome, the last a dedication to Hercules). Lollianus had been designated ordinary consul for 338 by Constantine (*JRS* 65 [1975], 40): his consulate in 355, therefore, should be regarded as a reward for loyalty to the Constantinian dynasty during the rebellion of Magnentius.

PRAEFECTI PRAETORIO

(1) Prefects attested as Christians

Junius Bassus, cos. 331, prefect 318–331
Flavius Ablabius, cos. 331, prefect 329–337
Ambrosius, attested as prefect in Gaul in 339, presumably therefore prefect
  of Constantinus 337–340
  Paulinus, *Vita Ambrosii* 2.2–4, cf. Ambrose, *De Exhortatione Virginitatis*
  12.82 (*PL* 16.376)
Septimius Acyndinus, cos. 340E, prefect of Constantius 338–340
Flavius Philippus, cos. 348E, prefect of Constantius 344–351
Thalassius, prefect of Gallus 351–353
  Athanasius, *Hist. Ar.* 22.1
Maiorinus, prefect of Constantius 351–354
  L. Robert, *Hellenica* 11/12 (Paris, 1960) 302–305
Strategius Musonianus, prefect of Oriens 354–358
  Eusebius, *VC* 3.62.1; Athanasius, *Apol. c. Ar.* 15.3; Ammianus 15.13.1/2
Honoratus, prefect of Gaul 355–357
  Sozomenus, *HE* 4.23.3, cf. R. von Haehling, *Religionszugehörigkeit* (1978)
  115.
Flavius Taurus, cos. 361, prefect of Italy 355–361
Flavius Florentius, cos. 361, prefect of Gaul 357–360, then of Illyricum 360–
  361
Helpidius, prefect of Oriens 360–361
  Jerome, *Vita Hilarionis* 14, cf. R. von Haehling, *Religionszugehörigkeit*
  (1978) 63/4.

(2) Prefects who were probably Christians

Flavius Constantius, cos. 327, attested as prefect 324–327
Valerius Maximus, cos. 327, attested as prefect in 327–328, 332–333 and on
  2 August 337
Evagrius, attested as prefect in 326, 329, 331 and 336
Gregorius, prefect in Africa 336/7
  Optatus 3.3
Flavius Domitius Leontius, cos. 344, prefect of Constantius 341/2–344
Nebridius, appointed prefect of Gaul by Constantius in 360

8 RELIGIOUS AFFILIATION OF CONSULS AND PREFECTS

(3) Prefects whose religious sympathies are unknown

Aemilianus, attested as prefect in 328

L. Papius Pacatianus, cos. 332, attested as prefect 332–336

Valerius Felix, prefect in Africa 333–336

C. Caelius Saturninus, prefect before 22 May 337, probably predecessor of Tiberianus

C. Annius Tiberianus, attested as prefect in 336

Nestorius Timonianus, attested as prefect in 336

Antonius Marcellinus, cos. 341, prefect of Constans 340–342

Eustathius, prefect in Rome 349

Domitianus, prefect of Gallus 353–354

Maecilius Hilarianus, cos. 332, prefect of Italy in 354

Anatolius, prefect of Illyricum 357–360

(Decimius Germanianus, acting prefect of Gaul in 361, was an appointee of Julian: Ammianus 21.8.1.)

(4) Prefects who were probably pagans

Hermogenes, *praefectus praetorio et urbis* 349–350

    The appointment of the easterners Ulpius Limenius, cos. 349, and Hermogenes to high office in the West is anomalous: see A. Chastaganol, "Remarques sur les sénateurs orientaux au IVe siècle," *Acta Antiqua* 24 (1978) 341–356, at 348; "La carrière sénatoriale du Bas-Empire (depuis Dioclétien)," *Epigrafia e ordine senatorio (Tituli* 4–5, 1982, pub. 1984) 167–193, at 181.

C. Ceionius Rufius Volusianus, prefect of Gaul 354–355

(5) Prefects attested as pagans

Valerius Proculus, cos. 340W, temporary prefect in Africa while proconsul in 332/3

Aconius Catullinus, cos. 349W, attested as prefect in 341, but probably appointed in 340

M. Maecius Memmius Furius Baburius Caecilianus Placidus, cos. 343W, prefect 342–c. 345, first of Constans and then of Italy

Anatolius, prefect of Illyricum 343/4–346

    Eunapius, *Vit. phil.* 10.6.1–3 (p. 490)

Vulcacius Rufinus, cos. 347W, prefect c. 345–354, first of Italy, then of Illyricum, and finally of Gaul

Fabius Titianus, cos. 337, prefect in Gaul 342–350

Ulpius Limenius, cos. 349W, *praefectus praetorio et urbis* 347–349

Q. Flavius Maesius Egnatius Lollianus, cos. 355, prefect of Illyricum 355–356

Hermogenes, prefect of Oriens 358–360
  Libanius, *Ep.* 21.1, cf. Ammianus 19.12.6 [6]
(Flavius Sallustius, cos. 363, was appointed prefect of Gaul in 361 by Julian
  in open defiance of the wishes of Constantius: Ammianus 23.5.4.)

PRAEFECTI URBIS ROMAE

(1) Prefects attested as Christians

Ovinius Gallicanus (316–317), cos. 317
Acilius Severus (325–326), cos. 323
Amnius Anicius Julianus (326–329), cos. 322
Publilius Optatianus (329, 333)
  Christian messages are woven into his *carmina intexta*, of which I-XX
  are to be dated to 324/5: "Publilius Optatianus Porfyrius," *AJP* 96
  (1975) 173–186.
Sex. Anicius Paulinus (331–333), cos. 325
Amnius Manius Caesonius Nicomachus Anicius Paulinus (334–335), cos.
  334
Naeratius Cerealis (352–353), cos. 358
Flavius Leontius (355–356)
  Epiphanius, *Pan.* 71.1.5
Junius Bassius (359)
  ILS 1286 (Rome), cf. A. Chastagnol, *Fastes* (1962) 150.

(2) Prefects who were probably Christians

Lucer./Locrius Verinus (323–325)
  D. M. Novak, *Ancient Society* 10 (1979) 299–301; T. D. Barnes, *New
  Empire* (1982) 118/9.
Petronius Probianus (329–331), cos. 322
Petronius Probinus (345–346), cos. 341

(3) Prefects whose religious sympathies are unknown

Septimius Bassus (317–319)
Maecilius Hilarianus (338–339), cos. 332
Q. Rusticus (344–345)

(4) Prefects who were probably pagans

M. Ceionius Julianus (333–334)
Hermogenes, *praefectus praetorio et urbis* (349–350)

---

[6] Wrongly identified as the Hermogenes whose career is described in Himerius, *Orat.*
48 by R. von Haehling, *Religionszugehörigkeit* (1978) 63/4.

10   RELIGIOUS AFFILIATION OF CONSULS AND PREFECTS

(5) Prefects attested as pagans

Valerius Maximus (319–323)
    On his identity as a western aristocrat who was a different man from
    the consul of 327, see *New Empire* (1982) 103, 117/8, 132; "Himerius
    and the Fourth Century," *CP* 82 (1987) 206–225, at 217/8.
Ceionius Rufius Albinus (335–337), cos. 335
L. Aradius Valerius Proculus (337–338), cos. 340
L. Turcius Apronianus (339)
    Both his sons were *quindecimviri sacris faciundis* (*PLRE* 1.817/8).
Fabius Titianus (339–341), cos. 337
Aurelius Celsinus (341–342)
    As proconsul of Africa in 338/9, Celsinus restored a *fanum dei Mercurii*
    (*CIL* 8.12272: Avita Bibba).
Q. Flavius Maesius Egnatius Lollianus (342), cos. 355
Aconius Catullinus (342–344), cos. 348W
M. Maecius Furius Baburius Caecilianus Placidus (346–347), cos. 343W
Ulpius Limenius, cos. 349W, *praefectus praetorio et urbis* (347–349)
Memmius Vitrasius Orfitus (353–355, 357–359)
    CIL 6.45 (= *ILS* 3222), 1739–1742 (1741 = *ILS* 1243; Symmachus, *Ep.*
    1.1.3. Note also the fragment of a ceremonial bowl inscribed *Orfitus
    et Costantia. in nomine Herculis Acerentino* [presumably an error for
    Acerentini] felices bibatis: D. B. Harden, *Glass of the Caesars* (Milan,
    1987) 280 no. 155.[7]
Tertullus (359–361)
    Ammianus 19.10.1–4

TABLES

In each of the following tables columns (1) to (5) correspond to the five
categories into which consuls and prefects have been divided, viz.,
    (1) men attested as Christians
    (2) men who were probably Christians
    (3) men whose religious sympathies are unknown
    (4) men who were probably pagan
    (5) men attested as pagans.

---

[7] Constantia is not in *PLRE* 1 (1971), but her name suggests that she may be related
to the Constantinian dynasty—and such a connexion would help to explain why the
pagan Orfitus held two long prefectures, the second beginning shortly before Constantius
visited Rome in the spring of 357. Orfitus was probably born c. 320 (cf. *PLRE* 1.651–
653) and hence will have married for the first or only time in the early 340s.

CONSULES ORDINARII

	(1)	(2)	(3)	(4)	(5)	
317–337	8	9	7	2	3	29
338–340	2	0	1	0	1	4
341–350E	1	1	3	0	0	5
341–350W	1	1	4	0	4	10
351–361	4	2	1	0	1	8
317–361	16	13	16	2	9	56

(The two consuls of 344 and 350 whose appointment cannot be assigned to either Constantius or Constans are excluded.)

PRAEFECTI PRAETORIO

	(1)	(2)	(3)	(4)	(5)	
324–337	2	4	6	0	1	13
337–350E	2	1	0	0	0	3
337–350W	1	0	2	1	6	10
351–361	7	1	3	1	2	14
324–361	12	6	11	2	9	40

PRAEFECTI URBIS ROMAE

	(1)	(2)	(3)	(4)	(5)	
317–337	6	2	2	1	3	14
338–350	0	1	1	1	7	10
352–361	3	0	0	0	2	5
317–361	9	3	3	2	12	29

(The prefects appointed by Magnentius in 350–352 are omitted.)

VIII

CHRISTIANS AND PAGANS IN THE REIGN OF CONSTANTIUS

II

In ancient history, what appear to be profound and subtle problems of historical interpretation often devolve into straightforward (if not always simple) issues of fact. With the religious policies of the emperor Constantine and the general religious atmosphere of his reign, a great deal depends on whether we accept Eusebius' clear statement that he prohibited pagan sacrifice. If he did so, then it is plausible to speak of the establishment of Christianity as the official religion of the Roman Empire, even of a Constantinian reformation comparable in significance with the great religious movement of the sixteenth century.[102] On the other hand, the majority of recent writers have deemed such an outright prohibition "very improbable":[103] for example, MacMullen has reaffirmed that Constantine's basic policy was that "everyone should respect everyone else's religion", while Lane Fox discounts the law prohibiting sacrifice with the observation that "this claim is highly contestable and was certainly not fulfilled", discusses Constantine's religious policies in 325 as if it never existed—and concludes that the emperor was tolerant in matters of religion.[104] Such interpretations are incompatible with the existence of the law which Eusebius reports. But can the factual issue be decided conclusively?

The evidence is clear and unambiguous. Eusebius reports a series of enactments by Constantine after the defeat of Licinius:

---

[102] See T. D. BARNES, "The Constantinian Reformation", in *The Crake Lectures 1984* (Sackville, N.B., 1986), 39-57.

[103] J. GEFFCKEN, *Der Ausgang des griechisch-römischen Heidentums* (Heidelberg ²1929), 39 f.

[104] R. MacMULLEN, *Christianizing the Roman Empire*, 50; R. LANE FOX, *Pagans and Christians*, 667; 635 ff. The latter asserts that "most of the governors" who had to enforce the disputed law "were themselves still pagans" (667).

1 two edicts sent to every province undid the effects of Licinius' persecution: one was sent to the churches and the other to non-Christians, and Eusebius quotes in full the copy sent to the provincials of Palestine;

2 the emperor began to appoint Christians as provincial governors, and forbade governors, *vicarii* of dioceses and praetorian prefects who were still pagan to perform sacrifice before conducting official business;

3 a law prohibited "the disgusting practices of idolatry practised of old in city and countryside, so that no-one should venture to erect cult-statues, consult oracles or sacrifice at all";

4 another law issued at the same time urged the enlarging of existing churches and the construction of new ones for the expected converts: it was put into effect by means of letters to governors and bishops arranging for the latter to draw freely on imperial funds, and Eusebius quotes the letter which he received;

5 a long and sometimes abusive letter to the eastern provincials, often described as an 'edict of toleration', implicitly reaffirmed the preceding prohibition of sacrifice.[105]

There is no call to reject Eusebius' reports (2,3) while accepting his quotations (1, 4 and 5): he does not quote the crucial law about cult acts because he did not possess a copy of Constantine's original pronouncement.[106] In 341 the emperor Constans threatened condign punishment for any who dared to sacrifice "against the law of the divine emperor our father and this order of our clemency".[107]

---

[105] Eus. *Vit. Const.* II 24-60.

[106] T. D. BARNES, "Constantine's Prohibition of Pagan Sacrifice", in *AJP* 105 (1984), 69-72.

[107] *CTh* XVI 10, 2.

That ought to suffice for proof. Why then is the existence of such a law so often denied?

The basic reason appears to be the weight of academic tradition: such a law contradicts the traditional picture of Constantine held by most historians from Gibbon to Lane Fox: therefore, it cannot have been issued.[108] More specifically, the general distrust of the *Life of Constantine*, evinced even by those who (like Jacob Burckhardt) accept Eusebius' authorship, seems to deprive its evidence of probative value.[109] Further, Libanius claimed that Constantine "made absolutely no change in the established forms of worship", that it was Constantius who prohibited sacrifice.[110] However, Libanius' assertion is special pleading for the benefit of Theodosius, while the relevant section of Eusebius' *Life of Constantine* is less a retrospective panegyric than part of what was intended as a documented ecclesiastical history of the last years of Constantine.[111] Furthermore, the religious history of the period between 324 and 361 makes more sense if Constantine prohibited sacrifice. Constantine conquered the East in 324 in a Christian crusade, a purge of prominent pagans (or at least persecutors) occurred, and the political situation allowed drastic action.[112] Constantine surely cannot have let such an opportunity slip. But enforcement of the law prohibiting sacrifice depended on local conditions and local initiative, Constantine was too canny a politician to send soldiers to suppress traditional cults throughout the East or to attack the existing rights of

---

[108] For a cautious recent formulation of this view, P. D. A. GARNSEY, "Religious Toleration in Classical Antiquity", in *Persecution and Toleration*, ed. W. J. SHIELS, Studies in Church History 21 (Oxford 1984), 1-27, esp. 18 n. 39.

[109] H. A. DRAKE, in *AJP* 103 (1982), 464 f.

[110] Lib. *Or.* XXX 6.

[111] For this analysis, see my "Panegyric, History and Hagiography in Eusebius' *Life of Constantine*" (now reprinted in this volume as no. XI).

[112] T. D. BARNES, *Constantine and Eusebius*, 208 ff.; 245 ff.

those who had become his subjects in 306, 312 or even 316/7. Hence the religious situation of the Roman Empire after 324 was a varied one—and it long remained varied: the East was more Christian than the West, and the West had an entrenched landowning aristocracy which was more resistant to Christianity than any other stratum of society.

The earliest evidence for Christian attacks on pagan holy places comes from the West: one of the canons of the Council of Elvira alludes to the smashing of pagan idols, probably c. 300.[113] Such aggressiveness, however, does not appear to have become common in the West until late in the fourth century.[114] In the East, matters moved more swiftly. Constantine conducted a systematic confiscation of temple treasures accumulated over the centuries, and also suppressed certain cult-centres which Christians found particularly offensive on moral grounds (most conspicuously the shrine of Aphrodite at Aphaca in Phoenicia).[115] Under Constantius, local bishops went further and attacked pagan holy places on their own initiative.[116] When Julian exiled

---

[113] Canon 60. In favour of a date c. 300, see the classic statement by L. Du-CHESNE, "Le concile d'Elvire et les flamines chrétiens", in *Mélanges Renier* (Paris 1887), 159-174, and my brief defence in *The Crake Lectures 1984*, 45; 55 n. 43. R. LANE FOX, *Pagans and Christians*, 664 ff., dates the council between 312 and 324 and argues that the canons "throw a sharp light on church life in Constantine's Christian era."

It is not clear exactly how to classify the removal of *cupae* and vinegar from a shrine of Serapis at Cirta apparently c. 303 (Optatus Milevitanus, ed. C. ZIWSA, Appendix I, p. 195, 20-24).

[114] When it is documented in Sulpicius Severus, *Vita Martini* 14, 1 ff.; cf. C. STANCLIFFE, *St. Martin and his Hagiographer. History and Miracle in Sulpicius Severus* (Oxford 1983), 328 ff.

[115] Eus. *Triac.* 8, 1 ff.; *Vit. Const.* III 54, 4 ff. (also recording the destruction of shrines at Aegeae in Cilicia and Heliopolis in Phoenicia). Eunapius observes in passing that Constantine pulled down the most celebrated temples (*Vit.phil.* VI 1, 5, p. 461 Didot).

[116] G. FOWDEN, "Bishops and Temples in the Eastern Roman Empire, A. D. 320-435", in *JThS* N.S. 29 (1978), 53-78.

Eleusius from Cyzicus, the charges included despoiling temples, defiling sacred precincts and persuading pagans to abandon their ancestral rites.[117] When he reached Tarsus, Julian was approached by the priest of Asclepius at Aegeae in Cilicia, who asked for the return of columns which the local bishop had taken from the temple and used in building a church.[118] Mark of Arethusa became a martyr: under Constantius he had destroyed a pagan shrine "according to the power then given to Christians" in order to build a church; under Julian he refused to restore the shrine or offer even a single obol in compensation despite prolonged tortures.[119] At Heliopolis in Phoenicia, again probably in the reign of Constantius, the deacon Cyrillus smashed many of the idols worshipped there: when Julian came to power, the pagans remembered this boldness, killed Cyrillus and (it is alleged) ate his liver.[120] Martyrdoms also occurred in Gaza where the pagans were enraged at those who "had damaged shrines and employed the preceding period to destroy and insult Hellenism".[121] Such activity is most fully reported for George of Alexandria. He was lynched soon after news came of Constantius' death, and Socrates plausibly makes his lynching an act of vengeance by pagans for riots which occurred when George excavated a disused Mithraeum and found human skulls there.[122] Julian then

---

[117] Soz. *HE* V 15, 4-10.

[118] Zonaras XIII 12, 30-34. The sanctuary had been destroyed by soldiers acting on the orders of Constantine (Eus. *Vit. Const.* III 56): on its history, see L. ROBERT, "De Cilicie à Messine et à Plymouth", in *Journal des Savants* 1973, 161-211, esp. 183-193. Robert notes the relevance of Libanius, *Ep.* 695, 2, which refers to "the war of the atheists against his (*sc.* Asclepius') temple, its destruction, the fire, the desecrated altars, the wrong done to suppliants no longer allowed a release from their ills."

[119] Greg. Naz. *Or.* IV 88-91; Soz. *HE* V 10, 5-14; Thdt. *HE* III 7, 6-10.

[120] Thdt. *HE* III 7, 3, where the majority of textual witnesses read ἐπὶ Κωνσταντίνου.

[121] Soz. *HE* V 9, 2.

[122] Socr. *HE* III 2.

wrote a letter of mild rebuke to the city which includes a description of George's misdeeds:

> Tell me by Serapis, for what injustices were you annoyed with George? You will doubtless say that he incited the blessed Constantius against you, then brought an army into the holy city, and that the general of Egypt (i.e. Artemius) siezed the holiest shrine of the god, stripping it of its statues, offerings and the ornaments in its sanctuaries. When you were quite justifiably enraged and tried to defend the god, or rather the god's possessions, he dared unjustly, illegally and impiously to send his heavily armed soldiers against you, perhaps because he feared George more than Constantius, who restrained himself so that he might deal with you from afar and appear to behave moderately and constitutionally, not like a tyrant.[123]

These six examples (be it observed) are known only because pagans exacted revenge under Julian. Similarly, Sozomenus notes that the Christians who formed the vast majority of the inhabitants of Caesarea in Cappadocia had destroyed the temples of Zeus and Apollo, but only in the context of Julian's punishment of the city and its citizens for such actions.[124] Bishops who destroyed temples but either died before Constantius or escaped notice under Julian simply do not show up in the surviving evidence. There were surely many of them. For Sozomenus speaks of Julian's general policy of "forcing those who had destroyed them to rebuild the temples dismantled in the reigns of Constantine and Constantius or to repay the cost of doing

---

[123] Iulian. *Ep.* 60 Bidez.
[124] Soz. *HE* V 4, 1-5.

so".[125] Julian himself makes a general accusation that the sons of Constantine demolished the ancestral temples which their father had despised and stripped of votive offerings, and that when the temples were destroyed, churches (his word is 'sepulchres') were built on new and old sites.[126]

The phenomenon was widespread. Even friends of Libanius profited from attacks on pagan shrines. Under Julian, Libanius wrote two letters to Belaeus, the governor of Arabia, on behalf of the Christian Orion, as well as interceding personally for him.[127] The letters are couched in polite and allusive language and set out to make a case. In some official capacity,[128] Orion had allowed the spoliation of pagan shrines: "he blamed rather than imitated those who used their power badly," and Libanius heard from the inhabitants of Bostra that "he neither waged war on the temples nor harried priests but alleviated the misfortunes of many by performing his office with great mildness." When Libanius wrote, however, Orion was despondent; he had been attacked by those whom he had protected, his brother was exiled, his family scattered, his land unsown, his furniture stolen—all because Julian had declared that anyone who possessed any holy objects should forfeit them. Libanius claims that, though a Christian, Orion is being wronged and asks Belaeus to protect him, above all not to turn him into a martyr like Mark of Arethusa. In the course of his pleading, however, Libanius admits that Orion received

---

[125] Soz. *HE* V 5, 5, cf. V 3, 1 (the reopening and restoration of temples and reconstruction of altars).

[126] Iulian. *Or.* 7, 228 BC Hertlein.

[127] Lib. *Ep.* 763; 819. Julian appointed Belaeus *praeses Arabiae* in 362 precisely because of his staunch paganism: there were riots in Bostra when Julian tried to enforce his religious policies there (Iulian. *Ep.* 114).

[128] Orion, who is not in *PLRE* I, is held to be a native of Bostra rather than a governor by G. R. SIEVERS, *Das Leben des Libanius* (Berlin 1868), 117; W. ENSSLIN, in *RE* XVIII 1 (1939), 1087.

some proceeds from pagan temples, which he has spent. We must surely suspect that many officials under Constantius had behaved like Orion.[129] Official policy was clear and there is evidence that pagan shrines were suppressed by local initiative. But how effective was action at either level? In one area at least, almost totally. Mithraism was a religion of soldiers and officials, prominent as late as 308 when, at the Conference of Carnuntum, Diocletian and Galerius declared on behalf of themselves and their imperial colleagues that the Roman Empire was under the protection of Mithras.[130] Yet after 312, only two Mithraic dedications seem to be known outside Rome.[131] When Eusebius records that, besides prohibiting sacrifice, consultation of oracles and the erection of cult-statues, Constantine forbade 'secret rites', it seems probable that he alludes to a law which specifically condemned Mithraism.[132] Soldiers and officials had little choice but to obey, whatever their private inclinations.

Pagans without ambitions to rise in imperial service had more freedom. Libanius' autobiographical oration provides some striking examples of non-conformity. Libanius' uncle Phasganius presided over the Olympic Games at Antioch in 328: he disregarded Constantine's recent prohibition and exhibited gladiators.[133] (There is no evidence that these games ever again included gladiators.[134]) As a student in

---

[129] Compare Libanius' defence of Theodulus for buying objects forcibly removed from a temple (*Ep.* 724).

[130] *ILS* 659.

[131] R. TURCAN, "Les motivations de l'intolérance chrétienne et la fin du mithriacisme au IVᵉ siècle ap. J.-C.", in *Actes du VIIᵉ Congrès de la F.I.E.C.* II (Budapest 1984), 209-226, esp. 222-3.

[132] Eus. *Vit. Const.* IV 25; cf. R. TURCAN, *art. cit.*, 220 ff.

[133] Lib. *Or.* I 5, cf. *CTh* XV 12, 1 (325); Eus. *Vit. Const.* IV 25.

[134] P. PETIT, *Libanius et la vie municipale à Antioche au IVᵉ siècle après J.-C.* (Paris 1955), 125.

330

Athens (336-339), Libanius himself travelled in Greece and went to Argos to be initiated into the local mysteries; he was probably also initiated into the mysteries at Eleusis. He formed a close friendship with Crispinus of Heraclea whose uncle was an ostentatious pagan:

> he consorted more with gods than with men on earth: even though a law banned it and the penalty for one who dared was death, nevertheless he journeyed through life in the company of gods and mocked that evil law and its impious enactor.[135]

Constantine could easily tolerate such harmless bravado. The eastern intelligentsia long continued to boast of outspoken pagans,[136] as did the Roman aristocracy. But both bodies were divided. Many pagan intellectuals could accept the prohibition of sacrifice with equanimity, for Porphyry had argued forcefully that sacrifice was not necessary for worshipping the gods, indeed that it hindered the higher forms of devotion.[137] In the reign of Constantius, the pagan Themistius composed commentaries on Aristotle, turned out official panegyrics and accepted a position of dignity in the Christian Senate of Constantinople, while the Christian Proaeresius taught rhetoric in the still pagan atmosphere of Athens.[138]

An outspoken claim for the continuing vitality of traditional cults in the East appears to be made in the *Expositio totius mundi et gentium*:

---

[135] Lib. *Or.* I 27. The "impious enactor" of the "evil law" is clearly Constantine: no need, therefore, to detect an anachronistic reference to the law of 341, as does A.F. NORMAN (ed.), *Libanius' Autobiography (Oration I)* (London 1965), 155, followed by P. PETIT (ed.), *Libanios: Discours I* (Paris 1979), 215.

[136] G. FOWDEN, "The Pagan Holy Man in Late Antique Society", in *JHS* 102 (1982), 33-59.

[137] R. TURCAN, *art. cit.*, 214 ff.

[138] *PLRE* I 731.

[in Egypt you have] men similarly noble who worship the gods eminently: for nowhere are the mysteries of the gods so performed as there from antiquity until now, and almost of itself [Egypt] taught the whole world to worship the gods... We know that the gods lived and still live there.[139]

To judge from his interests and enthusiasms, the author of the *Expositio* was a pagan merchant from Palestine.[140] His insights are not profound and what impressed him most about Egypt was its sacred architecture, including the Serapeum. In the passage quoted he speaks more as an awestruck tourist than as an acute observer of present reality.

In the West, Constantine probably did not even promulgate the prohibition of sacrifice formally. It was Constans who did so in 341, in a constitution addressed to Crepereius Madalianus, the *vicarius Italiae*.[141] That law had some immediate effect, since in the following year Constans instructed the *praefectus urbi* to protect temple buildings outside cities so that they could continue as the focus of games and contests.[142] Yet many Christians were dissatisfied at the pace of change. In 343, the senator Firmicus Maternus, who had in 337 addressed a treatise on astrology to a prominent aristocrat, urged the emperor to suppress traditional rites altogether. The bulk of Maternus' *On the Error of Profane Religions* rehearses apologetic arguments against paganism familiar from writers such as Tertullian and Arnobius with a fullness which makes the treatise a

---

[139] *Expositio* 34.
[140] J. ROUGÉ (ed.), *Expositio totius mundi et gentium*, Sources chrétiennes 124 (Paris 1966), 27 ff.
[141] *CTh* XVI 10, 1.
[142] *CTh* XVI 10, 2.

VIII

332

valuable source for religious history.[143] Maternus' purpose, however, was not a rational refutation of all varieties of paganism, but their forcible suppression. He urges Constantius and Constans to use the power given them by God to lay low the Devil, to extinguish idolatry. Better to save the unwilling by force than to let them destroy themselves. The adornments of the temples should be seized and turned into coin or arms, for God will reward such a destruction with even greater success than the emperors have so far enjoyed.[144]

Firmicus Maternus may have presented his work to Constans. The emperor was not impelled to action. On the contrary, Constans needed the cooperation of the Senate and appointed aristocrats to high office. And Magnentius, who supplanted him in 350, had even less cause to risk alienating potential supporters by attacking paganism: although he was a Christian himself and sought the support of eastern Christians who opposed Constantius (such as Athanasius), he relaxed the existing prohibition on nocturnal sacrifices.[145] When Constantius conquered the West, he introduced a more restrictive policy: he ordered the closure of all temples, the complete cessation of sacrifice and execution as the penalty for disobedience.[146] Yet in Rome itself, even Constantius needed to tread carefully. In 357, he entered the city with carefully staged ceremonial and made gestures of deference to the Senate.[147] As *pontifex maximus* he coopted new members into the traditional priesthoods,

[143] See the full commentary by R. TURCAN (éd.), Firmicus Maternus: *L'erreur des religions païennes* (Paris 1982).

[144] Firmicus Maternus, *Err.* 16, 4; 20, 7; 29, 3-4.

[145] *CTh* XVI 10, 5 (23 November 353).

[146] *CTh* XVI 10, 6 (19 February 356); XVI 10, 4. The transmitted date of the latter is 1 December 346, but the addressee is the praetorian prefect Taurus: the year, therefore, should be emended to 356, cf. O. SEECK, *Regesten der Kaiser und Päpste* (Stuttgart 1919), 41; 203.

[147] Amm. XVI 10, 1-17.

and he confirmed their endowments.[148] To balance this, however, he removed the altar of Victory from the senate-house where it had stood since the days of Augustus. The emperor clearly wished to prevent the possibility that any Christian senator might be compelled, by etiquette or social pressure, to participate in a pagan ritual.

III

The war of 324 and its consequences must have cowed pagans throughout the Roman Empire. As in 313, an emperor who persecuted the Christians had gone down to military defeat and, as in 313, the friends, relatives and sympathisers of the victims of the persecuting regime exacted revenge. For the purge of 313 only a handful of names can be recovered (of governors and priests),[149] but the bloodletting was widespread enough for Licinius to issue an edict making accusations for treason more difficult, of which copies survive from six eastern cities.[150] For the purge of 324 we have only the piously self-satisfied remark of Eusebius that the advocates of fighting God paid the appropriate penalty.[151] Yet lack of proper documentation should not blind us to the seriousness or importance of what may have been a systematic settling of accounts in Asia Minor and the East. It may help to explain the lack of Greek pagan literature for the next thirty years. The pagan Praxagoras produced a panegyrical history of Constantine,[152] and under Constantius the sophist Bemarchius,

---

[148] Symmachus, *Rel.* 3, 7.

[149] *Constantine and Eusebius*, 64.

[150] See now C. HABICHT and P. KUSSMAUL, "Ein neues Fragment des Edictum de Accusationibus", in *MH* 43 (1986), 135-144.

[151] Eus. *Vit. Const.* II 18.

[152] *FGrH* 219.

334

"though sacrificing to the gods", travelled the East reciting a panegyric on the glorious new church at Antioch.[153] Themistius and Libanius, born c. 317 and in 314 respectively, made their débuts as imperial panegyrists in 347 and 344 : it may be significant that Libanius' speech in praise of Constantius and Constans was composed and delivered at the behest of the Christian praetorian prefect Flavius Philippus.[154]

In the circumstances of 324/5 a puzzling fact cannot help exciting speculation. One of the ordinary consuls of 325 seems to have been disgraced in April or May and replaced by Julius Julianus, the former praetorian prefect of Licinius.[155] His name is indisputably documented as Proculus,[156] while a fragmentary papyrus can be restored to supply the *nomen* Valerius.[157] It is tempting, therefore, to see in Valerius Proculus as the presumed consul of 325 a Roman aristocrat involved in a pagan protest against Constantine, and to connect his disgrace with the murder of Licinius at Thessalonica.[158] All admittedly speculation—but there is a historical void to be explained.

Constantine's court was not closed to pagans. Yet they were not as prominent as is often supposed. Against the emperor's alleged favours to Sopater, the pupil of Iamblichus, must be set the fact that Constantine executed him for using magic to cause a food shortage in Constantinople.[159] And two favourite examples of pagans at the court of Constantine must be discarded: the pupil of Iamblichus, six of whose letters are transmitted under the name of the

---

[153] Lib. *Or.* I 39.

[154] Lib. *Or.* LIX 1 ff.

[155] *The New Empire...*, 102-3.

[156] *POxy.* 3125; *CTh* II 25, 1 = *CJ* III 38, 11 (29 April).

[157] *POxy.* 889, cf. T.D. BARNES and K.A. WORP, in *ZPE* 53 (1983), 276-278.

[158] *Constantine and Eusebius*, 214.

[159] Eunapius, *Vit.phil.* VI 2, 2-11, pp. 462-3 Didot; Zos. II 40, 3.

emperor Julian, went to the court of Licinius, not Constantine,[160] while the philosophical Hermogenes, whose career has been taken as a paradigm of pagans who prospered in the newly Christian empire,[161] probably served Gallus, Julian and Valens, not Licinius and Constantine.[162] The ethos of the court of Constantine was openly, perhaps even stridently, Christian.[163]

It is against this background that we must set the conversion of Julian from the Christianity in which he was brought up. In 351, at the age of twenty, Julian went to Pergamum and Ephesus. At Pergamum he listened to the Neoplatonic philosophers Aedesius, Chrysanthius and Eusebius. In Ephesus he met the wonderworker Maximus and underwent a conversion to the philosophy of Iamblichus and its theurgical practices.[164] According to Libanius, news of the event spread quickly and devotees of the Muses and the pagan gods flocked to see the prince.[165] Although Libanius made this claim after Julian's death, it should not be completely discounted.[166] Gallus was worried enough to send Aetius from Antioch to bring his brother to his senses.[167] Julian listened and behaved himself: for the next decade he studiously composed himself as a pious Chris-

---

[160] Iulian. *Ep.* 181; 183-187 Bidez; cf. T.D. BARNES, in *GRBS* 19 (1978), 99-106.

[161] F. MILLAR, in *JRS* 60 (1970), 216.

[162] T.D. BARNES, in *CPh* 82 (1987), 220 f. For the traditional picture of Hermogenes and Sopater as influential advisers of Constantine, L. de GIOVANNI, *Costantino e il mondo pagano* (Napoli ³1983), 155 ff.

[163] As argued in *Constantine and Eusebius*, 221 f.; 248 ff. For a different view, H.A. DRAKE, *In Praise of Constantine. A Historical Study and New Translation of Eusebius' Tricennial Orations* (Berkeley 1976), 12 ff.; 46 ff.

[164] J. BIDEZ, *La Vie de l'Empereur Julien* (Paris 1930), 67 ff.

[165] Lib. *Or.* XVIII 20 ff.

[166] J. BIDEZ, *op. cit.*, 93 ff.

[167] Philostorgius, *HE* III 27.

336

tian.[168] Yet his sympathy for the old religion was known: when the bishop of Ilium, conducted Julian round the shrines of his city, he revealed that he too was a worshipper of the gods obliged by the temper of the times to conform to the ascendant religion.[169] It would be mistaken, however, to imagine a 'pagan underground' actively working for the elevation of Julian.[170] On the contrary, when Julian became Caesar, Priscus and other philosophers refused to go to him in Gaul.[171] Oribasius of Pergamum attended as his physician, but only two other men came, of no real prominence (the African Euhemerus and the hierophant of the Eleusinian mysteries).[172]

It would be equally mistaken to imagine a group of pagans in Gaul working to manœuvre an unwilling Julian into rebellion in the winter of 359/60.[173] Julian possessed an unquenchable ambition to replace Constantius as emperor: though repressed at the conscious level, his aspirations broke through in matters such as his dream of two trees, one tall and about to collapse, the other young and vigorous, and his depiction of himself as Achilles to Constantius' Agamemnon.[174] Yet it seems clear that most eastern pagans had little confidence in Julian—or at least expected Constantius to defeat him. And many eastern pagans kept their distance even when Constantius unexpectedly died. Against

---

[168] G.W. BOWERSOCK, *Julian the Apostate* (Cambridge, Mass., 1978), 29 ff.

[169] Iulian. *Ep.* 79. Iulian was assiduously active on behalf of friends with pagan connections (*Ad Them.* 259 CD Hertlein).

[170] See J.F. DRINKWATER, "The "Pagan Underground", Constantius II's "Secret Service", and the Survival, and the Usurpation of Julian the Apostate", in *Studies in Latin Literature and Roman History*, ed. C. DEROUX, III, Collection Latomus 180 (Bruxelles 1983), 348-387.

[171] Iulian. *Ep.* 11-13.

[172] Iulian. *Ad Ath.* 277 C Hertlein; Eunapius, *Vit.phil.* VII 3, 7-8, p. 476 Didot.

[173] As does J.F. DRINKWATER, *art. cit.*, 370 ff.

[174] Iulian. *Ep.* 14; *Or.* 2, 49 C ff. Hertlein.

the shallow enthusiasm of Himerius, who hastened to the court of Julian, must be set the reluctance of the prudent Themistius, who had long before decided that there was a place for the traditions of Hellenism (correctly defined) in the new Christian Empire.[175] Indeed, it can be claimed that until the death of Constantius in November 361 Julian derived more political benefit from his support of catholic opponents of Constantius' ecclesiastical policies in the West than from the badly kept secret of his apostasy.[176] It was only when Constantius was removed that Julian dared to sacrifice openly as a declared pagan. He knew that to challenge Constantius as an avowed pagan would have been to ensure defeat in the strongly Christian Roman Empire of 361.

[175] On Himerius' career, see *CPh* 82 (1987), 206 ff.; for Themistius' attitudes, the massive study of G. DAGRON, *L'empire romain d'Orient au IVe siècle et les traditions politiques de l'hellénisme. Le témoignage de Thémistios*, Travaux et Mémoires 3 (Paris 1967), 1-242.

[176] *Athanasius and Constantius. Theology and Politics in the Constantinian Empire* (Cambridge, Mass., 1993), 153 ff.

IX

The Constantinian Settlement

Eusebius of Caesarea was born not long after 260 CE and died at the end
of May 339. He grew up and passed most of his life in the Roman province
of Palestine, and for a quarter of a century he was bishop of the city of
Caesarea, the residence of the provincial governor, the capital of the
province—and hence also its Christian metropolis. He was trained as a
biblical scholar and reached middle age in a period when Christianity, despite
its claims to uniqueness, had come to be accepted as one of the normal,
perhaps even traditional, religions of Roman provincial society. The appeal
by Christians to the emperor Aurelian, probably in 270, to oust a recal-
citrant bishop of Antioch who refused to accept his deposition by a church
council symbolizes the official toleration and social respectability of the
Christian church in the late third century (*HE* 7.30.19–20).[1]

I. Eusebius and Contemporary Politics

Imperial policy towards the Christians changed suddenly around 300.
Precisely why cannot be documented properly, since both court intrigues and
the formulation of imperial policy tend to be concealed from the inquisitive
gaze of outsiders. There survives, however, an account of imperial
persecution of the Christians between 303 and 313 and its political
background, written by an intelligent observer who had lived on the fringes
of the court of Diocletian in Nicomedia and became tutor to the eldest son of
Constantine, probably before the Battle of the Milvian Bridge. Lactantius'
pamphlet *On the Deaths of the Persecutors* plausibly makes the persecution
initiated by imperial edict in February 303 the result of political pressure
exerted in private on Diocletian by the Caesar Galerius, who in 298 inflicted
a spectacular defeat on the Persians.[2] Galerius invaded Armenia, descended
into Mesopotamia, captured Ctesiphon, and annexed territory to the Roman
Empire. Flush with military prestige, Galerius began to push Diocletian

towards persecution, even though the senior emperor had tolerated Christians for fifteen years, and was willing to appoint Christians as provincial governors (*HE* 8.1.2). Galerius' motives were personal, political, and dynastic. As matters stood in 300, it seemed clear who would be the next Roman emperors.

In 293 Diocletian had established a college of four emperors, himself and Maximian as Augusti, Constantius and Galerius as a pair of nominally subordinate Caesars. The four emperors were closely linked by marriage. Diocletian's only child was married to Galerius, whose only legitimate child was married to Maxentius, the only son of Maximian, as soon as their ages permitted. Maximian's adult daughter was married to Constantius, whose only adult son (Constantine) was perhaps expected to marry Maximian's second, much younger daughter.[3] Hence, by dynastic principles visible to all, Constantine and Maxentius were marked out as the next pair of emperors to be appointed to the imperial college—and were groomed as candidates for the purple, Constantine at the court of Diocletian, Maxentius at his father's court in the West. It may also be the case (the matter remains obscure and controversial) that Diocletian had already set a twenty-year limit for the rule of the two Augusti:[4] if so, the two senior emperors were due to abdicate in 305 and anyone who wished to upset Diocletian's arrangements for the succession needed to make haste. Galerius saw what might further his own ambitions and acted. Constantine and Maxentius were openly sympathetic to Christianity. The officially ordained persecution into which Galerius impelled Diocletian in the winter of 302/303 was intended (so at least it may be claimed) to make it politically impossible for the senior emperor to appoint as Caesars men known to oppose a policy on whose enforcement imperial prestige now came to rest. On 1 May 305, when Diocletian announced the names of the new Caesars, they were not Constantine and Maxentius, as was widely expected, but Severus and Maximinus, a protégé and the nephew of Galerius.

Constantine fled to his father, was proclaimed Augustus in his stead on 25 July 306, and by stages over the next eighteen years made himself the sole effective ruler of the whole Roman Empire. Eusebius, who had seen Constantine as a young man at the side of Diocletian as the imperial court traveled through Palestine in 301 or 302 (*Vita Const.* 1.19) became his subject in October 324. Thereafter, Eusebius probably saw Constantine on no more than four occasions in all: during the Council of Nicaea and the subsequent celebrations of the emperor's *vicennalia* in the summer of 325; at the Council of Nicomedia which rehabilitated Arius in the winter of 327/328; in November 335 when Eusebius and five other leading bishops traveled post-haste from the Council of Tyre in an unsuccessful attempt to forestall Athanasius' appeal to the emperor to set aside the decisions of the council; and finally during the Council of Constantinople in July 336 and the subsequent celebrations of the emperor's *tricennalia*, at which he delivered his surviving *Panegyric to Constantine*. Eusebius was never close to Constantine: he was a provincial bishop who saw and admired from afar. He was a scholar and a historian who did not write contemporary history in order to glorify an imperial patron, but primarily because he felt that God has entrusted him with the task of transmitting to posterity a reliable account of the persecution of the Christian church which he witnessed in his own day, and its subsequent political triumph.

Eusebius had already composed an *Ecclesiastical History* in seven books before the Diocletianic persecution.[5] He first proclaimed his vocation as a witness to the events of his own day in the preface to the long recension of the *Martyrs of Palestine*, which he wrote between June and November 311 in memory of his friends who had perished in eight years of persecution (*MP* (L) Pref.8). Shortly after Eusebius completed this work, Maximinus recommenced persecution in Asia Minor, Egypt, and the East: when persecution ceased again with the defeat and death of Maximinus in 313, Eusebius decided to rewrite his *Martyrs of Palestine* and incorporate it into the already existing *Ecclesiastical History*. He composed the short recension of the *Martyrs of Palestine* as an integral part of the *Ecclesiastical History*, which, together with the present ninth book (on Maximinus' renewal of persecution in 311–313), provided a survey of the ten years of persecution in the East. Later, dissatisfied with the excessively provincial viewpoint of even the rewritten *Martyrs*, Eusebius composed the present Book 8 of the *History* to replace it, and the replacement shows clear traces of its complicated origin.[6]

The edition of the *Ecclesiastical History* published ca. 315 concluded with a series of documents illustrating the new status of the Christian church under the Christian emperor Constantine and his colleague Licinius, whom Eusebius then believed to be equally sympathetic to his religion. After Licinius too had persecuted the church, albeit briefly and ineffectually, and had been defeated and deposed (October 324), Eusebius rewrote the end of the *Ecclesiastical History* to reflect his changed view of Licinius and to include recent events. Eusebius also (it seems) began to collect documents with a view to continuing his *History* beyond 324: the letters and edicts of Constantine that he assembled between the winter of 324/325 and the autumn of 328 form the nucleus of what was published after his death as Books 2 and 3 of the *Life of Constantine*.[7]

The defeat and abdication of the eastern emperor Licinius in October 324, and the subsequent purge of his most prominent pagan supporters, on whom the liberated Christians wreaked a bloody revenge for this recent oppression, produced a revolutionary situation. Constantine saw his opportunity and acted swiftly and decisively. In 324/325, he passed beyond the religious toleration for all which he had so far upheld, made Christianity the official religion of the Roman Empire, and began to dismantle the apparatus and practice of the traditional cults of the gods, at least in the newly conquered provinces of Asia Minor, Syria, Palestine, and Egypt. The cumulative effects of the new policies in the years following 324 amount to a "Constantinian reformation," in which the balance of wealth, political power, and social prestige shifted from the priests, devotees, and shrines of the traditional deities of the Greek-speaking provinces of the empire to the Christian church.[8] The Christians of Eusebius' generation, who grew up in a world where to be a Christian had ceased to be a crime, never forgot the perils and humiliations of the "Great Persecution" which came unexpectedly and lasted in Asia Minor, Syria, Palestine, and Egypt for ten years. Eusebius himself, in his historical writings, has left an invaluable record of the successive stages of imperial persecution, imperial toleration, and imperial patronage of the Christian church—and his optimistic *Commentary on Isaiah*, composed towards the end of his life, places the Constantinian settlement described in the *Life of Constantine* within the continuum of human history stretching from the Fall to the Last Judgment.

II. Persecution

The Christian church and individual Christians had enjoyed de facto toleration since 260, when the emperor Valerian, who had attempted to suppress Christianity in the higher strata of Roman society, was captured by the Persians and his son Gallienus disowned his policies, put an end to persecution, and recognized the rights of Christian communities to own cemeteries and church buildings (*HE* 7.13).[9] The next forty years have, with some plausibility, been styled "the triumph of the Church."[10] Eusebius asserts categorically (and there is no good reason to disbelieve him) that Diocletian appointed Christians as provincial governors and allowed them to omit the symbolic acts of sacrifice which normally preceded the transaction of all official business (*HE* 8.1.2).

The situation changed suddenly in 299. The emperors Diocletian and Galerius were sacrificing in Antioch (so at least Lactantius implies) for the purpose of divination. But the haruspices were unable to discover the normal marks on the entrails of the victims because Christians in the imperial household made the sign of the cross to ward off demons. When the cause was detected, the emperors ordered all members of the imperial court to sacrifice to the gods, then instructed military commanders that all men under their command were either to sacrifice to the gods or to be cashiered.[11] That sufficed for the moment. Galerius departed for the Danubian frontier, while Diocletian resided in Antioch until the autumn of 302, with a visit to Egypt in the preceding winter 301/302.[12] In the autumn of 302, the deacon Romanus came from Caesarea, saw the temples of Antioch crowded with worshipers, and protested by striding into the governor's court and urging those present not to sacrifice. The governor condemned Romanus to be burned alive, but Diocletian overruled him and ordered the protester's tongue to be cut out. This episode is known only from Eusebius' *Martyrs of Palestine*, and it is only the long recension of the *Martyrs* that records the vital fact of Diocletian's presence in Antioch—and hence establishes the date of Romanus' arrest (*MP* (L) 2). (He was eventually executed on 17 November 303.) The young Palestinian's protest demonstrates not only his own confident and provocative attitude but also Diocletian's extreme and continuing reluctance to execute Christians. It needed prolonged political pressure from Galerius to set the so-called Diocletianic persecution in motion.

Diocletian spent the winter of 302/303 in Nicomedia, where the Caesar joined him. Both Lactantius, who was in Nicomedia at the time, and Eusebius blame Galerius for instigating the series of edicts which Diocletian issued against the Christian church in 303 and 304. Their testimony has sometimes been questioned as sheer rhetorical exaggeration, the reflection of political propaganda, the product of ignorance and bias, or as an apologetic invention inspired by Galerius' later gruesome death.[13] That is not justifiable. It suited Constantine in the 320s to make Diocletian responsible and to ignore Galerius—but it also suited him, in the same context, to misrepresent his own age in order to preclude any criticism that he had not exerted himself on the Christians' behalf when persecution threatened (*Vita Const.* 2.51).[14] Lactantius and Eusebius undoubtedly both simplify and exaggerate, but to reject their explicit testimony on a central issue which affected them so closely, and on which Lactantius was well placed to discover the truth, would be to deny their credibility in general. Nothing in the ancient evidence—only modern scholarly tradition—prevents the history of the period from being reconstructed convincingly on the assumption that Lactantius and Eusebius are basically honest and trustworthy witnesses.[15]

The first persecuting edict was published on 24 February 303.[16] It forbade Christians to assemble for worship and attempted to dismantle their religion: churches were to be destroyed, all copies of the Bible and liturgical books surrendered and burned, church ornaments, ecclesiastical vestments, and the sites on which churches stood were to be confiscated, and private houses where any of the paraphernalia of Christian worship might be found were to be destroyed. More generally, the edict prescribed that every person without exception who appeared in any court of law, civil as well as criminal, should sacrifice to the gods before being heard—a requirement tantamount to depriving Christians of all their legal rights.[17] As a result, any Christian who was challenged and refused to sacrifice would automatically forfeit honor, rank, and status, incurring liability to torture. In addition, imperial freedmen who were Christians were reenslaved. (It seems preferable to regard these as corollaries of the edict rather than specific provisions contained in it.) This edict was promulgated throughout the Roman Empire, but applied with varying strictness. The Caesar Constantius contented himself with pro forma enforcement in Britain and Gaul, avoiding any bloodshed, whereas some provincial governors elsewhere (such as the proconsul of Africa and the *praeses* of Numidia) exceeded the terms of the edict by ordering that all Christians under their jurisdiction should sacrifice to the gods.[18]

In the western Roman Empire, neither the Caesar Constantius nor even the Augustus Maximian, who ruled Spain, Italy, and Africa, appears to have promulgated any further persecuting edict. In their territories persecution petered out altogether in less than two years (*MP* (S) 13.12),[19] and was legally ended in 306, when Constantine and Maxentius came to power.[20] In the East, however, persecution both persisted and intensified. Soon after the first edict, an imperial letter instructed provincial governors to arrest and imprison the Christian clergy. They filled the prisons, and soon orders were given to release all who sacrificed—or who could be physically constrained to do so (*HE* 8.6.8–10; *MP* (S) Pref.2; 1.3–4). Early in 304 came a second general edict or imperial letter which ordered the population of every city to sacrifice and make libations to the gods collectively (*MP* 3.1). Some show, at least, of enforcement was made throughout the eastern provinces.

On 1 May 305, Diocletian abdicated, Galerius added Asia Minor to his European territories, and his nephew Maximinus was appointed Caesar, receiving the diocese of Oriens to rule, i.e., Syria, Palestine, and adjoining regions, together with Egypt and Cyrene. Maximinus resided mainly in Antioch and Caesarea for the next six years. Hence Eusebius' account of the martyrs of Palestine between 305 and 311 also constitutes, for all practical purposes, an account of Maximinus' policies towards the Christians of the East. Unfortunately, there is no similar systematic source for Galerius in these years, since Lactantius (it seems) fled back to his native Africa, and fictitious *acta martyrum* tend to adopt a dramatic date before the abdication of Diocletian.[21] Consequently, the paradoxical thesis has recently been argued that Galerius relaxed persecution in 305.[22] The Christian traditions in Asia Minor, as used by Gregory of Nazianzus in his denunciations of Julian, contradict: in this area people remembered that, though Diocletian began the attack on the Christians (i.e., in 303–305), Galerius surpassed him when he succeeded him (i.e., in 305–311), and Maximinus who came after them was a greater persecutor than either.[23]

If the details of Galerius' treatment of the Christians in the Balkans and
Asia Minor between 305 and 311 are largely unknown,[24] Eusebius has
described the persecuting policies of Maximinus with some precision (*MP*
4–13). The new Caesar was determined that the edict enjoining universal
sacrifice should be obeyed. He instructed the magistrates of each city to
ensure enforcement, taking advantage of the fact that the new census rolls
prepared in early 306 listed, for the first time, the names of city dwellers
who owned no property as well as all landowners and the rural population.
Galerius had ordered this innovation to increase revenue; enforced everywhere, it was so unpopular in Italy that it sparked the revolt which brought
Maxentius to power.[25] Maximinus was to remove landless city dwellers
from the census rolls in 311, but in 306 he had no objection to using the
new full lists for a nonfiscal purpose. On the instructions of the governor,
heralds summoned the whole population of the cities to the temples of the
gods, while soldiers went from house to house summoning everyone by
name from the census list (*MP* 4.8). Unfortunately, Eusebius chose not to
describe the general effects of this policy even in Caesarea; instead he
concentrates on the protest and subsequent martyrdom of his friend
Apphianus (2 April 306).

Persecution continued. Eusebius records the execution of Christians
whom he knew in Caesarea to mark Maximinus' birthday on 20 November
306 and on various other occasions in 307 and 308. Then came a respite
(*MP* 9.1). Eusebius records no martyrs in Palestine between 25 July 308
and 13 November 309; it seems that Maximinus was preoccupied with his
political standing in the imperial hierarchy. Suddenly, however, Maximinus
issued an edict that local magistrates should rebuild disused temples and
ensure that all articles for sale in the market should be sprinkled with holy
water from libations made at sacrifices, and that no one might enter the
public baths without a ritual act of sacrifice (*MP* 9.2). The winter of
309/310 witnessed the severest bout of persecution in Palestine, as
Firmilianus closely followed imperial wishes. But it seems that persecution
ceased in Caesarea after the spring of 310, although executions continued
among the confessors deported, mainly from Egypt, to the copper mines at
Phaeno (*MP* 9.3–13.10).

In the spring of 311, the dying Galerius proclaimed an end to
persecution throughout the Roman Empire. Maximinus acquiesced in the
change of imperial policy grudgingly. Instead of publishing Galerius' edict
in the East, Maximinus instructed his praetorian prefect Sabinus to issue a
circular to provincial governors, which merely rescinded his own edict of
late 309 by declaring that Christians should be free of molestation and not
punished for their religion. This change of policy was no more than a
tactical move, designed to free Maximinus' hand for his seizure of territory

from Galerius' political heir. As soon as news came of the senior emperor's death, he invaded Asia Minor, traversed Anatolia rapidly to Nicomedia, and obtained Licinius' acceptance of his seizure of territory. It seems that Maximinus bid for political support by canceling the liability of landless city dwellers, first in the East, then in Asia Minor, to direct taxation.[26] As soon as he felt secure politically, he resumed persecution of the Christians.

This time, for purposes of justification and propaganda, the initiative came from below.[27] The city of Nicomedia requested its new ruler to rid it of Christians (*HE* 9.9a.4). It was perhaps in response to this request that Maximinus forbade Christians to assemble in cemeteries (*HE* 9.2.1). When other cities, including Antioch, made the same request as Nicomedia (*HE* 9.2–4), Maximinus resumed violent persecution. First, he executed prominent Christian leaders such as Peter the bishop of Alexandria (26 November 311) and the scholar Lucian of Antioch (7 January 312), whom he tried himself in Nicomedia (*HE* 7.32.31; 9.6.2–3).[28] Next, as he traveled south and east along the coast of Asia Minor towards Syria, Maximinus issued a general rescript rewarding and encouraging the cities that had submitted petitions against the Christians. Eusebius quotes long sections of the copy posted in Tyre (*HE* 9.7.3–14). His accuracy even in details of wording is confirmed by two inscriptions which preserve parts of the same text: one from Arycanda in Lycia has the end of Maximinus' rescript followed by the petition submitted by the provincial council of Lycia and Pamphylia,[29] the other the last fifteen lines of the rescript addressed to the people of Colbassa in the same province and issued from Sardis on 6 April 312.[30] Maximinus' windy rhetoric provided a flashy theological justification for persecution. But the nub of the matter was simple: Maximinus' subjects, as they had requested, were to free themselves from pollution by expelling the Christians from their cities and territory. In return, the emperor promised to grant any boon that they might desire.[31] According to Eusebius, the publication of this rescript reduced the Christians to despair and they sought deliverance from God alone (*HE* 9.7.15).

The political situation—and hence the situation of the Christians— changed completely within a few months. The winter rains of 312/313 failed in the East, bringing famine accompanied by plague (*HE* 9.8.1). Before that, in the autumn of 312, the Transtigritane principalities, which were heavily Christian, rebelled against the renewal of persecution and compelled Maximinus to wage an unsuccessful campaign in Mesopotamia (*HE* 8.8.2, 4).[32] Moreover, as soon as Constantine defeated Maxentius on 28 October 312, he wrote to Maximinus, with whom Maxentius had formed an alliance, and in his own name as senior Augustus and that of Licinius, ordered the cessation of persecution.[33] Before the end of December, Maximinus obeyed. Provincial governors published an imperial directive to Sabinus which combined a personal apologia with a reaffirmation of the policy proclaimed in June 311: violence and compulsion were no longer to be used to make any of the emperor's subjects worship the gods (*HE* 9.9a.1–9). After the disappointed hopes of 311, Christians remained cautious and apprehensive, not yet daring to assemble openly (*HE* 9.9a.10–11).

In the spring of 313, the politically isolated Maximinus attempted to forestall the attack that he expected from Licinius, who had cemented an alliance with Constantine by marrying his sister in Milan in February. The attempt failed miserably. Maximinus was defeated near Adrianople on 30 April and fled across Asia Minor towards Syria. He was finally defeated again and killed himself at Tarsus in the summer.[34] Before he died, he granted his Christian subjects freedom to worship their God, the right to build churches, and the restoration of all property seized in the persecution (*HE* 9.10.7–11). Elsewhere in the Roman Empire, Constantine, Maxentius and Licinius had already granted their Christian subjects all this before the 'Great Persecution' ended in the East.

III. Toleration and Restitution

Eusebius' Palestinian viewpoint determined his presentation not only of the persecution of the Christians between 303 and 313, but also of the stages by which they were granted toleration, restitution, and, finally, imperial recognition and support. For the ten years of persecution, he notes, travel between the different political jurisdictions of the Roman Empire was dangerous and unwise, since the unwary traveler risked torture and even execution upon suspicion of being a spy (*HE* 8.15). Under these circumstances, it was impossible for Eusebius to keep himself continuously well informed about events in the West after 303 and also, even in retrospect afterwards, difficult for him to reconstruct the earlier part of the decade of persecution in the West accurately. As a result, Eusebius both exaggerated the sympathy that Constantius showed for the Christians, mistakenly alleging that he took no part at all in the persecution and did not even destroy churches (*HE* 8.13.13; *Vita Const.* 1.15–17), and failed to appreciate the true significance of Constantine's accession for the Christians of the West. Modern historians of the period easily recognize (and hence correct) Eusebius' distortion of perspective in his account of Constantius: unfortunately, they have also tended to follow Euesbius in ignoring (and hence denying) the political support that Constantine gave the Christians long before 312. Lactantius was far better informed on events both in Nicomedia and in Gaul, where he resided for a period, probably from 310 to 313, and his clear statement that Constantine began his reign in 306 with a gesture of political support towards the Christians dovetails perfectly with what Eusebius reports for Maxentius, Galerius, and Licinius.

644

Constantine was proclaimed emperor at York on 25 July 306 in place of his father. He skillfully obtained recognition as a member of the imperial college from an unwilling Galerius, but at once began to pursue policies which distanced him from his eastern colleagues. As proof of both his religious sympathies and his political independence, he formally ended persecution in Britain, Gaul, and Spain, whose administration he had taken over from Constantius. Persecution appears to have petered out in the West in the winter of 304/305, but the edict of 24 February 303 was not repealed until Constantine ordained toleration for the Christians under his rule and the restoration of Christian property seized three years earlier. In Lactantius' words, "this was the first measure by which he sanctioned the restoration of holy religion."[35]

Maxentius came to power in Rome on 28 October 306 and soon established control over the whole of Italy and Africa. He too marked his accession by putting a formal end to persecution.[36] Unlike Constantine, however, he granted only toleration. The Christian churches of Italy and Africa had to wait until 311, when Maxentius went to war against Constantine, before they were authorized to recover confiscated ecclesiastical property, and the restoration was still incomplete when Maxentius was defeated and killed (28 October 312).[37]

The years 307 and 308 were a period of complicated political maneuvers. Aided by his father, who emerged out of retirement, Maxentius repulsed two attempts to dislodge him, the first by Severus, Augustus in the West since Constantius' death, whom he captured (early 307), the second by Galerius himself, who faced defeat before the walls of Rome but extricated himself and his army from Italy (autumn 307). Finally, after Maximian attempted to depose his son in April 308 and then fled to Constantine in Gaul, a college of four emperors was reestablished at the Conference of Carnuntum (11 November 308) with Galerius and the newly proclaimed Licinius as Augusti, Maximinus and Constantine as Caesars. The political implications of this new tetrarchy were clear: Licinius was expected to remove Maxentius, recover Italy, and become Augustus in the West. But events frustrated Galerius. Constantine and Maximinus refused to accept their inferior status, while Licinius proved incapable of fulfilling the function assigned to him, even though he appears to have attacked Italy in 309. In 310, Licinius was compelled to fight on the Danube and Galerius himself was stricken with a debilitating disease (perhaps cancer of the bowels). By April 311, Galerius knew that death was near, and he decided to solve at least one of Licinius' problems by ending the persecution in all the eastern parts of the Roman Empire.

Both Lactantius and Eusebius quote the "palinode" of Galerius, the former from the text posted in Nicomedia on 30 April 311, the latter a

Greek translation which preserves the full (and accurate) imperial titles of Galerius, Constantine, and Licinius.[38] The document has the form of a letter to provincials, though Lactantius calls it an edict. In it Galerius confesses that persecution has failed. The emperors in 303 (he states) had a noble end in view: devoted to ancient Roman traditions, they desired Christians to return to the religion of their forefathers. The result, however, was that most Christians were now not worshiping any god at all. Clemency required, therefore, that the Christians be allowed to exist again and to assemble again, provided that they were well behaved and prayed to their God for the public good. The edict thus removed all requirements in the edicts of 303 and 304 (and in Maximinus' subsequent enactments) that Christians participate in pagan ceremonies or cult, but it did not restore church buildings or property seized under the first edict.

The restitution of property which the Christian communities of the West had received in 306 and 311 was delayed in the East until 313, when Licinius granted it at the insistence of Constantine. Lactantius quotes a letter of Licinius to the governor of Bithynia published in Nicomedia on 13 June 313, while Eusebius quotes the Greek version of an almost identical text, presumably that posted in Caesarea later in the year.[39] It used to be fashionable to style this document "the Edict of Milan," and the fashion has not quite died out, despite general acknowledgement that the document is not an edict, that it was not dictated or promulgated in Milan, and that it was issued by Licinius, not Constantine. It is true that it was issued in the names of both Constantine and Licinius, in that order, but that merely reflects the normal protocol whereby all imperial enactments were issued in the name of all the emperors reigning at the time, listed in their order of seniority in the imperial college. It is also true that the preamble refers to the meeting of Constantine and Licinius at Milan at which they discussed "all matters which concerned the public advantage and safety." But the legal effect of the document was merely to give the Christian subjects of Licinius what those of Constantine had enjoyed since 306—a fact which the misleading designation "Edict of Milan" conceals and misrepresents.

What the document attests is that Constantine persuaded Licinius to extend his own legislation of 306 to the East, and that Licinius did so, first presumably at once in the Balkans, then in Asia Minor, and finally in Oriens and Egypt. The imperial letter of 313 proclaims complete freedom of religion both for Christians and, apparently, for all others. It orders that all property seized from the Christian church during the persecution be restored, but also provides compensation for its present owners who have bought such property from the imperial treasury or from an individual or received it as a gift. By the end of 313, therefore, the Christian church throughout the

Roman Empire had regained what it had lost in 303. It had also acquired an imperial patron who proclaimed allegiance to the Christian God.

IV. Imperial Patronage

Constantine had been sympathetic to Christianity at least since he was a young man at the court in Nicomedia, a city where he may well have known Lactantius and Lucian of Antioch.[40] Indeed, it has recently been argued that he was a Christian in his religious beliefs long before his "conversion" in 312.[41] Be that as it may, he began his reign in 306 by legislating an end to persecution in his domain. In 312 he went further. The army of Constantine that routed Maxentius at the Battle of Milvian Bridge on 28 October 312 fought under a Christian emblem.[42] When the victorious emperor entered Rome in triumph, he refused to ascend the Capitol to give thanks to Jupiter, as any pagan predecessor would have done.[43] He made his change of religious allegiance clear by commissioning a gigantic statue, which occupied an apse in the basilica of Maxentius and showed Constantine holding a cross or labarum, with an inscription proclaiming that by this salutary sign the emperor had liberated Rome from tyranny and restored the ancient splendor of the Senate and people of Rome (*HE* 9.9.10–11; *Vita Const.* 1.40.2). Eusebius alone reports the inscription: fragments of the statue including the head, hands, and feet survive and confirm his report.[44] From the start, the Christian emperor regarded his new religion as restoring and enhancing, not diminishing, all that was valuable in Greco-Roman culture.

Constantine rapidly reached a mutually advantageous political accommodation with the Roman Senate, which had supported Maxentius. Constantine forgave the Senate, reaffirmed its prestige, and reappointed to high office leading senators who had prospered under Maxentius. In return, the Senate recognized Constantine's claim to be the senior member of the imperial college, voted him honors as the liberator of Rome[45]—and raised no protests against his religious policies. Constantine issued *mandata* to the officials sent to Africa in November 312 which instructed them to provide money to the bishop of Carthage on request (*HE* 10.6). He gave freely from the imperial treasury for the building and decoration of churches: the list of Constantinian foundations in the *Liber pontificalis* indicates the scale of these benefactions.[46] More important, it was in the winter of 312/313 that Constantine began the process of remolding the institutional framework which defined the role of Christians and the Christian church within Roman society. The Christian clergy received immunity from public liturgies (*HE* 10.7.1–2) and perhaps from all forms of direct taxation; bishops received the right to preside over the manumission of slaves in church and acquired a formally defined legal jurisdiction in civil disputes involving Christians; and the church itself became a privileged legatee, able to accept unlimited bequests even if the deceased had only expressed their wishes verbally. Constantine made various symbolic innovations: he abolished crucifixion and enjoined the observance of Sunday as a day of rest. More fundamentally, he repealed the marriage legislation of Augustus which Septimius Severus had reasserted and attempted to enforce a century earlier. Whereas Augustus had encouraged and rewarded marriage and the procreation of children, Constantine removed all the penalties for celibacy or childlessness. He also made divorce far more difficult, allowing it only for a very small number of specific causes.[47]

The edition of the *Ecclesiastical History* which Eusebius published ca. 315 celebrated not only the end of persecution but also the increased prosperity of the church under imperial patronage. Eusebius had long since decided not to write the history of the church after ca. 280. The dissensions of bishops and "their unnatural conduct to one another before the persecution" filled him with distaste. Nor was he willing to write a full history of the persecution which chronicled the cowardice, compromise, flight, and disgrace of bishops: it was better to record only what might profit present and future generations (*HE* 8.1.7–2.3). As a result, Book 8 of the *Ecclesiastical History* is a very unsatisfactory account of persecution between 299 and 311, paradoxically more informative on imperial policy (about which Eusebius knew little) than on the sufferings of the Christians of the East, where emotional exaggeration and carelessness over chronology produce an undifferentiated vagueness (*HE* 8.7–13.8). Book 9, in contrast, which concentrates on the policies of Maximinus in 311–313, is sharply focused, chronologically precise, and alert to changes in imperial policy. It ends with a chapter describing the purge of Maximinus' family and supporters that followed his defeat (*HE* 9.11.3–9). Eusebius names a minister of Maximinus, a prefect of Egypt who had executed many Christians, and Theotecnus, who led the anti-Christian agitation in Antioch. Licinius himself tried Theotecnus and his associates, and his initial encouragement ensured that the purge had wide repercussions. On 1 January 314, however, Licinius felt obliged to stop the bloodletting: he issued an edict discouraging accusations, especially those for treason or by slaves and freedmen.[48] The fact that fragments of this edict have been found in five eastern cities (including Pergamon, Sinope, and Lyttos in Crete) ought to indicate the wide scope of the purge, whose victims must primarily have been those who had persecuted and harassed the Christians.

Eusebius approved of the punishment of the impious. But he approved still more of the benefits which Constantine and Licinius showered on the church. In the edition of ca. 315, the tenth book of the *Ecclesiastical History* comprised three sections: an introduction celebrating the end of persecution and the rebuilding of churches (*HE* 10.1–3); the panegyric which Eusebius himself delivered in the newly rebuilt church at Tyre (*HE* 10.4); and a series of imperial enactments documenting imperial favor towards the Christians (*HE* 10.5–7). The panegyric draws an elaborate threefold parallelism between the Temple in Jerusalem, the worldwide church which the Temple prefigured, and the new building constructed by the bishop Paulinus, which is the image of the worldwide church. Perhaps the most significant feature of the speech is its assumption that both emperors who have freed the Christians from oppression have abandoned paganism and adopted Christianity—Licinius no less than Constantine, to whose statue in Rome Eusebius alludes (*HE* 10.4.16, 60).

The documents quoted, all in translation from the Latin, were the following:

(1) the letter of Licinius granting toleration and restitution, presumably posted in Caesarea ca. August 313;

(2) a letter of Constantine to Anullinus, the proconsul of Africa, urging him to restore all Christian property forthwith (winter 312/313);

(3) a letter of Constantine to Miltiades, the bishop of Rome, and Mark, informing him that he has referred the Donatist complaint against Caecilianus to him (June 313);

(4) a letter of Constantine to Chrestus, bishop of Syracuse, about the forthcoming Council of Arles (spring or early summer 314);

(5) a letter of Constantine to Caecilianus, bishop of Carthage, about the administration of funds authorized for distribution to the churches (winter 312/313);

(6) a letter of Constantine to Anullinus releasing clergy from public liturgies (February 313).

What is the explanation for Eusebius' selection of documents? Apart from the first, their unifying feature appears to be relevance to Donatism. And why does Eusebius quote Constantine's letter to the insignificant bishop of Syracuse? Presumably, some personal contact procured Eusebius this otherwise inexplicable selection of documents from Syracuse itself.

V. The Church Triumphant

Eusebius was mistaken about Licinius' attitude towards his religion. In 313 and against Maximinus it was in the interest of this old associate of Galerius to appear to be a Christian. But when his political rival was Constantine, support of Christianity ceased to bring Licinius political benefits. Hence, although he never attempted a full-scale persecution, he drifted into policies which again produced Christian martyrs and confessors. He expelled Christians from the imperial palace, though Eusebius, the bishop of Nicomedia, retained an entrée to the court. He required all soldiers and officials to sacrifice, he canceled the tax privileges of the clergy and enrolled them in city councils, and he hindered the functioning of the church by prohibiting councils of bishops, by forbidding the sexes to worship together or women to receive instruction from men, and by ordering that the election of bishops be held outside the city in the open air (*HE* 10.8.10–19; *Vita Const.* 1.51–54). Moreover, Eusebius' *Demonstration of the Gospel*, written between ca. 318 and 324, makes it clear that provincial governors had recovered the power to punish Christians simply for being Christians.[49] It was not surprising, therefore, if Christians in Pontus had treasonable dealings with Armenia, which had been officially Christian since 314. Bishops in Pontus were executed and their churches destroyed. Hence there was plausibility in Constantine's claim that he made war on Licinius in 324 to prevent a general persecution of Christians in the East (*HE* 10.8.15–19; *Vita Const.* 2.1–3).

The campaign of 324 was swift and decisive. Constantine invaded Licinius' territory, forced a crossing of the River Hebrus, and defeated the opposing army, most of which surrendered (3–4 July), and advanced on Byzantium. Constantine's fleet, under Crispus, broke through the Hellespont; his army crossed the Bosporus and crushed Licinius outside Chalcedon (18 September). Licinius surrendered and abdicated: he was sent to Thessalonica, later to be executed for plotting (spring 325). The Christians were not in a forgiving mood. As in 313, it seems, they exacted vengeance on their recent tormentors. It is symptomatic of the poverty of our sources that the only evidence for the purge of 324 is Eusebius' coy observation that those who counseled war against God were removed with the tyrant and perished, paying the appropriate penalty (*Vita Const.* 2.18). But it is not rash to generalize from this one allusion: the defeat of Licinius created a revolutionary situation in which Constantine carried through a religious reformation in the East.[50]

The first step was to undo the effects of Licinius' persecution. Constantine sent a long letter to every province in which he first set out his own role as God's agent in liberating the Christians, then made detailed provision for the restoration of exiled Christians and the restitution of confiscated Christian property—without any compensation for its present owners who should count themselves fortunate to escape punishment for possessing it (*Vita Const.* 2.24–42). The next step was to make it clear that Christianity was now the established official religion of the empire. Not only did Constantine show an obvious preference for appointing Christians as provincial governors, but he forbade pagan officials at any level to perform the customary ritual act of sacrifice before conducting official business or hearing legal disputes—a symbolic reversal of the first persecuting edict of 303.[51] Moreover, he prohibited "the disgusting practices of idolatry practiced of old in city and countryside" which constituted the core of traditional religions: no more cult-statues were to be erected, no one should consult any oracle, and the ritual sacrifice of animals was to cease altogether (*Vita Const.* 2.45.1). Furthermore, when pagans protested, Constantine issued a long and abusive letter to the eastern provincials in the form of an address to God (*Vita Const.* 2.48–60). As a magnanimous concession, to avoid violence, he allowed pagans to keep their "shrines of falsehood" if they must, but implicitly reaffirmed the preceding prohibition of sacrifice. Even this concession was not absolute. Constantine ordered the forcible suppression of certain shrines which were considered particularly offensive, such as the shrine of Aphrodite at Aphaca in Phoenicia and the oracle of Apollo at Aegeae, famous for its association with Apollonius of Tyana. And he sent specially chosen commissioners to tour every province of the East confiscating all treasures, precious metals, and other items of value in temples and shrines in every city and the countryside.[52] The profits of this spoliation were then used to provide rich endowments for the church.

Eusebius set about bringing his historical and apologetic writings up to date. In 325/326, he added a brief account of Licinius' administration, persecution, and defeat to his *Ecclesiastical History* (*HE* 10.9–10), apparently removing the documents which concluded the edition of 315.[53] He revised his *Chronicle* and added a continuation from its original ending, probably in the second year of the emperor Probus (277/278) down to the *vicennalia* of Constantine. It was also probably shortly after 324 that he distilled the essence of his vast *Preparation for the Gospel* and *Demonstration of the Gospel* into the briefer *Theophany*, which has a protreptic rather than an apologetic tone. In these same years, Eusebius also began to collect documents with a view to writing an account of Constantine's establishment of Christianity in the East. Formal proof of this neglected but important fact comes in three manuscripts of the *Ecclesiastical History* which quote Constantine's letter of October 324, undoing the effects of persecution followed by the sentence:[54] "Let this stand here; but now come let us assemble together, making a fresh beginning, all the laws and letters on behalf of true piety of our God-loving and most gentle emperor." The letter now forms the centerpiece of Book 2 of the *Life of Constantine* (*Vita Const.* 2.24–42). Since, in addition, the *Life* quotes twelve letters of Constantine from the years 324–328 and three from 335/336, but none whatever from the intervening period, it is a cogent inference that Eusebius collected Constantinian documents in the late 320s and originally conceived (perhaps even wrote) the historical sections of the *Life* as a continuation of the *Ecclesiastical History* in the late 320s.[55]

Whatever the reason, Eusebius set the planned continuation of his *History* aside, though he returned to it after the death of Constantine (22

May 337). He directed his energies instead into ecclesiastical politics and his duties as bishop of Caesarea. It was doubtless the experience of preaching and instruction as bishop and head of the school of Caesarea that induced Eusebius to codify his interpretation of human history in his *Commentary on Isaiah*. Proof-texts from Isaiah had been prominent in Eusebius' speech at Tyre in 315 (*HE* 10.4.32, 48–52, 62); now he produced a full exegesis of the prophet which reflects the prosperity of the Christian church after 324. Large portions of the *Commentary on Isaiah* are preserved as marginal annotations in an eleventh-century manuscript of the Greek Old Testament now in Florence. The text, discovered in 1932, is not complete, even though it fills more than 400 pages in the *editio princeps*, published in 1975.[56] Jerome, who drew heavily on Eusebius for his own commentary on Isaiah, reports at least one interpretation which is not in the extant text and he refers to a title and an index, now lacking, which promised a historical interpretation. Jerome complains that Eusebius took refuge in allegory wherever history failed him, that "he promises a historical exposition in his title, but sometimes forgets his purpose and retreats to the precepts of Origen."[57] The charge is not quite fair. When Eusebius uses allegory, he does so in the service of an interpretation which is fundamentally historical.[58]

Modern scholarship and analysis has established that the Book of Isaiah is the product of a complicated process of composition. Three main blocs of material can be discerned, viz., (1) original prophecies of Isaiah the son of Amoz in the reign of Hezekiah (729–686 BCE) (chaps. 1–39); (2) an anonymous prophet in the period of the Babylonian exile who names the Persian King Cyrus (539–522) (chaps. 40–55); and (3) post-exilic materials from various hands. But the book has a real unity since a series of revisers and redactors have arranged and rewritten the earlier material so that it looks forward to the later.[59] Eusebius believed that the Holy Spirit spoke through Isaiah with foreknowledge of the whole course of human history from the prophet's own day down to the second coming of Christ to conduct the last judgment. Hence Eusebius can find in Isaiah predictions of such details as the identity of the disciple who betrayed Jesus (28.1 [179, 28, ed. Ziegler]), the feebleness of the youthful Jewish patriarchs of his own day who resided in Tiberias (3.4–11 [23, 15–19]), and the five orders or ranks in the Christian church, viz., bishops, priests, deacons, baptized laity, and catechumens (19.18 [133, 11–16]). But his exegesis concentrates on half a dozen nodal themes.[60] First, the deportation of Jews by Nebuchadnezzar, their exile and restoration. Second, the life, death, and resurrection of Jesus, including his descent into hell (46.10–11 [300, 26]). Third, the Jewish rejection of the Messiah and its twin corollaries, their own ruin, the sack of Jerusalem, and their continuing exclusion from their holy city set against the success and increasing prosperity of the Gentile church. Fourth, the persecution of Christians which Eusebius, here as always, regards as permitted by God to chastise and test his church (51.15–16 [325, 28–31]). Fifth, the demise of paganism and the flourishing of Christianity under imperial patronage in Eusebius' own day. Sixth, the second theophany, the glorious coming of Christ at the last judgment. All these themes recur again and again, and even where Eusebius sees two levels of meaning in Isaiah, the nonliterary, hidden, or allegorical meaning tends to coincide with one of his historical preoccupations. On the literal level, for example, all that Isaiah foretold in one passage happened in the reigns of Vespasian and Hadrian, but at the deeper level of meaning the prophet was speaking of the spiritual hunger and spiritual death which Jews still experience for lack of heavenly nourishment from the bread of life which they have rejected (5.11–17 [32, 1–4]).

The historical value of the *Commentary on Isaiah* lies principally in its unselfconscious reflection of the new Christian Empire. Eusebius construes events narrated in his *Ecclesiastical History* as the fulfillment of prophecy:

> And *kings*, who uttered many blasphemous, irreligious and impious things against him [sc. Christ] and persecuted his church, but then achieved nothing, finally after their vain labors *checked their mouths* and yielded to his teaching, vanquished in different ways on different occasions through being harried by lashings from God. We ourselves, the author of this commentary, have ascertained this by actual experience: some of them *checked their mouths*, while others uttered a palinode giving orders by laws and edicts to his church to build houses of prayer and conduct its usual business. (52.14–15 [333, 36–334, 8])

The *Commentary* celebrates the suppression of idolatry: those who used proudly to worship idols have been compelled to hide their lifeless cult-statues *in caves* in order to escape the imperial agents sent to strip them of their precious finery (2.18–21 [21, 1–5]). And the church now truly has *kings* as its *foster fathers* and *princesses* as its *nurses*: the emperor supports the church, while the governors of every province in obedience to his command provide supplies of grain to needy Christians (49.23 [316, 9–16]). Isaiah of course predicted the conversion of Constantine:

> Now seeing Roman emperors and *kings* in the flesh entering *the gates* of the Church of God, how could anyone deny that the prophecy is true? They will be received also into *the gates* of the kingdom of heaven. (60.10–12 [375, 21–25])

When Eusebius praised Constantine in Constantinople on the thirtieth anniversary of his accession (25 July 336) he did not conclude his oration with the traditional wish that the sexagenarian emperor enjoy many more years of life; instead he looked forward to Constantine's reception into heaven.[61]

Notes

References to Eusebius' *Ecclesiastical History*, to the *Life of Constantine*, and to the *Martyrs of Palestine* will usually be given in the text: where relevant, the long and short recensions of the *Martyrs* are denoted by *MP* (L) and *MP* (S) respectively. All other nonbiblical references are given in the notes.

The overall interpretation of Eusebius adopted here is that expounded more fully in my *Constantine and Eusebius* (Cambridge and London: Harvard University Press, 1981), supplemented by *The New Empire of Diocletian and Constantine* (Cambridge: Harvard University Press, 1982), and I have deliberately refrained from overloading the notes with continual cross-references to these two books.

[1]F. Millar, "Paul of Samosata, Zenobia and Aurelian: The Church, Local Culture and Political Allegiance in Third-Century Syria," *JRS* 61 (1971) 1–17.

[2]Lactantius, *Mort. pers.* 9–15. The work has recently been edited and translated into English with a good commentary by J. L. Creed (Oxford: Clarendon, 1984). On Lactantius' career, which it is difficult to reconstruct precisely, and in defense of his essential trustworthiness, see T. D. Barnes, "Lactantius and Constantine," *JRS* 63 (1973) 29–46; *Constantine and Eusebius*, 13–14, 291–92. For the alternative view that Lactantius remained in Bithynia continuously between 303 and 313 and then went to Gaul, see recently A. Wlosok, *Restauration und Erneuerung: Die lateinische Literatur von 284 bis 374 n. Chr.* (ed. Reinhart Herzog; Handbuch der lateinischen Literatur der Antike 5; Munich: Beck, 1989) 375–79 (with full bibliography).

[3]*Pan. Lat.* 7(6).6.2, a speech of 310 describing a mosaic in the imperial palace at Aquileia, whose dramatic date appears to be 293 (Barnes, *New Empire*, 41–43).

[4]F. Kolb, *Diocletian und die erste Tetrarchie: Improvisation oder Experiment in der Organisation monarchischer Herrschaft?* (Berlin and New York: De Gruyter, 1987) 139–58, 179.

[5]On the problem of disentangling and dating the various editions, see T. D. Barnes, "The Editions of Eusebius' *Ecclesiastical History*," *GRBS* 21 (1980) 191–201. That article has regrettably been ignored by some subsequent writers on the subject, such as T. Christensen, "The So-called *Appendix* to Eusebius' *Historia Ecclesiastica* VIII," *Classica et Mediaevalia* 34 (1983) 177–209; M. Gödecke, *Geschichte als Mythos: Eusebs "Kirchengeschichte"* (Europäische Hochschulschriften 23; Frankfurt and New York: Lang, 1987) 19ff.; D. Timpe, "Was ist Kirchengeschichte? Zum Gattungscharakter der Historia Ecclesiastica des Eusebius," *Festschrift Robert Werner* (Xenia 22; Konstanz: Universitätsverlag Konstanz, 1989) 171–204. The oversight is unfortunate because, whether the precise hypothesis argued there (and assumed here) is correct or not, the article establishes that the problem of the editions of the *Ecclesiastical History* cannot be solved without reference to the two recensions of the *Martyrs of Palestine*—a work which the three discussions cited leave totally out of account.

[6]For a fuller exposition, see Barnes, *Constantine and Eusebius*, chaps. 8 and 9.

654

[7]T. D. Barnes, "Panegyric, History and Hagiography in Eusebius' *Life of Constantine*," *The Making of Orthodoxy: Essays in Honour of Henry Chadwick* (ed. R. Williams; Cambridge: Cambridge University Press, 1989) 94–123.

[8]For this thesis, see Barnes, *Constantine and Eusebius*, chaps. 12–14; "The Constantinian Reformation," *The Crake Lectures 1984* (Sackville, NB: The Crake Institute, 1986) 39–57; "Christians and Pagans in the Reign of Constantius," *L'église et l'empire au IVe siècle* (Entretiens Hardt 34, 1989), 301–37. For a very different interpretation of Constantine, R. MacMullen, *Christianizing the Roman Empire (A.D. 100–400)* (New Haven: Yale University Press, 1984) 43ff.; R. Lane Fox, *Pagans and Christians* (Harmondsworth: Penguin, 1986 and New York: Knopf, 1987) 609ff.

[9]*P. Oxy.* 2673 (304) proves, by implication, that churches received both gifts and testamentary bequests before 303.

[10]W. H. C. Frend, *Martyrdom and Persecution in the Early Church* (Oxford: Blackwell, 1965) 440ff.

[11]Lactantius, *Div. Inst.* 4.27.4–5; *Mort. pers.* 10.1–5; Eusebius, *HE* 8.1.7, 4.2–4; Jerome, *Chronicle* (ed. Rudolf Helm, *Eusebius Werke*, Vol. 7: *Die Chronik des Hieronymus* [GCS; 3d ed.; Berlin: Akademie, 1984]) 227.9–11.

[12]Barnes, *New Empire*, 55, 63–64.

[13]For recent statements of this thesis, see Kolb, *Diocletian*, 113–14, 128–39; P. S. Davies, "The Origin and Purpose of the Persecution of 303 AD, " *JTS* n.s. 40 (1989) 66–94.

[14]The other ancient evidence points very strongly to 272 or 273 as the year of Constantine's birth (Barnes, *New Empire*, 40).

[15]As in Barnes, *Constantine and Eusebius*, chaps. 1–5.

[16]The precise contents of the first edict are nowhere reported fully, but must be deduced primarily from the following items of evidence: Lactantius, *Mort. pers.* 13.1; 15.5; Eusebius, *MP* (S) Pref.1; 2.1; *HE* 8.2.4; 9.10.8; Optatus, App. 1 (ed. Ziwsa, pp. 186–88); 2 (pp. 198–202); *Acta Felicis*. The classic treatment of the enforcement of the persecuting edicts of 303/304 remains that by G. E. M. de Ste. Croix, "Aspects of the 'Great Persecution,'" *HTR* 47 (1954), 75–109. For helpful surveys of legislation affecting the Christians between 303 and 313, see F. Millar, *The Emperor in the Roman World (31 BC–AD 337)* (London: Duckworth, 1977) 573–84; S. Mitchell, "Maximinus and the Christians in A.D. 312: A New Latin Inscription," *JRS* 78 (1988) 105–24, esp. 111–16.

[17]*P. Oxy.* 2601 reflects the application of this provision in a small town in Egypt: since "those who appear in court are being compelled to sacrifice," Copres informs his "sister" Serapias that he has appointed his "brother" to appear in court in his place.

[18]Lactantius, *Mort. pers.* 15.7; Optatus 3.8, App. 2 (pp. 198–99).

[19]De Ste. Croix, "Aspects," 84–96. Latin hagiography attests no martyrdom even in Africa later than December 304.

[20]Lactantius, *Mort. pers.* 24.9; *Div. Inst.* 1.1.13 (Constantine); Eusebius, *HE* 8.14.1; Optatus 1.18, App. 1 (p. 194) (Maxentius); cf. T. D. Barnes, "The Beginnings of Donatism," *JTS* n.s. 26 (1975) 13–22, esp. 18–20.

[21]Barnes, *New Empire*, 185–91, cf. H. Delehaye, *Les légendes hagiographiques* (Subsidia Hagiographica 18; 3d rev. ed.; Brussels: Bollandistes, 1927) 23: "Il y a aussi le type de persecuteur. C'est Dioclétien en tête...." It is particularly revealing that the *Passio Quirini* (*BHL* 7035) puts the death of Quirinus before 1 May 305 whereas the earliest evidence implies a date close to 310 (below, n. 24).

[22]Davies, "Origin," 67ff.

[23]Gregory of Nazianzus, Orat. 4.96.

[24]Note, however, that Jerome, Chronicle 229, 10–15, puts the martyrdom of Quirinus, the bishop of Siscia, in 308—though between two political events datable to summer 310 and spring 311. Prudentius is presumably drawing on Jerome when he similarly puts the execution of Quirinus "sub Galerio duce" (Peristephanon 7.6).

[25]Lactantius, Mort. pers. 23, 26.2–3; cf. Barnes, New Empire, 232–34.

[26]Lactantius, Mort. pers. 34–36; Eusebius, HE 8.17–9.1; CTh 13.10.2; cf. Barnes, New Empire, 232.

[27]Lactantius, Mort. pers. 36.3; Eusebius, HE 9.2.

[28]For the dates, and an explication of the chronology of Book 9 of the Ecclesiastical History, see Barnes, New Empire, 67–68.

[29]For the best edition, see E. Kalinka, Tituli Asiae Minoris 2.3 (Vienna: Hölder, Pichler, Tempsky, 1944) no. 785, with Mitchell, "Maximinus," 110–11.

[30]Published by Mitchell, "Maximinus," 108, with Plate XVI. In line 16, "II idus Aprilis" is a misprint; for the correct reading, see C. F. Konrad, Epigraphica Anatolica 13 (1989) 89–90.

[31]Mitchell ("Maximinus," 121–23) identifies the boon as the exemption of landless city dwellers from poll tax attested in CTh 13.10.2, which is transmitted with the date of 1 June 313 but which he follows A. Demandt, Gnomon 43 (1971) 693, in redating to 1 June 312 rather than 311 (as assumed above). But Christians too would automatically have benefited from this exemption unless physically expelled from the cities.

[32]Barnes, Constantine and Eusebius, 160–61, 359.

[33]Lactantius, Mort. pers. 44.10–12; Eusebius, HE 9.9.12; 9.9a.12. Lactantius, Mort. pers. 37.1, states that Constantine had written to Maximinus requesting him to desist from persecution in 311. This is conventionally dismissed as a mistaken anticipation of the letter of November 312: in favor of accepting it, see Barnes, "Lactantius," 44–45.

[34]Lactantius, Mort. pers. 45–47, 49; Eusebius, HE 9.10.

[35]Lactantius, Mort. pers. 24.9; Div. Inst. 1.1.13. Lactantius' statement is still dismissed as a legend by E. Heck, MH ΘEOMAXEIN: oder, Die Bestrafung des Gottes-verächters: Untersuchungen zu Bekämpfung und Aneignung römischer religio bei Tertullian, Cyprian und Lactanz (Studien zur klassischen Philologie 24; Frankfurt and New York: Lang, 1987) 214, while Mitchell ("Maximinus," 111–16) nowhere even mentions it in his recent survey of "Emperors and Christians 303–313."

[36]Eusebius, HE 8.14.1; Optatus 1.18, App. 1 (p. 194).

[37]Augustine, Brev. Coll. 3.18.34; Contra partem Donati post gesta 13.17 (CSEL 53.84, 113–14; Eusebius, HE 10.5.15–17.

[38]Lactantius, Mort. pers. 34; Eusebius, HE 8.17.3–10; cf. T. D. Barnes, "Imperial Campaigns A.D. 285–311," Phoenix 30 (1976) 174–93, esp. 188–90; New Empire, 22–23. R. M. Grant ("The Case against Eusebius, or, Did the Father of Church History Write History?" StudPatr [TU 115; Berlin: Akademie, 1975] 413–21) advanced the bizarre theory that the "palinode" was in fact issued by Maximinus in December 311 and that Eusebius dishonestly altered the heading by substituting the name of Galerius. He has repeated the theory in his recent paper, "The Transmission of Eusebius, H.E. VIII 17,3–5," Texte und Textkritik: Eine Aufsatzsammlung (ed. J. Dummer; TU 133; Berlin: Akademie, 1987) 179–85.

[39] Lactantius, *Mort. pers.* 44.2–12; Eusebius, *HE* 10.5.2–14.

[40] Barnes, *Constantine and Eusebius*, 74–75, 194.

[41] J. Szidat, "Konstantin 312 n. Chr.," *Gymnasium* 92 (1985) 514–25; T. G. Elliott, "Constantine's Conversion: Do We Really Need It?" *Phoenix* 41 (1987) 420–38; "Constantine's Early Religious Development," *JRH* 15 (1989) 283–91.

[42] Lactantius, *Mort. pers.* 44.1ff.; Eusebius, *Vita Const.* 1.27ff. On the political and military context of Constantine's action, see T. D. Barnes, "The Conversion of Constantine," *Classical Views* n.s. 4 (1985) 371–91. It continues to be seriously misrepresented by Lane Fox, *Pagans*, 618.

[43] See now A. Fraschetti, "Costantino e l'abbandono del Campidoglio," *Società romana e impero tardoantico* 2 (Rome and Bari: Laterza, 1986) 55–98, 412–38.

[44] J. D. Breckenridge, *Age of Spirituality* (ed. K. Weitzmann; New York: Metropolitan Museum of Art and Princeton University Press, 1979) 18–19, no. 11. Several art historians, it should be noted, date this colossal head of Constantine ca. 325 on stylistic grounds.

[45] Lactantius, *Mort. pers.* 44.11; *Pan. Lat.* 12(9).25.4; Victor, *Caes.* 40.26.

[46] *Liber Pontificalis* 34 (ed. Duchesne, pp. 170–89), cf. C. Pietri, *Roma Christiana* (Paris: de Boccard, 1976) 4–69.

[47] For the very varied (and sometimes problematical) evidence for the statements in this paragraph, see Barnes, *Constantine and Eusebius*, 48–53, 309–13. A recently published papyrus from Oxyrhynchus shows that the observance of Sunday instead of Thursday as the weekly legal holiday had been introduced into Egypt before October 325 (*P. Oxy.* 3759, cf. 3741).

[48] For the text of this edict, see now C. Habicht and P. Kussmaul, "Ein neues Fragment des Edict de Accusationibus," *Museum Helveticum* 43 (1986) 135–44. On its date, see Barnes, *New Empire*, 127–28.

[49] Eusebius, *DE* 3.5.78ff.; 5.3.11; 6.20.17ff.; cf. 2.3.155; 3.7.36ff.; 7.1.132; 8.1.61.

[50] Barnes, "Reformation," 39–57. The inference drawn there from Eusebius, *Vita Const.* 2.18 is rejected as "rather wild" in the review by T. G. Elliott, *Phoenix* 43 (1989) 94.

[51] *Vita Const.* 2.44. Eusebius' report is confirmed by the complete cessation of dedications to traditional deities by provincial governors, which had been frequent under Diocletian. (I owe this important point to W. Eck, who will shortly publish an article on the subject.)

[52] *Panegyric to Constantine* 8.1ff.; *Vita Const.* 3.54–59; Eunapius, *Vit. phil.* 6.1.5 (ed. Didot, p. 461); cf. Barnes, "Christians," 322ff.

[53] See Eduard Schwartz's discussion of the manuscript evidence for the different editions in GCS 9.3 (1909) xlviiff.

[54] Printed by Schwartz in the apparatus criticus to his edition of *HE* 10.9.9 (GCS 9.2 [1908] 904).

[55] Barnes, "Panegyric," 110–14.

[56] The discovery was reported by A. Möhle, "Der Jesajakommentar des Eusebios von Kaisareia fast vollständig wieder aufgefunden," *ZNW* 33 (1934) 87–89. The text is edited by J. Ziegler, *Eusebius Werke*, Vol. 9: *Der Jesajakommentar* (GCS; Berlin: Akademie, 1975).

[57]Jerome, *In Esaiam* 5.Prol. (CChrL 73.160); cf. 5.18.2; 5.22.2 (CChrL 73.190, 210).

[58]On Eusebius' principles of exegesis, see Barnes, *Constantine and Eusebius*, 94–104; M. Simonetti, "Esegesi e ideologia nel Commento a Isaia di Eusebio," *Rivista di storia e letteratura religiosa* 19 (1983) 3–44; C. Curti, "L'esegesi di Eusebio di Cesarea: Carattere e sviluppo," *Le trasformazioni della cultura nella tarda antichità* 1 (ed. C. Giuffrida and M. Mazza; Rome: Jouvence, 1985) 459–78. [On the hermeneutics of Eusebius see the essay by M. Hollerich in this collection. Eds.]

[59]M. A. Sweeney, *Isaiah 1–4 and the Post-Exilic Understanding of the Isaianic Tradition* (BZAW 171; Berlin and New York: de Gruyter, 1988) 11ff.

[60]Given both the nature of the work and Eusebius' congenital repetitiveness, it will perhaps be most helpful to give references (by page in Ziegler's edition) to some of the principal treatments of each of the six recurring themes identified here:

    (1) 51–53, 76–79, 194–206, 287–94

    (2) 15, 124–32, 178–81, 248–52, 344–47, 367–68

    (3) 13–15, 32–35, 42–43, 314, 364–66

    (4) 33, 203–4, 218, 294, 325

    (5) 20–21, 91, 110–12, 259–60, 273, 316, 333–34, 371–75

    (6) 95–98, 167–74, 369–71, 383–88, 407–11.

Numerous other discussions of these six themes can easily be found through Ziegler's excellent index of key words (447–75).

[61]*Panegyric to Constantine* 10.7. S. Calderone ("Eusebio e l'ideologia imperiale," *Le trasformazioni della cultura nella tarda antichità* 1 [ed. C. Giuffrida and M. Mazza; Rome: Jouvence, 1985] 1–26) detects much biblical language and a heavy Christian emphasis in the speech, which he holds to have been delivered in January 336 to an audience consisting exclusively of bishops. It seems more probable that Eusebius delivered it in July 336 to an audience which included both the imperial court and the bishops who had just deposed Marcellus of Ancyra (Barnes, *Constantine and Eusebius*, 253–55).

X

THE CONSECRATION OF ULFILA

ULFILA, who translated the Bible into the Gothic language, was
an important historical figure in his own time, and his presence at
the Council of Constantinople in January 360 which promulgated
the official homoean creed has an obvious (if not perhaps direct)
relevance to the 'Arianism' of the Visigoths and other invaders of
the Roman Empire in the fifth century. Unfortunately, the details
of Ulfila's career are largely beyond recovery.[1] Jerome did not
include Ulfila in his *De viris illustribus*, composed in 392, nine
years after the bishop's death, and nothing besides fragments of
his Gothic translation of the Bible appears to survive from his own
pen. There are two main sources for the life of Ulfila, viz. a letter
of Auxentius, the bishop of Durostorum, written shortly after his
death and incorporated in a fifth-century Latin Arian composition,[2] and Photius' ninth-century summary of a section in Philos-

[1] The relevant sources are conveniently collected in W. Streitberg, *Die gotische
Bibel* 1[2] (Heidelberg, 1919, often reprinted), pp. xiv–xxv. For a full recent
discussion of Ulfila's career, see H. Wolfram, *History of the Goths*[2], trans. T. J.
Dunlap (Berkeley, 1988), pp. 75–85.

[2] The *editio princeps* was by G. Waitz, *Über das Leben und die Lehre des Ulfila:
Bruchstücke eines ungedruckten Werkes aus dem Ende des 4. Jahrhunderts* (Hanover,
1840). The text of the *Dissertatio Maximini* (*Clavis*[2] no. 692) in *PLS* i (1958),
cols. 693–728 reprints the edition by F. Kauffmann, *Aus der Schule des Ulfila*
(Strassburg, 1899), pp. 67–90, but replaces Kauffmann's text of the letter of

542

torgius' *Ecclesiastical History*, which was written *c*.430. These two sources appear to contradict each other irreconcilably on the date at which Ulfila was consecrated bishop. The letter of Auxentius makes Ulfila's death contemporaneous with the Council of Constantinople which Theodosius convened in June 383 (Socrates, HE v. 10)[3] and refers three times to his completion of forty years as bishop—which has usually been construed as an exact figure reckoned from an erroneous terminal date of 381 or 382. On the other hand, Philostorgius stated explicitly that Ulfila was sent by the ruler of his tribe on an embassy in the time of Constantine and consecrated by 'Eusebius and the bishops with him' (HE ii. 5).

The majority of scholars who have written about Ulfila have connected his consecration as bishop with the 'Dedication Council' at Antioch of 341, and have explained Philostorgius' dating as due either to confusion of the names of Constantine and Constantius (in itself a very frequent phenomenon) or to a mistaken retrojection of later events.[4] But objections have also been raised. E. A. Thompson, though he ultimately acquiesced in the traditional date of 341, expressed deep unease at the arguments used in its favour and preferred a date under Constantine.[5] R. Klein rejected 341 in favour of 338 on the grounds that Philostorgius' phrase 'Eusebius and those with him' should refer to the Council of Constantinople which replaced Paul as bishop of that city with Eusebius of Nicomedia[6]—a council which in fact met in the autumn of 337, as the narrative of Socrates makes clear (HE ii.

Auxentius (*Clavis*[2] no. 691) with that of H. E. Giesecke, *Die Ostgermanen und der Arianismus* (Leipzig–Berlin, 1939), pp. 16–22. The letter is now edited critically by R. Gryson: (*a*) as 'Commentaires de Maximinus' paras. 42–63 in *Scolies ariennes sur le concile d'Aquilée* (*Sources chrétiennes* cclxvii, 1980), pp. 236–250, and (*b*) as *Maximini episcopi dissertatio*, paras. 24–40 in *Scripta Arriana Latina* I (*CCL* lxxxvii, 1982), pp. 160–6. Gryson's 1980 edition offers an alphabetical bibliography including work on Ulfila (pp. 15–22), his 1982 edition a chronological bibliography of editions of and studies on the Arian scholia to the acts of the Council of Aquileia (pp. xiii–xvi).

[3] For the proof, R. Gryson, *Scolies ariennes* (1980), pp. 149–61.

[4] For a clear statement of this view, see A. Lippold, *RE* ix A, 1 (1961), col. 515. Some more recent writers have been more guarded: for example, E. K. Chrysos, *Dacoromania* i (1973), p. 64; B. Brockmeier, *Bonner Jahrbücher* clxxxvii (1987), p. 97. H. Wolfram, *Goths*[2] (1988), pp. 76 ff., squares the discordant sources by means of the hypothesis that Ulfila came to Constantinople as a young man between 332 and 337, returned home and then travelled to Antioch to be ordained at the 'Dedication Council' in 341.

[5] E. A. Thompson, *The Visigoths in the time of Ulfila* (Oxford, 1966), pp. xiii–xviii.

[6] R. Klein, *Constantius II. und die christliche Kirche* (Darmstadt, 1977), pp. 254–7.

4–7).[7] Subsequently, K. Schäferdiek argued forcefully for 336: he diagnosed an error in the letter of Auxentius which makes Ulfila bishop for seven plus thirty-three years, i.e. a total of forty years in all, instead of what he held to be the correct total of seven plus forty, and deduced that Ulfila was bishop from 336 to 383.[8] The present note argues for the same chronology, but on entirely different grounds—and without attempting the laborious and unrewarding task of evaluating systematically what is valid and what fallacious in earlier statements of the case for or against the predominant dating to 341.

The central issue is whether the letter of Auxentius deserves the primacy of regard and status as a privileged witness which it has usually received since its first publication in 1840. In fact, the text is far more problematical than is normally allowed. What survives is not the original letter written by Auxentius of Durostorum in the 380s, but the version of his letter which Maximinus incorporated much later into his theological polemic against Ambrose. It cannot legitimately be assumed without argument either that Maximinus quotes the whole of the letter or that he has refrained from altering its text. B. Capelle long ago pointed out a number of coincidences in phraseology and theological vocabulary between the letter and Maximinus' sermons and drew the conclusion that Maximinus has systematically rewritten the letter.[9] Whether that inference is correct or not, the chronology of the letter is concerned less with pedantic accuracy than with biblical typology. Ulfila began his episcopal career at the age of thirty: the text makes explicit the parallels with David, Joseph in Egypt, and Jesus. Ulfila's role in the Gothic crossing of the Danube resembled that of Moses rescuing his people from the violence of Pharaoh and the Egyptians—and then he withdrew to a mountain *secundum sanctorum imitationem*. And the forty-year episcopate, with seven years in Gothic territory and thirty-three on Roman soil, corresponds, though this is not explicitly stated, to David's seven and a half

---

[7] *AJAH* iii (1978), p. 66. The erroneous date of 338 appears still to be assumed in the recent discussion by R. P. C. Hanson, *The Search for the Christian Doctrine of God* (Edinburgh, 1988), p. 589.

[8] K. Schäferdiek, 'Wulfila. Vom Bischof von Gotien zum Gotenbischof', *ZKG* xc (1979), 253–92, at pp. 254–6.

[9] B. Capelle, 'La lettre d'Auxence sur Ulfila', *Revue bénédictine* xxxiv (1922), 224–33. Capelle further argued that the Gothic crossing of the Danube to which the letter refers is the large migration of 376 wrongly placed in 350. That was misplaced scepticism, cf. J. Zeiller, 'Le premier établissement des Goths chrétiens dans l'Empire d'Orient', *Mélanges offerts à M. Gustave Schlumberger* i (Paris, 1924), 3–11. Cyril of Jerusalem, *Cat.* 10. 19 (*PG* xxxiii, col. 688) referred to Gothic as well as Persian martyrs in the 340s.

544

years as king in Hebron followed by thirty-three in Jerusalem (2 Sam. 2: 11, 5: 4–5; 1 Kgs. 2: 11). The biblical analogies inevitably cast doubt on the exactness of the chronology of the letter, whether it be due to Auxentius himself or to Maximinus.

Philostorgius, by contrast, provides precise information and he appears to draw on good sources. On Ulfila's background, for example, he plausibly reports descent from Cappadocians captured and deported in a third century raid from Sadagolthina, a village in the territory of the city of Parnassus.[10] The context in Photius' summary of Philostorgius' *Ecclesiastical History* (nearer the beginning than the end of Book Two) indicates that the name of Constantine is not likely to be an error in transmission for that of Constantius, and the mention of an embassy seems in fact to point to a very precise occasion for the consecration of Ulfila, viz. the Council of Constantinople held in the summer of 336 which deposed Marcellus of Ancyra, attempted to force Alexander the bishop of Constantinople to accept Arius into communion, and then celebrated the *tricennalia* of Constantine.

The evidence for this council is sparse, as it is for all the other councils which treated Arius' theological views as less than obviously heretical. But it is consistent and clearcut.[11] The case against Marcellus was prepared by Eusebius of Caesarea who, after the ecclesiastical business was concluded, delivered the extant *Panegyric to Constantine* on 25 July 336 and saw the ambassadors of the Blemmyes, Indians and Ethiopians whose presence he later noted in his *Life of Constantine* (iv. 7, cf. iv. 56). The scene described by Eusebius bears a strong resemblance to Virgil's description of Augustus receiving gifts from submissive representatives of the nations of the world on the shield of Aeneas (*Aeneid* viii. 720–31).[12] It seems probable, therefore, that Constantine orchestrated the celebration of his *tricennalia* in a way which deliberately evoked the memory of Augustus, just as he built a bridge over the Danube, reconquered Dacia and took the title *Dacicus maximus* in obvious and conscious imitation of Trajan.[13] In July 336 Constantine was preparing to invade Mesopotamia as the professed champion of the Christians of

[10] The site of Parnassus was identified by J. G. C. Anderson, *JHS* xix (1899), 107–109, with map facing p. 52.

[11] *Constantine and Eusebius* (Cambridge, Mass., 1981), pp. 240–2, 253.

[12] B. H. Warmington, 'Virgil, Eusebius of Caesarea and an Imperial Ceremony', *Studies in Latin Literature and Roman History*, iv (*Collection Latomus* cxcvi, 1986), pp. 451–60. *P. Abinnaeus* 1 confirms the presence of ambassadors of the Blemmyes, who had been escorted to Constantinople by Flavius Abinnaeus, cf. *Phoenix* xxxix (1985), pp. 369/70.

[13] *Constantine and Eusebius* (1981), pp. 250, 271.

Persia.[14] It may be suggested that he associated the consecration of Ulfila with the celebration of his *tricennalia* in order to give the traditional clichés of Roman imperialism a specifically Christian colouring.[15]

[14] See 'Constantine and the Christians of Persia', *JRS* lxxv (1985), 126–36.
[15] I am most grateful to Mr Andrew Gillett for bibliographical and other assistance.

Panegyric, history and hagiography in Eusebius' *Life of Constantine*

Eusebius' *Life of Constantine* has an obvious relevance to the making of Christian orthodoxy. It has often seemed to be a peculiarly problematical text. I had the great good fortune to be introduced to the *Life* and its problems many years ago by Henry Chadwick, who pronounced, in that grave and rational tone of voice which all who have known him will recall so well, that Eusebius' authorship was the only plausible hypothesis – an opinion which he later reiterated in print.[1] At the time, I was wrestling with the problem of trying to understand Tertullian under Henry's temporary guidance, but I never forgot the remark. When I began to work seriously on the Constantinian period, I consciously adopted the transmitted and traditional attribution of the *Life* as a working hypothesis, which came to seem more strongly based the more I penetrated the period. Hence it is with deep gratitude and pleasure that I offer the following essay on the occasion of Henry Chadwick's seventieth birthday – all the more so since the first article which I wrote about Constantine was published in a volume celebrating the seventieth birthday of Sir Ronald Syme.[2] Debate has moved on since 1973: here I shall be less concerned to demonstrate partially novel interpretations of Constantine and Eusebius than to apply hypotheses which I have developed elsewhere to the work which has for ever linked their two names.[3]

The problems posed by the *Life of Constantine* are both literary and historical. The literary and historical problems are of course inextricably linked to each other, since proof of anachronisms would exclude Eusebius' authorship of the whole, while Eusebian authorship confers on the *Life* a certain status as evidence. Yet clarity demands that the literary and historical problems be considered separately – a procedure which reveals that the traditional 'problem of the *Life of Constantine*' in large part arose from confusing the two.[4] Progress has been made, and can still be made, when the two questions are asked separately: does the *Life* as transmitted in the manuscripts come entirely from the pen of Eusebius, or is it wholly or partly the work of a later hand? And what is the historical value of the extant *Life* as evidence for the actions and personality of Constantine? Even the former question, however, when posed in these terms, is misleading when the four books of the *Life* are considered as if they were designed to stand by themselves. Since its structure and literary genre are both problematical, the *Life* must not be considered apart from the three speeches appended to it, for Eusebius makes it clear that he intended them to stand as an integral complement to the *Life* (4.32,46), the four books and appended speeches forming a single literary whole.

The *Life* itself has a messy structure which can *prima facie* be analysed roughly as follows:

1.1–11 Introduction
1.12–19 Constantine at the court of Diocletian
1.20–5 Proclamation as emperor (306)
1.26–38 The war against Maxentius (311–12)
1.39–48 From Constantine's entry into Rome (29 October 312) to his *decennalia* (315/16)
1.49–2.18 War against Licinius: the two wars, of 316/17 and 324, are deliberately fused together as a single war
2.19–60 The consequences of Constantine's victory in 324 for Christians and pagans
2.61–3.23 The controversy over Arius and the Council of Nicaea (325), interrupted by comparison of Constantine with Licinius (3.1–3)
3.24–66 Actions of Constantine relating to Christianity and the Christian church
4.1–13 Constantine's qualities as emperor (1–6) and his fame beyond the empire (7), illustrated by his correspondence with the Persian King (8–13)
4.14–39 Constantine's Christianity and Christian legislation
4.40–52 Constantine's last years: introduced by an explicit reference to his *tricennalia* (40)
4.53–73 Death and burial
4.74/5 Epilogue

To this are appended three speeches:

1 Constantine's *Speech to the Assembly of the Saints*, styled Book v in two manuscripts. The authenticity of this speech has often been denied or disallowed, but it now seems certain that Constantine delivered it either shortly before or shortly after his defeat of Licinius in 324 in Thessalonica, Serdica, Nicomedia or possibly Antioch, and that what Eusebius preserves is an official (though not highly skilful) Greek translation of a Latin original which was often obscurely expressed.[5]

2 *Panegyric to Constantine*, delivered by Eusebius in Constantinople on the occasion of Constantine's *tricennalia*. Since the speech alludes to Dalmatius Caesar, who was not proclaimed a member of the imperial college until 18 September 335 (*Laus Constantini* 2.4, cf. *MGH.AA* 9.235), the date of delivery must be 25 July 336 (not July 335).[6]

3 *Treatise on the Church of the Holy Sepulchre*, delivered by Eusebius to the Council of Jerusalem in mid September 335 as part of the bishops' dedication of Constantine's magnificent new church.[7]

It would be unenlightening as well as depressing to describe yet again the history of the controversy over the authorship and authenticity of the *Life of Constantine*. Friedhelm Winkelmann's survey published in 1962 removes any necessity,[8] and it is clear that three turning points have now transformed the long and sterile debate. First, A. H. M. Jones (acting on a suggestion from C. E. Stevens) identified a fragmentary papyrus dated palaeographically between c. 320 and c. 340 as containing part of a document in the *Life* (2.24–42) which hostile critics had most confidently pounced upon as a manifest forgery.[9] Consequently, since the early 1950s the authenticity of all the documents has generally and correctly been conceded, as has Eusebius' authorship of the *Life*, despite some isolated denials.[10] Second, the first war between Constantine and Licinius has been convincingly re-dated from 314 to 316/17: on the traditional chronology, which held sway unchallenged from 1665 to 1953, Eusebius' account of the hostilities between the two emperors seemed to commit at least one gross error by putting the start of hostilities between them after Constantine's *decennalia* in 315 (1.49, cf. 48). The date of 316/17, which had prevailed before 1665,[11] was reinstated by Patrick Bruun in 1953 on the basis of the Constantinian coinage of Arelate:[12] when other numismatists demurred, Christian Habicht proved that the literary and documentary evidence also heavily favours 316, while Bruun demonstrated the same for the coinage of all the imperial mints.[13] The correct chronology not only removes the error in the *Life of Constantine*, but necessitates a fresh approach to Lactantius' *On the Death of the Persecutors*, which can now be used as a basis for writing the history of the Constantinian period.[14]

The third turning point is one whose importance was realized only slowly and is still sometimes denied. In 1910, Giorgio Pasquali demonstrated that the *Life of Constantine* is unfinished.[15] But other scholars exhibited a curious failure to understand Pasquali's thesis. His conclusions were totally misreported, not only at once by the French scholars Jules Maurice and Pierre Batiffol, but also in 1930 by Norman Baynes, in an influential study still regarded by many as the best introduction to the Constantinian period.[16] Baynes performed the agile feat of first refuting what he presented as Pasquali's thesis, then appropriating and arguing Pasquali's main conclusion as if in opposition to him. Henri Grégoire (it is amusing to observe) was not deceived, though he let the misrepresentation pass for tactical reasons.[17] Scholars who were more trusting (and perhaps too busy to read Pasquali for themselves) accepted Baynes' false report until 1962, when Winkelmann documented and exposed the misrepresentation. Since the reprint of Baynes' study of Constantine (published in 1972) charitably refrains from taxing Baynes with the error, a restatement of Pasquali's thesis will be apposite. Too much modern writing about Constantine has an air of unreality, as if the protagonists in the controversy prefer shadow-boxing to grappling with the real issues.

Pasquali began from Ivar Heikel's edition of the *Life of Constantine*, which he reviewed at length for the Göttingen Academy.[18] He therefore knew and accepted Heikel's demonstration, in the preface to his edition, that the language and style of the documents quoted in the *Life* is very different from that of the text – from which it follows that Eusebius himself cannot have invented them.[19] Pasquali then observed a curious, undeniable and significant phenomenon: the *Life* contains at least one clear and substantial doublet, since Book II first summarizes an edict of Constantine in some detail (20–1: more than twenty lines), then quotes the document just summarized verbatim and in full (24–42). Pasquali made a comparison of the quoted text and its preceding summary the cornerstone of a proof that, whatever the *Life* may be, it cannot be a finished literary product composed and articulated by Eusebius as a unitary composition. Accordingly, after identifying other indications that the *Life* contains 'two drafts or at least the remains of two drafts', Pasquali suggested an explanation in terms of two changes of plan and unfinished composition. On Pasquali's hypothesis, as soon as Eusebius learned that the emperor had died on 22 May 337 (i.e. in June), he composed a panegyric of the dead emperor in the style and manner deemed appropriate to a *basilikos logos* in Greek rhetorical handbooks.[20] However, when Eusebius discovered that his enemy Athanasius was being restored from exile, he began to remodel the encomium as more of a polemical pamphlet. Finally, when news came of the dynastic murders of the summer of 337 and the proclamation of Constantinus, Constantius and Constans as Augusti on 9 September, Eusebius revised the almost-finished work at the beginning and end to take account of the new political situation.

Pasquali argued that Eusebius died in May 338, before he had time to prepare the *Life* properly for publication. His concluding paragraph, tersely expressed in limpid German, deserves quotation:

Then someone came and published the work at once, as he found it: perhaps Acacius, Eusebius' successor in the see of Caesarea was the editor, but the name does not matter. The work was published with the same piety and the same lack of understanding as Plato's *Laws* were by Philippus of Opus. With the *Life*, political considerations too affected the publication.[21]

The analogy ought to have made the conclusion perfectly clear. Pasquali did not believe the *Life* to be interpolated in the normal sense, as Maurice, Batiffol and Baynes alleged: on the contrary, he held that the 'interpolations' which he identified were all inserted by Eusebius himself into his own earlier draft.

Pasquali's central thesis was never refuted, merely misreported or ignored. It cannot be refuted, for it corresponds to and explains the observable phenomena. Moreover, even though not all the doublets and inconsistencies which Pasquali identified really are what he claimed them to be, other features of the *Life* which he did not discuss support his central contention that a posthumous editor published the *Life* after Eusebius died. The following briefly annotated list includes passages adduced by Pasquali, by Winkelmann (in the preface to his edition of the *Life*)[22] and by the present writer:

Chapter headings Eusebius normally equipped his historical and apologetical works with chapter headings (*kephalaia*) before each chapter and lists of contents in the form of a consolidated list of the relevant chapter headings before each book (which it is convenient to style an 'index').[23] The chapter headings and index to the *Life* use the third person (not the first) to describe the author's activity in composition (1.11 *keph.*: 'That he has now related only the god-loving actions of Constantine'; 4.33 *keph.*: 'How he stood to listen to the rhetorical display of Eusebius about the tomb of the Saviour').

1.11.1 Eusebius promises to omit Constantine's victories in war and his peaceful measures for the good of the whole commonwealth: in fact, the *Life* contains passages which depict the emperor with the traits of the traditional good ruler with little or no allusion to his Christianity (e.g. 1.25, on campaigns *c.* 307; 1.45, on campaigns *c.* 314; 4.1–7, on his generosity, his military prowess against the northern barbarians and his world-wide reputation). Moreover, these passages are matched by two others which denounce Licinius as a tyrant (1.54.2–55) and compare the two emperors point by point (3.1–3).

1.18.2 This passage praises Constantius, the father of Constantine, for surpassing other emperors in fertility by raising 'a large chorus of male and female children'. Eusebius is unlikely to have written that after the two surviving sons of Constantius were killed in the summer of 337,[24] though he may well have forgotten to delete the already written sentence. Everywhere else in the *Life*, Eusebius reflects the political realities of September 337 when the three sons of Constantine and Fausta were proclaimed Augusti after the elimination of their dynastic rivals, who included the Caesar Dalmatius.

1.23 Eusebius declares that he has decided to avoid sullying his work with accounts of the rulers who waged war on the church, but the first book of the *Life* closes with long accounts of the painful deaths of Galerius in 311 and Maximinus in 313, partly transcribed almost word for word from the *Ecclesiastical History* (1.57–9, cf. *HE* VII.16.3–4, 17.1; IX.10.2–3; X.14–15).

2.13 This is a clear insertion into its context: 14.1 (*tauta men oun*) follows on from 12.2, while 13.2 contradicts the closing sentence of 12.2, alleging that Constantine spared opposing soldiers even in the heat of battle, whereas the earlier passage boasts that his men slaughtered the enemy vigorously until victory was won.

2.20–1 These describe the document quoted in 24–42, and 23.1

follows on 19.3. As Pasquali showed, Eusebius cannot have intended both passages to stand in the same work.[25]

3.1–3 This *synkrisis* of Constantine and Licinius interrupts a context which moves from the Arian controversy (2.61–72) to the Council of Nicaea (3.5–21).

3.4 This chapter repeats the last sentence of 2.72 and the substance of 2.62, inelegantly introducing the Melitians for a second time. It was (I believe) added by the editor of the *Life*, who betrays himself by using a pastiche of phrases from elsewhere in the *Life* with words Eusebius does not normally use.[26]

3.22 Eusebius speaks here about Constantine's letters from the Council of Nicaea as if he had not already quoted one of them (as he does in 17–20).

3.25 The chapter follows logically on the description of the Council of Nicaea: 'These things being so, the god-lover began another accomplishment worthy of memory in the province of Palestine.' What immediately precedes (viz. 23–4) is intrusive to its present context.

3.41–2 and 43.1–4 These form a doublet on Helena's foundation of churches to mark the places of Christ's nativity in Bethlehem and ascension from the Mount of Olives.

4.8 The introduction to Constantine's letter to Shapur (especially the words *kai touto parastēsei*) implies that Eusebius has just quoted another document, while the sentence which follows the letter refers to Constantine's conquest of the East in 324 (14.1): Eusebius surely intended this letter to follow those quoted in 2.24–60.

4.23 Eusebius summarizes in one brief sentence ('similarly a law went to all provincial governors [ordering them] to honour the Lord's day') an enactment which he has just paraphrased at length (4.18–19: about twenty-five lines).

4.23–5 In this messy passage, two successive brief chapters inelegantly begin with the same words (*enthen eikotōs*): of them, 4.24 seems to follow on the first sentence of 4.23, while 4.25 seems to follow on the second sentence of the same chapter.

4.33–8 The abrupt changes of subject, from a speech which Eusebius

delivered before Constantine while the emperor insisted on
standing (33) to two letters of Constantine, the one thanking
Eusebius for a treatise on the date of Easter (35), the other asking
him to prepare copies of the scriptures for liturgical use in
Constantinople (36), may well indicate the lack of a final revision.
Moreover, 38 seems to be an alternative version of 37.

4.46 This chapter, describing two speeches which Eusebius intends
to append to the work, interrupts a context devoted to the Council
of Jerusalem in September 335, and the opening words of 47
('*tautēn megistēn hōn ismen sunodon deuteran*') read awkwardly after 46
and refer back to 45.

4.50 This is a doublet of 4.7.

4.54 This passage has a totally different tenor from any other passage
in the *Life*. It is angry, defensive and polemical, inspired (as
Pasquali saw) by the restoration of Eusebius' ecclesiastical enemies,
especially Athanasius, from exile in the summer of 337.[27]
   I suspect that the first sentence of 55 ('*alla tous men ouk eis makron
hē theia metērcheto dikē*') represents the editor's attempt to connect 54
to its context. The rest of 55 would follow on after the first lacuna
in 37.

Treatise on the Church of the Holy Sepulchre The hypothesis of
posthumous publication resolves the notorious conundrum posed
by the fact that the speech on the Church of the Holy Sepulchre
which stands in the manuscripts of the *Life* does not correspond to
the speech which the text of the *Life* promises to quote. For the
Life promises a speech describing the church and its costly
decoration (4.46.1), whereas the extant *Treatise* avoids physical
description in order to concentrate on Constantine's theological
motives in building the church. The discrepancy can most readily
be explained by the following hypothetical reconstruction:[28]

1 In September 335, Eusebius delivered the extant *Treatise* in
   Jerusalem (11.2) during the ceremonies marking the dedication
   of the Church of the Holy Sepulchre by the Council of Tyre
   (cf. *Life* 4.45.3).

2 In November 335, Eusebius delivered another speech on the same
   subject to Constantine in the imperial palace in Constantinople
   (4.33, 46.1).

3 Eusebius intended to append the later speech to the *Life* (4.46.1).

4 The editor of the *Life* attached the earlier speech, either through careless error or because he failed to find a copy of the later one among Eusebius' papers.

It is important to distinguish clearly between what Pasquali proved and what he did not. He demonstrated that the *Life of Constantine*, as extant, represents a conflation of two drafts and that someone else published the still unfinished work after Eusebius died. He did not, however, attempt to relate the *Life* to other works from the end of Eusebius' life, and he did not define precisely or accurately enough the nature of the two drafts which he distinguished.

Between the death of Constantine and his own, Eusebius was busy on works of contemporary polemic as well as on the *Life*, viz. *Against Marcellus* and *Ecclesiastical Theology*, which are both theological 'hatchet-jobs'.[29] The former was written to justify the deposition of Marcellus of Ancyra by the Council of Constantinople in 336, apparently when Marcellus returned from exile in 337: at all events, it refers to Constantine as dead and as having approved the condemnation of Marcellus.[30] The latter work (it seems) was designed to prepare the way for Marcellus' second deposition, which probably occurred at the Council of Antioch in 338/9 which deposed Athanasius as bishop of Alexandria and replaced him with the Cappadocian Gregory, probably under the presidency of Flaccillus the bishop of Antioch, the dedicatee of the *Ecclesiastical Theology*.[31]

The day of Eusebius' *depositio* or burial is certified as 30 May: it may be deduced, with something close to certainty, that the bishop of Caesarea died in late May 339.[32] This is very relevant to the *Life of Constantine*. Eusebius was not cut off as abruptly as Pasquali imagined (for he put his death in May 338). Moreover, the genesis of the *Life* may be more complicated than Pasquali believed. Even though the *Life* does indeed contain two different drafts or conceptions, of which one is a conventional commemoration of a dead monarch, it is not immediately obvious to which ancient literary genre the other belongs.

In what sense is the *Life of Constantine* a biography? Wilamowitz was characteristically forthright: it neither is nor claims to be a life.[33] For once Wilamowitz was correct as well as pungent, even though Averil Cameron has recently uttered a flat contradiction.[34] His verdict is strengthened by Pasquali's demonstration of posthumous publication.

The manuscripts present the title of the work in two forms. First, preceding the list of chapter headings:

kephalaia tou kata theon biou tou makariou Kōnstantinou basileōs.

Second, at the head of the text:

Eusebiou tou Pamphilou eis ton bion tou makariou Kōnstantinou basileōs.

Neither designation comes from Eusebius himself, and neither promises a proper biography. The phrase 'life according to God' echoes Eusebius' statement that he will record only Constantine's acts of piety (1.10.4), only what tends to produce a god-loving way of life (1.11.1). The preposition in the second title ('on the life of the blessed Emperor Constantine') may imply a partly non-biographical selection of material,[35] or could in theory be intended to suggest similarity to the *Life of Apollonius of Tyana*, a work certainly known to Eusebius, to which Philostratus give a similar title ('*ta eis ton Apollōnion ton Tuanea*').[36] But, whereas Philostratus described his work as a life of Apollonius,[37] the text of Eusebius' so-called *Life of Constantine* never uses the terms appropriate to a formal biography. It is wrong to claim that the work is 'at the same time a biography, a panegyric and an idealisation.'[38] As Wilamowitz saw, it is not a 'life' at all in the ancient sense of the term. It is equally mistaken to supply a noun and then construe the title as signifying 'Reflections of the Life of Constantine'.[39] On the contrary, Eusebius twice describes his work as a history: he protests that to collect and include all Constantine's correspondence with bishops and Christian congregations would interrupt 'the body of our present history' (3.24.2: '*hōs an mē to sōma tēs parousēs hēmin diakoptoito historias*'), and he refers to himself as 'the writer of this history' (3.51.2: '*hēmin de tois tēnde graphousi tēn historian*').

Literary analysis confirms. In his classic study of Greek and Roman biography as a literary genre, Friedrich Leo characterized the *Life* as 'an encomium in four books, with a half-biographical title, half-historical content, completely rhetorical style and ecclesiastical bias', in fact 'an ecclesiastical history of his time centred around the person of Constantine', in which 'the material and its depiction are a mixture of panegyric and history'. Nevertheless, Leo emphasized biographical elements in the *Life*, declaring that 'the thread is biographical' and detecting 'the Suetonian descriptive section' in the way Eusebius sums up Constantine's life before describing his death (4.53–5).[40] Leo's analysis is not quite subtle enough. In ancient writing, the line dividing biography from panegyric, especially encomiastic biography from large-scale panegyric, was narrow and frequently crossed.[41] It follows that what Leo identified as biographical elements may in fact be constituent pieces of the unfinished panegyric.

The arrangement of the *Life* in four books comes from the posthumous editor, not the author. It is necessary, therefore, before a detailed literary analysis can proceed, that passages of the abandoned panegyric be identified. On internal grounds, the following connected passages would be appropriate to a speech composed by Eusebius during 337, presumably begun when he heard of Constantine's death on 22 May but revised after news came that his sons alone had been proclaimed Augusti on 9 September:

1.1–9 Exordium in several sections, viz.

> 1–3 Eusebius draws a parallel with the panegyrics of Constantine which he composed in 325 and 336 (1.1) and argues that Constantine alone of all Roman emperors became 'a shining example of a pious life to all men'.
>
> 4–6 God was Constantine's protector.
>
> 7–8 Comparison of Constantine with Cyrus and Alexander the Great.
>
> 9 Summary of main themes and prayer for God's help in composition.

1.12–25 Constantine's origin, youth and accession as emperor, introduced by a comparison to Moses at the court of Pharaoh (12). Eusebius concentrates on Constantine's father, whom he presents as an ideal emperor, using a traditional story first found in Xenophon's *Cyropaideia* (14: he kept his treasury empty, but his friends supplied abundant funds as a gift when he needed them),[42] and as a Christian who refused to persecute his subjects in any way at all in 303 (13.3: disproved as exaggeration by Lactantius, *De mortibus persecutorum* 15.7). Moreover, he follows the advice of the rhetorical handbooks for a *basilikos logos*, ignoring both Constantine's birthplace and his low-born mother: since neither Naissus nor the ignoble Helena increased the emperor's glory, Eusebius simply omitted them.

1.47 God's preservation of Constantine against plots, first by Maximian in the summer of 310, then by other relatives, i.e. the alleged plot by Bassianus, the husband of Anastasia, in 316 (*Origo Constantini imperatoris* 15, cf. *Life* 1.50).[43]

The opening words of 47 ('*en toutois d'onti autō(i')* follow on
perfectly from 25, which refers to the emperor crossing to Britain
– as Constantine in fact did both in 307 and late in 310.

3.1–3 A systematic comparison of the good and pious Constantine
with Licinius, to whom Eusebius always applies a generalizing
plural (*hoi men … ho de*).

4.1–7 A panegyrical survey of Constantine as a good emperor in the
traditional mould, with only a slight Christian colouring.
Constantine showered *beneficia* on his subjects in the form of gifts
of money, property and statues (1.2), he remitted taxes and
assessed fairly (2–3), he compensated the losing parties in law-suits
(4), he defeated the Goths and Sarmatians (5–6, with clear
reference to campaigns waged in 332 and 334), and he received
homage from the ends of the earth (7, describing the *tricennalia* of
336). The passage is a miniature *speculum principis*.[44]

In marked contrast to these flowing passages which observe the rules
laid down in the handbooks for speeches in honour of rulers stand slabs
of documentary history with a clear exposition of a theme:

2.24–60 The establishment of Christianity as the official religion of
the Roman empire. Eusebius quotes documents in which
Constantine repairs and restores the effects of Licinius' persecution
in the East (24–42), provides for a massive programme of building
churches (46) and defines his policy towards paganism (48–60), viz.
to allow pagans to keep their 'shrines of falsehood' while
implicitly reiterating the prohibition of sacrifice, consulting oracles
and erecting new cult-statues which Eusebius records (45.1), along
with a previous law forbidding magistrates and governors to
sacrifice before performing public business (44).[45]

2.61–73 and 3.5–21 The Council of Nicaea. Eusebius introduces the
theological controversy over the views of Arius allusively (2.61),
for he is determined never to name Arius himself or to refer to
him openly, and he lays more stress on the controversy over the
date of Easter (3.5), though also alluding to the Melitian schism
(2.62). The whole account was shown up as hopelessly lacunose,
tendentious and self-serving by the discovery of a Syriac
translation of the synodical letter of a Council of Antioch which
met early in 325 and excommunicated Eusebius.[46]

In the present context, it need only be noted that Eusebius has structured his account around two letters and a speech which he had heard: he quotes Constantine's letter to Alexander and Arius which was sent to Alexandria in the winter of 324/5 (2.64–72), his opening speech to the Council of Nicaea (3.12) and his letter to the churches on the correct date of Easter (3.17–20). In describing the Council, Eusebius concentrates on ceremony (10, 15), Constantine's personal behaviour (13–14, 16, 21–2) and the size and variety of the assembly (7–9) – which matched the crowd at the first Pentecost (Acts 2:5–11).

3.59–66 Constantine's beneficial interest in the affairs of the church, illustrated by his letters concerning the election of a bishop to the see of Antioch (60–2) and his letter or edict urging heretics to join the catholic church (64–5).

To the same concept or draft belong five other passages:

1.10–11 A full and formal preface promising a work exclusively devoted to these actions of Constantine that 'conduce to the life of piety'.

1.26–46 Constantine's war against Maxentius and its consequences. Eusebius presents Constantine's victories as the consequence of his piety. First, needing superhuman aid against Maxentius, Constantine decided to pray to the God of his father Constantius (27), saw a vision in the sky, made the labarum, took theological instruction – and prosecuted the war fortified with good hopes (28–32). Maxentius' tyranny and Constantine's victory over him are then described in a long passage which largely repeats the *Ecclesiastical History* (33–41, cf. *HE* VIII.14.2, 17.3–6; IX.9.2–11). Next comes Constantine's showering of benefits on the Christian church (42–3) and his concern for its internal welfare, with clear allusions to his presence at the Council of Arles in September 314 (44)[47] and to his subsequent attempts to compose the Donatist schism in Africa (45.2–3).

1.48–2.19 Constantine and Licinius. Despite some intrusive passages which belong to the panegyric proper (2.6.2, 11, 13), this section of the *Life* falls into four clearly articulated parts, viz:
1 Introduction: Constantine celebrated his *decennalia* in a Christian fashion (1.48).

2 Licinius' treacherous treatment of Constantine (1.49–50).
3 Licinius' tyranny in the East (1.51–2.2).
4 Constantine's war against him (2.3–19).
The style of presentation is historical: Eusebius quotes a speech of Licinius to his troops, which he claims to know from those who heard it (2.5.2–5). But part 3 is badly arranged, with some incoherence as well as a large amount of repetition from the *Ecclesiastical History*: Eusebius passes from Licinius' anti-Christian legislation (1.51–4, cf. *HE* x.8.8, 10–11), to his fiscal and moral oppression of his subjects (55, cf. *HE* x.8.12–14), then back to his treatment of bishops (56) and his forgetfulness of the dreadful fates of Galerius and Maximinus, which are described (57–8), and back again to his persecution of bishops sympathetic to Constantine (2.1–2, expanding on 56.1).

An overlap with the panegyrical section which opens Book III is highly significant. Licinius' lust for money was insatiable:

apōdureto ptōcheian, Tantaleiō(i) pathei tēn psuchēn truchomenos (1.55.2);

chrēmatōn hēttous huperchon Tantaleiō(i) pathei tēn psuchēn dedoulōmenoi (3.1.7).

Nothing could illustrate more clearly the fact that the two treatments of Licinius are alternative presentations of the same material, not designed to stand together in the same work.

4.8–14 Constantine's letter to Shapur (9–13), with its introduction and epilogue, stands between a panegyrical section (1–7) and a section of mixed character (15–55). Eusebius intended the letter closely to follow other documents (8).

4.56–75 A connected narrative of Constantine's last illness, death and burial, which begins with his preparations for an expedition against Persia during the winter of 336/7 (56: the lacuna between 56.3 and 58 is due to a purely accidental textual loss in transmission). There is no compelling evidence of two drafts here, one written before September 337, the other after:[48] here, as elsewhere, allowance must be made for Eusebius' normal and undoubted repetitiousness as a writer.

The one passage not so far classified (4.15–55) is a miscellany where fragments from the two drafts are jumbled together in some confusion. To the panegyric may be assigned the following:

15–17 The power of Constantine's faith in God.

21 The labarum (whose origin and power are described in the narrative sections 1.28–31, 2.7–9).

23, 25 Christian legislation (25.1 repeats 2.45.1).

27.3²–28 Constantine's generosity to the church.

31 Constantine's *philanthropia* (of a piece with the claim that he spared the lives of enemy soldiers in 2.13).

38–39 Examples of church building.

53 The length of Constantine's life and reign and his good health (with implicit reference back to 1.7–8)

Interspersed with these brief treatments of large themes are fragments of a more grandiose and detailed exposition and of connected narrative:

18–20 Legislation prescribing the observance of Sunday and prayers for the army.

22 Constantine's private devotions (the opening sentence follows on 20.2).

24 His respect for bishops as evidenced in a remark made at dinner.

26.2–6 Reform of Augustus' marriage legislation and of testamentary law.

27.1–3¹ Jews forbidden to own Christian slaves; decisions of church councils given legal force.

29–30 Constantine's study of Christian theology.

32 His speech *To the Assembly of the Saints* (this brief chapter belongs after 29, p. 131.26 Winkelmann).

33–37¹ Constantine and Eusebius.

37²: Constantine's treatment of Constantia in Palestine.

40–50 The Councils of Tyre and Jerusalem, set in the context of the celebration of the *tricennalia* in 335 (40) and in July 336 (49–50).

51–2 The territorial responsibilities and courts of Constantine's three sons as Caesars.

55 Constantine's readiness for death.

A more general question must now be raised. What familiarity did Eusebius possess with either the theory or the practice of ancient historiography? The question can be answered easily, since the contents of his library can be described with some precision. The library of Caesarea had been formed by Pamphilus, an intellectual disciple of Origen, and it reflects his interests, with a heavy emphasis on philosophy, especially Plato and the Platonic tradition.[49] The *Preparation for the*

Gospel and the *Proof of the Gospel*, composed on a vast scale between 313 and 324, deliberately flaunt Eusebius' erudition. Among the large array of philosophical authors quoted appear only a few historians, all of them adduced for very ancient history: Abydenos, Philo of Byblos on Phoenician religion, Alexander Polyhistor, Diodorus Siculus on Egyptian religion. The *Chronicle* admittedly displays a wider knowledge of historical or quasi-historical writers, but some of it is second-hand, cribbed from the Christian Julius Africanus.[50] Even here, however, the only imperial writers named are Phlegon of Tralles, Cassius Longinus and Porphyry.[51] There is no sign that Eusebius was familiar either with recent Greek historians of the Roman Empire such as Cassius Dio, Herodian and Dexippus or with the classics of Greek historiography such as Herodotus, Thucydides, Xenophon and Polybius.

It is as an outsider, therefore, that Eusebius comments on the contrast between his account of Constantine and traditional histories:

Would it not be disgraceful if, while the memory of Nero and certain impious and godless tyrants far worse than he wins bold writers who have beautified the accounts of base actions with pretty exposition and consecrated them in histories of many books, we should be silent whom God himself has deigned to bring together with such an emperor as the whole of history has never described, and to come to see, know and converse with him? Wherefore it would befit us above all others to proclaim the rich tidings of good to all in whom the imitation of virtue arouses a yearning for the love of God. For they (i.e. the historians of emperors like Nero), collecting lives of frivolous men and deeds unprofitable for moral improvement from favour or hatred towards individuals, and perhaps I suppose in order to display their own learning, have unnecessarily dignified the accounts of base affairs by pompous verbal rhetoric, becoming, for those fortunate enough through God not to have any part in the evil, instructors in deeds which are not good, but which deserve to be buried in oblivion, darkness and silence. Even if my skill as a writer (*ho tēs phraseōs logos*) is overawed by the magnificence of the facts described, let it nevertheless be joyful at the bare reporting of good deeds, and the recollection of a god-loving narrative will provide an acquaintance with them which is not unprofitable but extremely life-enhancing to those whose souls are well prepared. (1.10)

Despite some obvious points of contact with Greek and Roman historians (most obviously the accusations of bias and flashy writing),[52] Eusebius has strayed far from the paths of traditional historiography. Moreover, what he says about Nero indicates that he had either misremembered or else not read historical accounts of his reign, for Nero rapidly became a text-book example of a tyrant. The hostile Latin tradition given shape by Fabius Rusticus, Pliny the Elder and Cluvius Rufus is evident in the pages of Tacitus, Suetonius and Dio, and Josephus early observed that Nero's madness, murders and cavorting on the stage were hackneyed themes.[53] *A fortiori*, there is even less reason to imagine that Eusebius studied imperial biographies.

If the *Life of Constantine* is not a 'life' in the ancient sense, and if it was written without familiarity with Greek historiography, what then is its literary genre? Portions of the *Life*, it has been argued, belong to an imperial panegyric, a genre with which Eusebius was acquainted. What of the rest? The more historical design may perhaps be regarded as an experiment in hagiography. The fourth century saw a rapid proliferation of literary and semi-literary accounts of martyrs and lives of saints, which edified and entertained a new Christian reading and listening public. For this new hagiography, existing pagan literature could provide only partial models, not normative rules of composition. Hence the wide variation in the literary form of saints' lives, from the *Life of Antony*, originally written (it seems) in Coptic but soon adapted for a Greek audience in Alexandria, to Sulpicius Severus' biography of Martin of Tours and the letters and dialogues which supplemented it.[54] It is in a hagiographical sense that Eusebius surely intended readers to construe his statement that he would include only those actions of Constantine which conduce to the life of piety (1.11.1). Among Eusebius' voluminous writings, it is the *Martyrs of Palestine*, originally composed in 311 to commemorate friends who had died in persecution, that in some ways shows the closest thematic similarity to the *Life*. Both works are inspired by Eusebius' burning desire to leave a permanent record of important events for posterity.[55]

If the *Life of Constantine*, in its extant state, represents a conflation of a panegyric and a documentary history of a hagiographical nature, it must next be asked which of the two conceptions came first? It seems natural and obvious to suppose that Eusebius wrote the panegyric first, then abandoned it for the more grandiose design. So Pasquali, and (with divergences in detail) the present writer.[56] Another view of the genesis of the work is possible, preferable and perhaps imposed by Eusebius' choice of documents to quote. Scholarly discussion of the documents in the *Life* has concentrated on whether or not they are authentic. Since that controversy is now settled, attention should be transferred to the more revealing question of how Eusebius assembled them.

Besides speeches and brief quotations, the *Life* contains no fewer than fifteen letters and edicts of Constantine quoted entire.[57] A list of their dates and addressees reveals how personal is Eusebius' choice of what documents to quote:

1 2.24–42 To the provincials of Palestine in October 324, undoing the effects of Licinius' persecution. Since the letter closes with the instruction 'let it be posted up in our eastern territories' (42), a text was presumably posted publicly in Caesarea. Eusebius specifically states that he reproduces the text from an original copy with a *subscriptio* in the emperor's own hand 'preserved among us' (23.3).

2 2.46 To Eusebius, urging him to build churches (shortly after October 324).

3 2.48–60 To the eastern provincials, probably in 325 or 326, allowing them to retain their 'shrines of falsehood' but implicitly reaffirming the prohibition of sacrifice of 324/5 (45.1). Presumably also posted publicly in Caesarea.

4 2.64–72 To Alexander, the bishop of Alexandria, and Arius, urging them to treat their theological quarrel as a philosophical disagreement, not an occasion for schism. This letter was taken to Alexandria in the winter of 324/5 by a trusted envoy, and presumably circulated by each of the recipients among their allies as they prepared for the Council of Nicaea.[58]

5 3.17–20 Circular letter to all churches, written from Nicaea in June or July 325 to announce the Council's decisions about the date of Easter.

6 3.30–2 To Macarius, bishop of Jerusalem, instructing him to build the church of the Holy Sepulchre, dated to 326 or shortly thereafter by a reference to the *vicarius* Dracilianus (31.2).[59]

7 3.52–3 To Macarius and the other bishops of Palestine, instructing them to root out pagan ceremonies at the Oak of Mamre, where God appeared to Abraham, and build a church on the site. Eusebius received a copy of the letter (51.2), which was probably written *c.* 328.[60]

8–10 3.60–2 Three letters concerning the election of a bishop to the see of Antioch in 328: to the church of Antioch (60), to Eusebius (61), and to the bishops assembled at Antioch (62). The letter to

Eusebius implies that Constantine sent him copies of the other two letters (61.3).

11 3.64–5 To heretics excluding them from all benefits conferred on the catholic church: apparently an edict (65.3: 'let it be posted'), certainly issued before 25 September 326 (cf. *CTh* 16.5.2).

12 4.9–13 Letter to Shapur asserting Constantine's position as protector of the Christians of Persia, written *c.* 325.[61] Eusebius specifically states that Constantine wrote it in his own hand, and that he possessed a copy of the letter in Latin, but he leaves it unclear how he obtained a copy or who translated it.

13 4.35 To Eusebius, thanking him for his treatise on the date of Easter.[62] Eusebius dates this and the following letter to the time when he was returning to Palestine from his visit to Constantinople in November 335 (34).

14 4.36 To Eusebius requesting copies of the Bible for use in the churches of Constantinople.

15 4.42 Letter to the Council of Tyre, of which Eusebius was a member, brought by the *notarius* Marianus (4.44 *keph.*) and read at the opening session in August 335.

This is not a random collection of Constantine's letters and edicts. Two of the documents from the years 324–6 contain instructions for publication (nos. 1 and 11), which implies that they were posted in Caesarea and copied by Eusebius at the time, in exactly the same way as he had copied down letters of Galerius, Maximinus and Licinius in 311–13 for quotation in the *Ecclesiastical History*. Another four are letters addressed to Eusebius personally (nos. 2, 9, 13, 14) and it is known that he was sent a copy of two more (nos. 8, 10), while he belonged to the collective body addressed in another three (nos. 5, 7, 15). In addition, it is easy to see how Eusebius obtained a copy of Constantine's letter to Alexander and Arius (no. 4), while Macarius doubtless advertised his commission to build a splendid church in Jerusalem (no. 6). But what of Constantine's letter to Shapur? How did Eusebius obtain a copy, in Latin, of a diplomatic letter to a foreign ruler? The answer to that question may turn out to be the key to the genesis of the *Life of Constantine*. There are only two possibilities: either Constantine circulated the letter, or Eusebius obtained a copy for himself. The former hypothesis has historical plausibility: Constantine could have circulated the letter, in which he poses as the champion of the Christians of Persia, for purposes of propaganda in 336/7 as he prepared to mount an invasion of Mesopotamia.[63] But in that case Eusebius would surely have seen an official Greek translation specially made for the purpose. The fact that Eusebius possessed a copy of the letter in Latin suggests rather that he obtained one for himself.[64] Further, since Eusebius was not an habitué of the court, he either wrote to ask for a copy (which hardly seems plausible) or obtained one during one of his visits to the imperial court. Since Constantine wrote to Shapur *c.* 325, it may be suggested that Eusebius learned of the letter and obtained a copy in 325 while he was at court to attend the Council of Nicaea. Why then did he decide to request a copy from the emperor? Presumably because he was already thinking ahead to the day when he would compose a sequel to the *Ecclesiastical History* which he had recently brought down to 324, that is, a documented history of Constantine as a Christian emperor and protector of the Christian church.

That hypothesis will explain the odd chronological distribution of the letters and edicts quoted in the *Life* and the appended speeches. The majority of these documents belong to the first years of Constantine's rule of the East: eight were written between October 324 and 326 (nos. 1–6, 11, 12), and Constantine's *Speech to the Assembly of the Saints*, whatever its precise date of delivery, would have come into Eusebius' hands no later than 325. Of the remaining letters, six were sent to Eusebius himself, four *c.* 328 (nos. 7–10) and two in the winter of 335/6 (nos. 13, 14). The only other documents quoted are Constantine's letter to the Council of Tyre, read by the *notarius* Marianus in August 335 (no. 15), and Eusebius' two speeches, which he delivered in July 336 and September 335 respectively. Why are so few documents quoted from the central period of seven years during which Constantine ruled the East (from autumn 328 to summer 335)? It looks as if Eusebius collected letters and edicts of Constantine assiduously in 325 and 326, then stopped. Perhaps he decided that his *Commentary on Isaiah*, composed largely in these years, was a more appropriate medium for celebrating the Constantinian empire.[65] Perhaps he had some other reason. At all events, whatever his motive for dropping the project, it appears that Eusebius had begun to think about the work which eventually became the *Life of Constantine* as soon as the emperor conquered the East.[66] When Constantine died, Eusebius already had a preliminary collection of material on hand – and perhaps an inchoate narrative for the period down to 326.

The hypothesis just adumbrated receives confirmation from a well-known fact which seems never to have been exploited in this context. In three manuscripts of Eusebius' *Ecclesiastical History*, Constantine's letter to the provincials of Palestine in October 324 (no. 1) stands as an appendix to that work. It was certainly put there by Eusebius himself, since it is followed by the sentence:

Let this stand here; but come now let us assemble together, making a fresh beginning, all the laws and letters on behalf of true piety of our god-loving and most gentle emperor.[67]

Moreover, the text offered by the manuscripts of the *Ecclesiastical History* is superior in minor details to that in the manuscripts of the *Life*, which accordingly reveals itself as a secondary version.[68] That ought to count as a positive proof that the *Life of Constantine* originated as a continuation of or sequel to the final edition of the *Ecclesiastical History*. Book IX of that work provided the model for a narrative of an emperor's actions (there Maximinus in 311–13) centred around and illustrated by an array of documents quoted entire.[69]

A long scholarly tradition, whose recent representatives include Arnaldo Momigliano and Peter Brown, has presented Eusebius as a court writer, virtually an imperial propagandist.[70] Hence the *Life of Constantine* has been saluted as the only court biography still extant, a combination of 'Christian *Cyropaedeia* and novel', propounding the ideal of a Christian emperor for imitation by his successors and full of rhetorical and novelistic devices.[71] The exegetical premiss is totally false. Eusebius was no habitué of Constantine's court, which he visited only four times, always on ecclesiastical business in the company of other bishops.[72] He was a provincial bishop who resided at Caesarea in Palestine, far from the centre of political events. He was a scholar whose earlier historical works evince an honest desire to write a reliable history of his own day – an aspiration which the *Life* reiterates (2.23.2).[73]

No historian ever completely fulfils his aspirations to or professions of impartiality and fairness. How far short of the ideal does Eusebius fall? The traditional verdict on him has been harsh, and it is still argued that the *Life of Constantine* must be unreliable because it is 'a self-confessed panegyric'.[74] Recent research, however, has done much to rehabilitate the good faith of Eusebius. On issue after issue, Eusebius' testimony, so often dismissed or disregarded, either receives positive confirmation from other evidence or else deserves to be regarded as inherently plausible. Eusebius knew the precise date at which Constantine took the title *victor* (2.19.2),[75] and that Constantine instituted the office of *peraequator census* (4.3).[76] He presumably saw in Constantinople in 336 the Blemmyes whose presence there is incidentally attested by a papyrus (4.7.1, cf. 1.8.3).[77] And his reports that Constantine prohibited pagan sacrifice altogether in 324 (2.45.1, cf. 4.25.1) and forbade Jews to own Christian slaves (4.27.1) deserve credence: a constitution of Constans confirms the former,[78] while correct prosopography shows that the prohibition on Jews owning Christian slaves was indeed issued by Constantine, not under his sons.[79] Similarly, when Eusebius states that the new city of Constantinople contained no pagan cults (3.48), that should not be written off as one of his 'notorious distortions and falsehoods'.[80] A speech of the pagan Himerius, delivered in the city in 362, provides precise confirmation.[81]

On the other hand, gross tendentiousness in some areas cannot be denied. Eusebius consistently writes as if Constantine only had three sons and only proclaimed three Caesars: Crispus, Caesar from 317 until his execution in 326, and Dalmatius, who was appointed Caesar on 18 September 335 and killed in 337, are totally ignored. More serious, Eusebius totally misrepresents both the theological disputes and the ecclesiastical politics of the reign of Constantine in a partisan fashion. Yet his viewpoint can be defined, understood and discounted. Writing after September 337, he could avoid repeating the official view of Constantine's dynastic intentions only by writing a different sort of work. Nor did his contemporaries have any doubt where Eusebius stood within the church: he was instrumental in deposing such champions of Nicene orthodoxy as Eustathius of Antioch in 326 and Marcellus of Ancyra in 336.[82] The *Life* itself displayed its sympathy for Arius openly for all who could catch an allusion: when Eusebius complimented Constantine for a policy which brought back into the church in herds the ecclesiastical exiles who recognized their mother, the church (3.66.3), he echoed words used by Arius and Euzoius when requesting readmission to the catholic church in late 327[83] – a request granted by the Council of Nicomedia which Eusebius records and praises (3.23).[84]

The contrast between verifiable accuracy on many matters and flagrant bias on others prompts the question whether the *Life* contains hidden assumptions which pervade the work and impair its value as evidence for Constantine. That view has been argued recently with some subtlety.[85] Yet, as formulated, it relies upon dismissing as 'over-mechanical' (and therefore, presumably, erroneous) Pasquali's proof that the *Life* is a conflation of two generically different drafts. Perhaps a full literary analysis of the *Life* can restate the theory in a valid form. Certainly, there is need for structural analyses which will lay bare Eusebius' patterns of thought (note, for example, the schema of satanically inspired envy as the sudden cause of contemporary disputes within a peaceful church).[86] But such analyses must respect the observable phenomena. The so-called *Life of Constantine* is a combination of conventional panegyric and something daringly original which hovers between ecclesiastical history and hagiography. To treat it as a work cut from a single cloth is as misleading as it would be to suppose that Charles Dickens intended both endings of *Great Expectations* to stand side by side.[87]

NOTES

1 H. Chadwick, 'The Origin of the Title "Oecumenical Council"', *JThS*, n.s. 23 (1972), 132–5, at 133.

2 'Lactantius and Constantine', *JRS*, 63 (1973), 29–46.

3 Viz. in *Constantine and Eusebius*, Cambridge, Mass. 1981, henceforth referred to as *Constantine*, and *The New Empire of Diocletian and Constantine*, Cambridge, Mass. 1982, henceforth referred to as *New Empire*. For the sake of brevity, uncontested dates and facts documented there are not annotated here.

4 As was clearly stated by N. H. Baynes, *ByZ*, 39 (1939), 468, reviewing H. Grégoire, 'Eusèbe n'est pas l'auteur de la "Vita Constantini" dans sa forme actuelle et Constantin ne s'est pas "converti" en 312', *Byz*, 13 (1938), 561–83.

5 R. Lane Fox, *Pagans and Christians*, Harmondsworth 1986 pp. 627–35, argues for delivery in Antioch on Good Friday (i.e. 16 April) 325, against my arguments in favour of Serdica in 321 (*Constantine* 323 n. 115, modifying Barnes, 'The Emperor Constantine's Good Friday Sermon', *JThS*, n.s. 27 (1976), 414–23) or Thessalonica in 323 or 324 (as argued by A. Piganiol, 'Dates constantiniennes', *RHPhR*, 13 (1932), 360–72, at 370ff.). I am doubtful whether that hypothesis can be squared with what else is known about events preceding the Council of Nicaea which opened in June. The correct answer to the conundrum may be delivery on Good Friday 325 in Nicomedia, as argued in an unpublished doctoral thesis by D. Ison, 'The Constantinian Oration to the Saints – Authorship and Background', dissertation, University of London 1985, 207ff.

That the extant Greek is a translation from a Latin original was proved in a long series of articles by A. Kurfess: see now D. N. Wigtil, 'Towards a Date for the Greek Fourth Eclogue', *Classical Journal*, 76 (1981), 336–41.

Lane Fox, *Pagans and Christians*, p. 778 n. 9, cf. p. 630, promises a proof that Constantine both delivered and composed the *Speech* in Greek.

6 H. A. Drake, 'When was the *De Laudibus Constantini* delivered?', *Historia*, 24 (1975), 345–56.

7 'Two Speeches by Eusebius', *GRBS*, 18 (1977), 341–5. Although the two speeches precede the *Life* in the manuscripts, Eusebius intended them to follow it (4.46: '*meta tēn parousan tēs graphēs hupothesin ekthēsometha*').

8 F. Winkelmann, 'Zur Geschichte des Authentizitätsproblems der Vita Constantini', *Klio*, 40 (1962), 187–243.

9 A. H. M. Jones, 'Notes on the Genuineness of the Constantinian Documents in Eusebius' *Life of Constantine*', *JEH*, 5 (1954), 196–200. Jones had earlier presented his identification at the First International Patristic Conference in Oxford in 1951. For other discussions of the papyrus (*P. Lond.* 878), see T. C. Skeat, 'Britain and the Papyri', in *Aus Antike und Orient, Festschrift W. Schubart*, Leipzig 1950, pp. 126–32; W. Schubart, 'Zu Skeat: Britain and the Papyri', in *Festschrift für F. Zucker*, Berlin 1954, pp. 343–8. It had originally been identified as a 'literary fragment, perhaps of an oration' by F. G. Kenyon and H. I. Bell, *Greek Papyri in the British Museum* 3, London 1907, p. xlii.

The authenticity of the document in 2.24–42 had been denied by A. Crivellucci, *Della fede storica di Eusebio nella Vita di Constantino*, Livorno 1888, pp. 5off.; *Studi Storici*, 3 (1894), 369–84, 415–22: V. Schultze, 'Quellenuntersuchungen zur *Vita Constantini* des Eusebius', *ZKG*, 14 (1894), 503–55; A. Mancini, 'Osservazioni sulla Vita di Costantino d'Eusebio', *RFIC*, 33 (1905), 309–60: P. Batiffol, 'Les documents de la Vita Constantini', *BALAC*, 4 (1914), 81–95.

10 H. Grégoire, commenting on A. H. M. Jones' discussion of *P. Lond.* 878, in the 'Rapports des séances de la société "Theonoé"', *La nouvelle Clio*, 5 (1953), 215; 'L'authenticité et l'historicité de la *Vita Constantini* attribuée à Eusèbe de Césarée', *BAB*, Classe des Lettres, 5th Series, 39 (1953), 462–79; M. R. Cataudella, 'La "persecuzione" di Licinio e l'autenticità della "Vita Constantini"', *Athenaeum*, n.s. 48 (1970), 48–83, 229–50.

11 See C. Baronius, *Annales Ecclesiastici*, vol. 3, Antwerp 1623, p. 157: the erroneous date of 314 only became canonical with Gothofredus' prolegomena to his edition of the Theodosian Code (*Chronologia Codicis Theodosiani*, Lyons 1665, xiii).

12 P. Bruun, *The Constantinian Coinage of Arelate*, Finska Fornminnesföreningens Tidskrift, 52:2, 1953, pp. 17ff.

13 C. Habicht, 'Zur Geschichte des Kaisers Konstantin', *Hermes*, 86 (1958), 360–78; P. Bruun, *Studies in Constantinian Chronology*, Numismatic Notes and Monographs, 146, 1961, pp. 10ff.; *Roman Imperial Coinage*, vol. 7, London 1966, pp. 76ff.

14 As argued in Barnes, 'Lactantius and Constantine', *JRS*, 63 (1973), 29ff.;

Constantine, pp. 13f., cf. the recent commentary by J. L. Creed, *Lactantius: On the Deaths of the Persecutors*, Oxford 1985. However, the date of 314 continues to find defenders: so, recently, I. König, *Origo Constantini: Anonymus Valesianus*, Teil 1, *Trierer Historische Forschungen*, 11 (1987), 119–23.

15 G. Pasquali, 'Die Composition der Vita Constantini des Eusebius', *Hermes*, 46 (1910), 369–86.

16 J. Maurice, 'Sur la vie de Constantin d'Eusèbe', *BSNAF* (1913), 387–96, at 387f.; Batiffol, *BALAC*, 4 (1914), 94 n. 2; N. H. Baynes, *Constantine the Great and the Christian Church*, London 1931; 2nd edition, with preface by H. Chadwick, Oxford 1972, pp. 42ff. Baynes delivered the text of his paper as a lecture on 12 March 1930, then expanded it by the addition of 'a few bibliographical notes', amounting to some seventy-five pages, for publication in *PBA*, 15 (1929, published 1931), 341–442.

17 H. Grégoire, *Byz*, 13 (1938), 578.

18 Review of I. A. Heikel, *Eusebius Werke* 1 (Leipzig, 1902), *GGA*, 171 (1909) 259–86.

19 Heikel, *Eusebius Werke* 1 (*GCS* 7, 1902), pp. lxvi–lxxxii.

20 Heikel had detected the same model (ibid, pp. xlviff.).

21 Pasquali, *Hermes*, 46 (1910), 386 (my translation).

22 F. Winkelmann, *Eusebius Werke* 1.1.[2] (*GCS* 1975), pp. xlixff. The list omits cases where Pasquali and Winkelmann seem to me to fail to demonstrate doublets.

23 *JThS*, n.s. 27 (1976), 418–20, cf. R. T. Ridley, 'Anonymity in the Vita Constantini', *Byz*, 50 (1980), 241–58.

24 Viz. Flavius Dalmatius, consul in 333, and Julius Constantius, consul in 335 and *patricius*.

25 Pasquali, *Hermes*, 46 (1910), 369ff.

26 Eusebius nowhere uses the word *sumplēgas*; the verb *suntarattō* occurs only in quotations or where Eusebius is paraphrasing the Septuagint (*Praep. ev.* 6.8.23, from Diogenianus; *PG* 23.173, 560, 636, in the *Commentary on the Psalms*).

27 Pasquali, *Hermes*, 46 (1910), 383.

28 Proposed in Barnes, 'Two Speeches by Eusebius', *GRBS*, 18 (1977), 344f.

29 For a brief description of those works and their context, see *Constantine*, 264f.

30 *c. Marcellum* 2.4.29, cf. Barnes, 'Emperor and Bishops, A.D. 324–344: Some Problems', *AJAH*, 3 (1978), 53–75, at 64f.

31 See *Athanasius of Alexandria. Theology and Politics in the Constantinian Empire* (Cambridge, Mass., 1993), ch. IV.

32 *PO* 10.15, cf. Barnes, *Constantine*, p. 263.

33 U. von Wilamowitz-Moellendorf, 'Ein Bruchstück aus der Schrift des

Porphyrius gegen die Christen', *ZNW*, 1 (1900), 101–5, at 105 n. 1; 'die Schrift *eis Kōnstantinon*, die ein *bios* weder heisst noch ist'.

34 Averil Cameron, 'Eusebius of Caesarea and the Rethinking of History', *Tria Corda. Scritti in onore di Arnaldo Momigliano* (Como 1983) pp. 71–88, esp. pp. 82–3: 'not a straightforward panegyric but a *bios*, a *Life*, akin in some ways to the moralising *Lives* of classical authors, but with a very different purpose'. A footnote dismisses Pasquali's thesis as 'over-mechanical' (p. 83 n. 57, cf. pp. 71–2 n. 2).

35 Heikel, *Eusebius Werke* 1 (1902), p. xlv: 'nicht Vita Constantini (Das Leben Constantins), sondern De Vita Constantini (Über das Leben Constantins)'.

36 The testimony of the MSS. of the *Vita Apollonii* is confirmed by Philostratus, *Vitae sophistarum* 2.5.1. E. Schwartz, *RE*, 6 (1909), 1423, detected the influence of Philo in Eusebius' formulation of his aims (1.3.4) and his comparison of Constantine to Moses (1.12, 19–20; 2.12).

37 Philostratus, *Vita Apollonii* 1.9.1; Eunapius, *Vitae philosophorum* 2.1.2, p. 454; *Suda* A 3420 (1.307 Adler).

38 R. Farina, *L'impero e l'imperatore cristiano in Eusebio di Casarea*, Zürich 1966, p. 19.

39 W. Telfer, 'The Author's Purpose in the Vita Constantini', *Studia Patristica*, 1, *TU* 63, 1957, pp. 157–67. He asserts 'we clearly have to do with panegyric, not historical biography' appealing to Photius' description of the work as '*hē eis Kōnstantinon ton megan basilea egkōmiastikē tetrabiblos*' (*Bibliotheca* 127).

40 F. Leo, *Die griechisch-römische Biographie nach ihrer litterarischen Form*, Leipzig 1901, pp. 311–13.

41 H. Homeyer, 'Zu den hellenistischen Quellen der Plutarch-viten', *Klio*, 41 (1963), 145–57.

42 H. Kloft, 'Zur *Vita Constantini* I 14', *Historia*, 19 (1970), 509–14, adducing Xenophon, *Cyropaedia* 8.2.15–22. The story is also applied to Constantius in exactly the same way by Praxagoras (*FGH* 219), Libanius, *Orationes* 59.15 and Eutropius, *Breviarium ab urbe condita* 10.1.2.

43 So Habicht, *Hermes*, 86 (1958), 374 n. 5, correctly repudiating the allusion to Fausta and Crispus (i.e. to 326) postulated by other scholars (e.g. F. Vittinghoff, 'Eusebius als Verfasser der Vita Constantini', *RMP*, n.f. 96 (1953), 330–373, at 347ff.).

44 Note the use made of the passage by F. Millar, *The Emperor in the Roman World (31 B.C. – A.D. 337)*, London 1977, esp. 10, 117, 139, 278.

45 On this section of the *Life*, see recently C. Pietri, 'Constantin en 324: Propagande et théologie impériales d'après les documents de la *Vita Constantini*', *Crise et redressement dans les provinces européennes de l'Empire (milieu du IIIe – milieu du IVe siècle ap. J.-C)*, Strasbourg 1983, pp. 63–90; T. D. Barnes, 'Constantine's Prohibition of Pagan Sacrifice', *AJP*, 105 (1984), 69–72.

46 Published by E. Schwartz, 'Zur Geschichte des Athanasius', *NAWG*, hist. Klasse, 1905, 257–99, cf. L. Abramowski, 'Die Synode von Antiochien 324/25 und ihr Symbol', *ZKG*, 86 (1975), 356–66.

47 For other evidence attesting Constantine's presence at the Council, *New Empire*, pp. 72, 242.

48 Against Pasquali, *Hermes*, 46 (1910), 380–2, see N. H. Baynes, *Constantine the Great and the Christian Church*, London 1931, p. 44.

49 K. Mras, 'Die Stellung der "Praeparatio Evangelica" des Eusebius im antiken Schrifttum', *AöAWPH*, 209–17; Barnes, *Constantine*, pp. 93f., 182f.

50 On the sources used by Eusebius, see A. A. Mosshammer, *The 'Chronicle' of Eusebius and the Greek Chronographic Tradition*, Lewisburg, Pa. and London 1979, pp. 113ff. (not entirely convincing).

51 *Chronicle*, ed. J. Karst in *GCS* 20, 1911, p. 126, quoted and translated in Barnes, *Constantine*, 118.

52 For those motifs, G. Avenarius, *Lukians Schrift zur Geschichtschreibung*, Meisenheim/Glan 1956, pp. 40ff., 59ff.

53 Josephus, *BJ* 2.250/1. Josephus' later reference to those who were careless of the truth out of gratitude toward Nero (*AJ* 20.154) should be construed in a comparative rather than an absolute sense: Cluvius Rufus, who had been an habitué of Nero's court and to whom Josephus should here refer, provided a lurid enough account of the emperor's sexual escapades (Tacitus, *Annales* 14.2.1).

54 See, respectively, 'Angel of Light or Mystic Initiate? The Problem of the *Life of Antony*', *JThS*, n.s. 37 (1986), 353–68; C. Stancliffe, *St. Martin of Tours and his Hagiographer. History and Miracle in Sulpicius Severus*, Oxford 1983, pp. 86 ff.

55 On the nature of the *Martyrs* (which is often misunderstood), see Barnes, *Constantine*, pp. 154f.

56 Pasquali, *Hermes*, 46 (1910), 384–6; Barnes, *Constantine*, p. 265.

57 I. Daniele, *I documenti costantiniani della 'Vita Constantini' di Eusebio di Cesarea*, Analecta Gregoriana 13, 1938, pp. 5ff.

58 Neither the text of the *Life* nor the chapter headings name the envoy. Socrates, *HE* 1.7.1, identified him as Ossius of Cordoba, who certainly went to Alexandria during the winter of 324/5 (Athanasius, *Apologia contra Arianos* 74.4). Virtually all recent writers have accepted Socrates' identification. However, B. H. Warmington, 'The Sources of Some Constantinian Documents in Eusebius' *Ecclesiastical History* and *Life of Constantine*', *StPatr*, 18 (1986), 93–8, has argued from the similarities of *Life* 2.63, 73 to 4.44 that the envoy should instead be identified as the *notarius* Marianus, who performed similar duties in 335.

59 Barnes, *New Empire*, pp. 141, 246. Constantine alludes to the discovery of the 'true cross' (30.1). Eusebius' silence, which has puzzled so many

modern scholars, is due to his resentment towards Macarius, who undoubtedly used his discovery to bolster his claims to episcopal primacy within Palestine over the metropolitan bishop of Caesarea.

60 Constantine refers to the *comes* Acacius (53.2), who is attested in Macedonia on 21 February 327 (*Codex Theodosianus* 11.3.2) and in the East in 328 (*Life* 3.62.1).

61 'Constantine and the Christians of Persia', *JRS*, 75 (1985), 126–36.

62 A partial text is preserved by Nicetas of Heraclea (*PG* 24.693–706), but nothing in it fixes the date.

63 Wide distribution is assumed in Barnes, 'Constantine and the Christians of Persia', *JRS*, 75 (1985), 131.

64 Warmington, *StPatr*, 18 (1986), 94f., suggests that Eusebius obtained both a copy of the letter and the information that the emperor wrote it in his own hand from the *notarius* Marianus. The hypothesis that Eusebius obtained his copy at court shortly after Constantine wrote the letter owes much to discussion with Mr John Harstone.

65 Published in full by K. Ziegler (*GCS*, 1975): see now M. Simonetti, 'L'Esegesi e ideologia nel Commento a Isaia di Eusebio', *RSLR*, 19 (1983), 3–44.

66 The notion that Eusebius began work before Constantine died goes back to P. Meyer, 'De vita Constantiniana Eusebiana', *Festschrift dem Gymnasium Adolfinum zu Moers* (1882), pp. 23–8. For a detailed argument that Eusebius conceived the *Life* in 335 and began composition in 336/7 see H. A. Drake, 'What Eusebius knew: the Genesis of the *Vita Constantini*', *CP*, 83 (1988), 20–38.

67 See E. Schwartz, *Eusebius Werke* 2.2 (*GCS* 9.2, 1908), p. 904. The passage is quoted by Daniele, *Documenti*, p. 32; F. Winkelmann, *Eusebius Werke* 1.1[2] (1975), p. xviii.

68 Heikel, *Eusebius Werke* 1 (1902), pp. xx–xxiv; F. Winkelmann, *Die Textbezeugung der Vita Constantini des Eusebius von Caesarea*, TU, 84 (1962), 121–31.

69 Pietri, *Crise et redressement*, p. 68, notes the similarity of the *Life* to the *History*; for the structure of Book IX see Barnes, *New Empire*, pp. 67f.

70 A. Momigliano, 'Pagan and Christian Historiography in the Fourth Century A.D.', *The Conflict between Paganism and Christianity in the Fourth Century*, Oxford 1963, p. 85; P. Brown, *The World of Late Antiquity*, London 1971, pp. 82, 86. The famous denunciation of Eusebius as 'the most objectionable of all eulogists' by J. Burckhardt, *Die Zeit Constantins des Grossen*, 2nd edn, Leipzig 1880, pp. 223ff., is more circumspect.

71 H. Peter, *Die geschichtliche Litteratur über die römische Kaiserzeit bis Theodosius I und ihre Quellen*, Leipzig 1897 1.405ff., 452; 2.279ff.

72 Viz. in the summer of 325, the winter of 327/8, November 335 and the summer of 336. H. A. Drake, *CP*, 83 (1988), 20–38, suggests that Eusebius

may have remained in Constantinople from the summer of 336 until at least Easter 337.

73 For the provincial viewpoint and basic honesty of Books VIII to X of the *Ecclesiastical History*, see Barnes, *Constantine*, pp. 155ff.

74 Averil Cameron, 'Constantinus Christianus', *JRS*, 73 (1983), 184–90.

75 For the inscriptional evidence, A. Chastagnol, 'Un gouverneur constantinien de Tripolitaine: Laenatius Romulus, *Praeses* en 324–326', *Latomus*, 25 (1966), 539–52, 543ff.; E. Guadagno and S. Panciera, 'Nuove testimonianze sul governo della Campania in età constantiniana', *Rendiconti della Accademia Nazionale dei Lincei*, 8th series, 25 (1970), 111–29, 111 ff.; G. Camodeca, 'Iscrizione inedite di Pozzuoli', *Atti dell' Accademia di Scienze Morali e Politiche, Napoli*, 82 (1971), 24–48, 30ff.

76 Probably in 321, cf. Barnes, *Constantine*, p. 69, adducing L. Aradius Valerius Proculus, consul in 340, who was *peraequator census provinciae Gallaeciae* shortly after 320 (*ILS*, 1240–2).

77 *P. Abinnaeus* 1, cf. Barnes, 'The Career of Abinnaeus', *Phoenix*, 39 (1985), 368–74.

78 *CTh* 16.10.1 (341), cf. Barnes *AJP*, 105 (1984), 69–72. The traditional view that Constantine issued no such prohibition is restated by P. Garnsey, 'Religious Toleration in Classical Antiquity', *Persecution and Toleration* (Studies in Church History 21, 1984), pp. 1–27, at p. 18, n. 39. The absence of the law reported by Eusebius from the Theodosian Code is in no way suspicious, cf. Pietri, *Crise et redressement*, p. 69.

79 *CTh* 16.9.2. is addressed to the praetorian prefect, Evagrius, on whom see *PLRE*, 1 (1971), 284f.; Barnes, *New Empire*, pp. 131f. O. Seeck, *Regesten der Kaiser und Päpste für die Jahre 311 bis 476 n. Chr.*, Stuttgart, 1919, p. 187 accepted the MSS. date of 339 for *CTh* 16.9.2, which is assumed to be correct by K. L. Noethlichs, *Die gesetzgeberischen Massnahmen der christlichen Kaiser des vierten Jahrhunderts gegen Häretiker, Heiden und Juden*, dissertation, Cologne 1971 , p.46; Winkelmann, *Eusebius Werke* 1.1² (1975), note on p. 130.8ff.; M. Avi-Yonah, *The Jews of Palestine*, New York 1976, pp. 161ff., 174ff.; C. D. Reichardt, 'Die Judengesetzgebung im Codex Theodosianus', *Kairos*, 20 (1978), 16–39; F. Blanchetière, 'L'evolution du statut des Juifs sous la dynastie constantinienne', *Crise et redressement* (1983), pp. 127–41.

80 Cameron, *Tria Corda*, p. 85.

81 Himerius, *Orationes* 41.8: 'temenē men egeirōn theois, teletas de theias kathidruōn tē(i) polei xenas'. G. Dagron, *Naissance d'une capitale. Constantinople et ses institutions de 330 à 451*, Paris 1974, p. 376 translates: 'en relevant les temples des dieux, en instituant des initiations jusqu'ici étrangères à cette cité'. That narrows considerably what Himerius is really saying, viz. that Julian introduced pagan religious rites into a city which was a Christian foundation.

82 On Eusebius' reputation, F. Winkelmann, *Byzantinische Beiträge*, ed. J. Irmscher, Berlin 1964, pp. 91–119.

83 H. G. Opitz, *Urkunden zur Geschichte des Arianischen Streites 318–328, Athanasius Werke* 3.1, Berlin/Leipzig, 1934, no. 30.

84 For this council (whose existence is often denied) and its context, see Barnes, *Constantine*, pp. 229–31. A full survey of the problem is given by R. Lorenz, 'Das Problem der Nach-synode von Nicäa (327)', *ZKG*, 90 (1979), 22–40.

85 Cameron, *Tria Corda*, pp. 82ff.

86 Eusebius uses this pattern in his accounts of the Arian controversy (2.61.3, 73; 3.4.1 (argued above to be an editorial addition)), the disputed election at Antioch in 328 (3.59.1), the Council of Tyre (4.41.1) – and of Licinius' disloyalty to Constantine (1.49.2; 3.1.1).

87 A preliminary version of the present essay was delivered as a lecture at the University of California in Santa Barbara in February 1987: the version published here owes much to the kind comments of Harold Drake who, through his courteous disagreements over many years, has taught me more than anyone else about the *Life of Constantine*.

XII

THE TWO DRAFTS OF EUSEBIUS' *LIFE OF CONSTANTINE*

I

In 1910 GIORGIO PASQUALI established four central facts from which any interpretation of Eusebius' *Life of Constantine* must proceed:

(i) the *Life* contains at least one certain pair of doublets, since a letter of Constantine is first summarised at length in some twenty lines (2.20/21), then formally introduced (2.23) and quoted in full without any reference whatever to the summary which immediately precedes (2.24–42);

(ii) both this doublet and others which Pasquali also detected in the *Life* come from the hand of Eusebius himself and are not the result of later interpolation;

(iii) the *Life* is consequently not a literary unity, but fuses together parts of two generically different drafts or concepts;

(iv) the *Life* owes its present form of four books followed by three speeches to an editor who published it after Eusebius' death (and whom Pasquali plausibly identified as Acacius, his successor as bishop of Caesarea).[1]

Pasquali's article suffered the unfortunate fate of being misreported by influential and normally accurate scholars. Pierre Batiffol spoke of Pasquali as believing in a continuator who enriched the text and brought it up to date,[2] while the standard German handbook to later Greek literature states that Pasquali proved that the original form of the *Life* was considerably enlarged by additions, above all by the inclusion of documents between the death of Eusebius and its final redaction in the form in which it survives.[3] Finally, Norman Baynes added his immense authority to the misrepresentation,[4]

---

[1] G. Pasquali, "Die Composition der Vita Constantini des Eusebius," *Hermes* 46 (1910) 369–386. The stylistic contradiction in the *Life* is elegantly stated by A. Dihle, *Die griechische und lateinische Literatur der Kaiserzeit* (Munich, 1989) 433: "Merkwürdigerweise sind auch in dieses Werk höfischer Panegyrik ganz gegen die Formgesetze der Gattung Urkunden im Wortlaut eingefügt."

[2] P. Batiffol, "Les documents de la Vita Constantini," *Bulletin d'ancienne littérature et d'archéologie chrétiennes* 4 (1914), 81–95, at 94 n. 2: "nous inclinerions plutôt à croire (avec M. Pasquali, p. 386) que la V.C. laissée inachevée, a été achevée, enrichie, mise au point, par un continuateur, peu après la mort d'Eusèbe."

[3] W. Christ, W. Schmid and O. Stählin, *Geschichte der griechischen Litteratur* 2[6] (Munich, 1924) 1369.

[4] N. H. Baynes, *Constantine the Great and the Christian Church* (London, 1931) 42–45—not corrected in the second edition, with a new preface by H. Chadwick (Oxford,

2   THE TWO DRAFTS OF EUSEBIUS' *LIFE OF CONSTANTINE*

with the result that several subsequent scholars faithfully repeated his perversion of Pasquali's views without (it appears) taking the trouble to read the original article for themselves.[5] Hence Pasquali's analysis of the literary problem of the *Life* played no role in discussions of "the Constantinian problem" or "the problem of the *Life of Constantine*" for fifty years. Misrepresentation prevailed over truth until Friedhelm Winkelmann in 1962 called the bluff of the second-hand scholars and drew attention to what Pasquali actually wrote.[6] Since then more doublets and signs of revision or of the hand of a posthumous editor have been detected, both by Winkelmann himself in the preface to his edition of the *Life* (published in 1975) and by the present writer.[7] Even so, intelligent and normally careful scholars still classify Pasquali among those who denied Eusebius' authorship.[8]

One reason why Pasquali's analysis failed to obtain widespread acceptance may be that, although he proved that the *Life* comprises parts of two generically different treatments of Constantine, his reconstruction of the precise process of composition was not convincing. Pasquali held that Eusebius began work on a formal panegyric commemorating the recently deceased monarch as soon as he heard of the death of Constantine (on 22 May 337), and that he composed it according to the rules laid down in rhetorical handbooks for the *basilikos logos*. Then, in the late summer or early autumn, when he learned of the return of Athanasius from exile, Eusebius started to turn the panegyric into a polemical pamphlet which quoted documents and even included criticism of Constantine (in 4.54), but he had not completed either draft before he died in May 338.[9] On this analysis, however, it is hard to see how most of the non-panegyrical sections of the *Life* relate to the "pamphlet"—and Pasquali wrongly classified the second preface (1.11) as deriving from the abandoned panegyric.[10]

1972), despite an acknowledgement that Baynes was wrong to date the defeat of Licinius to 323 (with E. Schwartz) instead of 324 (as argued by O. Seeck and E. Stein).

[5] E.g., D. S. Wallace Hadrill, *Eusebius of Caesarea* (London, 1960) 45: "A. (*sic*) Pasquali had argued in 1910 that the original text of Eusebius was at a later date altered."

[6] F. Winkelmann, "Zur Geschichte des Authentizitätsproblem der Vita Constantini," *Klio* 40 (1962) 187–243, at 208–210.

[7] F. Winkelmann, *Eusebius Werke* 1 (*GCS* 1975) xlix–xxx; T. D. Barnes, "Two Speeches by Eusebius," *Greek, Roman and Byzantine Studies* 18 (1977) 341–345; "Panegyric, History and Hagiography in Eusebius' *Life of Constantine*," *The Making of Orthodoxy. Essays in honour of Henry Chadwick*, ed. R. Williams (Cambridge, 1989) 94–123, at 98–102.

[8] Thus S. Calderone, "Il pensiero politico di Eusebio di Cesarea," *I cristiani e l'impero nel IV secolo*, ed. G. Bonamente and A. Nestori (Università degli Studi di Macerata: Pubblicazioni della Facoltà di Letter e Filosofia 47, 1988) 50: "il ben noto attacco, da Crivellucci a Pasquali a Grégoire, contro l'autenticità della Vita Constantini."

[9] *Hermes* 46 (1910) 384: "ein stilgerechtes Enkomion . . . ein zur Lektüre bestimmtes Enkomion"; 385: "das Encomium bekam einen immer stärkeren Anstrich von Pamphlet."

[10] *Hermes* 46 (1910) 384.

Closer to the truth, but still far from satisfactory, is the analysis of the *Life* into a panegyric and a biography.[11] Parts of the *Life* are indeed readily identifiable as imperial panegyric, but, since it is panegyric of a dead emperor, the genre should be defined as an *epitaphios logos*, which the writers of rhetorical handbooks recognised as a separate sub-genre closely akin to and observing the same rules of composition as the encomium of a living person.[12] More serious, the other concept in the *Life* can hardly be an imperial biography, a life of the recently deceased emperor, for two reasons. First, the *Life of Constantine*, as Wilamowitz crisply stated, "neither is nor claims to be a life."[13] Second, ancient panegyric and ancient biography were not in fact distinct literary genres. Their similarities were recognised in Greek literature from Xenophon's *Agesilaus* and Isocrates' *Evagoras* onward,[13] and Polybius drew an explicit contrast between the favourable presentation of his hero which had been appropriate in his *Life of Philopoemen* and the impartiality required of him when he was writing history rather than biography:

ὥσπερ γὰρ ἐκεῖνος ὁ τρόπος[15] ὑπάρχων ἐγκωμιαστικός, ἀπῄτει τὸν κεφαλαιώδη καὶ μετ' αὐξήσεως τῶν πράξεων ἀπολογισμόν, οὕτως ὁ τῆς ἱστορίας, κοινὸς ὢν ἐπαίνου καὶ ψόγου, ζητεῖ τὸν ἀληθῆ καὶ τὸν μετ' ἀποδείξεως καὶ τῶν ἑκάστοις παρεπομένων συλλογισμῶν.

Just as that genre, being encomiastic by nature, demanded a summary account with amplification of his deeds, so the genre of history, which distributes praise and blame impartially, demands a true account supported by reasoning and the considerations accompanying each action. (10.21.8 = *FGrH* 173 F 1)[16]

[11]Recently reiterated by R. Leeb, *Konstantin und Christus. Die Verchristlichung der imperialen Repräsentation unter Konstantin dem Grossen als Speigel seiner Kirchenpolitik und seines Selbstverständnisses als christlicher Kaiser* (*Arbeiten zur Kirchengeschichte* 58, 1992) 172: "Sie vereinigt Elemente des Panegyrikos (βασιλικὸς λόγος) und der Biographie, ist sozusagen eine 'Mischform'." The analysis in *Constantine and Eusebius* (Cambridge, Mass., 1981) 265–271, more cautiously identified the two components of the *Life* as a formal panegyric and "an account of Constantine's religious activities illustrated by documents quoted in their entirety" or "something which more closely resembled biography."

[12]Menander Rhetor, ed. D. A. Russell and N. G. Wilson (Oxford, 1981), 76–95 (*basilikos logos*), 171–179 (*epitaphios logos*). Note that Libanius entitled his long panegyric of the dead Julian ἐπιτάφιος ἐπὶ Ἰουλιανῷ (*Orat.* 18).

[13]U. von Wilamowitz-Moellendorf, "Ein Bruchstück aus der Schrift des Porphyrius gegen die Christen," *ZNW* 1 (1900) 101–105, at 105 n. 1: "die Schrift εἰς Κωνσταντῖνον, die ein βίος weder heisst noch ist."

[13]See, in general, W. Kroll, *RE*, Supp. 7 (1940) 1128–1135; G. Avenarius, *Lukians Schrift zur Geschichtsschreibung* (Diss. Frankfurt, pub. Meisenheim am Glan, 1956) 13–16, 157–163.

[15]S. A. Naber, "Polybiana," *Mnemosyne* 6 (1857) 113–137, 225–258, 341–363, at 244, comparing 1.2.8, 9.1.4, 29.6a.4, 39.1a.4. The ms. reading τόπος was retained by the Teubner editor T. Büttner-Wobst, *Polybii Historiae* 3 (Leipzig, 1893), 85.

[16]The text is quoted from the recent Budé edition by E. Foulon, *Polybe: Histoires* 8 (Paris, 1990) 78, while my English translation reflects both Foulon's French version and

4   THE TWO DRAFTS OF EUSEBIUS' *LIFE OF CONSTANTINE*

Since the two literary genres are so similar, large-scale panegyric cannot be distinguished from small-scale biography on grounds of either content or literary style.

The preceding essay in the present volume argued that the two literary genres which can be detected in the *Life of Constantine* are not a panegyric and a biography, but a panegyric commemorating the recently deceased Constantine which Eusebius drafted shortly after the emperor's death on 22 May 337 and a treatment of Constantine's religious policies in the style of the *Ecclesiastical History*, which Eusebius began as a continuation of his earlier work c. 325, laid aside before 330, then resumed shortly before his own death in May 339. The essay addressed itself to the task of assigning passages of the *Life* to one draft or the other (or, occasionally, to the posthumous editor who must be postulated), but the analysis was presented in several stages and unsystematically, and by an oversight it omitted the greater part of Book Three. The present paper sets out to repair that omission, and provides a schematic summary of the analysis argued for the whole *Life*. It also comments on two recent discussions of specific problems in the *Life* whose conclusions, if valid, would tend to undermine the overall interpretation of both the *Life* and of Constantine propounded in this volume and elsewhere.

II

Book Three begins with a panegyrical *synkrisis* of Constantine to Licinius (1–3). Then, after a transitional chapter added by the editor (4),[17] it turns to the Council of Nicaea, which is treated at some length (5–21). The rest of the book may be analysed as follows:

22 + 24 Letters written by Constantine after the council.
          24 follows on 22, with τούτοις in 24.1 referring back to the letters of 22 rather than the γραφή of 23. In 24.2 Eusebius declines to include the text of these letters. The sentence is correctly rendered as: "il faudrai avoir le temps de réunir les lois dans un recueil particulier pour ne pas romper le cours de notre histoire" by M. J. Rondeau, who was preparing a new edition with French translation for the series *Sources chrétiennes* with C. Piétri before the latter's death.[18]

---

the discussion of the passage by F. W. Walbank, *Polybius* 2 (Oxford, 1967) 221–223. It diverges widely from the Loeb translation of W. R. Paton, *Polybius: The Histories* (London, 1925) 155.

[17]To the linguistic arguments adduced in the preceding essay (XI 100, 118 n. 26) may be added the fact that Eusebius avoids the adjective φρενοβλαβής (only *PE* 13.18.16, in a quotation from Philo, *De specialibus legibus* 1.20), even though he uses the corresponding noun φρενοβλάβεια ten times.

[18]See C. Piétri, "Constantin en 324. Propagande et théologie impériales d'après les documents de la Vita Constantini," *Crise et redressement dans les provinces européennes*

In the main clause, one should read σχολῆς δ'ἂν δέοιτο with Heikel in place of the transmitted γένοιτο, which Winkelmann retains. In the subordinate clause, the phrase τὸ σῶμα τῆς παρούσης ... ἱστορίας should not be rendered lamely as "the body of our present history": σῶμα is virtually a literary technical term,[19] so that L. Tartiglia is correct to translate it into Italian as "la trama di questa nostra storia."[20]

23   Constantine's presence at the Council of Nicomedia, which met in December 327.[21]

25–39 The finding of the holy cross and the construction of the Church of the Holy Sepulchre.

These chapters form a connected, coherent and internally consistent narrative, and their introductory phrase (25.1: τούτων δ'ὧδε ἐχόντων) looks back to the harmony achieved at the Council of Nicaea in 325 (5–21). Moreover, the discovery to which the letter of Constantine to Macarius, the bishop of Jerusalem, alludes (30.1, 4) probably occurred in the autumn of 326.[22]

40   The decoration of the Church of the Holy Sepulchre

This chapter declines to provide the detailed description of the church which has in fact just been given in 35–39. It appears, therefore, to be an alternative to these chapters—and it may be suspected that the back-reference in its opening words (τόνδε μὲν οὖν τὸν νεών) owes something to the editor.

41–42 and 43–47.3

Two parallel accounts of Helena's visit to Palestine in 326/7 and her foundation of the Churches of the Nativity in Bethlehem and of the Ascension on the Mount of Olives.[23]

47.4   Transition

48–50 Construction in Constantinople, Nicomedia and Antioch.

---

de l'empire romain (milieu du IIIe au milieu de IVe siècle ap. J. C.), ed. E. Frézouls (Strasbourg, 1983) 63–90, at 70. On the same page, Piétri explicitly states that the division into books is "postérieure à Eusèbe" (70 n. 30).

[19] G. Avenarius, *Lukians Schrift* (1956) 105–113.

[20] L. Tartiglia, *Eusebio di Cesarea: Sulla Vita di Costantino* (*Quaderni di* KOINΩNIA 8, 1984) 137.

[21] *The New Empire of Diocletian and Constantine* (Cambridge, Mass., 1982) 77.

[22] See my review (*JEH*, forthcoming) of S. Borgehammar, *How the Holy Cross was Found. From Event to Medieval Legend* (Bibliotheca Theologiae Practicae / Kyrkovetenskapliga studier 47, 1991) and J. W. Drijvers, *Helena Augusta. The Mother of Constantine the Great and the Legend of Her Finding of the True Cross* (Brill's Studies in Intellectual History 27, 1992).

[23] On Eusebius' presentation of the building of these churches, see recently P. W. L. Walker, *Holy City, Holy Places? Christian Attitudes to Jerusalem and the Holy Land in the Fourth Century* (Oxford, 1990) 184–194. The *Panegyric of Constantine* groups them with the Church of the Holy Sepulchre as a triad of "three sites revered for mystical caves" (9.15–17).

6   THE TWO DRAFTS OF EUSEBIUS' *LIFE OF CONSTANTINE*

51–53 The new church at the Oak of Mamre.

54–58 Measures against "the superstitious error of the pagans," partly based on the *Panegyric of Constantine* delivered in Constantinople in July 336 (54.4–55.5 < *Laus Constantini* 8.1–7).[24]

59–62 Constantine's intervention when an attempt was made to elect Eusebius bishop of Antioch (in 328).[25]

63–66.2 The treatment of schismatics as illustrated by Constantine's letter "to the heretics" (325/6).

Both logically and chronologically (63.1: ἔνθεν μεταβάς) this section should immediately follow the Council of Nicaea (5–21). In 66.1/2 Eusebius describes the effects of the law against heretics: when it produced both genuine and pretended converts from heresy to orthodoxy (66.1), the leaders of the churches rejected the false converts, but admitted those with a genuine change of heart into their congregations after an appropriate period of penitence (66.2).

66.3   After a transition marked by a phrase which Eusebius uses often (ταῦτα μὲν οὖν), the text turns to an entirely different subject from that of 66.1/2—the readmission of those who, though advocating no impious teachings, had been extruded from the church through the fault of schismatics. Eusebius alludes obliquely but unmistakeably to the readmission of Arius to communion at the Council of Nicomedia in December 327: the clause τὴν μητέρα τὴν ἐκκλησίαν ἐπεγίνωσκον echoes the letter which Arius and Euzoius wrote to Constantine in the autumn of 327 affirming their orthodoxy and requesting the emperor's good offices in reuniting them to their mother, the church (Opitz, *Urkunde* 30.5: ἐνοῦσθαι ἡμᾶς ... τῇ μητρὶ ἡμῶν, τῇ ἐκκλησίᾳ δηλάδη).

The editor has mistakenly combined two fragments on different subjects into a single chapter and provided a chapter-heading ("How, when illegal books were found in their possession, many of the heretics returned to the catholic church") which summarises only the first part of the chapter (66.1/2).

---

[24] The textual similarities between the *Theophany* and the *Panegyric* imply that the passages in the *Life* which closely resemble *Panegyric* are in fact transcribed and adapted from it, not vice versa: see H. Gressmann, *Studien zu Eusebs Theophanie* (*Texte und Untersuchungen* 23.3, 1903); *Eusebius Werke* 3.2 (*GCS* 1904) xii*–xx*; I. A. Heikel, *Kritische Beiträge zu den Constantin-Schriften des Eusebius* (*Texte und Untersuchungen* 36.4, 1911) 81–97; T. D. Barnes, *Constantine* (1981) 186–188.

[25] T. G. Elliott, "Constantine and 'the Arian reaction after Nicaea'," *JEH* 43 (1992) 169–194, at 174, dates this council to 327 and the earlier Council of Antioch which deposed Eustathius to 326. His argument rests explicitly on dating the Council of Serdica to 342 instead of 343: in favour of the latter date, see now *Athanasius and Constantius. Theology and Politics in the Constantinian Empire* (Cambridge, Mass., 1993), Chapters 7–9.

III

The following overall schematic analysis of the *Life of Constantine* may now be offered. It assigns the whole of the *Life* to its three constituent parts, viz. (A) the unfinished funeral speech of summer 337, (B) the continuation of the *Ecclesiastical History* begun c. 325, then abandoned but resumed in the autumn of 337 or later, and (C) the additions of the editor who published the *Life* after Eusebius died on 30 May 339:

(A)	(B)	(C)
		κεφάλαια
1.1–9	1.10–11	
1.12–25[26]	1.26–46	
1.47	1.48–59.1	?first sentence of 1.55.1 (τοιαῦται Λικινίου αἱ διατάξεις)
		1.59.2[27]
	2.1–12	
2.13	2.14–19	
2.20–22		?last sentence of 2.22 (ἀλλ' οἱ μὲν ὧδε ἐφρόνουν)
	2.23–73	
3.1–3		3.4
	3.5–39	?the opening words of 3.40 (τόνδε μὲν οὖν)
3.40–42	3.43–66.2	
3.66.3		
4.1–7	4.8–14	
4.15–17	4.18–20	
4.21	4.22	
4.23	4.24	
4.25–26.1	4.26.2–27.3[1]	
4.27.3[2]–28	4.29–30	
4.31	4.32–37	
4.38–39	4.40–52	

[26] On 1.12, see now M. J. Hollerich, "Myth and History in Eusebius's *De Vita Constantini: Vit. Const.* 1.12 in its Contemporary Setting," *HTR* 82 (1989) 421–445.

[27] Apart from Maxentius, whom Constantine defeated in 312 and whom Eusebius needed to identify by name for his eastern readers, Licinius is the only villain named in the *Life*, although Eusebius freqently uses descriptive periphrases to refer to Diocletian, Maximian, Galerius, Maximinus and Licinius himself: hence I suspect the hand of the editor in these two passages. The editor may also have added the name of Helena in 3.43.4 and the names of Constantine's sons, Constantinus, Constantius and Constans, in 4.40.1, where the explanation of each of the three names renders their actual occurrence otiose and even jarring.

8   THE TWO DRAFTS OF EUSEBIUS' *LIFE OF CONSTANTINE*

4.53	4.54	4.55[1]

4.55[2]-76

Constantine, *Speech to the Assembly of the Saints*
Panegyric of Constantine
Treatise on the Church of the Holy Sepulchre

IV

R. M. Errington has recently argued that, although Constantine did in fact prohibit sacrifice in 324/5, the law reported by Eusebius (*Life* 2.45.1) "can only have had a validity of at most a few months," since it was soon superseded and nullified by Constantine's letter to the eastern provincials (quoted in 2.47–60), which "insisted firmly on peacefulness and universal toleration."[28] Errington's argument explicitly sets out to combine and reconcile what he regards as valid in the present writer's interpretation of Constantine[29] with the traditional picture of a Constantine tolerant in religious matters as restated by H. A. Drake.[30] His case rests upon the explicit assumption that the *Life of Constantine* "is after all not a history and does not aspire to historical canons of accuracy" (315). It also has two other, equally fatal flaws.

(1) Errington takes Constantine's reference to "the shrines of falsehood" (2.56.2: τὰ τῆς ψευδολογίας τεμένη) which pagans are allowed to retain as metaphorical, not concrete, as referring to "the total complex of paganism" rather than to the temples and sacred enclosures of the traditional gods of the Greco-Roman world. The argument as stated considers only the transmitted Greek version of Constantine's words. But the whole document is translated from Latin, so that any precise linguistic argument must take account of the presumed or probable Latin original— which was surely *fana falsitatis*. Errington does not consider whether this (or any other Latin phrase which might lie behind the Greek translation) can bear the metaphorical interpretation which he applies to the phrase τὰ τῆς ψευδολογίας τεμένη. The *Thesaurus Linguae Latinae* registers only one metaphorical use of the noun *fanum*—by Zeno of Verona on the repentant sinner at his baptism (2.29 [2.42].3 [*CCL* 23.203]: quem noveris idololatriae

---

[28]R. M. Errington, "Constantine and the Pagans," *Greek, Roman and Byzantine Studies* 29 (1988) 309–318.

[29]Especially, on this issue, *Constantine* (1981) 210/1, 254/5; "Constantine's Prohibition of Pagan Sacrifice," *AJP* 105 (1984) 69–72.

[30]*AJP* 103 (1982) 462–466, reviewing *Constantine* (1981); "Suggestions of Date in Constantine's *Oration to the Saints*," *AJP* 106 (1985) 335–349; "What Eusebius Knew: the Genesis of the *Vita Constantini*," *CP* 83 (1988) 20–38. Errington also appeals to Averil Cameron, *JRS* 73 (1983) 189.

fanum, gaudeas dei templum).[31] There seems to be no parallel to the use which Errington's interpretation requires: therefore, until the contrary is proved, Constantine's words must be taken to refer to pagan temples and shrines.

(2) Although Errington correctly breaks with scholarly tradition and refuses to believe Libanius' claim, advanced in 386 in the speech *Pro Templis*, that Constantine made no changes in the "normal ritual programme" of the temples and that "Constantine took no action against sacrifice" (*Orat.* 30.6, 37), he fails to discuss a very relevant passage in the same writer's *Autobiography*.[32] Libanius reports that during his stay in Greece in the late 330s he struck up a friendship with Crispinus of Heraclea, whose uncle

consorted more with gods than with men on earth: despite the law which banned it and the death penalty inflicted on any who dared to do so, he yet went his way through life in the company of the gods, and laughed to scorn that evil law and its sacrilegious enactor. (*Orat.* 1.27)[33]

It is wrong to detect an anachronistic reference to the prohibition of sacrifice issued to the *vicarius Italiae* by Constans in 341 (*CTh* 16.10.1).[34] That interpretation can only be described as a *petitio principii*: in its context, the plain meaning of Libanius' remark is that the law prohibiting sacrifice and the consultation of oracles which Eusebius reports that Constantine issued shortly after October 324 was legally operative in the late 330s.

v

T. G. Elliott has recently discussed a number of acknowledged misrepresentations in the *Life*, such as Eusebius' acceptance of Constantine's claim to be much younger than he really was, which is reflected in contemporary panegyric,[35] in order to accuse Eusebius of "a willingness to invent in order to mislead" in the closing chapters of Book Three:

Eusebius' chronological displacement, his inadequate treatment of the provision regarding the Novatians, and his suppression of the ban on Arius' books indicate that he tried to mislead his readers about this matter. He selected for

---

[31] *TLL* 6 (1912–1926) 271–275.

[32] Brought into the argument in the paper "Christians and Pagans in the Reign of Constantius," *L'Église et l'empire au IVe siècle (Entretiens sur l'Antiquité Classique* 34, 1989) 301–337, at 330. Errington's article was completed in November 1988.

[33] Translation of A. F. Norman, *Libanius' Autobiography (Oration I)* (London, 1965) 21.

[34] As Norman, *ib.* 155: "this law may be *CTh* 16.10.2 of A.D. 341."

[35] *New Empire* (1982) 39–42.

XII

quotation a letter about an edict which did not mention Arians simply because it antedated Nicaea, inserted it into his text in such a way as to imply that Constantine had no policy against Arianism after Nicaea, and claimed
that he had banned the books of the named heretics, instead of those of
Arius.[36]

The argument again rests upon a vulnerable assumption—in this case, that
Eusebius himself is responsible for the order and arrangement of material in
the *Life*. Something specific can also be said about three aspects of Elliott's
indictment.

First, the chronology of the end of Book Three of the *Life* is indeed
confused. For the text passes from Eusebius' refusal to allow himself to be
elected bishop of Antioch in 328 (60–62) to the measures against Novatianists, Valentinians, Marcionites, Paulianists, Montanists and other heretics
(64–65), which must be earlier than the imperial constitution of 25 September 326 exempting the Novatianists from them (*CTh* 15.5.2),[37] yet a linking
chapter implies that the edict against the heretics is later than the letters
quoted immediately before (63.1: ἐπεὶ δὲ ... ἔνθεν μεταβὰς ἄλλο τι γένος ἀθέων
ἀνδρῶν ...). But the unfinished state of the *Life* makes it hazardous to infer that Eusebius intended 3.64–65 to stand where it does, still less to infer
that he chose the present arrangement of material in order deliberately to
mislead.

Second, it is true that Eusebius makes no mention of the later ban on
Arius' writings (Opitz, *Urkunde* 33: 333). But that is merely one of a long
series of omissions of the reverses and humiliations suffered by Eusebius
himself and his ecclesiastical allies: most obviously, the account of the
Council of Nicaea in the *Life* not only suppresses the Council of Antioch
in the winter of 324/5 which excommunicated Eusebius but also omits the
council's condemnation of Arius.[38]

Third, Elliott's charge that Constantine did not in fact ban the books
of the heretics named in his letter because "there is no other evidence of a
Constantinian ban on the books of a heretic" apart from Arius raises a real
and serious question. But what Eusebius quotes is a letter of Constantine to
the heretics themselves, not the edict or letter to officials which gave precise
legal instructions. Eusebius himself refers to the two separate documents
when he distinguishes between (1) "an order sent to the governors in every
province" which drove out "all the race of such men," and (2) the "lifegiving
lesson" (ζωοποιὸν διδασκαλίαν) which Constantine addressed in addition to
the law to the heretics urging them to repent of their errors (3.63.3). It

[36]T. G. Elliott, "Eusebian Frauds in the *Vita Constantini*," *Phoenix* 45 (1991) 162–
171, esp. 168 (the passage quoted).
[37]*Constantine* (1981) 224.
[38]*Constantine* (1981) 270/1.

seems hypercritical to deny that Eusebius correctly reports the content of the former document, which he knew but did not quote.[39]

VI

The analysis of the *Life of Constantine* propounded in the present and the preceding essay was anticipated by Friedhelm Winkelmann and L. Tertiglia. In the long preface to his edition of the *Life*, the former observed that the documents and the chronological arrangement of the major part of the *Life* show that the author was a historian and he correctly adduced the final books of the *Ecclesiastical History* as its literary model.[40] In the introduction to his Italian translation, the latter identified the components of the *Life* as encomium, biography and history, noted that more than one passage shows "l'atteggiamento dello storico," and that "alcune parti della *Vita Constantini* assumono un andamento storiografico piuttosto che biografico" and use the same historical method as the *Ecclesiastical History*.[41] It will be appropriate, therefore, to conclude with the verdict on the *Life* which Tartiglia quotes from Franchi de' Cavalieri: it is tendentious, passionate, partial, deliberately lacunose, but not knowingly mendacious.[42]

---

[39] H. Dörries, *Das Selbstzeugnis Kaiser Konstantins* (*Abh. Göttingen*, Phil.-hist. Klasse³ 34, 1954) 82/3, cf. Valesius' note on the passage, reproduced at *PG* 20.1144 n. 15.

[40] F. Winkelmann, *Eusebius Werke* 1 (*GCS* 1975) li–lii.

[41] L. Tartiglia, *Sulla Vita di Costantino* (Naples, 1984) 7–13, esp. 11/12, noting that Eusebius calls his work ἱστορία (3.24.2, 51.2) and πραγματεία (1.11.1).

[42] P. Franchi de' Cavalieri, *Constantiniana* (*Studi e Testi* 171, 1953) 20: "io stimo la *Vita Constantini* qualche cosa di mezzo fra la biografia e il panegirico, in altri termini, una narrazione storica tendenziosa, passionata, parziale, deliberatamente lacunosa; ma non vedo motivi per ritenerla menzognera, *scientemente menzognera*."

PRAETORIAN PREFECTS, 337-361

The nature of the praetorian prefecture in the reign of Constantine has been a matter of
scholarly disagreement, which epigraphic discoveries continue to clarify.[1] It can now be
regarded as established that Constantine did not create the four regional prefectures of the late
fourth century as Zosimus alleged (2.33.1-2), repeating the views and probably the words of
Eunapius.[2] The prefectures were created piecemeal under Constans and Constantius,[3] but
the system had not yet crystallised into its final form by 361, when the latter died. For,
whereas Claudius Mamertinus, the consul of 363, was honoured as 'per Italiam ac Inlyricum
praefecto praetorio' under the emperor Julian (ILS 755: Concordia), his colleague Salutius
Secundus was not praetorian prefect of the East (as is often assumed),[4] but an old-style
prefect who accompanied the emperor wherever he went: Ammianus styles him pointedly
and correctly 'praefectus Salutius praesens' (23.5.6).

1. The nature of the prefecture, 335-361
Discussion of the praetorian prefects of the sons of Constantine must start from the
college of five prefects attested by a pair of dedications to Constantinus Caesar from near

---

[1] See A.Chastagnol. 'Les préfets du prétoire de Constantin', REA 70,1968,321-354 (on the importance of
inscriptions published since 1960); L'évolution politique, sociale et économique du monde romain 284-363,
Paris 1982,249-253; 'Les inscriptions africaines des préfets du prétoire de Constantin', L'Africa romana. Atti
del III convegno di studio, Sassari, 13-15 dicembre 1985, Sassari 1986,263-273 (principally on the
significance of AE 1981.878); 'Un nouveau préfet de Dioclétien: Aurelius Hermogenianus', ZPE
9,1989,165-68.

[2] The New Empire of Diocletian and Constantine, Cambridge, Mass. 1982, Chap. VIII, cf.
A.Chastagnol, L'évolution, 1982,251.
A college of five prefects is attested while Domitius Zenophilus was proconsul of Africa (AE 1981.878
[Ain Rchine]), i.e., between 328 and 332 (New Empire 1982,106,171). The names of the first three prefects
are unambiguously preserved on the stone, viz., (1) Valerius Maximus, consul in 327, (2) Ju[nius Bassus]
and (3) [F]lavius Ablabius, the consuls of 331. Therefore, since Bassus became prefect several years before
Maximus (New Empire 1982,129,132), the order of names does not reflect simple seniority within the
college. Rather, first come the prefects of consular rank in the chronological order of their consulates, then
prefects who have not been consuls in the order of their appointment as prefects.
The fifth name is totally lost, but the fourth begins with the letters Va[. T.Grünewald, Constantinus
Maxius Augustus, Wiesbaden 1990, 202, on no.133, has recently suggested that he was Valerius Felix. But
Felix only became prefect of Africa in 333, i.e., after Bassus had left office (New Empire, 1982,133). Hence,
unless the college contains an otherwise unknown prefect, the fourth and fifth names should be those of (4)
Evagrius, whose nomen is unknown but who is attested as praetorian prefect in 326, 329, 331 and 336, and
(5) L.Papius Pacatianus, who had probably been prefect since 329 (cf. New Empire, 1982,131/2, 135).
Moreover, since Evagrius never held the consulate, whereas Pacatianus became consul on 1 January 332, the
fact that Evagrius precedes Pacatianus implies that the inscription cannot be later than 331.

[3] 'Regional Prefectures', Bonner Historia-Augusta-Colloquium 1984/1985 (1987), 13-23.

[4] E.g., PLRE 1. 814-817, 1050.

Carthage and Antioch.[5] The African inscription has been known since 1924 and has oft
been dated to 337: the name of the third prefect, erased on this stone but now attested by t
parallel text from Antioch published in 1985, fixes the date as earlier than 9 October 33(
The college is as follows: -

(1) L.Pap(ius) Pacatianus, consul in 332, otherwise attested as prefect and in some w
responsible for the city of Rome between April 332 and April 335;

(2) Fl(avius) Ablabius, consul in 331, attested as prefect from 329 to 337 and active
court or in Constantinople;

(3) Val(erius) Felix, praetorian prefect of the African diocese from 333 to 336;

(4) C.Annius Tiberianus, praetorian prefect in Gaul;

(5) Nestorius Timonianus, otherwise unknown.

Publishing the Antioch text, D.Feissel argued that the occasion of the joint dedication of t
prefects to Constantinus was probably his vicennalia as Caesar on 1 March 336.[7] Th
hypothesis has the unwelcome consequence that the Caesar Dalmatius, who was proclaim
on 18 September 335, had no praetorian prefect, even though literary sources imply that
was assigned a portion of the Empire to supervise in the same way as the other Caesars.[8]
would be preferable, therefore, to identify the occasion of the dedications as the marriage
Constantinus, which probably took place in the summer of 335.[9] (The presumed attestati
of Annius Tiberianus as vicarius Hispaniarum on 15 July 335 is more than doubtful on oth
grounds.)[10] In that case, the functions of the prefects in 335 can be identified as follows: -

(1) L.Papius Pacatianus, prefect of Constans;

(2) Flavius Ablabius, prefect of Constantine;

(3) Valerius Felix, prefect in Africa (and responsible for the dedication at Tubemuc);

(4) C.Annius Tiberianus, prefect of Constantinus;

(5) Nestorius Timonianus, prefect of Constantius (and responsible for the dedication
Antioch).

Since the order of names must here reflect seniority of appointment within the colleg
Pacatianus must have become prefect before Ablabius, who seems to be first attested on

---

[5] The number of prefects has often been misstated as four: e.g., L.Poinssot and T.Lantier, 'Quatre préf
du prétoire contemporains de Constantin', CRAI 1924,229-233 (the original publication); W.Ensslin, I
22,1954,2430; PLRE 1. 1048; C.Vogler, Constance II et l'administration impériale, Groupe de recherc
d'histoire romaine de l'Université de Strasbourg: Études et travaux 3, Strasbourg 1979,111; A.Demandt, I
Spätantike, Munich 1988,77 n.79.

[6] D.Feissel, Travaux et Mémoires 9,1985,421ff. For other evidence for each of these prefects, N
Empire, 1982,131ff., where a date of 337 for AE 1925.72 = ILT 814 (Tubemuc) is mistakenly assumed.

[7] D.Feissel, Travaux et Mémoires 9,1985,434, cf. L.Poinssot and R.Lantier, CRAI 1924. 232.

[8] Origo Const. Imp. 35; Epit. de Caes. 41.20.

[9] Eusebius, VC 4.49, implies a date before 336. Constantinus was born on 7 August 316: the identity
his wife appears to be unknown (New Empire 1982,44/5).

[10] See New Empire, 1982,145 n.17, arguing that CTh 3.5.6, though published in Spain in 336, m
have been issued to Tiberianus as vicarius Hispaniarum on 15 July 332.

May 329 (CTh 11.27.1[S]). He will have administered Italy (and perhaps part of the Balkans) as a quasi-regional prefect until the Caesar Constans received Italy, Africa and Illyricum to supervise in 335.[11] In 335, therefore, each emperor had a praetorian prefect attached to his person, and there was one additional prefect administering the African provinces.

After Constantine died on 22 May 337, Flavius Ablabius was dismissed, then later put to death (Eunapius, Vit. phil. 6.3.8-13, p.464). The prefect of Dalmatius was presumably killed with him during the summer of 337, and, since there is no good evidence that an African prefecture ever existed under the sons of Constantine, it may be presumed that this prefecture lapsed in 337. The prefects who held office between the proclamation of the sons of Constantine as Augusti on 9 September 337 and the death of Constantius on 3 November 361 fall into two categories: those who were attached to emperors and in effect served as deputy emperors, and those who supervised the administration of a region of the empire.

Constantinus ruled precisely the area of the later Gallic prefecture, viz. Britain, Gaul and Spain, so that his prefect appears to span the two categories of deputy emperor and regional prefect. Between 337 and 340, one prefect of Constantinus is known and the only source to name him describes him as a regional prefect: Paulinus' Vita Ambrosii states that its hero's father was administering the prefecture of the Gauls when his son was born in 339 (2.3).[12] Since Paulinus was writing many years after 340, his description of Ambrosius' title or function may be anachronistic: hence, like Annius Tiberianus before 337, Ambrosius may legitimately be regarded as the praefectus praetorio praesens of Constantinus.

Constantius employed prefects of the old type in the East until 354. The ecclesiastical historian Socrates specifically reports that his prefect Philippus, whom he describes as δευτέρῳ μετὰ βασιλέα χρηματίζοντι, commanded troops in Constantinople in late 344 (HE 2.16.2, 8), and a statue of Philippus as prefect wearing a sword still stood in Chalcedon two centuries later (John Lydus, Mag. 2.9, p.64 Wuensch). Moreover, in 351 Constantius appointed Thalassius to serve the Caesar Gallus as prefect, guide and counsellor, together with the quaestor Montius Magnus (Passio Artemii 12 = Philostorgius, HE 3.26[a]). As Constantius became ruler of the West in stages between 350 and 353, however, he took over the regional prefectures already developed there by his brother Constans, and after 354 he began to extend the system to the eastern empire.

When Constans acquired the territories of Constantinus in 340, he appointed a praetorian prefect to administer them, as may safely be deduced from the fact that he had two prefects in the early 340s. Two colleges of prefects are attested from these years. The earlier (of late 341 or early 342) comprises the following three names:

(1) Antonius Marcellinus, consul in 341;

---

[11] Two of the four constitutions addressed to Pacatianus concern the city of Rome (CTh 14.4.1 [8 March 334]; 8.9.1 [17 April 335]).

[12] For the date, J.R.Palanque, Saint Ambrose et l'empire romain, Paris 1933, 480-482; F.H.Dudden, The Life and Times of St.Ambrose 1, Oxford 1935, 2 n.2.

(2) Domitius Leontius, consul in 344;

(3) Fabius Titianus, consul in 337 (ILS 8944: Traiana in Thrace).

The other college is known from a pair of letters which the prefects jointly wrote to Flavi Felicianus, ex-comes and the priest of Apollo at Delphi, probably in 342:

(1) Fl(avius) Domitius Leontius;

(2) Fabius Titianus;

(3) Furius Placidus, i.e. M.Maecius Memmius Furius Baburius Caecilianus Placidu consul in 343.[13]

In each case, the eastern prefect Leontius has two western colleagues at a time whi Constans was sole emperor of the West. Moreover, a survey of all the known prefects Constans establishes that by c.345 he had three prefects, not merely two, and the eviden indicates that each of the western prefects of the later 340s operated in one of the thr geographical areas of Gaul, Italy and Illyricum.[14]

On the basis of these facts, the genesis of the regional prefectures becomes readi comprehensible in terms of political events and administrative logic. When Consta appointed a second prefect in 340 to supervise the former territories of Constantinus, created the praetorian prefecture of Gaul. By implication, he limited the area in which k existing praetorian prefect normally exercised jurisdiction to Italy, Africa and Illyricum. T third prefect was created during or shortly after Constans' expedition to Britain in the win of 342/3. Henceforward, one praetorian prefect resided in Trier and administered Britai Gaul and Spain, another resided at Sirmium and administered Illyricum, while a third Milan administered Italy and Africa. Thus the first of the four regional prefectures of the la fourth century came into existence in 340 as the result of a sudden and unexpected politic change: the new praetorian prefect of Gaul administered exactly those territories whi Constantinus had ruled as Caesar and then Augustus with a praefectus praetorio praesens his deputy. The decisive step came in 343 or shortly thereafter, when Constans replaced h other praetorian prefect, who presumably still functioned in the old way, with two prefects whom he assigned the civil administration of, respectively, Illyricum and Italy with Africa.

---

[13] Delphi, Inv. nos. 1647, 4077, reported by A.Chastagnol, REA 70,1968,336, from C.Vatin, Delphe l'époque impériale, Diss. Paris 1965,258/9. It is unfortunate that the full text of this pair of inscriptic seems not to have been published, for they show that Felicianus had requested the protection of the prefects avoid harassment in the performance of his priestly duties.

[14] Bonner Historia-Augusta-Colloquium 1984/1985 (1987), 17ff.

[15] Bonner Historia-Augusta-Colloquium 1984/1985 (1987), 21/2.

2. Attested Prefects, 337-361

Since the praetorian prefecture changed greatly between 337 and 361, it would be
isleading to draw up a single list of prefects.[16] The list which follows, therefore, is divided
rst by the type of prefect, then within each category by the emperor served or the region
administered. Where the prefecture itself is unproblematical, mere references or a summary
description will be given, fuller treatment being reserved for those cases where the date or
ature of the prefect's office is not clearly and unambiguously documented.[17]

PREFECTS ATTACHED TO EMPERORS

CONSTANTINUS

39 Ambrosius
    Paulinus, Vita Ambrosii 2.3-4

CONSTANTIUS

38-340 Septimius Acindynus, cos. 340
    Attested on 27 December 338 (CTh 2.6.4) and by papyri with the consular date of 340.[18]

41 or 342-344 Flavius Domitius Leontius, cos. 344
    Leontius is securely attested in the Theodosian Code from 11 May 342 (11.36.6) to 6
uly 344 (13.4.3), but an incomplete or abbreviated subscription may attest Leontius as early
s 11 October 340 (7.9.2S).[19] The inscriptional evidence which records Leontius as prefect
: not dated precisely, but ILS 8944 (Traiana) confirms that he had become prefect by late

---

[16] For earlier lists and discussions, which there would be no point in criticising in detail, H.M.Gwatkin,
tudies of Arianism[2], Cambridge 1900,283-289; J.R.Palanque, Essai sur la préfecture du prétoire au Bas-
empire, Paris 1933,17-36; W.Ensslin, RE 22, 1954, 2431-2434, 2496-2500; J.R.Palanque, 'Les préfets du
rétoire sous les fils de Constantin', Historia 4,1955,257-263; PLRE 1. 1049/50; R.von Haehling, Die
eligionszugehörigkeit der hohen Amtsträger des römischen Reiches seit Constantins I. Alleinherrschaft bis
am Ende der Theodosianischen Dynastie, Bonn 1978,52, 56-64,95,99-101,284/5,290-295,331/2,335-338;
'ogler, Constance, 1979,110-130 (who postulates a separate regional prefecture of Africa from 347 to 355).
here is also much scattered discussion in W.Kuhoff, Studien zur zivilen senatorischen Laufbahn im 4.
ahrhundert n.Chr. Ämter und Amtsinhaber in Clarissimat und Spektabilität, Frankfurt/Bern 1983: note the
assages listed in the index (462/3).

[17] The present reconstruction assumes that Flavius Eugenius, who was honoured as ex praefecto
raetorio, consuli ordinario designato when Constantius and Julian restored his statue in Rome, presumably
a 357 (ILS 1244), was an honorary praetorian prefect, who received the title and rank on or after his
etirement as magister officiorum, as argued by E.Stein, Byzantion 9,1934,331/2. Vogler, Constance,
979,123ff., argues that he governed a separate prefecture of Africa from 12 June 347 to early 350.

[18] R.S.Bagnall, Alan Cameron, S.R.Schwartz and K.A.Worp, Consuls of the Later Roman Empire,
atlanta 1987,215. The anecdote repeated by Augustine, Sermo domini in monte 1.12.50 (PL 34. 1254) both
mplies that Acindynus was a Christian and locates him in Antioch in 340.

[19] CTh 7.9.1 names the consuls of 340: the subscription to 7.9.2 appears to read 'dat. v id. Oct. consss.',
which O.Seeck, Regesten der Kaiser und Päpste für die Jahre 311 bis 476 n.Chr. Vorarbeit zu einer
rosopographie der christlichen Kaiserzeit, Stuttgart 1919,188, expanded to 'conss. s(upra) s(criptis)'.

341 or early 342. (ILS 1234 [Berytus] honours Leontius as both prefect and consul in th lifetime of Constans, i.e., between 344 and 350.)

344-351 Flavius Philippus, cos. 348

The long praetorian prefecture of Flavius Philippus has a meagre and problematic attestation in the Theodosian Code, from 28 July 346 (CTh 11.22.1) to 20 September 34 (3.13.1 + 8.13.1+2).[20] Philippus is comparatively well attested, however, in literar sources, by inscriptions and on papyri with the consular date of 348.[21] The date at which h became prefect can be deduced from Socrates' account of his expulsion of Paul c Constantinople (HE 2.16): the movements of Paul, who was with Athanasius at the court c Constans by the spring of 345 (HE 2.22.5), exclude a date later than the final months c 344.[22] Philippus was still prefect in 351, when Constantius and Gallus honoured him with statue at Chytrae in Cyprus (ILS 738). He died, it appears, shortly before the Battle c Mursa on 28 September 351. The date and circumstances of his death must be inferred from three separate sources which each give part of the story: -

(a) Philippus was 'dismissed from his office with great dishonour, in such a way that h was mocked by those whom he did not wish after becoming a private citizen' and died as a outlaw (Athanasius, Hist.Ar. 7.6);

(b) Constantius sent Philippus to Magnentius as an ambassador: after Magnentiu advanced into Pannonia in the summer of 351, Philippus addressed his troops and almos persuaded them to desert, but Magnentius kept Philippus with him (Zosimus 2.46.2-47.2 48.2, 48.5);

(c) Philippus persuaded Silvanus to desert from Magnentius to Constantius shortly befor the Battle of Mursa (scholiast on Julian, Orat. 2, 97c).[23]

The easiest combination of these three incomplete accounts is to suppose that Philippu: death came about from his abuse of his privileged position as an ambassador. Athanasiu

---

[20] See A.H.M.Jones, 'The Career of Flavius Philippus', Historia 4,1955,229-233. Seeck, Regester 1919,199-200, had emended the date of CTh 11.22.1 as well as those of CTh 8.7.2 and 11.30.20, whos transmitted dates are 3 November 326 and 9 June 340 respectively, to show Philippus as still in office a prefect in 353. Even though Jones expressly observed that Athanasiu, Hist.Ar. 7.6 unambiguously date Philippus' death to 351, Vogler, Constance, 1979, 122,123,129, revives the impossible notion that he wa still alive and in office in 353 (in her view, as prefect of Italy).

[21] For Philippus as consul, Bagnall, Cameron, Schwartz and Worp, Consuls, 1987,230/1. On I.Ephese 41, in which Constantius orders Philippus to be honoured with statues in the cities of Asia, see the origina publication by L.J.Swift and J.H.Oliver, 'Constantius II on Flavius Philippus', AJP 83,1962,247-264.

[22] Athanasius and Constantius. Theology and Politics in the Constantinian Empire, Cambridge, Mass 1993 Chapter X with App.8.

[23] First published in advance of his edition by J.Bidez, REA 27,1925,314. Not noted in the account c his career in PLRE 1. 696/7 - though the entry for Silvanus has it (840/1).

nay seem to imply dismissal and execution by Constantius, but his words will also cover an attempt by Magnentius to seize Philippus and his subsequent death in flight.[24]

etween 351 and 354 Maiorinus
   Prefect before 357 (Libanius, Ep. 560, cf. 1510, written in 365): probably identical with he praetorian prefect Maiorinus attested by a group of inscriptions from a family tomb of the sixth century in the Trachonitis (W.H.Waddington, Inscriptions grecques et latines de la Syrie, Paris 1870, nos.2474-2477, republished with the correct identification of Maiorinus, by L.Robert, Hellenica 11/12, Paris 1960,302-305).[25]

CONSTANS

340-342 Antonius Marcellinus, cos. 341
   Attested by the Theodosian Code on 29 April (11.12.1) and 28 June 340 (6.22.3). Still in office in late 341 or early 342 (ILS 8944).

342-344 M.Maecius Memmius Furius Baburius Caecilianus Placidus, cos. 343
   Attested as prefect from 342[26] to 28 May 344 (CTh 12.1.37). An inscription which records Placidus' career confirms that he was already prefect when he became ordinary consul on 1 January 343 (ILS 1231: Puteoli). During the last part of his tenure, perhaps from 343 and into 345, Placidus was probably prefect in or of Italy.[27]

MAGNENTIUS

350 Nunechius
   cυγκλητικὸc ὕπαρχοc, sent by Magnentius with proposals for peace to Constantius, who arrested him (Petrus Patricius, frag. 16, cf. Zonaras 13.8). The nature of Nunechius' prefecture is totally unclear.

GALLUS

351-353 Thalassius
   Appointed as praetorian prefect in 351 and given the task of supervising the Caesar Gallus together with the quaestor Montius Magnus (Passio Artemii 12 = Philostorgius, HE 3.26a).[28] He was in Antioch in 352/3 (Libanius, Ep. 16) and is styled praefectus praetorio

---

[24] PLRE 1. 697 assumes that Philippus was dismissed and disgraced by Constantius and construes I.Ephesos 41 as attesting his posthumous rehabilitation. That is pure fantasy: the present tenses in Constantius' praise of Philippus indicate that he was then alive and in office, cf. H.Wankel, Die Inschriften von Ephesos 1a, Bonn 1979,258.
[25] The identification was also made independently in PLRE 1. 537/8.
[26] Above, at n.13.
[27] PLRE 1. 705.
[28] On the latter, see PLRE 1. 535/6.

praesens by Ammianus (14.1.10), who records his death in office in 353 (14.7.9), which occurred after 3 July (CTh 16.8.7^S: 357 mss.).

353-354 Domitianus
Successor of Thalassius, lynched by the troops in Antioch after provocative behaviour towards Gallus (Ammianus 14.7.9-11.17).[29]

REGIONAL PREFECTS

GAUL

341 Aconius Catullinus, cos. 349[30]
CTh 8.2.1 = 12.1.31 (issued at Lauriacum on 24 June 341). It should be noted that the functions of Catullinus and Marcellinus are not expressly attested: the Prosopography of the Later Roman Empire argues that Marcellinus, Catullinus and Furius Placidus were successors in the same prefecture of Italy and Illyricum.[31]

342-350 Fabius Titianus, cos. 337
Appointed prefect no later than 342 (ILS 8944), Titianus served Constans in Gaul until the very end of his reign (Jerome, Chronicle 236^d: 'apud Gallias'; CTh 9.24.2 [12 November 349]), when he transferred his allegiance to Magnentius, who made him praefectus urbi at Rome on 27 February 350 (Chr.min. 1. 66).[32]

?353-354 Vulcacius Rufinus, cos. 347
CTh 9.23.1^S (8 March 354: 356 mss.); Ammianus 14.10.4 (dismissed in spring 354).

354-355 C.Ceionius Rufius Volusianus
Zosimus 2.55.3 (summer 354); CTh 11.34.2 (1 January 355); CJ 6.22.6 (18 February); CTh 3.12.3 (30 April); 11.30.26 + 36.12 (29/30 July); Ammianus 15.5.4-5, 13 (dismissed in 355).[33]

---

[29] For other sources which record his death with less precise detail, PLRE 1.262.
[30] CIL 6. 1780 establishes his nomen as Aconius, not Aco (as is commonly assumed), cf. Bagnall Cameron, Schwartz and Worp, Consuls, 1987, 232.
[31] PLRE 1. 1049.
[32] Also attested as praetorian prefect on 30 June 343 (CTh 12.1.36) and probably on 27 May 349 (CTh 7.1.2 + 8.7.3, cf. Jones, Historia 4,1955,232/3).
[33] Also perhaps CTh 13.3.1 (321 or 324 mss.), cf. JRS 65,1975,47.

355-357 Honoratus
Libanius, Ep. 386 (written in 358); Jerome, Chronicle 241[e] (both retrospective references to Honoratus as prefect of Gaul). He had been comes Orientis in 353 (Libanius, Ep. 386; Ammianus 14.1.3, 7.2).

357-360 Flavius Florentius, cos. 361
Ammianus 16.12.14; 17.3.2-6; 18.2.4; 20.4.2-8, 8.20; Julian, Ep.ad Ath. 280a-c; Libanius, Orat. 18.84-85.

360-361 Nebridius
Quaestor sacri palatii of Julian as Caesar, appointed praetorian prefect by Constantius to succeed Florentius (Ammianus 20.9.5, 8; 21.1.4, 5.11-12, 8.1; Libanius, Ep. 1315).

361 Decimius Germanianus
Acting prefect (Ammianus 21.8.1).

361-363 Flavius Sallustius, cos. 363
Ammianus 21.8.1; 23.5.4.

ITALY
343-c.345 M.Maecius Memmius Furius Baburius Caecilianus Placidus, cos. 343
CTh 12.1.37 (28 May 344).

c. 345-347 Vulcacius Rufinus, cos. 347
Rufinus served continuously as prefect from before his consular year until 354, and he began as prefect in or of Italy (CTh 9.23.1[S] [received at Cirta on 8 March 346: the mss. have 356]; 11.1.6 [issued in 353 or 354, but referring to a decision concerning Italy made by Rufinus as praetorian prefect under Constans];[34] ILS 1237 [Rome, but implying activity at Ravenna]). However, there is no evidence for the precise beginning or end of his Italian prefecture.

350 Anicetus
Praetorian prefect of Magnentius, Anicetus resisted Nepotianus in Rome in June 350 and was killed (Zosimus 2.43.3; Victor, Caes. 42.6, where the transmitted text has urbi praefecto in error).

---

[34] On this constitution, where 'iuxta statutum Constantii fratris mei' must be emended to 'Constantis', see PLRE 1. 782.

354 Maecilius Hilarianus, cos. 332
  CTh 6.4.3 + 4^S (March 354: 339 mss.); 6.4.7^S (14 March 354: 353 mss.).

355-361 Flavius Taurus, cos. 361
  Praef(ectus) praet(orio) per Italiam atque Africam (AE 1934.159: Rome, between 364 an(
367) from at least 6 April 355 (CTh 7.4.2) to 29 August 361 (CTh 8.4.7 + 12.1.49). In th(
summer of 361 Taurus fled to Illyricum, then to Constantius (Ammianus 21.9.4; Passi(
Artemii 19 = Philostorgius, HE 6.5^a; Zosimus 3.10.4, cf. Julian, Ep.ad Ath. 286b).

PRAEFECTI PRAETORIO ET URBIS

347, June 12-349, April 8 Ulpius Limenius
  Chronographer of 354 (Chr.min. 1. 68); CTh 9.21.6 (12 February 348); 9.17.2 (2(
March 349).

349, April 8-May 19 Eustathius
  An imperial constitution with the transmitted date of 8 March 349 is addressed t(
Eustathius as praetorian prefect and was subsequently published at Rome (CTh 2.1.1 -
11.7.6). It is tempting to emend the date from viii id. Mart. to viii id. Mai., i.e. 8 May, an(
to regard Eustathius as a stand-in during the interval between Limenius and Hermogenes(
when the Chronographer of 354 reports that 'cessaverunt praefecturae' (Chr.min. 1. 68).[35]

349, May 19-350, February 27 Hermogenes
  Chronographer of 354 (Chr.min. 1. 68-69).

ILLYRICUM

343 or 344-346 Anatolius
  Nicknamed Azutrio, attested as prefect on 23 May 346 (CTh 12.1.36) and described as
praetorian prefect of Illyricum recently arrived from Gaul, i.e. from the court of Constans, i(
an anecdote whose content points to a date not long after 343 (Eunapius, Vit.phil. 10.6.4
10.7.6, pp.490-492). To be carefully distinguished from the Anatolius, also a native o(
Berytus, who was prefect of Illyricum from 357 to 360.[36]

---

[35] PLRE 1. 311.
[36] A.F.Norman, 'The Illyrian Prefecture of Anatolius', Rh.Mus., N.F. 100,1957,253-259, cf. Vogle(
Constance, 1979,115ff.; R.Penella, Greek Philosophers and Sophists in the Fourth Century A.D. Studies i
Eunapius of Sardis, Leeds 1990,90/1, 96-98, 130-132.
  A.Groag, Die Reichsbeamte von Achaia in spätrömischer Zeit, Budapest 1946,32-33, had already note
that Eunapius implies a date no later than 345/6. For a restatement of the traditional view that the tw(
Anatolii are one, V.Neri, 'Le prefetture del pretorio in occidente nel periodo 346-350 d.C.', Rivista storic(
dell'antichità 4,1974,89-111. They are also conflated by R. von Haehling, Religionszugehörigkei(
1978,99/100; PLRE 1. 59/60.

347-?353 Vulcacius Rufinus, cos. 347

Active as prefect at Savaria in Pannonia Secunda before 350 (ILS 727).[37] Attested on 28 December 349 (CJ 6.62.3), prefect under Vetranio (Petrus Patricius, frag. 16) and then under Constantius: Epiphanius, Pan. 71.1.5, implies his presence in or near Sirmium in the spring of 351, and he is attested in office on 26 February 352 (CJ 6.22.5).[38]

355-356 Q.Flavius Maesius Egnatius Lollianus, cos. 355

Attested as praetorian prefect in July 355 (CTh 6.29.1; 11.30.25 + 36.11). Ammianus locates him in Illyricum as prefect in 356 (16.8.5-7).

357-360 Anatolius

Attested as prefect by numerous letters of Libanius from 357, 358 and 359.[39] Ammianus described him as 'regente tunc per Illyricum praefecturam' in 359 (19.11.2) and notes his death in office in 360 (21.6.5).

360-361 Flavius Florentius, cos. 361

Successor of Anatolius (Ammianus 21.6.5), he fled to Constantius when Julian invaded Illyricum in the summer of 361 (Ammianus 21.9.4; Zosimus 3.10.4).

ORIENS

354-358 Strategius Musonianus

Successor of Domitianus, 'Orientem praetoriani regebat potestate praefecti' (Ammianus 15.13.1) from 354 to 358: attested by plentiful evidence.[40]

358-360 Hermogenes

Succeeded Musonianus before 24 August 358 (Libanius, Orat. 1.115/6; Ep. 21, cf. Ammianus 19.12.6). He apparently left office in the winter of 359/60 (Libanius, Ep. 138), so that Ammianus must be mistaken when he states that Hermogenes died in office early in 361 (21.6.9).

---

[37] Vogler, Constance, 1979,120-121, dates the inscription before Rufinus' consulate and deduces that he succeeded Anatolius in 346.

[38] On Rufinus as prefect of Illyricum, see J.R.Palanque, 'Du nouveau sur la préfecture d'Illyricum au IVe' Hommages à M.Renard 2, Brussels 1969,600-606. For laws transmitted with other dates which may originally have been addressed to Rufinus as prefect of Illyricum in 352 or 353, PLRE 1. 783.

[39] O.Seeck, Die Briefe des Libanius, Leipzig 1906,59-66.

[40] PLRE 1. 611/2.

360-361 Helpidius

Successor of Hermogenes (Ammianus 21.6.9): attested in office on 4 February 360 (CT♭ 11.24.1: office not stated),[41] but dismissed by Julian at the end of 361 (Amianus 22.3.1, cf Libanius, Orat. 37.11; Ep. 740).

---

[41] For laws which explicitly attest Helpidius as prefect, PLRE 1. 414.

XIV

Two Victory Titles of Constantius.

In any period of the Roman Empire, official commemorations of victories
provide important evidence for military history, from the twenty one imperatorial salutations of Augustus to the cognomina devictarum gentium with
which Justinian advertised the conquests of his generals in Africa and
Italy.[1] Such evidence becomes more important, the scrappier and more tendentious are the surviving narrative sources. For periods such as the reigns
of Diocletian and Constantine, indeed, the formal evidence of imperial titles
can (and must) be pressed into service in order to obtain a coherent outline
of the course of events.[2] The obscure period of sixteen years between the
death of Constantine and the year 353, where the extant detailed political
and military narrative of Ammianus Marcellinus begins, requires the use of
similar extrapolations and inferences. In particular, the victory titles of
Constantius, as attested by two inscriptions, assume great significance.

*   *   *

A marble cippus found in the Forum of Trajan at Rome and published by
R. Paribeni in 1933 contains the opening of an imperial letter to the consuls,
praetors, tribunes and Senate of Rome which commends the noble pedigree and
virtues, both private and public, of one Proculus (AE 1934.158).[3] The imperial college in whose joint name the letter was sent comprises Constantine
as Augustus, and four Caesars, viz. Constantine's sons Constantinus, Constantius and Constans, and his half-nephew Dalmatius (whose name has subsequently been erased). Now Constantine is described as "trib. potest.
XXXIII consul VIII imp. XXXII." Since Constantine held his eighth and last
consulate in 329, became imperator for the thirty second time on 25 July 336,
entered on his thirty third tribunicia potestas on 10 December 336, and died
on 22 May 337, it follows that the letter must be dated between December 336
and spring 337. It seems a reasonable conjecture, therefore, that the letter,
most of whose text is lost, was written not merely to commend C. Aradius
Valerius Proculus to the Roman Senate, but to announce his appointment as

---

1. The survey of victory titles by P. Kneissl, Die Siegestitulatur der
römischen Kaiser (Hypomnemata 23, 1969) is unfortunately not an adequate
treatment of the theme. On Augustus' imperatorial salutations, JRS 64 (1974),
21ff.

2. Phoenix 30 (1976), 176ff.; ZPE 20 (1976), 149ff.; The New Empire of
Diocletian and Constantine (1982), 49ff.

3. Notizie degli Scavi[6] 9 (1933), 489 no. 165, with Tavola XIV. The
heading is now reedited in New Empire (1982), 23 no. 8.

praefectus urbi, a post which he assumed on 10 March 337 (Chr. min. 1.67).[4] This inscription, whose protocol emanates directly from the imperial chancellery, gives Constantine four victory-titles, three with iterations, and styles the Caesar Constantinus Alamannicus, but registers no victory titles at all for the other three Caesars.

Another inscription, which records military construction near Troesmis under Constantinus, Constantius and Constans as Augusti, gives Constantius the two victory titles Sarmaticus and Persicus, and Constans the single victory title Sarmaticus (ILS 724 = CIL 3.12483).[5] Since the three surviving sons of Constantine became Augusti on 9 September 337 (Chr. min. 1.235), while Constantinus was killed in the spring of 340, it is an easy inference that the military achievements which these titles reflect occurred between February 337 and early 340.[6] Further, since the emperors who ruled between 284 and 337 formally assumed victory titles only for victories won by an emperor in person,[7] the titles of Constantius and Constans appear to imply that the former had won (or claimed) victories over the Sarmatians and Persians, the latter a victory over the Sarmatians between the engraving of the two inscriptions. Hence the hypothesis of a joint campaign of Constantius and Constans on the Danube in the second half of 337 or the early months of 338.[8] However, Constantius returned to Antioch for the winter of 337/8 (Socrates, HE 2.7, cf. Libanius, Orat. 59.75ff.). It is advisable, therefore, to disjoin the Sarmatian victories of the brothers, and to date Constantius' campaign against the Sarmatians to the summer of 337, before Constantius conferred with his brothers over how the Empire should be divided between them, the Caesar Dalmatius having been killed.[9] The title of Persicus on the inscription presumably reflects Constantius' restoration, in summer 338 of Arsaces to the throne of Armenia (Julian, Orat. 1, 20-21). To be sure, no fighting is recorded, nor any victory of Constantius over the Persians in the field until several years later.[10] But the inscription of Troesmis reflects a provincial view of Constantius' victory titles, not necessarily the emperor's own official view. As for the Sarmatian victory of Constans, the year 338 appears probable.[11]

---

4. ZPE 20 (1976), 150 n. 2.
5. All is not clear in this inscription, divergent readings being offered by J. Toutain, MEFR 11 (1891), 243 (whence AE 1891.148); H. Dessau, ILS 724; and A. von Domaszewski, CIL 3.12483 (accepted by Dessau in his addenda vol. 3, p. clxxii). It seems certain, however, that the three titles discussed here are adequately attested.
6. A. Arnaldi, Epigraphica 39 (1977), 91ff.
7. Phoenix 30 (1976), 177ff.
8. ZPE 20 (1976), 154.
9. Phoenix 34 (1980), 162.
10. In fact, not until 343: Athanasius, Hist. Arian. 16,2; Festus, Brev 27, cf. Phoenix 34 (1980), 163.
11. A. Arnaldi, Epigraphica 39 (1977), 93f.; T.D. Barnes, Phoenix 34 (1980), 164.

The titles of Constantius and Constans, as attested in one inscription
of spring 337 and another inscription engraved within three years, imply
that between 337 and 340 both emperors won victories over the Sarmatians,
and at the same period the coinage of Siscia proclaims a "victoria Constanti
Aug(usti)" and then, somewhat later, a "victoria Constantis Aug(usti)" (RIC
8, 349-352 Siscia 8, 17, 33-38).[12] The reality was less glorious. Battles
may have been won, but the ultimate outcome of the campaigns of Constantius
and Constans was unfavourable to Rome. Constantine had reconquered territory
north of the Danube, an achievement for which he took the title Dacicus
maximus (AE 1934.158).[13] Shortly after he died, these conquests were lost:
according to Julian, they withered as fast as the gardens of Adonis (Caes.
329 B-D).

*　*　*

These inferences, and the reconstruction which they entail, have been
impugned by Dr. J. Arce, in a brief but closely argued paper, which contends
that Constantius took both the titles on the inscription of Troesmis in the
lifetime of his father, becoming Sarmaticus in 334 at the same time as his
father Constantine assumed the title of Sarmaticus maximus for the second
time, Persicus for a campaign in 336 in which he killed the Persian prince
Narses.[14] This chronology, as Dr. Arce emphasises, is not a new one, but a
reassertion of the chronology adopted (with minor divergences) by Otto Seeck,
Joseph Vogt, Jacques Moreau and others.[15] Therein lies its fatal weakness,
for it was formulated before the inscription from Rome (published in 1933)
attested the victory titles of Constantius and his father and brothers in
early 337. Since Dr. Arce pronounces the traditional chronology "the only
possible one," he must deal rather brusquely with the inconvenient testimony
of the inscription from the Forum of Trajan. He alleges that because Constantine lacks certain victory titles attested elsewhere and because the
name of the Caesar Dalmatius has been erased, the inscription should be
regarded "not as a complete and faithful document." He affirms, moreover,
that Constantinus alone of Constantine's sons possesses a victory title
because he was "at the time the inscription was set up, the only senior and
principal successor of Constantine in his plans for an heir in the Empire."

---

12. Also a "victoria Constantini Aug(usti)" (RIC 8.348-9, Siscia 1-4,
12-13) - which is relevant to the appearance of Germanicus maximus among
Constantinus' titles in Domaszewski's revision of the inscription from
Troesmis (CIL 3.12483, accepted by Dessau in his addenda to ILS 724).

13. D. Tudor, Revista Istorică Romană 11-12 (1941-42), 134ff.

14. J. Arce, ZPE 48 (1982), 245ff.

15. O. Seeck, RE 4 (1900), 1045; J. Vogt, Constantin der Große und sein
Jahrhundert (1949), 242; J. Moreau, JAC 2 (1959), 164; P. Bruun, RIC 7 (1966),
74; G. Sabbah, Ammien Marcellin 2 (Budé, 1970), 186 n. 111. Some of these
scholars preferred a date in late 335 or 336 to one in 334.

Objections must be raised to these arguments, on more levels than one. Constantine's dynastic actions imply, not that he intended Constantinus to succeed him as senior emperor with authority over his colleagues, but that he planned to leave the empire divided territorially among four emperors (viz. his three sons and his half-nephew Dalmatius).[16] Moreover, the inscription in question carries the beginning of a formal imperial letter fro Constantine to the Roman Senate, drafted with care in the imperial chancellery, transmitted direct from emperor to recipient, and engraved by the lat ter within weeks of its receipt. It thus belongs to a small group of author itative documents which provide the primary and most reliable evidence for the imperial titulature of Diocletian, Constantine and their imperial colleagues.[17] The inscription of Troesmis, engraved on the orders of the dux limitis Scythiae, is a far less authoritative document. Unlike the imperial letter, which contains Constantine's official statement of the imperial titles of himself and his Caesars, the inscription from Troesmis reflects merely the view of provincial officials about the emperors' titles. It is implausible in the extreme to argue that the later, less authoritative statement of Constantius' titulature attests victory titles officially take before 337 and deliberately omitted from the earlier, more authoritative document. Furthermore, the subsequent erasure of Dalmatius' name after his death in the summer of 337 is patently irrelevant to the accuracy of what was engraved in the spring of 337. Finally, the claim that the Roman inscri tion omits some of the victory titles of Constantine himself appears to res on a failure to realise that these omitted titles appear only on two notoriously problematical African inscriptions, which attribute to Constantine victory titles which he never officially assumed (ILS 8942; 696).[18]

The attempt to impugn the inferences from the Roman inscriptions of 33 and the inscription from Troesmis fails. By the normal criteria of historic proof, Constantius lacked any official victory titles in spring 337. Before 340, however, he had performed actions which led the dux limitis Scythiae (or whoever else authorised the wording on the inscription from Troesmis) t style him both Sarmaticus and Persicus. The hypothesis that the title Sarma ticus commemorates a victory of Constantius in 337, while the title Persicu reflects his activities in Armenia in 338 proceeds from the acceptance of both inscriptions as valid evidence.

*   *   *

16. Constantine and Eusebius (1981), 251f.

17. New Empire (1982), 17ff.

18. J. Arce, o.c. 249, appeals to R. Paribeni, o.c. 490, for the proposition that in AE 1934.158 "i cognomina ex virtute non sono elencati tutt But Paribeni adduces only ILS 8942 and 696, on which, see now New Empire (1982), 81 n. 145. Some scholars (it may be observed) had argued that these inscriptions reproduce the victory titles of Constantine's father, not of Constantine himself.

A formal argument from two inscriptions, however valid, may not suffice
to still all doubts. It remains to review other relevant evidence, and to
ask how far it supports the inferences drawn from the two stones. Panegyrics
of Constantius by Libanius and Julian may be adduced, as well as a Syriac
text written in Mesopotamia in 337.

Libanius' panegyric on Constantius and Constans, composed in late 348
or early 349 and his earliest extant speech,[19] betrays the hand of an ap-
prentice as it labours through the traditional topics of speeches addressed
to emperors. After introduction, Constantius' family and education, Libanius
comes at last to the Persian war. It began (he explains) in the reign of
Constantine and the Persians were the aggressors (Orat. 59.62ff.). After
some diplomatic exchanges, Constantine set out for war, but died before he
could achieve anything:

When he had just begun the journey and was in this city
(i.e. Nicomedia), the Mighty One saw that, whereas his name
was engraved on many trophies, it was necessary that the one
of his two sons who was facing the Persians should gain glory
through victories over barbarians. After resolving thus, he
summoned the father on high to himself, and transferred the
war to the son (Orat. 59.72).

God ordained that Constantine should die in order that his son might win
glory from fighting the Persians: Libanius clearly did not believe that Constantius had already won a Persian victory, for which he had earned the
title of Persicus maximus, in the lifetime of his father.

Julian's panegyric of 355 is equally explicit on the Persian war. According to this speech, Constantine first made his youthful son an emperor
over the Celts or Gauls, then transferred him to sole command against the
Persians (Orat. 1, 11D-12A; 13B). Julian stresses that a war was already
smouldering on the eastern frontier and about to burst into flame, but that
Constantius engaged in no fighting until his father was dead and he had conferred with his brothers in Pannonia c. September 337 (13B, 18Dff.). Admittedly, the notion that Constantius was Caesar in Gaul, though widely accepted by recent historians of the period, appears to be erroneous.[20] And
it must be conceded that Julian, who commends Constantine for giving Constantius experience of ruling as Caesar without the risks of war, because he arranged that the barbarians whom his son faced be at peace with his subjects
(12A), has omitted Constantius' campaign against the Sarmatians, whether it
occurred in 334 or 337. Nevertheless, Julian presents a picture of the early
stages of the Persian war which is both unambiguous and consonant with the
other evidence: serious fighting began only after the death of Constantine.

---

19. For the date, R. Foerster, Libanii Opera 4 (Teubner, 1908), 201 n. 2.
20. New Empire (1982), 84f.

XIV

Strong confirmation comes from a source not normally adduced by Roman historians. The Christian Aphrahat, who lived in Persian territory, composed ten treatises in the Seleucid year 648 (which ran from October 336 to September 337). The fifth of these, written in the spring of 337, looks forward to a great war which is about to begin.[21] Aphrahat identifies the combatants as Rome and the Persian king, and he argues that in the coming conflict Rome will win. Aphrahat alludes to Constantine, of whose death he has not yet heard, and to the military preparations of Shapur (Dem. 5.1). But he consistently states and assumes that the war has not yet commenced: if a Roman emperor had recently taken the field against the Persians and won a victory, Aphrahat is completely unaware of that fact.

Festus, the magister memoriae of the emperor Valens, writing in 370, presents a similar picture. He lists nine serious battles against the Persians under Constantius, stating that the emperor was present in person at only two, both near Singara, apparently in 343 and 348 (Brev. 27).[22] Again that seems to exclude a campaign in 336 in which Constantius earned the title Persicus maximus on the field of battle.

To sum up. The very varied evidence of Libanius, Julian, Aphrahat and Festus confirms the inference drawn from the heading to Constantine's letter to the Roman Senate: Constantius did not officially take the titles Sarmaticus or Persicus during his father's lifetime.

* * *

Problems nevertheless remain. Most obviously, when did Constantius first officially assume the title of Sarmaticus maximus? It must be before 358, for Ammianus Marcellinus, narrating an expedition north of the Danube which the emperor conducted in that year, records his appellation by the soldiers as Sarmaticus for the second time (17.13.25, 33). That the first official salutation belongs to the 330's has been the standard assumption (despite disagreement about the precise year). Yet the evidence available hardly suffices for proof, and a milestone of 354 or 355 from the vicinity of Sirmium omits the title altogether: Constantius is presented as "Germanicus Alamamnicus maximus, Germ. max., Gohticus maximus, Abiabin. max." (ILS 732). Besides the careless spelling, omission or error may readily be surmised.[23] The mile-

21. Edited, with a Latin translation, by J. Parisot, Patrologia Syriaca 1.1 (1894), 183-228.

22. Phoenix 34 (1980), 163 n. 16.

23. On this inscription, see A. Arnaldi, Epigraphica 39 (1977), 94ff. A date in 354 or 355 is established by the fact that Constantius is "consul VII". But the text printed by Th. Mommsen on the authority of Z. Gruić (CIL 3.3705) and reproduced by Dessau also styles him "tribuniciae potestatis XXXII imp. XXX" - which seems to be an impossible combination, cf. New Empire (1982), 252f.

stone deserves little more authority as a precise statement of Constantius' official titles than the inscription of Troesmis. That fact counsels a doubt and prompts a conjecture. Constantius could have taken the title Sarmaticus maximus officially for the first time as late as 352. He defeated the usurper Magnentius at Mursa on 28 September 351 (Chr. min. 1.237), and yet delayed his entry into Italy for most of a year.[24] The delay requires explanation - which the hypothesis of a Sarmatian campaign would provide.

More puzzling still is an item in a late writer concerning warfare in Mesopotamia. Theophanes asserts that, in the same year as Constantine deposed Licinius and his son (i.e., 324/5), Narses, the son of the Persian king, raided Mesopotamia and captured Amida (p. 20.20-22 de Boor). The notice has been identified as deriving from a fourth century source,[25] and hence deemed worthy of credence as attesting a Persian capture of Amida in 334 or 335.[26] The inference, though hazardous, could conceivably be correct. For Amida only gained strategic importance when Constantius fortified it and made it a military strong-point: previously it had been little more than a village (Ammianus 18.9.1). A Persian capture before 337 would have lacked the significance of the well-attested capture in 359. Were it to be conceded, however, that the Persians ravaged Amida under Constantine, the date given by Theophanes would need serious consideration. A Persian raid into Mesopotamia in 324 during the war between Constantine and Licinius cannot be ruled out. After that war, there were those who spoke as if Constantine might soon lead an expedition against Persia (Publilius Optatianus Porfyrius, Carm. 18.4).

These uncertainties, however, are a minor matter. The traditional view that Constantius took the titles Sarmaticus and Persicus in his father's lifetime was deduced from their appearance on an inscription engraved shortly after Constantine's death.[27] Explicit and direct attestation of Constantius' titles at the very end of his father's reign was lacking; when it was published in 1933, the traditional view was disproved. It is no service to scholarship to dismiss new evidence merely because it disproves existing beliefs.

---

24. O. Seeck, Regesten der Kaiser und Päpste für die Jahre 311 bis 476 n.Chr. (1919), 198f.

25. J. Bidez, Philostorgius Kirchengeschichte (1913), 204, in an appendix entitled "Fragmente eines arianischen Historiographen."

26. W. Ensslin, RE 16 (1935), 1757; Klio 29 (1936), 106.

27. O. Seeck, RE 4 (1900), 1045.

XV

THE CAREER OF ABINNAEUS

FOR SEVERAL YEARS in the reign of Constantius, Flavius Abinnaeus served as *praefectus* of the *Ala Quinta Praelectorum* and commander of the fort at Dionysias in the Arsinoite nome which it garrisoned. He would be totally unknown to history but for a happy accident of survival. After his service at Dionysias, Abinnaeus appears to have retired to Philadelphia, also in the Fayyûm, taking with him papers relating to his years of military command. In 1892 and 1893 some eighty papyri which had belonged to Abinnaeus were offered for sale in Egypt. Almost all of them found their way into the libraries of the British Museum and the University of Geneva, and in 1962, after most had been published with other papyri from those two collections, virtually the whole of the archive which has survived received exemplary publication under the supervision of Sir Harold Idris Bell.[1]

The reconstruction of Abinnaeus' career offered by the editors of the *Abinnaeus Archive* was subsequently adopted in the first volume of the *Prosopography of the Later Roman Empire*.[2] Since its chronology is partly founded on the false proposition that the imperial audience which Abinnaeus had in Constantinople "can have been granted only in the latter part of 337 or the spring of 338,"[3] pedantry alone might recommend a re-examination. Moreover, the search for greater accuracy and greater precision of detail may permit Abinnaeus' career to be linked to better known events and more famous personages.

---

[1]H. I. Bell, V. Martin, E. G. Turner, and D. van Berchem, *The Abinnaeus Archive. Papers of a Roman Officer in the reign of Constantius II* (Oxford 1962), cited here as *Archive*. The first section of the introduction, by V. Martin, describes the origin and discovery of the archive (1 ff.).

One papyrus was included which does not belong to the archive, viz. *PGen.* 60 = *PAbinn.* 65: see H. Cadell, "P. Genève 60, B.G.U. II, 456 et le problème du bois en Égypte," *Cd'E* 51 (1976) 331–348, who republishes the whole contract of which it forms part (*BGU* 456 + *PAbinn.* 65 + *PBerlin inv.* 8001). And one papyrus must be added, R. Rémondon, "Un papyrus inedit des archives d'Abinnaeus," *JJurPap* 18 (1974) 33–37.

I am most grateful to Roger Bagnall for his observations on an earlier version of the present article.

[2]*PLRE* 1 (1971) 1–2, with J. R. Martindale, "Prosopography of the Later Roman Empire: addenda et corrigenda to Volume I," *Historia* 23 (1974) 246–252, at 246. Also in the article by R. Rémondon, "Militaires et civils dans une campagne égyptienne au temps de Constance II," *JSav* 1965.132–143.

[3]E. G. Turner, *Archive* 8.

I

Abinnaeus is first attested as commander of the *ala* at Dionysias on 29 March 342 by a petition to him found among the papers of Aurelius Sakaon (*PTheadelphia* 23 = *PAbinn.* 44 = *PSakaon* 47). Among the papers of Abinnaeus himself is the draft of an earlier petition in Latin, in which Abinnaeus recounts the events leading to his appointment as *praefectus alae* at Dionysias, and requests the emperors Constantius and Constans to ensure that he be permitted to assume the post to which they have promoted him (*PAbinn.* 1).

Abinnaeus' origin and the first stage in his career are lost in a lacuna, but he seems to say that he served for thirty-three years in the *vexillatio* of Parthian archers stationed at Diospolis in the province of the Upper Thebaid (lines 4–5). He came to the imperial court when Senecio, the *comes limitis* of the province, directed him to escort certain *refugae* of the tribe of the Blemmyes to Constantinople: Abinnaeus went with the *comes* and ambassadors of the Blemmyes, whom he presented to Constantius —"whereupon your divinity ordered me, from the station of *ducenarius*, to adore your venerable purple" (lines 5–8), i.e., the emperor or emperors bestowed on Abinnaeus the honorary rank of protector (as implied by lines 1–3, cf. *PAbinn.* 55). The precise date can be ascertained. Abinnaeus found Constantius in Constantinople. But Constantius never resided in that city except as a child: from 335 until 350, his capital and normal residence was Antioch, whence he regularly set forth on campaign against the Persians in the spring of each year from 338 onwards.[4] He visited Constantinople on only two occasions between 335 and the winter of 341/2. In the summer of 336 Constantius was on hand for the tricennalia of his father, when Eusebius documents his presence in the city on 25 July (*Vita Const.* 4.49, cf. *Triac.* 3.4). In the following year, the death of Constantine and the ensuing political and dynastic crisis necessitated a longer visit to western Asia Minor and Europe. Constantius arrived in Nicomedia shortly after his father's death on 22 May, and probably spent some time in Constantinople before conferring with his brothers in Pannonia in the late summer: he then passed through the city again in the autumn on his way to Antioch for the winter of 337/8.[5]

Eusebius happens to record that he saw ambassadors from many foreign nations, including the Blemmyes, outside the imperial palace, on an occasion which can only be the tricennalia of Constantine in July 336 (*Vita Const.* 4.7.1). Abinnaeus (it should be deduced) came to Constantinople in

[4]See, provisionally, *The New Empire of Diocletian and Constantine* (Cambridge, Mass. 1982) 85 f. (to 337); *Phoenix* 34 (1980) 162–166 (337–350).

[5]For the evidence, *New Empire* 86. The most explicit items upon which this reconstruction rests are Julian *Orat.* 1 16d, 19a, 20c; Socrates *HE* 2.7; Zonaras 13.4.

the summer of 336. When he speaks of a journey *ad sacra vestigia pietatis vestrae* and an order from *divinitas vestra*, he does not mean either that he saw both Constantius and Constans in Constantinople or that he came to Constantius alone and saw no other emperor. Of the five emperors then reigning, only Constantine himself and Constantius were present in Constantinople during the celebration of Constantine's tricennalia in July 336: presumably, therefore, Abinnaeus performed *adoratio purpurae* before Constantius and his father. On the other hand, the joint address to Constantius and Constans does not imply that Abinnaeus sent his petition to both emperors. Emperors who ruled jointly formed a college: in accordance with the etiquette of imperial collegiality, Abinnaeus addressed both the emperors ruling in 340 or 341 when he sent his petition to Constantius alone.

In Constantinople, Abinnaeus received instructions to conduct the ambassadors of the Blemmyes back to their native land. Abinnaeus spent a period of three years with the ambassadors (he presumably includes the journey as well as his time in the country of the Blemmyes); then he visited the imperial court again, bringing recruits from the province of the Thebaid which he delivered at Hierapolis (lines 8–10). This audience probably belongs to 339 or 340. For time must be allowed before the audience for Abinnaeus' *trienne tempus* with the ambassadors of the Blemmyes, including two long journeys, from the Bosporus to the southern frontier of Egypt and from there to northern Syria, while after the audience lengthy delays occurred before Abinnaeus took command at Dionysias, where he is attested on 29 March 342 (*PAbinn.* 44). Constantius' precise whereabouts are not on record between 27 December 338, when he was at Antioch (*CTh* 2.6.4) and 12 August 340 when he was at Edessa (*CTh* 12.1.30, with Seeck's emendation of the place of issue from *Bessae* to *Edessae*). Abinnaeus' delivery of recruits may be relevant to a sometimes neglected literary text.[6] The author of the so-called *Itinerarium Alexandri* set forth the examples of Alexander and Trajan for Constantius to emulate in a Persian campaign which he was about to undertake—and in which (so the writer fervently declared) he would at last make the servile Persians free citizens of the Roman Empire. The *Itinerarium Alexandri* was composed shortly after the death of Constantinus in the late winter or spring of 340. It could well be that its author heralds the campaign for which Abinnaeus helped to bring Constantius a much-needed supply of Egyptian recruits. That was a standard procedure before an eastern emperor embarked on any aggressive expedition: monastic hagiography describes what seems to be Maximinus' enrolling of Egyptian recruits in 312/3 prior to his attack on Licinius.[7]

[6]On its importance and context, *JRS* 75 (1985) 135.

[7]*Sancti Pachomii Vita Prima* 4, ed. F. Halkin, *Sancti Pachomii Vitae Graecae* (Brussels

At Hierapolis, Abinnaeus was released from active service under colours and appointed *praefectus* of the *ala* at Dionysias. On his return to Egypt, however, when he submitted his letter of appointment to the *comes* Valacius, the bureau of the *comes* replied that other men had produced letters of this type and refused to act upon his imperial letter (lines 12–14). Abinnaeus accordingly composed a petition to Constantius: a copy survives among his papers solely because he was dissatisfied with the initial formulation of his request and therefore dictated an amended version of the all-important clause. In his first formulation, Abinnaeus invited the emperor to contemplate his past labours and begged him to ensure his daily sustenance (lines 13–14). On second thoughts, Abinnaeus substituted for this the request that, since the others had been promoted *ex suffragio*, while he had an imperial patent, the emperor should order those who had promotion *per suffragium* to be removed and Abinnaeus to take up the post (written above lines 12–13). Whether, how, and to what immediate effect the petition was submitted are unknown, but at all events Abinnaeus obtained his desire and reward: by 29 March 342 he had become *praefectus* of the *ala Quinta Praelectorum* and commander of the garrison at Dionysias.

Abinnaeus' petition sheds a disturbing light on the administration of Constantius, and it is highly unfortunate that some recent discussions of *suffragatio* in the emperor's reign pass over this interesting document in silence.[8] Abinnaeus makes a firm distinction between appointment *ex suffragio* and appointment *iudicio sacro*, between those who hold their positions *per suffragium* and one like himself, who has an imperial letter of appointment (*apices vestros*). He thus assumes that those who obtained posts by *suffragium* did not receive appointment by or from the emperor, but only from their patrons. On the other hand, when the bureau of Valacius received the imperial letter (*sacrae litterae*) which Abinnaeus submitted, it refused to act on the strength of it, on the grounds that others too had submitted exactly similar letters. Since Abinnaeus denounces the latter as beneficiaries of *suffragium*, it seems to follow that the officials of

---

1932, Subsidia Hagiographica 19) 3. The *vita* states that it was Constantine under whom Pachomius enlisted for a war against a "tyrant:" for the correct date, D. J. Chitty, *Studia Patristica* 2 (Berlin 1957, Texte und Untersuchungen 64) 379 f.

[8]There is no mention of *PAbinn.* 1 in C. Collot, "La pratique et l'institution du *suffragium* au Bas-Empire," *RHistDroit*[4] 43 (1965) 185–221; W. A. Goffart, "Did Julian combat venal 'suffragium'?," *CP* 65 (1970) 145–151; C. Vogler, *Constance II et l'administration impériale* (Strasbourg 1979) 244 ff. Vogler's omission is all the more inexplicable because her survey of sources notes that *PAbinn.* 2 documents the use (and abuse) of *suffragium* under Constantius (73 f., 80). Abinnaeus' petition is, however, briefly discussed by D. Liebs, "Ämterkauf und Ämterpatronage in der Spätantike. Propaganda und Sachzwang bei Julian dem Abtrünnigen," *ZSav*, Rom. Abt. 95 (1978) 158–186, at 172 f.

Constantius' court issued letters of appointment in his name without obtaining the emperor's explicit authorisation.

II

Some time during the consular year 344 Valacius, the *dux et comes* of Egypt, sent Abinnaeus a brusque letter of dismissal (*PAbinn.* 2). Valacius tells Abinnaeus that another ex-protector has been appointed to succeed him *iuxta divinitus sancita*, since Valacius has been informed that the prefect has completed the term of his command (*eo quod [impe]rii iam tempora c[o]nplesse suggereris*). The justificatory phrase *iuxta divinitus sancita* is slippery: though it suggests (and was doubtless intended to suggest) that Valacius was acting "in virtue of orders from imperial headquarters,"[9] a strict construction of his words might reveal a claim merely to be acting "in accordance with statutory procedures" (to put ancient bureaucratic jargon into recognisable modern form). Abinnaeus was not deceived and refused to be supplanted easily. He set off again for the imperial court, obtaining two promissory letters dated 1 and 2 February 345 in which friends undertook to reimburse him for expenses incurred in furthering their interests. In the one, the president of the local council of Arsinoe contracts for the obtaining of an *epistula exactoriae* (*PAbinn.* 58),[10] while in the other a veteran of Dionysias contracts for the promotion of his son to be *decurio* of the camp at Dionysias (*PAbinn.* 59).

Abinnaeus succeeded in obtaining reinstatement, and he is attested as camp commander from 1 May 346 (*PAbinn.* 47) until 11 February 351 (*PAbinn.* 55). It does not necessarily follow, however, that he journeyed all the way to court and appeared before Constantius.[11] For his enemy Valacius perished suddenly and unexpectedly. Riding with the prefect Nestorius on the road just outside Alexandria, he was thrown from his mount and bitten by his companion's horse, dying of his wounds within three days.[12] Valacius' accident probably occurred in 345: at all events the *dux* was clearly dead before Athanasius returned to Alexandria on 21 October 346.[13] With Valacius' death, Abinnaeus may have been able to obtain reinstatement without needing to travel to the emperor in Syria: he

---

[9]So the phrase is translated in *Archive* 38.

[10]The meaning of the term is disputed: see V. Martin, *Actes du Ve Congrès de Papyrologie* (Brussels 1938) 260–285; J. D. Thomas, *Cd'E* 34 (1959) 124–140, at 132 ff.; A. H. M. Jones, *The Later Roman Empire* (Oxford 1964) 728.

[11]As argued by E. G. Turner, *Archive* 12.

[12]*Vita Antonii* 86; Athanasius *Historia Arianorum* 14.

[13]The Festal Index registers Palladius as prefect at Easter 344, Nestorius as prefect from 345 to 352; unfortunately, no contemporary document helps to date the beginning of Nestorius' tenure more precisely, the earliest being an imperial letter of summer 346 quoted by Athanasius (*Apol. c. Ar.* 56.2–3).

had an imperial letter of appointment which stated no fixed term for his command, while his supplanter may have had nothing more efficacious than a letter from the *dux et comes* Valacius.

III

The preface to the *Archive* declares that "it is impossible to pronounce definitively" on the question whether Abinnaeus was a Christian, then detects a slight indication (in *PAbinn.* 32) that he was not. Moreover, it argues that "the presence of a statue of Fortune in the place of honour in the camp of Dionysias does not speak in favour of a preponderance of Christianity among the soldiers."[14] The archaeological argument is not cogent, since there seems to be no evidence for the date at which the apparently second-century statue of Nemesis or Victory ceased to be a cult-object.[15] It is more significant that the petitions to Abinnaeus never name a single pagan deity and refer almost thirty times to God (singular) or divine providence rather than to plural gods: the plural occurs only once, and apparently by carelessness or inadvertence, since the petitioner, who is a slave of Abinnaeus himself, closes with the salutation "I pray for your health in the Lord for many years" (*PAbinn.* 36). Moreover, a petition to Abinnaeus published in 1974 implies that he will regard the priest of the village of Hermopolis as a particularly trustworthy witness—and hence indirectly that the prefect is himself a Christian.[16]

The latest document in the archive of Abinnaeus is a petition in which Aurelius Heron, a deacon from the village of Berenice in the Arsinoite nome, accuses one Euporus from the village of Philagris of breaking and entering his house, and stealing his clothing (*PAbinn.* 55). After outlining his complaint, Heron asks for restitution of his property and informs Abinnaeus that he is a deacon of the catholic church (lines 14–15). That remark is more pointed than appears at first glance. In the Egypt of the late 340s "catholic" was not a neutral term with an innocuous meaning such as "worldwide."[17] The word conveyed a claim: clergy of the catholic church did not merely belong to the worldwide church as opposed to a heretical or schismatic group, but enjoyed privileges which Constantine and his sons had bestowed on them as clergy of the catholic church. These privileges were not granted to all who called themselves Christians. As early as 313

---

[14]V. Martin, *Archive* 30 ff., esp. 33.

[15]J. Schwartz, "Une forteresse construite sous Dioclétien: Qasr-Qarun," *CRAI* 1951.90–96; *Qasr-Qarun/Dionysias 1950* (Cairo 1969) esp. 61 ff.

[16]R. Rémondon (above, n. 1) esp. 37. There is no good reason for assigning to the archive the aggressively Christian Strasbourg papyrus published by J. Lesaulnier, "Un nouveau papyrus des archives d'Abinnaeus," *ZPE* 3 (1968) 155–156 (whence *SB* 10755).

[17]As the editors of the *Archive* appear to assume (116), with their appeal to S. Eitrem, *Papyri Osloenses* 3 (Oslo 1936) 165, on *POsl.* 113.15 (a security of 346).

Constantine explained to the proconsul of Africa that his bounty was confined to "the catholic church over which Caecilianus presides" (Eusebius *HE* 10.7.2).[18] In Egypt, the definition of "catholic" changed twice in the dozen years before Heron suffered burglary.[19] In 339 Gregorius and his supporters became the recipients of privilege in place of the dispossessed Athanasius and his. Seven years later, when Athanasius returned to Alexandria, Constantius wrote to the prefect of Egypt and to the governors of the other Egyptian provinces annulling any earlier instructions detrimental to those who communicated with Athanasius and restoring to them the freedom from liturgies which they used to enjoy, without removing the exemption of the clergy not in communion with Athanasius (*Apol. c. Ar.* 56.2–3).

The enmity which Valacius showed towards Abinnaeus may not be totally unconnected with ecclesiastical politics. Valacius, the enemy of Abinnaeus, was also the enemy of Athanasius and the monk Antony: he supported Gregorius when the latter replaced Athanasius as bishop of Alexandria, and it was alleged that he whipped monks and assaulted bishops and virgins in order to secure cooperation with the new bishop (Athanasius *Hist. Ar.* 12). Abinnaeus may have been an ally and supporter of Athanasius: after he had successfully overcome Valacius' attempt to oust him, he retained his post at Dionysias without known hindrance or challenge while Athanasius, after his return to Alexandria in 346, was building up a power-base in Egypt strong enough to defy the emperor for a decade.

---

[18]For further evidence, T. D. Barnes, *Constantine and Eusebius* (Cambridge, Mass. 1981) 224 ff.; T. G. Elliott, "The Tax Exemptions granted to Clerics by Constantine and Constantius II," *Phoenix* 32 (1978) 326–336.

[19]In the papyri, the phrase "catholic church" seems to be restricted to churches directly dependent on bishops within the ecclesiastical hierarchy subordinate to the bishop of Alexandria, cf. E. Wipszycka, *Les ressources et les activités économiques des églises en Égypte du IVe au VIIIe siècle* (Brussels 1972, Papyrologica Bruxellensia 10) 25 f.

HIMERIUS AND THE FOURTH CENTURY

T HE SOPHIST HIMERIUS finds few readers on the score of his merits as a writer. He has a justly deserved reputation for practicing eloquence as an end in itself, for concentrating on rhetorical ornamentation at the expense of serious content:[1] as the *Oxford Classical Dictionary* puts it, "Himerius in the main displays a talent for saying nothing gracefully and at length."[2] Yet Himerius has recently received a sympathetic portrayal as an early Byzantine orator.[3] And he has undeniable value to classical scholars, both for his quotations from and allusions to early Greek lyric poets, such as Sappho and Ibycus,[4] and as a quarry for literary commonplaces which help to elucidate passages in Hellenistic poetry or Roman elegy.[5] Moreover, much as he preferred to avoid contemporary reality in his speeches, Himerius inevitably lets slip some valuable remarks about the Roman Empire of his own day—for example, the exclusively Christian character of Constantine's new city of Constantinople before Julian introduced pagan cults (*Or.* 41. 8).[6]

Himerius' writings survive in three main ways.[7] First, Photius describes a corpus of some seventy-five speeches, which he knew and had read

I am most grateful to Alan Booth, Christopher Jones, and the Editor for their kind advice and criticism, and to audiences at Toronto and Stanford who helped me to clarify the exposition of a complicated subject.

1. W. von Christ, W. Schmid, and O. Stählin, *Geschichte der griechischen Literatur,* vol. 2.2⁶ (Munich, 1924), p. 1000: "reiner Dekorationsredner"; H. Gärtner, "Himerios," *Der kleine Pauly,* vol. 2 (Munich, 1975), col. 1149: "die gänzlich unpolitische Beredsamkeit des Himerios."

2. *OCD²,* s.v. "Himerius," p. 516.

3. G. A. Kennedy, *Greek Rhetoric under Christian Emperors* (Princeton, 1983), pp. 141–49.

4. C. Teuber, *Quaestiones Himerianae* (Ph.D. diss., Breslau, 1882); G. E. Rizzo, "Saggio su Imerio il sofista," *RFIC* 26 (1898): 513–63; J. Mesk, "Sappho und Theokrit in der ersten Rede des Himerios," *WS* 44 (1925): 160–70; J. D. Meerwaldt, "Epithalamica 1. De Himerio Sapphus imitatore," *Mnemosyne* 7 (1954): 19–38; L. E. Woodbury, "Ibycus and Polycrates," *Phoenix* 39 (1985): 193–214, at pp. 209–13.

5. J. C. Yardley, "The Roman Elegists, Sick Girls, and the Soteria," *CQ* 27 (1977): 400.

6. The passage is adduced, but undervalued, by G. Dagron, *Naissance d'une capitale: Constantinople et ses institutions de 330 à 451* (Paris, 1974), p. 376: "L'éloge vibrant qu' Himérios vient prononcer à Constantinople n'est que rhétorique."

7. See the edition by A. Colonna (Rome, 1951), upon which all statements made here about the text are based, except where otherwise noted. On the excerpts, see A. Colonna, "Disputationes Himerianae," *Bollettino del Comitato per la preparazione della Edizione nazionale dei classici greci e latini* 1 (1941): 147–69; and on the reliability of Photius, A. Colonna, "Il testo di Imerio nella 'Bibliotheca' di Fozio," in *Miscellanea G. Galbiati,* vol. 2, Fontes Ambrosiani 26 (Milan, 1951), pp. 95–106. There have been important discoveries since Colonna's edition: S. Eitrem and L. Amundsen, "Fragments from the Speeches of Himerios. P. Osl. inv. no. 1478," *C&M* 17 (1956): 23–30 (papyrus fragments, esp. of *Or.* 46); A. Guida, "Frammenti inediti di Eupoli, Teleclide, Teognide, Giuliano e Imerio da un nuovo codice del Lexicon Vindobonense," *Prometheus* 5 (1979): 210–14 (excerpts in another Naples manuscript, Bibl. Naz. gr. II D 29).

(*Bibl.* cod. 165). Second, Photius excerpted a large number of rhetorical flosculi from Himerius (*Bibl.* cod. 243), and numerous brief extracts are preserved elsewhere, in a fourteenth-century manuscript at Naples (Bibl. Naz. gr. II C 32) and in the lexicon of Andreas Lopadiota. Finally, some thirty-two speeches are extant in their own right. Unfortunately, the most important manuscript, of the thirteenth century (Paris. supp. gr. 352), which originally contained the full text of thirty-two speeches, was extensively trimmed in the fifteenth or sixteenth century, so that the text of several speeches which it preserves is extremely lacunose. (The other two manuscripts offer, respectively, nine and three of the same thirty-two speeches.) However, besides the text of the speeches themselves, the historian can use the headings that an ancient editor supplied, from which the titles given by Photius and found in the Naples excerpts are derived: these headings sometimes provide authentic information that cannot be deduced from the speech itself.[8] The medieval manuscripts, the excerpts, and Photius' reports all appear to derive from a collected edition made, presumably by a pupil, shortly after Himerius died.

The sophist Himerius was not a totally insignificant figure in his own day. He addressed proconsuls and, it appears, spoke before the emperor Constantius (frag. 1. 6). He became acquainted with Julian in 355, when the young prince studied briefly in Athens, and he traveled to the imperial court at Constantinople when Julian, now sole emperor, was about to undertake the restoration of Hellenism. At the lowest count, therefore, it would be a useful exercise to reconsider what Himerius reveals about his career and about the Roman governors whom he addressed, because a careful winnowing of his verbiage should allow the gleaning of something new, interesting, and important. But there is also some prospect that a fresh examination of the speeches may begin to build up a coherent career and personality for one of the most elusive writers of the fourth century.

I

Himerius' birth is normally set very early in the fourth century.[9] The standard date appears to derive from, or at least to be heavily influenced by, B. Keil's contention that Himerius was born ca. 300.[10] Keil deduced his date from Himerius' address to the city of Constantinople early in 362 (*Or.* 41); but though a date for Himerius' birth can indeed be deduced from this speech, it is one significantly different from that proposed by Keil. Himerius refers to his studies in Athens and to an earlier visit to the city on the Bosporus (*Or.* 41. 2):

8. E.g., the names of the *vicarius* Musonius and the *consularis* Calliopius (*Or.* 39, heading). Observe, however, that the title printed by Colonna for *Or.* 39 on the basis of the Naples excerpts is misleading: the speech is not a λαλιά addressed to the emperor Julian and Musonius but an address to the city of Thessalonica.

9. H. Schenkl, "Himerios (1)," *RE* 8 (1913): 1624–25 (ca. 303); Christ-Schmid-Stählin, *Geschichte* 2.2⁶:1000 (ca. 310); *OCD*², "Himerius" (ca. 310); *PLRE* 1:436 (early in the fourth century).

10. "Zwei Identificationen," *Hermes* 42 (1907): 548–63, at pp. 551–56.

My speeches, as if by some superior fate, have long (ἄνωθεν ἄρα)[11] been destined to belong to the city. The proof, a very strong one, is as follows. When it was time, after my contests in Athens and the great garlands of Athena Parthenos, for my words to plow and seed the rest of the world with Attic discourse, fate did not lead them to the western Rhine or direct their foreign travels to the legendary sea of Ocean but brought them to you still in the flower of youth, green with their first downy beard, so that they might weave a hymn to the city with still-fresh flowers. But since, on this second occasion, white is their hair and white already their locks, they have praised the emperor in private,[12] so that the city again may become the prologue of hymns in his praise.

Keil argued that Himerius' white hairs proved him already an old man: he saw in the Rhine and Ocean allusions to Constantine's court at Arles ca. 316, and hence he inferred that Himerius was probably born between ca. 300 and ca. 304.[13] But Keil felt able to advance this argument only because he assumed that no datable event in Himerius' life need be later than 368/69. That assumption appears to be mistaken, since the proconsul Flavianus, to whom Himerius addressed three speeches (*Or.* 12, 36, 43), was almost certainly the proconsul of Asia for 383/84.[14] The dating of these three speeches to 383 should be regarded as one of the few fixed points for establishing the chronology of Himerius' life: hence, an allusion to Himerius as a young man ca. 316 becomes implausible.

The passage in fact alludes, not to the court of Constantine, but to the court of his son Constans at Trier. K. Münscher, criticizing Keil, detected the specific reference.[15] Himerius contrasts himself implicitly with his rival in Athens, the sophist Proaeresius, who made a famous journey to Trier in or shortly after 343 (Eunap. *VP* 10. 7, p. 492). But why does Himerius mention both Rhine and Ocean? Münscher omitted to discuss that detail, while Schenkl hesitantly and unconvincingly suggested an allusion to Spain[16]—which would have no obvious point. The mention of Ocean surely alludes to Constans' expedition to Britain in the winter of 342/43, after which the emperor's crossing of the English channel and his overcoming of Ocean and the elements provided an obvious and easy

---

11. I am uncertain whether ἄνωθεν ἄρα should be translated "from on high" or "from long ago": both meanings are appropriate to the context and are found ın Himerius (cf., respectively, *Or.* 32. 1, 46. 8 and *Or.* 36. 18, 39. 5). The sophist also uses ἄνωθεν to mean "inland" (*Or.* 1, 39. 6).

12. Accepting Wernsdorf's emendation καθ᾽ ἑαυτούς for the transmitted καθ᾽ ἑαυτόν, which Colonna defends as meaning "for himself." Keil, "Identificationen," p. 552, n. 1, diagnosed deeper corruption: "Das corrupte καθ᾽ ἑαυτὸν kann ich nicht heilen; der Sinn verlangt οἴκοι ᾄδειν ἐπήνεσεν (d.h. die εἱμαρμένη)."

13. Two centuries earlier, it was possible for a Lucian or an Aelius Aristides to go to Gaul to teach; cf. C. P. Jones, *Culture and Society in Lucian* (Cambridge, Mass., 1986), pp. 11–12. The evidence of Libanius and Eunapius shows that Eastern sophists no longer did so in the fourth century.

14. See section IV, below, on *Or.* 12, 36, 43. Schenkl, "Himerios," col. 1625, rejected the identification altogether, whereas O. Seeck, "Flavianus (11)," *RE* 6 (1909): 2506, and "Flavianus (15)," *RE* 6 (1909): 2512, identified the Flavianus of *Or.* 12 as the proconsul of Asia in 383/84 but made the addressee of *Or.* 36 a proconsul of Africa; the latter identification, including Seeck's erroneous date of 361 (instead of 357/58), is repeated by R. Henry, ed., *Photius: "Bibliothèque,"* vol. 6 (Paris, 1971), pp. 124–25. That all three speeches are addressed to the younger Nicomachus Flavianus is assumed at *PLRE* 1:345.

15. "Bericht über die Literatur zur zweiten Sophistik (rednerische Epideiktik und Belletristik) aus den Jahren 1905–1909," *Bursians Jahresbericht* 149 (1910): 157.

16. "Himerios," col. 1622.

theme for any who wished to praise or flatter him.[17] But if that is so, then the two allusions to Rhine and Ocean coincide closely in time, and hence imply that Himerius completed his studies in Athens in the early 340s. His birth, therefore, should fall ca. 320 rather than at the very beginning of the fourth century. That his hair was white by 362 provides no counterargument, as many a middle-aged man will reluctantly testify.

II

Photius preserves a series of miscellaneous excerpts from speeches that he does not identify (between his extracts from *Or.* 11 and 12). One of them clearly comes from a speech addressed to Constantius between 351 and 354 (frag. 1. 6):

> O brightest eye of your race, you who have become for your family exactly what your ancestor Helios has often been for you! For of this fine pair, the one, like the morning star at dawn, has risen with you who illumine the great thrones, imitating your bright rays with his reflected lights; while the other, shining forth from the herd of young men, like some high-spirited bull that leads the herd, has leapt in the meadows of the Muses, like a young horse full of divine spirit who holds his neck high, and has imitated the young man in Homer, the son of Thetis, having become a good speaker of words and doer of deeds (*Il.* 9. 443).[18]

Behind this rodomontade there may lurk something highly significant, though otherwise unattested. The allusions to Constantius, Gallus, and Julian seem indisputable.[19] The language suggests that Gallus has recently become Caesar (morning star) to Constantius as Augustus (sun); indeed, Himerius speaks as if he is celebrating the *ortus* of a new emperor—and sun-imagery was all the more appropriate for a young Caesar just summoned to court from the obscurity of a private station.[20] Further, Himerius speaks as if Gallus and Julian are present (τῆς γὰρ συνωρίδος ταύτης δὴ τῆς καλῆς ὁ μέν . . .). In brief, the fragment implies that Himerius was in Sirmium on 15 March 351, when Constantius appointed Gallus Caesar (*Chron. min.* 1:238)—and that Julian was there too, as an honored guest at the proclamation of his brother. That Julian nowhere vouchsafes any hint is no counterargument to the admittedly tenuous deduction drawn here: on the contrary, his silence could be construed as an example of his mendacity when he writes about Constantius.

As concerns Himerius, the fragment has implications entirely independent of any hypothesis about the exact date and occasion of the speech from which it comes. It implies that he traveled to Constantius and spoke before him. But it is not certain that he did so on behalf of Athens, the city where he resided and taught for many years, and where he recited most, though not all, of his surviving speeches.

17. Firm. Mat. *Err. prof. rel.* 28. 6; Lib. *Or.* 59. 139 ff.
18. Translated into French by J. Bidez, *La vie de l'empereur Julien* (Paris, 1930), p. 95. He appears to date the speech to the period when Gallus was already residing in Antioch.
19. Colonna, "Testo," p. 97.
20. E. Kantorowicz, "Oriens Augusti—Lever du Roi," *DOP* 17 (1963): 119–77; S. G. MacCormack, *Art and Ceremony in Late Antiquity* (Berkeley and Los Angeles, 1981), pp. 20–21, 199.

III

Himerius was the son of the rhetor Ameinias from Prusias in Bithynia (*Suda* I.348 [2:633 Adler]). It has been argued so far that he was born ca. 320, came to Constantinople after his studies at Athens in or shortly after 342/43, and delivered a panegyric before Constantius, probably on 15 March 351. It may now be suggested that in his teaching positions both at Constantinople and later at Athens he followed in the footsteps of the Antiochene Libanius. To establish that proposition, it will be necessary to digress in order to consider Libanius' career between 340 and 353.

The accepted chronology for the career of Libanius between his departure from Athens in 340 and his permanent return to his native Antioch derives from the work of G. R. Sievers over a century ago, whose conclusions O. Seeck accepted and employed in his standard treatment of Libanius' correspondence.[21] It needs a critical reexamination, since Sievers expressly deduced his date of 342/43 for Libanius' departure from Constantinople from the supposed fact that Constantius suppressed the riots that preceded his departure (Lib. *Or.* 1. 44) during the winter of 342/43.[22] But Constantius' journey to Constantinople belongs to the preceding winter (i.e., 341/42).[23] Moreover, the recent accounts of Libanius' career given by A. F. Norman and the *Prosopography of the Later Roman Empire* entail the impossible corollary that Libanius delivered in Constantinople a speech whose text states that it was delivered in the city where Constantine died, i.e., in Nicomedia (Lib. *Or.* 59. 72).[24]

Libanius began to teach in Constantinople at the beginning of the winter of 340/41 (Lib. *Or.* 1. 31-33). He was compelled to leave the city by Limenius, who had recently replaced Alexander, after that proconsul had been wounded in a riot and forced to flee to Perinthus (Lib. *Or.* 1. 44-47). Neither the riot nor Libanius' departure can be at all precisely dated. The riot in which the proconsul was wounded should be different from the more famous riot of early 342, in which the military commander Hermogenes was lynched when he attempted to expel the bishop Paul (Jer. *Chron.* 235[f] Helm; *Historia acephala* 1. 4 Martin; Soc. *HE* 2. 13. 1-5; *Chron. min.* 1:235). And the proconsulate of neither Alexander nor Limenius is dated independently of Libanius—unless an adventurous emendation be permitted to show the latter proconsul in office on 27 August 342.[25] Nor can anything precise be discovered about Libanius' subsequent brief sojourn in Nicaea (Lib. *Or.* 1. 48).

---

21. Sievers, *Das Leben des Libanius* (Berlin, 1868), pp. 42-71; Seeck, *Die Briefe des Libanius zeitlich geordnet*, Texte und Untersuchungen 30.1-2 (Leipzig, 1906); cf. R. Förster and K. Münscher, "Libanios," *RE* 12 (1925): 2488-91.

22. *Leben*, p. 53, n. 10.

23. T. D. Barnes, "Imperial Chronology," *Phoenix* 34 (1980): 160-66, at p. 163.

24. *Libanius' Autobiography (Oration I)* (London, 1965), p. vii; *PLRE* 1:505. In his commentary, however, Norman correctly dates Libanius' departure from Nicomedia to 349 (pp. 161, 169).

25. Barnes, "Chronology," p. 164, emending the addressee and date of *CTh* 11. 39. 4 (transmitted date: 27 August 346).

XVI

After Libanius left Nicaea, however, he spent five years in Nicomedia, which he later proclaimed the best five years of his life (Lib. *Or.* 1. 51). Libanius presumably reckons by academic years running from autumn to summer,[26] and these five years almost certainly run from 344 to 349. The one fixed point is provided by Libanius' panegyric on the heroic deeds of Constantius and Constans (Lib. *Or.* 59), which he delivered in Nicomedia in late 348 or 349.[27] Libanius' quinquennium in Nicomedia, therefore, must include the academic year 348/49 and hence cannot have begun before 344. Soon after delivering the speech, Libanius returned to Constantinople when the praetorian prefect Philippus, who had earlier allowed Libanius to resist persuasion, compelled him to move by means of an imperial letter (Lib. *Or.* 1. 74). It seems natural to assign Libanius' return to Constantinople to 349.

Libanius' second departure from Constantinople is also problematical. His autobiographical speech records that in two successive summers his love for Bithynia led him to revisit his old haunts (Lib. *Or.* 1. 77); then Strategius, whom Constantius had appointed governor of Greece "after the removal of the usurpers, one by persuasion, the other by force," persuaded the Athenians to invite Libanius back to a chair of rhetoric there (Lib. *Or.* 1. 81-84). The accepted chronology of this stage of Libanius' career rests on the deduction that, since Strategius was appointed after the removal of both Vetranio and Magnentius, he was therefore appointed proconsul of Achaea in A.D. 353.[28] But Constantius gained control of the Balkans when Vetranio abdicated on 25 December 350, and he defeated Magnentius at the battle of Mursa on 28 September 351.[29] Strategius could have been appointed after Mursa for the proconsular year 352/53, or even before the battle for 351/52. Either of these dates seems to fit the explicit indications in Libanius better than the accepted date of 353: in 350 and 351 Libanius revisited Bithynia; in 352 he was offered a chair in Athens; and he then visited Antioch before returning there permanently during the winter of 353/54 (Lib. *Epist.* 386; cf. Amm. Marc. 14. 7. 2).[30]

Himerius (it is known) visited Bithynia while Libanius was teaching in Nicomedia.[31] Photius reports a speech given "in Nicomedia at the urging of Pompeianus, the governor there" (p. 9. 75-76 Colonna). The speech is

26. On the importance of "années scolaires," see P. Petit, *Les étudiants de Libanius* (Paris, 1957), pp. 48-59; A. D. Booth, "À quel âge Libanius est-il entré à l'école du rhéteur?" *Byzantion* 53 (1983): 157-63.

27. R. Förster, *Libanii Opera,* vol. 4 (Leipzig, 1908), p. 201. This speech has so far not received the systematic historical analysis that it deserves.

28. Seeck, *Briefe,* pp. 282-83; id., "Strategius (1)," *RE* 4A (1931): 182; Norman, *Autobiography,* p. 169; *PLRE* 1:611.

29. For full narratives, see O. Seeck, *Geschichte des Untergangs der antiken Welt,* vol. 4 (Berlin, 1911), pp. 96-120; J. Sasel, "The Struggle between Magnentius and Constantius II for Italy and Illyricum," *ZAnt* 21 (1971): 205-16.

30. On this stage of Libanius' career, "between Constantinople and Antioch," see R. A. Kaster, "The Salaries of Libanius," *Chiron* 13 (1983): 37-59, at pp. 41-50.

31. On the problem of distinguishing between different men called Himerius in the correspondence of Libanius, see H. Schenkl, "Zur Biographie des Rhetors Himerios," *RhM* 72 (1917-18): 34-40.

lost, but it appears to have been given on an occasion described by Libanius in a letter of 362 (*Epist.* 742):

> When I was enjoying that happiness in Nicomedia, not enjoying greater riches than others but having leisure for speeches, the governor of Bithynia was Pompeianus, a noble and just man, who in no way despised poverty, who honored genuine eloquence and rejected its opposite. Surely you do not forget how he mocked that finely tailored fellow from Athens, forcing him to speak against his wishes and intending to show his feebleness.

This is good-natured banter rather than barbed insult. If "the finely tailored fellow from Athens" is Himerius (as appears to be entailed by external testimony),[32] then the description would be apt only if the Bithynian were newly arrived from Athens—which suggests that the episode should be located early in Libanius' sojourn in Nicomedia.

In an earlier letter, of 355/56, Libanius had written to Gorgonius, an assessor of the governor, to ask him to aid Himerius in a lawsuit involving property in Armenia (*Epist.* 469):

> An opportunity has arrived that enables you to do good to the whole Greek world (ἅπαν τὸ Ἑλληνικόν). Himerius' life is education, and the place of his teaching (τόπος τῆς συνουσίας) is Athens, but he has property in Armenia.

At the time of the letter, Himerius was a teacher of rhetoric at Athens. There he taught two youths who later became Christian bishops, Basil of Caesarea and Gregory of Nazianzus, and probably also, very briefly in the spring of 355, the future emperor Julian (Soc. *HE* 4. 26. 6, whence Soz. *HE* 6. 17. 1).

The evidence considered so far is consistent with the hypothesis that Himerius taught rhetoric in Constantinople from 343 to 352 and that he only began to teach at Athens in the latter year. It now becomes necessary to inquire what a prosopographical study of the speeches Himerius addressed to Roman officials and governors can contribute to an understanding of his career.

IV

The speeches of Himerius, even in their often lamentable state of preservation, sometimes disclose information about Roman governors and officials that has not always been correctly evaluated or exploited. The following notes discuss the named proconsuls and other officials whom Himerius addresses: the order reflects the first occurrence of each name in the relevant speeches in Colonna's edition.[33]

Severus (*Or.* 9 and 24). Severus was a native of the province of Diospontus who studied with Himerius: the orator composed an epithalamium for his marriage in Athens to a woman from Philippopolis

---

32. Schenkl, "Biographie," pp. 39–40, halfheartedly questions the identification.
33. Colonna's edition contains some egregious errors: it turns a praetorian prefect into a lowly *praeses* (p. 176, on *Or.* 42) and makes the addressee of *Or.* 12, 36, and 43 a proconsul of Achaea (p. 178).

(*Or.* 9, esp. 5, 13–14, 17). Α second speech, whose title is reported as εἰς Σεβῆρον ἑταῖρον (*Or.* 24), describes his official career in a passage among the most lacunose in the whole corpus. Himerius alludes to his addressee's Pontic origin (line 26), to the relationship of master and pupil (lines 10–20), and to Severus' official career. At least four posts or honors receive mention.[34] First, "Galatians were a prelude of his honors" (line 36), i.e., Severus was governor of Galatia.[35] Then, "Bithynians after them"—the text breaks off, resuming after a gap of some thirty-two letters with another reference to Bithynia or Bithynians (lines 36–37): Severus, therefore, was *consularis* of Bithynia. It was presumably after this that Severus became a *comes* of the emperor. Himerius' allusion seems clear enough, despite the lacunae (lines 32–33): "they opened to him the imperial . . . having . . . they at once enrolled [him] among the emperor's friends." Finally comes a post that should be last in time, though mentioned first by Himerius. Severus obtained "the authority of a prefect" (line 29: τὴν ὕπαρχον ἐξουσίαν): Himerius' allusions to the Bosporus and Rome (lines 27, 28), and what appears to be a conceit based on the fact that, as prefect, Severus was close to Bithynia (line 37), make it certain that the post in question is that of *praefectus urbi* at Constantinople. That establishes a firm terminus post quem for Himerius' speech: the first city prefect of Constantinople was Honoratus, appointed on 11 December 359 (*Chron. min.* 1:239; cf. Jer. *Chron.* 241ᵉ Helm; Soc. *HE* 2. 41. 1), and there is no substantial gap in the fasti of the prefecture before 366.[36] Himerius could have addressed Severus in Constantinople as prefect between 366 and 372 (when the next prefect is attested). If the chronology proposed in the present article for Himerius' career is correct, then the epithalamium cannot be earlier than ca. 353—which implies that the whole of Severus' public career falls after that date. The epithalamium, it should be noted, describes Severus as a youth rather than as a mature adult (*Or.* 9. 15).

The speech whose title Photius reports as εἰς Σεβῆρον νέηλυν ἐπιστάντα συμπληγάδι (p. 9. 48–49 C.), i.e., "to Severus the new arrival on the occasion of a quarrel," can hardly be addressed to the same Severus, unless it is much earlier than the epithalamium.

Flavianus (*Or.* 12, 36, 43). Photius styles the addressee of *Oratio* 12 "consul of Asia" (*Bibl.* cod. 165, p. 8. 40 C.): this muddled information (Photius means "proconsul") derives from the heading to the speech in the collected edition whose contents Photius summarizes. Unfortunately, all three speeches are extremely fragmentary, and the fragments of only one contain a clear reference to Asia (*Or.* 12. 30). Nevertheless, the preserved details cohere with the supposition that all are addressed to the same man; and Photius also identifies the addressee of *Oratio* 43 as a

---

34. O. Seeck, "Severus (24)," *RE* 2A (1923): 2004, notes only three; *PLRE* 1:832, but two.
35. The evidence for the title of the governor of Galatia in the mid-fourth century is inconclusive. The rank of the governor of Bithynia was raised from *praeses* to *consularis* ca. 325 (*AE* 1969–70, 116).
36. See *PLRE* 1:1056.

proconsul (p. 9. 66–67 C.). Flavianus was a young man (*Or.* 43. 3), who had recently been in Africa (*Or.* 36. 1, 3, 5, 11). If he was on his way to Asia, then he must be the younger Nicomachus Flavianus, proconsul of Asia for the year 383/84 (*CTh* 7. 18. 8 + 9. 29. 2, 12. 6. 18; Symm. *Epist.* 2. 24);[37] and that identification dates the speeches to March or April 383 (cf. *Or.* 36. 1). But what had Flavianus been doing in Africa? The inscription that records his career is silent about any African office (*ILS* 2948 [Rome]): presumably, therefore, *legatus* to a recent proconsul who was a relative or a friend of his family. Nicomachus Flavianus had been *consularis* of Campania before 382, and Himerius duly presents his proconsulate as his second governorship (*Or.* 12. 16: πάλιν γὰρ σκῆπτρα, πάλιν τῆς δίκης οἱ θρόνοι. . .).

Why did Himerius compose three speeches for a man who merely passed through Greece en route to Asia? Flavianus' prominent pagan sympathies ought to be relevant. Despite the headings that style *Oratio* 12 προπεμπτήριος and *Oratio* 36 προπεμπτικός, *Oratio* 36 appears to be a speech of welcome on behalf of the provincial council of Achaea (*Or.* 36. 12).[38] *Orationes* 12 and 43 should therefore be speeches on the occasions of Flavianus' welcome to and departure from Athens.

Musonius (*Or.* 20 and 39). Two homonyms must be carefully distinguished:

(1) the addressee of *Oratio* 20, who was proconsul of Achaea at the time of that speech and who later was present when Himerius delivered *Oratio* 39 in Thessalonica in the winter of 361/62 (*Or.* 39. 14–15, and heading);

(2) a sophist, *vicarius* of Macedonia in 361/62 (*Or.* 39, heading), who was killed by Isaurian brigands ca. 367/68 (Amm. Marc. 27. 9. 8; Eunap. frag. 45 Müller = 43 Blockley).

The proconsulate of the former Musonius seems to belong before 356: like Ampelius (see below), he was *magister officiorum* as well as proconsul of Achaea; but unlike Ampelius, he was proconsul before becoming *magister officiorum*, in which post he is first attested in June 356 (*CTh* 8. 5. 8S).[39]

Ursacius (*Or.* 23). A *comes,* and from Illyria (*Or.* 23. 5): Himerius compares him to Abaris, who, though a northerner and Scythian in dress and appearance, was nevertheless Greek in language and character (*Or.* 23. 4, 7). Perhaps the same as Ursacius, *magister officiorum* in 364 and 365, whom Ammianus denounced as a rude Dalmatian (26. 4. 4, 5. 7). However, to judge from the scanty surviving fragments of the speech, Himerius praised his Ursacius as a soldier by profession.

---

37. For the date (instead of 382/83), see B. Malcus, "Die Prokonsuln von Asien von Diokletian bis Theodosius II," *OAth* 7 (1967): 118; T. D. Barnes, "Proconsuls of Africa, 337–392," *Phoenix* 39 (1985): 144.

38. *Or.* 36 A 3 seems to imply delivery at Corinth: for the attribution of the fragment to this speech, see Colonna, "Disputationes," pp. 159–62.

39. M. Clauss, *Der "magister officiorum" in der Spätantike (4.-6. Jahrhundert),* Vestigia 32 (Munich, 1980), p. 171, adducing Lib. *Epist.* 558.

Scylacius (*Or.* 25). Proconsul of Achaea (heading): Himerius alludes to his claim to descend from the Aeginetan hero Aeacus (lines 47 ff.) and to two earlier posts, one at court (line 33), the other in Ionia (lines 33–34) and by the River Maeander (lines 68 ff.), in which he pursued Pisidian bandits (lines 68, 95 ff.). The former post defies inquiry, but Scylacius is attested as *vicarius* (sc. of Asiana) by an inscription recording his building activities at Laodicea ad Lycum;[40] and an imperial constitution addressed to him on 24 February 343 establishes the date (*CTh* 11. 30. 22). Since Constans ruled Achaea until his death early in 350, Scylacius was presumably proconsul after this date.[41]

Athenaeus (*Or.* 28). Photius, reporting the lost title, styles Athenaeus a *comes* (*Bibl.* cod. 165, p. 9. 54 C.). Two fragments of the surviving text suggest rather an official with clearly defined territorial responsibilities:

> Of virtue in governing there are two proofs, the votes of an emperor and the desires of the governed (4);
> These are the first fruits of your friendship and words: the words, being prophetic and also clever at predicting such things and better, proclaim good luck, rule over Greeks (σκῆπτρα Ἑλλήνων), honors from the emperor, and praise (9).

Athenaeus may have been *vicarius* of Macedonia.

Ampelius (*Or.* 29, heading; *Or.* 31, 50). Proconsul in 359/60 (*Syll.*³ 905). The building activities that *Oratio* 31 stresses are documented by several inscriptions from Sparta, Chalcis, and Aegina.[42] One phrase that Himerius uses in a list of Ampelius' virtues is problematical (*Or.* 31. 13): "Honored by emperors, an object of fear to tyrants (τυράννοις εὐλαβής), affable to ordinary people, respected by the wise, most pleasing to the old, an object of affection to all conditions and ages alike." The passage survives only in the Naples collection of brief excerpts from Himerius. When publishing the excerpts, H. Schenkl emended the manuscript's εὐβλαβής to εὐλαβής (also printed by Colonna) but declined to explain what he thought Himerius meant by the phrase τυράννοις εὐλαβής.[43] If the adjective has its normally favorable connotation, then τυράννοις will have to have the rare, though well-attested, sense of "foreign princes" or "minor princelings."[44] In that case, however, it is hard to see how Himerius could expect an audience to divine his meaning. It is better to suppose that he uses εὐλαβής in the unfavorable sense which the corresponding verb often has:[45] τυράννοις can then have its normal

---

40. Published and discussed by L. Robert, *Laodicée du Lycos: Le Nymphée. Campagnes 1961–1963* (Québec and Paris, 1969), pp. 339–51, no. 15, with an elucidation of lines 72 ff. in Himerius' speech as describing Scylacius' construction of canals and dikes at Miletus.

41. E. Groag, *Die Reichsbeamten von Achaia in spätrömischer Zeit*, Dissertationes Pannonicae I, 14 (Budapest, 1946), p. 34.

42. Quoted by Groag, *Reichsbeamten*, p. 42.

43. "Neue Bruchstücke des Himerios," *Hermes* 46 (1911): 424.

44. The word is used of the rulers of Axum in the heading to the imperial letter quoted by Athanasius, *Apol. ad Const.* 31. 1; cf. A. Dihle, *Umstrittene Daten: Untersuchungen zum Auftreten der Griechen am Roten Meer* (Cologne, 1964), p. 53.

45. For the meaning "fear," see G. W. H. Lampe, *Patristic Greek Lexicon* (Oxford, 1961), p. 567. Himerius uses the verb in this sense in *Or.* 6. 17: νῦν δὲ τῶν μὲν εὐλαβηθεὶς τὴν τόλμαν, τῶν δὲ αἰσχυνθεὶς τὸν πόλεμον, αὐτὸς οἴκοι μένειν ἐβουλεύσατο.

meaning of "usurper" or "evil ruler." Ampelius was an Antiochene who had been *magister officiorum* (Amm. Marc. 28. 4. 3). Himerius could be alluding to dealings with Magnentius—which would imply that Ampelius served as *magister officiorum* some years earlier than is normally supposed.[46] An allusion to Gallus as Caesar in Antioch seems tasteless and improbable. In any event, the difficult phrase alludes to an otherwise unknown episode in Ampelius' career.

Anatolius (*Or.* 32). Himerius salutes Anatolius as "the great prefect" (*Or.* 32. 3; cf. Phot. *Bibl.* cod. 143). He was, therefore, praetorian prefect: presumably the Anatolius who was prefect of Illyricum from 357 to 360, not the homonym who visited Athens while praetorian prefect not long after 343 (Eunap. *VP* 10. 6, pp. 490–91).[47]

Alexander (*Or.* 33). *Oratio* 33 is addressed to Phoebus, the son of the proconsul Alexander. It is tempting to identify this Alexander with the proconsul of Constantinople who supported Libanius (*Or.* 1. 44–45).[48] That would date the speech to ca. 342 and imply that Himerius went to Constantinople before Libanius was forced to leave. The title of the speech implies otherwise: "To [Phoebus], the son of the proconsul Alexander [lacuna of ten letters] to him by his father after the schools in Corinth." Moreover, the implicit comparison of Himerius' teaching Phoebus with Isocrates' teaching Nicocles, whom Evagoras, the ruler of Cyprus, sent to him in Athens (lines 14 ff.), may suggest that the speaker is resident in Athens. Alexander could well be an otherwise unattested proconsul of Achaea.[49]

Arcadius (*Or.* 34). Doctor and *comes* (heading).

Cervonius (*Or.* 38). The heading identifies Cervonius as proconsul and states that "this is the first λαλιά that (Himerius) delivered in the *praetorium* at Athens." Cervonius is independently attested as proconsul at Thespiae (*SEG* 15. 323 = *IG* 7. 1855). On the chronology argued here for Himerius' career, that would imply that Cervonius was proconsul of Achaea in 353/54.

Calliopius (*Or.* 39). *Consularis* (sc. of Macedonia), present when Himerius delivered the speech in Thessalonica during the winter of 361/62 (title). As *consularis* he dedicated an altar at Thessalonica "under the most pious and restorer of cults, the lord and conqueror of every barbarian nation, Claudius Julianus, the all-powerful and only sovereign of the inhabited world."[50]

Salutius (*Or.* 42). Prefect (i.e., praetorian prefect): therefore, Salutius Secundus, the praetorian prefect of Julian. Himerius presumably pre-

---

46. "Possibly in 358," according to *PLRE* 1:56. Clauss, *Magister,* p. 145, suggests 355–56.
47. On the necessity of distinguishing the two, see A. F. Norman, "The Illyrian Prefecture of Anatolius," *RhM* 100 (1957): 253–59. His conclusions are disputed by V. Neri, "Le prefetture del pretorio in Occidente nel periodo 346–350 d.C.," *RSA* 4 (1974): 89–113.
48. So *PLRE* 1:40; Dagron, *Naissance,* p. 221.
49. As G. Wernsdorf supposed, in his edition of Himerius (Göttingen, 1790).
50. D. Feissel, *Recueil des inscriptions chrétiennes de Macédoine du IIIᵉ au VIᵉ siècle,* BCH Supp. 8 (Paris, 1983), p. 247, no. 86 bis.

sented this διάλεξις or θεωρία when he arrived at court in 362. It is significant that Himerius speaks of success in military commands: Salutius was not (as is often supposed) a civilian praetorian prefect of the East, but a prefect of the old type who accompanied the emperor wherever he went and acted as his deputy.[51]

Basilius (*Or.* 46 and 47). Proconsul and son of Basilius (*Or.* 46, heading), a westerner and pagan: Himerius speaks of a report that when it senses the approach of Dionysus, the land flows with honey and milk (*Or.* 46. 6).[52] Four men, whose lives span the fourth century, are relevant to the identification of Himerius' addressee:

(1) Valerius Maximus *signo* Basilius, *praefectus urbi* from 319 to 323;
(2) Valerius Maximus, consul in 327 and attested as praetorian prefect between 327 and 337;[53]
(3) Maximus, appointed *praefectus urbi* at Rome by Julian late in 361 (Amm. Marc. 21. 12. 24; *AE* 1904, 33 [362]; *CIL* 6. 31401; Symm. *Rel.* 34. 5);
(4) Basilius, *praefectus urbi* at Rome in 395 (*CTh* 7. 24. 1).

Himerius probably addressed his two speeches to the last-named, even though there are problems in establishing the identification securely.[54]

Himerius seems to say that the proconsul's father had been ordinary consul (*Or.* 46. 8)—which could be taken as proof that the *praefectus urbi* of 319–23 is identical with the consul of 327.[55] But there are extremely strong grounds for rejecting the identification of prefect and consul, and the fact that the proconsul's father was still alive and in the West at the time of the speeches (*Or.* 46. 11) makes it highly unlikely that he is either the *praefectus urbi* of 319–23 or the consul of 327.

Himerius alludes to an official post of the proconsul's father, in a passage whose manuscript text has been improved by a papyrus of the fifth century (*Or.* 46. 10):

> You come to the Greeks bringing us, not golden arms, but a certain golden Justice and Right, these assessors of your father (τὰς τοῦ πατρὸς παρέδρους),[56] which received you in their bosom at your birth and reared you from your cradle, not with

---

51. Ammianus styles him "praefectus Salutius praesens" (23. 5. 6). It is highly unfortunate that modern studies of the praetorian prefecture in the fourth century have paid insufficient attention to Ammianus' careful distinction between such prefects (cf. 14. 1. 10, on Thalassius) and regional prefects.

52. On this notion (dropped in Jewish writing, despite its biblical authority, because of its pagan associations), see J. D. M. Derrett, "Whatever Happened to the Land Flowing with Milk and Honey?" *Vig. Chr.* 38 (1984): 178–84.

53. For these two men, and on the necessity of distinguishing between them, see T. D. Barnes, *The New Empire of Diocletian and Constantine* (Cambridge, Mass., 1982), pp. 103, 117–18, 132. Observe, however, that the deleted name on *ILT* 814 is now known to be Valerius Felix, otherwise attested as praetorian prefect of Africa from 333 to 336: see the parallel text from Antioch published in G. Dagron and D. Feissel, "Inscriptions inédites du Musée d'Antioche," *T&MByz* 9 (1984): 421–31.

54. Groag, *Reichsbeamten,* pp. 51–54.

55. *PLRE* 1:149 makes Basilius the son of the consul of 327, "who was in turn presumably a relative of Valerius Maximus Basilius": the two are held to be identical by A. Chastagnol, *Les fastes de la préfecture de Rome au Bas-Empire* (Paris, 1962), p. 73.

56. Colonna prints Duebner's supplement τὰς τοῦ πατρὸς <τῶν θ>εῶν παρέδρους: the correct reading is established by *POsl.* inv. 1478, line 89 (fifth century): cf. Eitrem and Amundsen, "Fragments," p. 28.

any bees' honeycombs, but with lawfulness and words, by which the nature of a soul is nourished and watered.

The honorific epigrams of the later Roman Empire often laud Dike and Themis as the assessors of officials (their statues often stood outside the judgment chamber), whether provincial governors, *vicarii,* or praetorian prefects.[57] The proconsul's father had clearly held high office. Himerius salutes Basilius as the son of a distinguished father (*Or.* 46. 8). In the crucial phrase, the transmitted reading is ὦ πατρὸς ὑπάτου βλάστημα, which ought to mean "offspring of a father who has been consul." No ordinary consul is available as the proconsul's father, once the identity of Valerius Maximus, consul in 327, with the *praefectus urbi* of 319–23 is denied—as appears to be necessary on other grounds. Can the phrase be translated "offspring of a most noble father"?[58] It seems unlikely in a context referring to Roman officials. But, on prosopographical grounds, it is reasonable enough to identify the proconsul as the son of a *praefectus urbi.* If that is correct, then an easy emendation to the text resolves the historical difficulty. Read ὑπάρχου in place of ὑπάτου, and translate the invocation as follows: "O child of a divine man! O offspring of a father who has been prefect! You who have received the scepter of your paternal virtue." If the proconsul in Himerius is the Basilius who was *praefectus urbi* in 395, then Maximus, *praefectus urbi* in 361–62, was his father and possessed the *signum* Basilius: presumably, therefore, he was a Valerius Maximus *signo* Basilius like his presumed father, who had been *praefectus urbi* from 319 to 323. The date of Himerius' speech must be later than 364, probably considerably later: what is known about the usual ages of proconsuls and *praefecti urbi* points to a date in the 370s. Basilius was *comes sacrarum largitionum* in 382/83.[59]

Hermogenes (*Or.* 48). Also attested as proconsul at Corinth (*IG* 4. 209 [undated]), Hermogenes is the subject of the longest and most elaborate speech to survive intact. Himerius gives a high-flown and ornate account of Hermogenes' career before his proconsulate. First, he served at the court of a tyrannical ruler. Himerius defines Hermogenes' post as follows (*Or.* 48. 16):

Being at the imperial court in his earliest youth, he was deemed worthy of such great trust that he was considered the only worthwhile guardian of secrets. And on the one hand he performed this service on their behalf to the gods (ὑπὲρ ἐκείνων τοῖς θεοῖς), while on the other he transported the divine utterances to the one who sent him. He became an expounder of the best laws and customs, always wishing to mollify the purpose of the ruler, just as they say Pythagoras of Samos did, when he attended Phalaris in Sicily.[60]

57. L. Robert, *Hellenica,* vol. 4 (Paris, 1948), esp. pp. 24–25, 99–105. For the pairing of Dike and Themis as personified qualities, Robert aptly adduces Himer. *Or.* 38. 9, 48. 6.
58. As suggested implicitly by Groag, *Reichsbeamten,* p. 52, n. 2.
59. *PLRE* 1:149.
60. Pythagoras is brought into contact with Phalaris only in very late texts, such as Iamb. *VP* 32; *Epist. Phalaridis* 23, 56, 74 (R. Hercher, ed., *Epistolographi Graeci* [Paris, 1873], pp. 413–14, 422, 428). In contrast, Phalaris finds no mention in Porphyry's *Vita Pythagorae.*

Hermogenes, however, showed himself superior to Pythagoras because, whereas the latter despaired and left Sicily, Hermogenes "spoke out in conversations to such effect that he made the ruler's rule milder, by narrating ancient myths and stories from poetry and history" (*Or.* 48. 19). Next, when he reached manhood, Hermogenes retired to study philosophy (*Or.* 48. 20–28). Then he went to Constantinople in order to volunteer his services to "an emperor with profound respect for the law and noble by nature, with whom it was possible to use his preparation in knowledge" (*Or.* 48. 28). The emperor welcomed Hermogenes and at once made him an adviser, thereby enabling him to confer benefits widely (*Or.* 48. 30):

> What laws ventured by him were not generous? What men in peril did not escape danger through him? What men deserving office failed to obtain it through him? What men with a request for anything did not take refuge with him? For standing as an intermediary between the emperor and those under his rule, he provided him with the needs of his subjects, and them with his commands—just as the myths say that Hermes is the messenger of Zeus and reports his will to gods and men while learning theirs.

Finally, "god and time" made Hermogenes ruler of Greece (*Or.* 48. 31), though only after he had been to the Danube (*Or.* 48. 36).

Reconstructions of Hermogenes' career have proceeded from identifying the tyrannical ruler whom he first served as Licinius and the emperor who gave him a post in Constantinople as Constantine.[61] But what Himerius says about the cruel ruler evokes the Caesar Gallus rather than Licinius. Hermogenes was a *notarius* entrusted with taking messages from the emperor whom he served to another who, at the time Himerius was writing, was both dead and commonly styled *divus:* the generalizing plural "to the gods" means "to a deified emperor"—and has nothing to do with the consultation of oracles.[62] The dead emperor could as easily be Constantius as Constantine himself. Moreover, the emperor who welcomed Hermogenes to Constantinople resembles the philosophical Julian more than Constantine: the analogies with antiquity that Himerius draws (particularly that of Alcibiades and Socrates) discountenance the idea of a youthful Hermogenes counseling an elderly Constantine at the end of his life.

What was Hermogenes' post in Constantinople? Himerius' description might suggest that he was *quaestor sacri palatii.*[63] But Jovius held that

---

61. Seeck, *Briefe,* p. 173; Schenkl, "Himerios," col. 1622; Groag, *Reichsbeamten,* pp. 36–38; *PLRE* 1:424–25; F. Millar, *The Emperor in the Roman World (31 B.C.–A.D. 337)* (London, 1977), p. 100; cf. id., rev. of R. MacMullen, *Constantine,* in *JRS* 60 (1970): 216. A. Piganiol, *L'empire chrétien* (Paris, 1947), p. 69, even detected the hand of Hermogenes as *quaestor sacri palatii* in Constantine's legislation. That notion is considered and rejected by F. Amarelli, *Vetustas-innovatio: Un' antitesi apparente nella legislazione di Costantino,* Pubblicazioni della Facoltà giuridica dell' Università di Napoli 162 (Naples, 1978), pp. 100–102.
62. As assumed by A. Alföldi, *The Conversion of Constantine and Pagan Rome* (Oxford, 1948), pp. 57, 99; *PLRE* 1:424.
63. Millar, *Emperor,* pp. 100–101.

post under Julian in 361 and early 362 (Amm. Marc. 21. 18. 1, 22. 8. 49)—
and doubtless retained it beyond the last attested date of his tenure, 23
March 362 (*CTh* 11. 39. 5). Nor can Hermogenes have held the same
post as the sophist Nymphidianus of Smyrna, the brother of the
philosopher Maximus: Julian "entrusted the emperor's tongue to him"
by putting him in charge of imperial letters composed in Greek (Eunap.
VP 18, p. 497). Himerius' stress on petitions perhaps provides the vital
clue: Hermogenes may have been *magister libellorum* under Julian.

Himerius also alludes to Hermogenes' recent presence on or near the
Danube (*Or*. 48. 36). Again, a later date than is usually adopted furnishes
a natural explanation: shortly before he came to Greece, Hermogenes
may have visited the court of Valens, who was on campaign on the
Danube frontier from spring 367 until early 370.[64]

Plocianus (*Or*. 49). The speech is known only from Photius, who calls
Plocianus proconsul (*Bibl*. cod. 165, p. 9. 71–72 C.): presumably proconsul of Achaea.

Praetextatus (*Or*. 51). Himerius' speech to Praetextatus as proconsul
of Achaea is known only from Photius' report of its title (*Bibl*. cod. 165,
p. 9. 73–74 C.). Praetextatus was in Constantinople in January 362,
having been appointed proconsul of Achaea by Julian, presumably to
take office in the spring (Amm. Marc. 22. 7. 6): Himerius, it may be
deduced, delivered the speech in Constantinople. Praetextatus was still
proconsul of Achaea in September 364 (Zos. 4. 3. 3; cf. *CTh* 9. 16. 7): he
was proconsul, therefore, for the triennium 362–65.

Pompeianus (*Or*. 53). The speech is completely lost, but Photius
reports that Himerius delivered it in Nicomedia at the behest of
Pompeianus, who was governor there (*Bibl*. cod. 165, p. 9. 75–76 C.).

?Strategius Musonianus (*Or*. 62. 6). A speech apparently composed in
Constantinople refers to a man named after the Muses and a devotee of
culture who happens to be governing at the time (ὅσῳ καὶ ἄνδρα αὐτῶν
[sc. the Muses] ἐπώνυμον καὶ ταῖς ἐκείνων τελεταῖς σκιρτήσαντα
ἡγεῖσθαι τῆς πόλεως συμβαίνει). On purely formal grounds, the
name could be Musonius.[65] But neither of the Musonii before whom
Himerius delivered speeches (*Or*. 20 and 39) is as attractive a candidate
as Strategius Musonianus, who earned his second name (hence perhaps
ἐπώνυμον rather than ὁμώνυμον) through cultural activities in the service
of Constantine (Amm. Marc. 15. 13. 1–2).[66] Moreover, Himerius' language (ἡγεῖσθαι) suggests a proconsul rather than a prefect of the city of
Constantinople. Musonianus must have held the post before his proconsulate of Achaea in 352/53.

V

Eunapius never met Himerius, even though he studied in Athens for
four or five years (*VP* 10. 1. 1–2, p. 485; 10. 8. 3, p. 493; 14. 1, p. 494).

---

64. O. Seeck, *Regesten der Kaiser und Päpste für die Jahre 311 bis 476 n. Chr.* (Stuttgart, 1919),
pp. 231–39.

65. For the uncertainty, cf. *PLRE* I:611, 612.

66. Seeck, "Strategius," col. 182.

Himerius left Athens in the winter of 361/62 and attached himself to the court of Julian: when Julian was killed in June 363, Himerius continued to reside elsewhere until after his rival Proaeresius was dead (*VP* 14. 1, p. 494). Since Proaeresius died "not many days" after Eunapius departed from Athens (*VP* 10. 8. 4, p. 493), Himerius' absence from the city must have lasted at least five years. The conventional modern chronology assumes that Eunapius arrived in Athens in 361/62, and hence that Proaeresius died in 366/67 or 367/68.[67] On the other hand, a recent study, which seeks to extract precision out of vague phrases in the *Lives of the Philosophers,* argues that Eunapius arrived in Athens ca. 25 September 364 and left in the spring or summer of 369.[68] If that conclusion is correct, then Himerius could not have returned to Athens in 368 (as has sometimes been supposed)[69] but will have stayed away at least until 369.

Eunapius gives a hostile account of Himerius' journey to the court of Julian at Constantinople: he went in order to declaim in the hope that the emperor would regard him with favor because of his dislike for Proaeresius (*VP* 14. 1, p. 494). The headings to the relevant speeches present a different picture, which their text tends to confirm. Himerius was summoned by the emperor, he delivered speeches en route at Thessalonica and at Philippi (*Or.* 39 and 40), the former before Musonius, the *vicarius* of the diocese of Macedonia, and Calliopius, the *consularis* of the province of Macedonia, with a former proconsul of Achaea also present. When he arrived in Constantinople, Himerius produced a panegyric of the city (*Or.* 41), but only after a significant ceremony, to which its opening words allude (*Or.* 41. 1):

> After I have purified my soul to Mithras Helios and have already through the gods' agency been with the emperor who is a friend of the gods, come let me kindle not a lantern, but a speech to the emperor and city. For an Attic law orders initiates to carry a light to Eleusis and handfuls of grain, the tokens of civilized life: for our initiates let a speech serve as the thank-offering, since the same Apollo is also (I think) Helios and speeches are children of Apollo.

The passage has been duly noted by students of Julian's Mithraism, though perhaps not fully exploited.[70] The occasion and the prominence that Himerius gives to his initiation mark it as a significant event. Himerius was teaching in Athens when Julian studied there briefly in 355,[71] and the young prince will not have missed the opportunity to attend his lectures. Himerius traveled to Constantinople when Julian was about to embark upon a revival of Hellenism: it may without difficulty be surmised that he received an urgent invitation to come to

---

67. W. Schmid, "Eunapios (2)," *RE* 6 (1907): 1121; W. Ensslin, "Proairesios (1)," *RE* 23 (1957): 32; *PLRE* 1:296, 731; cf. Christ–Schmid–Stählin, *Geschichte,* 2⁶: 986, 1034.
   68. R. Goulet, "Sur la chronologie de la vie et les oeuvres d'Eunape de Sardes," *JHS* 100 (1980): 60–72.
   69. F. Schemmel, "Die Hochschule von Athen im IV. und V. Jahrhundert p. Chr. n.," *Neue Jahrbücher* 22 (1908): 494–573, at p. 499.
   70. P. Athanassiadi-Fowden, *Julian and Hellenism* (Oxford, 1981), p. 48.
   71. Soc. *HE* 4. 26. 6, whence Soz. *HE* 6. 17. 1. Himerius appears in these ecclesiastical histories because he taught Basil and Gregory, later bishops of Caesarea and Nazianzus.

court similar to that which Julian sent to the philosopher Maximus (*Epist.* 26 Bidez). When Himerius arrived, Julian honored him by initiating him into the mysteries of Mithras. The speech that Himerius then delivered in praise of the emperor and the city of Constantinople stresses that Julian had altered its Christian character by founding shrines and introducing pagan cults (*Or.* 41. 8–15).

VI

After the winter of 361/62, precise evidence for the career of Himerius is lacking for several years. It may well be that Himerius accompanied Julian to Antioch in 362 and remained in the East until the late 360s: the next firm indication of his whereabouts appears to locate him in Constantinople praising the *praefectus urbi* Severus shortly after 366 (*Or.* 24), though he was certainly back in Athens when Hermogenes served as proconsul of Achaea (*Or.* 48), probably no later than 370/71. At a more speculative level, Himerius' speeches can be held to imply that he passed through Cappadocia and visited Egypt.

Himerius had become a citizen of Athens (*Or.* 7. 2) and had married into one of the leading families of the city: his son, who was enrolled in the council of the Areopagus at the age of two (*Or.* 8. 15),[72] was a descendant of Plutarch, Minucianus, and Nicagoras, and could also claim Musonius Rufus and Sextus of Chaeronea among his forebears (*Or.* 7. 4, 8. 21). Presumably, therefore, since Himerius will probably have married in the 350s, his wife was a granddaughter of Nicagoras, torchbearer of the mysteries at Eleusis, who had visited the syringes at Thebes in Egypt in 326.[73] Nicagoras' father was the rhetor Minucianus, who was active in the 260s: he claims descent from the philosophers Plutarch and Sextus on an extant inscription at Eleusis (*IG* 2². 3814 = *Syll.*³ 845).[74] Himerius and his wife had two known children: a daughter, who outlived her father; and a son, Rufinus, whose premature death was the occasion of an extant threnody (*Or.* 8).

Rufinus died very young while Himerius was absent from Athens (*Or.* 8. 22): "Receive then these libations, which I pour for you by the River Melas, which ... has truly now become grim and black for me, and more hateful than Cocytus and Acheron." By the side of which river named Melas was Himerius when news came of his son's death? Possibly the river in Boeotia, since Himerius exclaims that Cithaeron is vanquished by his misfortunes (*Or.* 8. 8)—and some have imagined the sophist living the life of an exile in Boeotia as a result of academic quarrels in Athens.[75] But there were also rivers with the name Melas in

---

72. In lines 133–34, read τρίτον οὔπω γεγονὼς ἔτος . . . ἐξέπληξας, not ἐξέπληξα.

73. J. Baillet, "Constantin et le dadouque d'Eleusis," *CRAI* 1922: 282–96; cf. P. Graindor, "Constantin et le dadouque Nicagoras," *Byzantion* 3 (1926): 209–14.

74. See O. Schissel, "Die Familie des Minukianos: Ein Beitrag zur Personenkunde des neuplatonischen Athen," *Klio* 21 (1927): 361–73; F. Millar, "P. Herennius Dexippus: The Greek World and the Third-Century Invasions," *JRS* 59 (1969): 16–17.

75. Schenkl, "Himerios," col. 1624. His additional argument, that Himerius was close to Athens because he was preparing for Rufinus' arrival (*Or.* 8. 2–3), is clearly invalid.

Thessaly, Thrace, Bithynia, Pamphylia, and Cappadocia.[76] This last river Melas lay north of Caesarea (Strabo 538/39; Ptol. 5. 6. 7), on or close to the route that Julian and the imperial court took across Asia Minor in the early summer of 362.[77] It is an attractive, if extremely uncertain, conjecture that Himerius received tidings of his son's death in Cappadocia in May 362.[78]

As for Egypt, the evidence lies in the nuances of Himerius' rhetorical elaborations. An early speech delivered before 352 begins with a reference to the colossus of Memnon at Thebes in Egypt as "making a musical marvel at the dawn of the day," but the words are conventional and Himerius explicitly appeals to hearsay (*Or.* 62. 1). Later in life, however, when he praised Hermogenes, Himerius was able to describe the flooding of the Nile in concrete detail and with an implicit appeal to autopsy (*Or.* 48. 8–9):

> When the Egyptians, after sacrificing to Demeter, labor on threshing, then pouring down violently from Ethiopia it suddenly makes the whole of Egypt into a sea. You would see, you would see then also the great wonders in that country: on the same plot of land the same man as sailor and farmer, cattle grazing and shortly afterwards cargo ships, and what was formerly a city in the middle of dry land an island.

And in a speech for the birthday of a friend, which is otherwise undatable, Himerius appears to allude to their presence together in Egypt (*Or.* 44. 5):

> You know the loves of the Nile, having been a hearer and again a witness of the wonder; you know too his bedfellow, who is pregnant with and gives birth to a crop of varied fruits. . . . Someone stood looking at the size of the pyramids, and wondered at the Apis who was a foreteller of the future in the guise of a bull. The din of Meroe and the noise of the Cataracts has often detained travelers with wonder. Memnon, that crystalline rock emitting a living sound with inanimate voice, was considered (ἐνομίσθη) a god addressing the god Helios.[79] These are the finest things of Egypt: these adorn your celebration.

The mention of the Apis bull, to which Himerius recurs in one of his speeches to Nicomachus Flavianus (*Or.* 43. 6), suggests that Himerius may have gone to Egypt while Julian was in Antioch: an Apis bull was found in the autumn of 362 (Amm. Marc. 22. 14. 6).

VII

I have argued that Himerius was born ca. 320 at Prusias in Bithynia and studied in Athens, and that his career falls into four distinct stages:

---

76. For these rivers, see F. Stählin, "Melas 14," *RE* 15 (1931): 439; Oberhummer, "Melas 16," *RE* 15 (1931): 439; W. Ruge, "Melas 19–22," *RE* 15 (1931): 440.

77. For Julian's movements in 362, see Seeck, *Regesten*, pp. 209–11.

78. Schemmel, "Hochschule," p. 499. But *Or.* 8. 2–3 is hard to reconcile with the view that Himerius was traveling at the time, and especially with the view that he was accompanying the imperial court.

79. On the date at which the famous sound ceased to be audible, see G. W. Bowersock, "The Miracle of Memnon," *BASP* 21 (1984): 21–32. The evidence of Himerius confirms the conclusion that the miraculous music had ceased well before the end of the fourth century.

(1) teaching as a sophist in Constantinople from 343 to 352;
(2) teaching in Athens from 352 to December 361;
(3) absent from Athens, first at the court of Julian, then in the East and Asia Minor with a visit to Egypt, from December 361 to ca. 369;
(4) teaching in Athens again, from ca. 369 until the 380s.

The speeches can be assigned to the various stages of Himerius' career as follows:

(1) *Or.* 53 (between 344 and 349), 62 (before 352), frag. 1. 6 (?15 March 351);
(2) *Or.* 7 (not long before December 361), 9, 20 (before 356), 23, 25, 29 (359/60), 31 (359/60), 32 (between 357 and 360), ?33, 38 (?353/54), 50 (359/60);
(3) *Or.* 3 (possibly 362/63),[80] 8 (possibly early summer 362), ?10,[81] 24 (between 366 and ca. 369), 39–41 (winter 361/62), 42 (?early 362), 51 (ca. January 362), 52 (either ca. December 361 or late summer 362);[82]
(4) *Or.* 12, 36, 43 (all spring 383), 44, 46–47 (between 370 and 380), 48 (ca. 370); either (2) or (4): *Or.* 6, 28, 30, 34, 35, 49, 59, 60, 68 (all apparently delivered in Athens).[83]

VIII

The general picture that emerges is a disappointing and depressing one of an academic who attempted to achieve political prominence by attaching himself to Julian, then suffered disgrace (though not complete disaster) when Julian failed so spectacularly and the Roman Empire again became officially Christian. Himerius must be imagined pathetically championing the lost cause of the old religion whenever a sympathetic proconsul (like Hermogenes) came to Achaea. It is significant that his latest datable activity belongs to the spring of 383, when he composed no fewer than three speeches for the younger Nicomachus Flavianus on his way to be proconsul of Asia (*Or.* 12, 36, 43). It will be worth speculating about why Himerius considered the brief visit of Flavianus en route to Asia important enough to celebrate with three separate speeches. A group of Cretan inscriptions may suggest an answer to the question. Oecumenius Dositheus Asclepiodotus, *consularis* of Crete between 379 and 383 (*I. Cret.* 4. 284), erected at Gortyn a whole series of statues of prominent Roman aristocrats honored by the provincial κοινόν of Crete or the local βουλή of Gortyn, clearly at his instigation. The following names occur on the inscribed bases that have survived:

(1) Anicius Bassus, proconsul of Campania (*I. Cret.* 4. 314);
(2) Valerius Severus, *praefectus urbi* at Rome (315);

80. *Or.* 3 is an attack on Epicurus, particularly for denying providence: Himerius may be echoing Julian's disapproval of his philosophy; cf. Julian *Letter to Themistius* 255C, 259B; *Letter to a Priest* 301B.
81. *Or.* 10. 13 may allude to the emperor Julian.
82. It is not clear whether Photius' words (p. 9. 74–75 C.: πρὸς τὸν βασιλέα Ἰουλιανὸν ἀπαίρειν μέλλων) refer to Himerius' departure from Athens or from Julian's court.
83. Most of the otherwise undatable speeches that are extant either wholly or in substantial fragments should probably also be assigned to Himerius' years in Athens, viz. *Or.* 1, 2, 4, 5, 26, 27, 45, 54, 61, 64–66, 69, 74.

(3) Agorius Praetextatus, ex-prefect (316);
(4) Fl(avius) Hypatius, ex-consul and formerly praetorian prefect (317);
(5) Petronius Probus, ex-consul and formerly praetorian prefect for the third time (318);
(6) Vettius Probianus (the *nomen* is restored), ex-prefect of the city of Rome (319);
(7) Anicius Paulinus, ex-proconsul and formerly *praefectus urbi* at Rome (320);
(8) and (9) similar fragmentary inscriptions honoring an ex-prefect of the city (321) and Anicius Claudius (322).

These dedications form a homogeneous group, and the official titles of the Roman aristocrats all appear to be correct for 382/83.[84] None of these men had ever visited Crete, though they may have possessed property there. Why then are they so conspicuously honored? The fact that they are all honored at Gortyn suggests that the leading men of Crete felt a need for their patronage. Their fears may have concerned religion: in 384 the pious Cynegius, as praetorian prefect of the East, was to commence a rampage against pagan temples and shrines.[85] Himerius' speeches to Flavianus and Asclepiodotus' honoring of Roman aristocrats can be construed as evidence of a closing of pagan ranks against the dominant Christian orthodoxy. In a very real sense, Himerius speaks with the voice of dying Hellenism.[86]

After the spring of 383, no more is heard of Himerius. It is reported that he went blind in old age and died of epilepsy, leaving behind a daughter.[87] He was no longer among the living when Eunapius composed his *Lives of the Philosophers and Sophists* at the very end of the fourth century.

University of Toronto

84. Alan Cameron, "Anicius Claudius (I. Cret. iv. 322)," *ZPE* 57 (1984): 147–48.
85. J. F. Matthews, *Western Aristocracies and Imperial Court A.D. 364–425* (Oxford, 1975), pp. 140–42.
86. J. Geffcken, *Der Ausgang des griechisch-römischen Heidentums* (Heidelberg, 1929), p. 168 = *The Last Days of Greco-Roman Paganism,* trans. S. MacCormack (Amsterdam–New York–Oxford, 1978), p. 178: "a professor of upright sentiments, who under Christian emperors composed his face into that expression of sorrow which we already know, who rejoiced ecstatically under Julian, and when the times became worse again contented himself with a gesture of protest."
87. *Suda* I.348 (2:633 Adler); Eunap. *VP* 14. 2, p. 494.

XVII

HILARY OF POITIERS ON HIS EXILE

Hilary of Poitiers was condemned by the Council of Baeterrae in 356 and departed into exile in Asia Minor.[1] But the charge on which Hilary was condemned is nowhere explicitly recorded and there is consequently some divergence of modern opinions on what it was—and a scholar who knows the author exceptionally well has even maintained that he was never formally condemned and deposed at all.[2]

The traditional view has been that the 'Athanasius of the West' was deposed and exiled because he supported Nicene orthodoxy in the face of the attempts of Constantius to secure western acceptance of a non-Nicene credal formula at the Councils of Arles (353/4) and Milan (355).[3] But some eminent scholars have taken a less heroic and less creditable view. Long ago H. M. Gwatkin asserted that 'the charge seems to have been one of immorality, but we are not told exactly what it was', though he declined to offer any precise evidence or arguments in support of his assertion.[4] Subsequently, Alfred Feder, the excellent editor of the historical fragments deriving from Hilary's lost work against Ursacius and Valens, argued that Hilary's offence was political rather than either theological or moral, and suggested specifically that it was suspicion of disloyalty to the emperor.[5]

Gwatkin's view seems to have found no favour at all, but Feder's conclusion was rescued from long neglect by Henry Chadwick, who in 1959, in a standard work of reference, stated outright as if it were demonstrated fact that Hilary was condemned for high treason.[6] Moreover, in a recent and provocative study of Hilary, Hanns Christof Brennecke has adapted and extended Chadwick's thesis by denying the theological background which Feder and Chadwick both took for granted: he sets the exile of Hilary against the general political and military situation of Gaul in the mid-350s, denies that theological issues played any part at all in his condemnation, and contends that only the hypothesis that he was condemned on suspicion of subversive activities ('wegen des Ver-

130

dachts politischer Umtriebe') explains what Hilary himself says about his exile.[7]

The most recent discussion, however, reaches the agnostic conclusion that, while the traditional view is the product of hagiographical elaboration without demonstrable basis in fact, the political interpretation in its turn cannot be sustained because of the lack of direct evidence in its favour: hence the reasons for Hilary's condemnation and exile must remain a mystery.[8] Consequently, there is little likelihood that all aspects of the manifold problems which the exile of Hilary raises can be tackled, let alone solved, in a brief compass. Nevertheless, some progress towards clarifying the central question of the charge on which Hilary was condemned may become possible, if it is allowed at the outset that the public statements which Hilary made about his own exile could be deeply misleading.[9]

Hilary composed his *In Constantium* shortly after the Council of Constantinople, which in January 360 ratified the homoean creed finally agreed upon after the Councils of Ariminum and Seleucia.[10] It was written at white heat in fury at the outcome of the council and before Hilary heard of the proclamation of Julian as Augustus in February 360: the total absence of any detectable allusion to this important event is surely decisive in a work which argues that Constantius has ceased to be a legitimate emperor (27). The exordium begins in anger:

> Tempus est loquendi, quia iam praeteriit tempus tacendi. Christus expectetur, quia obtinuit antichristus. clament pastores, quia mercennarii fugerunt. ponamus animas pro ovibus, quia fures introierunt et leo saeviens circuit. ad martyrium per has voces exeamus etc.

Then, immediately after the introduction, Hilary claims that he had long foreseen the present situation:-

> ego, fratres, ut mihi omnes, qui me vel audiunt vel familiaritate cognitum habent, testes sunt, gravissimum fidei periculum longe antea providens, post sanctorum virorum exilia Paulini, Eusebi, Luciferi, Dionisi, quinto abhinc anno a Saturnini et Ursaci et Valentis communione me cum Gallicanis episcopis separavi, indulta ceteris consortibus eorum resipiscendi facultate, ut nec pacis abesset voluntas et principalium morborum fetida et in corruptione totius corporis membra proficientia desecarentur, si tamen hoc ipsum beatissimis confessoribus Christi edita decreta tum a nobis manere placuisset.[11] qui postea per factionem eorum pseudoapostolorum ad Biterrensem synodum compulsus, cognitionem demonstrandae huius haereseos obtuli. sed hi timentes publicae conscien-

tiae, audire ingesta a me noluerunt, putantes se innocentiam suam Christo
posse mentiri, si volentes nescirent quod gesturi postmodum essent
scientes. atque exinde toto hoc tempore in exilio detentus, neque deceden-
dum mihi esse de Christi confessione decrevi, neque honestam aliquam ac
probabilem ineundae unitatis rationem respuendam. (2.1-20 Rocher)

Hilary here makes certain claims or statements about himself.[12] First,
he dates the action which led to his exile to the fifth year before the time
of writing ('quinto abhinc anno'): since the *In Constantium* belongs to
the early months of 360, while the Council of Baeterrae met in the
spring of 356, Hilary presumably reckons in calendar years. Second, he
took the action which he proceeds to describe after the exiles of
Paulinus the bishop of Trier, Eusebius of Vercellae, Lucifer of Cagliari
and Dionysius of Milan: Paulinus was deposed by the Council of Arles
in 353/4, the other three at the Council of Milan in the summer of 355.
Third, Hilary and the Gallic bishops 'separated themselves from communion with Saturninus of Arles, Ursacius of Singidunum and Valens
of Mursa'—whatever that means or is supposed to mean. Fourth,
Hilary was subsequently compelled to attend the Council of Baeterrae,
where he attempted to expose heresy, but the council refused to allow
his submission to be heard. Fifth, Hilary was exiled and is still in exile.

Much will become clearer if this passage, in which Hilary talks mainly
about his own exile, is juxtaposed with another in which he is totally
silent about himself. A later, carefully structured chapter of the *In Constantium* (11) begins by calling the emperor 'a rapacious wolf' and
inviting him to listen to the results of his actions. It concludes with the
proposition that if Hilary is lying Constantius is a sheep, but that if the
emperor is indeed engaged upon such a course of action, then he is the
(or an) Antichrist. Hilary first adduces Alexandria, 'ravaged by so many
wars', where prefects have been changed, generals chosen, people
bribed and legions mobilised, all in order to prevent Athanasius from
preaching Christ. The allusions to Athanasius' deposition in 339 and to
his flight in 356 are clear. In the winter of 338/9 Philagrius was reappointed prefect of Egypt to install Gregory as the new bishop of Alexandria after a council at Antioch had deposed Athanasius, and in
February 356 all the troops of Egypt and Libya were mobilised under
the *dux* Syrianus in an attempt to arrest him: precisely these details are
emphasised in other early accounts of the two episodes.[13] Passing over
the lesser cities throughout the East that have been terrorised or
attacked, Hilary then turns to Constantius' activities in the West:-

132

(i) postque[14] omnia contulisti arma adversum fidem Occidentis et exercitus tuos convertisti in oves Christi: fugere mihi sub Nerone licuit! (ii) at tu Paulinum beatae passionis virum blandimento sollicitatum relegasti et ecclesiam sanctam Treverorum tali sacerdote spoliasti. edictis fidem terruisti. ipsum usque ad mortem demutasi exiliis et fatigasti, extra christianum quoque nomen relegasti, ne panem aut de horreo tuo sumeret aut de Montani Maximillaeque antro profanatum expectaret. (iii) Mediolanensem piissimam plebem quanto furoris tui terrore turbasti! tribuni tui adierunt sancta sanctorum et viam sibi omni per populum crudelitate pandentes protraxerunt de altario sacerdotes. levius te putas, sceleste, Iudaeorum impietate peccasse? effuderunt quidem illi Zachariae sanguinem, sed quantum in te est, concorporatos Christo a Christo discidisti. (iv) vertisti deinde usque ad Romam bellum tuum, eripuisti illinc episcopum, et — o te miserum,[15] qui nescio utrum maiore impietate relegaveris quam remiseris! (v) quos tu deinde in ecclesiam Tolosanam exercuisti furores! clerici fustibus caesi, diacones plumbo elisi, et in ipsum, ut sanctissimi mecum intellegant, Christum manus missae. (vi) haec, Constanti, si ego mentior, ovis es, si vero tu peragis, antichristus es. (11.14-37 Rocher)

The passage deserves to be analysed in full detail,[16] but the present exposition must confine itself to the most important points. (For convenience of reference, the sections into which the passage can logically be divided are marked with Roman numerals: no modern edition has yet divided the chapter into sections.)

(i) The logic of this sentence requires careful elucidation. As the first word, or first two words, the manuscripts offer *post quae* and *postquam*. Like Coustant (*PL* 10.558), the most recent editor prints *postquam*. Yet he translates *postquam* as 'après quoi', i.e., as an adverb rather than a conjunction.[17] That seems liguistically implausible. Yet his translation gives the required sense: it renders *post quae* perfectly, if the relative pronoun is taken as connective, as in the context it must be. But *post quae* has the disadvantage of making the word which immediately follows potentially ambiguous, since grammatically *omnia* could be linked to the immediately preceding *quae* rather than, as must in fact be the case, to the noun *arma* which follows after the verb.[18] Since the train of thought requires: 'Afterwards (or after this) [i.e., after terrorising the East] you concentrated all your arms against the faith of the West and turned your armies against the sheep of Christ', I formerly inclined to read *postea*,[19] but P. Smulders has pointed out that *postque* not only gives the required sense, but also explains the readings transmitted in the manuscripts while conforming to Hilarian usage.[20]

The second half of the first sentence has usually been rendered as if Hilary were saying: 'in the reign of Nero it would have been permissible for me to flee!'[21] But the precise nature of the reference of the phrase *sub Nerone* to the historical Nero needs definition. There is a subtle linguistic point at issue which has not always been recognised: it is one which Alfred Gudeman elucidated in his commentary on Tacitus' *Dialogus de Oratoribus* (3.3), although all his examples were of individuals referring to themselves by name in the third person:[22] the phrase means, not 'under Nero', but 'under a Nero' or 'under someone like Nero', i.e., in the present context, under a persecutor openly hostile to the Christians. Hilary has already styled Constantius a *persecutor fallax*, a *hostis blandiens*, an *antichristus* (5), and he is about to complain that he used flattery (*blandimento*) on Paulinus of Trier (ii). This sentence repeats the same contrast between open and covert persecution in different words, sharpening the effect: under a pagan, openly hostile persecutor of the Christians (like Nero), Hilary would have been allowed to flee, but Constantius did not allow his victims that liberty. Constantius is not a 'new Nero',[23] but a persecutor worse than Nero: Hilary is restating the point he made earlier when he expressed the wish that God had allowed him to confess his faith in the days of Nero or Decius (4) and proclaimed that he is saying to Constantius exactly what he would have said to Nero, to Decius and to Galerius (7).

(ii) Paulinus of Trier was deposed by the Council of Arles which met while Constantius was residing in the city for the winter of 353/4, with the emperor either present or closely following the proceedings.[24] The edicts with which Constantius terrorised the faith should be identified as his requirement that the Council of Arles ratify the decisions of the Council of Sirmium of 351, which condemned Athanasius, Marcellus and Photinus and promulgated a new creed.[25] After Paulinus was deposed for his refusal to endorse the Sirmian decisions, the emperor exiled him to Phrygia: hence Hilary's jibe that he had to be moved from his first place of exile because the emperor neither wished to feed him from an imperial granary nor to take the risk that he would beg food from the cave of Montanus and Maximilla. But where was Paulinus sent from Phrygia? Hilary phrase *extra christianum nomen* implies a totally pagan area. Where was such to be found in the Roman Empire of the middle of the fourth century, except perhaps (allowing for exaggeration) in Isauria.[26] However, it should not be assumed that Paulinus ever reached his destined second place of exile: Hilary's words suggest rather that he died on the journey from Phrygia.

(iii) The allusion to the arrest of Dionysius the bishop of the city during the Council of Milan in the summer of 355 is clear. Sulpicius Severus stresses that the laity of Milan 'preserved the catholic faith with outstanding enthusiasm' (*Chron.* 2.39.4).

(iv) Hilary's references to the exile of Liberius, the bishop of Rome, and to his return from exile in 357 are unmistakeable. Since he makes the temporal progression clear, the passage is very relevant to the dates of Liberius' arrest and return to Rome, which some recent writers have put in 356 and 358 respectively.[27] Hilary sets the arrest of Liberius between the Council of Milan (iii) and the Council of Baeterrae (v), i.e., between late summer 355 and late spring 356. What he says perfectly suits a date in the autumn of 355—which is in fact the date indicated by Ammianus Marcellinus, who puts the arrest of Liberius by the *praefectus urbi* Leontius before the proclamation of Julian as Caesar on 6 November 355 (15.7.6-10).[28]

(v) Rhodanius, the bishop of Toulouse, was forcibly expelled from his see against the opposition of the clergy and laity of his city after the Council of Baeterrae.[29] Admittedly, Jerome states that Rhodanius was exiled with Paulinus of Trier, i.e., at the Council of Arles (*Chronicle* 239[f], cf. 239[i] Helm), while Rufinus (*HE* 10.21) and Sozomenus (*HE* 4.9) both connect his exile with the Council of Milan. But these writers have merely conflated the depositions of different bishops at three different councils which met within the space of three years, viz. Arles (353/4), Milan (355) and Baeterrae (356). Now the name of Rhodanius appears to stand in a list of bishops who attended the Council of Milan,[30] even though he subsequently repented of his acceptance of its decisions.[31] The passage of the *In Constantium*, which is remarkable in appearing to equate Rhodanius with Christ, provides the principal indication that Rhodanius was condemned by the Council of Baeterrae.[32].

(vi) Hilary turns away from the bishops whom Constantius has exiled in the past and urges him to change his policies towards the church.

There is thus a systematic parallelism between the two passages:-

In Constantium 2	*In Constantium* 11
the exile of Paulinus	the exile of Paulinus (ii)
the exiles of Eusebius, Lucifer and Dionysius	the Council of Milan (iii)
	the arrest of Liberius (iv)

the exile of Hilary at the Council   the expulsion of Rhodanius (v)
of Baeterrae

Significantly, one passage mentions Hilary but not Rhodanius, the
other Rhodanius but not Hilary, even though both were condemned by
the same council.

The heading of the letter to the Gallic bishops, traditionally known
as the *De Synodis*, which Hilary wrote towards the end of 358,[33] can
now be exploited. Hilary excepts certain Gallic bishops from his general
salutation:-

> dilectissimis et beatissimis fratribus et coepiscopis provinciae Germaniae
> primae et Germaniae secundae et primae Belgicae et Belgicae secundae et
> Lugdunensis primae et Lugdunensis secundae et provinciae Aquitanicae et
> ex Narbonensi plebibus et clericis Tolosanis et provinciarum Britanniarum
> episcopis Hilarius servus Christi in deo et domino nostro aeternam
> salutem.[34]

If the words *et provinciae Aquitanicae*, which are missing from
several manuscripts, are original and not interpolated, then Hilary
includes in his greeting the bishops of all the Gallic provinces of the 350s
except the small province of Sequania in Upper Germany, the two
mountain provinces of Alpes Graiae et Poeninae and Alpes Maritimae,
the province of Viennensis—and the bishops of Narbonensis, whose
omission is highlighted by his greeting to the lay congregations of the
whole province and the clergy of the city of Toulouse.[35] Why does
Hilary do this? An obvious, though conjectural, explanation is that it
was the bishops of Narbonensis who deposed Hilary and Rhodanius at
the Council of Baeterrae. If that is the case, then the Council of Baeterrae was a provincial synod of the province of Narbonensis. If this
inference is correct, a further corollary can also be drawn concerning its
date. The fifth canon of the Council of Nicaea laid down that provincial
councils should be held twice a year, once in the spring between Easter
and Ascension and once around the time of the harvest in the early
autumn: since Easter was celebrated on 7 April in 356, the Council of
Baeterrae presumably met between that date and 17 May.

If Hilary of Poitiers and Rhodanius of Toulouse were condemned
and deposed together at the Council of Baeterrae, then it is surely
implausible to argue, in default of explicit evidence, that they were

deposed for entirely different reasons. Hilary's claim to Constantius in Constantinople in 360 that he was still a bishop despite his exile (*Ad Const.* 2) must be either disingenuous or a wilful refusal to accept the validity of his deposition.[36] What then of the silence of Athanasius, who never includes Hilary among the western bishops exiled for resisting heresy and refusing to subscribe to his own condemnation? It was tempting to deduce that both men could not be adherents of the same orthodoxy before 359[37]—a deduction which appeared to support the thesis that theological issues played no more than a small part in Hilary's exile. But the silence of Athanasius can be explained more convincingly in another way. When Hilary argued in his *De Synodis* that homoousians and homoiousians are in fundamental agreement, he praised the creeds of both the 'dedication council' of Antioch in 341 and of the Council of Sirmium in 351 (28-33, 37-63). Both these councils had condemned Athanasius, and that fact alone will fully explain his failure to mention Hilary. Since Athanasius constantly and stoutly contended that he had never been validly condemned by any church council, it would have been inconsistent and potentially damaging for him to enroll as an ally someone whose praise of the councils of 341 and 351 so obviously implied that their condemnation and deposition of the bishop of Alexandria was canonically valid.

It need not be presumed that Hilary attended either the Council of Arles in 353/4 or the Council of Milan in 355, or ever himself accepted the decisions of the Council of Sirmium when they were presented to him for his endorsement in Poitiers. But Constantius' policy of obtaining subscriptions from bishops in their own cities, which is most fully described by Athanasius (*Hist. Arian.* 31.3-6), provides the immediate historical background to his exile—a background which is too often forgotten or overlooked.[38] It is not easy to understand Hilary's protestations of his innocence, when he claims that he was exiled by a faction and false reports of the council to Constantius, and that Julian endured more insults from his exile than the bishop suffered real injury (*CSEL* 65.198.2-15). For already in 358 he had implied that theological issues were involved (*Syn.* 2), and by 360 he could claim that in 356 'together with the bishops of Gaul I withdrew myself from communion with Saturninus, Ursacius and Valens' (*In Const.* 2).[39]

Hilary's allusiveness tends to conceal precisely what action it was that led to his condemnation by the Council of Baeterrae.[40] Yet an item of evidence which was published only recently may help to decide the issue.

Many manuscripts of the *De Synodis* preserve interpolated in the text what were originally marginal notes added by Hilary himself in a copy of the work which he sent to Lucifer of Cagliari. In his still standard edition of 1693, Coustant recognised these notes for what they really are and gathered them together under the title 'Apologetica ad Reprehensores libri de Synodis Responsa' (*PL* 10.545-548). In 1978 P. Smulders published two more of these *Apologetica Responsa*:[41] the first reveals that Hilary thought of the *De Synodis* as a letter (which is indeed its literary form), while the second refers directly to the circumstances of his exile:-

> Caput omne hoc si diligentius lectum ab Hilario esset vel intellectum, scisset quid esset pro omousion pugnare et arrianos damnare, neque me diaconus inauditum episcopum absentem rescissae impiae damnationis vestrae et defensae dominicae causa fidei exulantem damnasset.

Here Hilary protests against the misunderstanding of his work by the deacon Hilarius, who is a well-attested associate of Lucifer.[42] The intransigent deacon has condemned the bishop Hilary, who was absent and not given an opportunity to defend himself,[43] even though he is in exile for 'tearing up the impious condemnation' of Lucifer himself and for 'defending the faith in our Lord'. The natural inference from these words, which were meant to be read by Lucifer in private, is that Hilary tore up a document which contained both a condemnation of Lucifer and a doctrinal statement:[44] such a document could hardly be anything other than a copy of the synodical letter of the Council of Milan which the agents of Constantius presented to Hilary in Poitiers for him to subscribe—perhaps very shortly after his consecration as bishop.[45]

NOTES

[1]   The classical form of the name is Baeterrae (M.Ihm, *RE* 2 [1984], 2763/3), but I retain the later spelling Biterrae in quotations.

[2]   P. Smulders, *Gestalten der Kirchengeschichte* 1 (Stuttgart, 1984), 254: 'ein eigentliches Synoden-Urteil scheint nicht gefällt worden zu sein, denn Hilarius wird nicht formell abgesetzt'.
   Similarly, R. P. C. Hanson, *The Search for the Christian Doctrine of God. The Arian Controversay 318-381* (Edinburgh, 1988), 462, argues that Hilary was not deposed by the Council of Baeterrae since eight years later he 'protested vigorously that he had not been deposed'. That is not quite what the relevant passage in fact seems to say (*Contra Auxentium* 7 [*PL* 10.614]), and Auxentius stated categorically that Hilary had been deposed as well as condemned (*Contra Auxentium* 13 [*PL* 10.717]).

138

³ To choose one example out of many: the entry in the *Oxford Dictionary of the Christian Church*, ed. F. L. Cross (1957), 638, begins: 'Hilary of Poitiers, St. (c. 315-367), the "Athanasius of the West". A convert from Neoplatonism, he was elected bp. of Poitiers c. 353 and became at once involved in the Arian disputes. His defence of orthodoxy led to his condemnation at the Synod of Biterrae (356)...'. The passage stands unchanged in the second edition of 1974 and its subsequent reprints.

For fuller expositions of this view, see C. F. A. Borchardt, *Hilary of Poitiers' Role in the Arian Struggle* (Diss. Leiden, pub. 's-Gravenhage, 1966), 18-37; J. Doignon, *Hilaire de Poitiers avant l'exil* (Paris, 1971), 428 ff. ('L'épreuve de foi d'Hilaire'). Doignon has recently characterised the Council of Baeterrae which exiled Hilary as 'ein Ketzergericht' (*Handbuch der lateinischen Literatur der Antike* 5 [Munich, 1989], 448).

⁴ H. M. Gwatkin, *Studies of Arianism* (Cambridge, ²1900), 154.

⁵ A. Feder, *Studien zu Hilarius von Poitiers III. Überlieferungsgeschichte und Echtheitskritik des sogenannten Liber II ad Constantium, des Tractatus mysteriorum, der Epistula ad Abram filiam, der Hymnen. Kleinere Fragmenta und Spuria. Sitzungsberichte der kaiserlichen Akademie der Wissenschaften in Wien*, Philosophisch-historische Klasse 169, Abhandlung 5 (1912), 14-16, esp. 15: 'Wahrscheinlich wurde Hilarius—und auch Julian wegen seiner Stellungnahme in dem kirchlichen Streite—der politischen Untreue gegen Konstantius verdächtigt. Solche Verdächtigungen fanden bei diesem um so leichter Glauben, als Gallien gerade um diese Zeit für ihn eine unsichere Provinz war, wo jeder bedeutende Mann gefährlich werden konnte'.

⁶ H. Chadwick, *Religion in Geschichte und Gegenwart* 3 (Tübingen, ³1959), 317: 'Als Konstantius 353/55 vom Westen die Verurteilung des Athanasius forderte, leitete Hilarius den Widerstand, zu dem sich 355 bei einer Revolte des Silvanus, magister militum in Köln, eine günstige Gelegenheit bot. Aber Silvanus wurde ermordet, Hilarius 356 wegen Hochverrat verurteilt und nach Kleinasien verbannt'.

⁷ H. C. Brennecke, *Hilarius von Poitiers und die Bischofsopposition gegen Konstantius II. Untersuchungen zur dritten Phase des arianischen Streites (337-361) (Patristische Texte und Studien* 26, Berlin and New York, 1984), 210-243. He repeats his interpretation more succinctly in his article on Hilary in *TRE* 15 (1986), 315-322, where he makes the logical structure of his case even clearer than in his book: 'Hilarius selbst sagt (Ad Const. 2), dass er aufgrund falscher Verdächtigungen durch Saturnin von Arles von Julian verurteilt worden sei. Das schliesst eine Verurteilung wegen Verweigerung der Unterschrift unter die Beschlüsse von Mailand aus. Wahrscheinlich wurden gegen Hilarius politische Verdächtigungen, u.U. im Zusammenhang mit dem gerade niedergeschlagenen Silvanus-Putsch, vorgebracht' (316).

⁸ D. H. Williams, 'A Reassessment of the Early Career and Exile of Hilary of Poitiers', *JEH* 42 (1991), 202-217, esp. 212.

⁹ Hilary's reticence and evasiveness are not always taken sufficiently into account: in particular, against his protestations to Constantius that he is still a bishop in 360 (*Ad Const.* 2.1 [*CSEL* 65.197.17-198.2]) must be set the fact that his earlier *De Synodis* (2 [*PL* 10.481]) contains the revealing phrase that he is writing 'quasi episcopus episcopis',which can mean either 'as a bishop' or 'as if a bishop'.

¹⁰ Jerome, *De vir.ill.* 100, dates the work after the death of Constantius on 3 November 361, even though its text consistently assumes that he is both alive and active (2.20-22, 5, 7, 26.1-2, 27.15-27 Rocher). Hence Brennecke, *Hilarius* (1984), 218, appeals to Jerome in order to establish that Hilary wrote the whole work in Gaul in the autumn of 361, while

A. Rocher, in the introduction to his recent edition, *Hilaire de Poitiers: Contre Constance (Sources Chrétiennes* 334, 1987), 29-38, postulates a gradual and complicated genesis comprising some five stages spread over fully two years. It is simpler and more justifiable to suppose Jerome mistaken: the tone and contents of the work indicate that it is a unitary composition written in January or February 360, as argued in *JTS*, N.S. 39 (1988), 610.

[11] This clause is extremely difficult to understand: although I print Rocher's text, either a lacuna or textual corruption should be suspected, cf. *JTS*, N.S. 39 (1988), 610.

[12] For full discussion of the passage, J. Doignon, *Hilaire de Poitiers avant l'exil* (Paris, 1971), 454-478.

[13] Athanasius, *Hist. Arian.* 9.2-10.1; *Historia acephala* 1.10 Martin.

[14] For this reading, see below, at n. 20.

[15] In favour of reading *miserum* rather than the better attested *miser*, see J. Doignon, 'L'*impietas* de l'empereur Constance à l'égard du pape Libère (Hilaire de Poitiers, *In Const.* 11)', delivered in Oxford on 21 August 1991 and to appear in *Studia Patristica* (forthcoming).

[16] See the careful discussion by H. Crouzel, 'Un "résistant" toulousain à la politique pro-arienne de l'empereur Constance II: l'évêque Rhodanius', *BLE* 77 (1976), 173-190.

[17] A. Rocher, *Sources Chrétiennes* 334 (Paris, 1987), 188, 191.

[18] See the discussion of the passage by Y. M. Duval, *Athenaeum*, N.S. 48 (1970), 259/60, who reads *quae* and leaves the reference of *omnia* open.

[19] *JTS*, N.S. 39 (1988), 610, where *postea* was mistakenly printed as two separate words and wrongly presented as having manuscript attestation.

[20] For Hilary's use of *postque* as the first word of a sentence, cf. *Trin.* 9.36.6, 10.37.4.

[21] E.g., Y. M. Duval, *Hilaire et son temps* (Paris, 1969) 52 n. 3: 'Il faut ... le traduire exactement: "Sous Néron il m'*aurait été* permis de fuir" '.

[22] A. Gudeman, *P. Cornelii Taciti Dialogus de Oratoribus*² (Leipzig and Berlin, 1914), 199.

[23] As seems to be suggested by Duval, o.c. 254.

[24] *CSEL* 65.102.8-13, cf. Brennecke, *Hilarius* (1984), 133-146.

[25] On Constantius' ecclesiastical policy in the West after the defeat of Magnentius, see *Athanasius and Constantius. Theology and Politics in the Constantinian Empire* (Cambridge, Mass., 1993), Chapter XIII.

[26] A. Rocher, *Sources Chrétiennes* 334 (1987), 239.

[27] C. Piétri, *Roma Christiana* (Paris, 1976), 212/3; Brennecke, *Hilarius* (1984), 265-297; D. H. Williams, *JEH* 42 (1991), 216.

[28] On Ammianus' care for correct chronology, see briefly *HSCP* 92 (1989), 413-422 (on Book XIV).

[29] H. Crouzel, *BLE* 77 (1976), 173-188.

[30] Published from a manuscript 'in Archivo Ecclesiae Vercellensis' by Cardinal Baronius: see, most accessibly, his *Annales Ecclesiastici* 4 (Antwerp, 1865), 537: anno 355, para. 22, where he prints the twenty fourth name as 'Rotamus (Rodanius)'.

[31] Sulpicius Severus, *Chron.* 2.39.7, states of Rhodanius: 'qui natura lenior non tam suis viribus quam Hilarii societate non cesserat Arrianis'. Crouzel, *BLE* 77 (1976), 186, plausibly saw in *lenior* 'quelque sous-entendu' designed to veil the fact that Rhodanius had subscribed to the decisions of the Council of Milan.

[32] Crouzel, *BLE* 77 (1976), 187/8. The heading to *De Synodis* (quoted below) implies

that all the bishops of the province of Narbonensis except Rhodanius condemned Hilary at the Council of Baeterrae.

[33] The work refers to the cancellation of the council which was to meet at Nicomedia after an earthquake devastated the city on 24 August 358 (*Syn.* 8, cf. Ammianus 17.7.2; *Chr. min.* 1.239). The *terminus ante quem* is given by the fact that Hilary describes the period which has elapsed between his deposition and the time of writing as *toto iam triennio* (2), i.e., the three consular years 356, 357 and 358.

[34] *PL* 10.479, reedited by J. Doignon, *REA* 80 (1978), 95/6. Both Coustant and Doignon print the dative *Lugdunensi* in both its occurrences. But, even if the better manuscripts support the dative, the sense requires the genitive, which I accordingly print.

[35] On the interpretation of the phrase *ex Narbonensi plebibus et clericis Tolosanis*, see J. Doignon, *REA* 80 (1978), 96-103. Hilary's enumeration of Gallic provinces corresponds closely to Ammianus' survey of Gaul in 355 (15.11) and other contemporary evidence: see *The New Empire of Diocletian and Constantine* (Cambridge, Mass., 1982), 212/3, 215, 217/8.

[36] *CSEL* 65.197.17-198.2, cf. above, n. 9.

[37] *Studia Patristica* 21 (1989), 392.

[38] See *Athanasius* (1993), Chapter XIII.

[39] From which some scholars have deduced that Hilary issued a decree to which many signatories appended their names: e.g., Borchardt, o.c. 24/5.

[40] On the proceedings of the council, see now Brennecke, *Hilarius* (1984), 230-243. It is normally assumed that Saturninus of Arles presided, but neither Hilary nor Jerome states explicitly that he did so—and Hilary's use of the phrases *minister vel auctor gestorum omnium* and *cuius ministerio exulo* (*CSEL* 65.198.9/10,19/20) to describe Saturninus' actions in fact implies that he did not.

[41] P. Smulders, 'Two Passages of Hilary's "Apologetica Responsa" rediscovered', *Bijdragen. Tijdschrift voor Philosophie en Theologie* 39 (1978), 234-243, reprinted in *Texte und Textkritik. Eine Aufsatzsammlung*, ed. J. Dummer. *Texte und Untersuchungen* 133 (Berlin, 1987), 539-547.

[42] Liberius, *Ep. ad Constantium* = Lucifer, *Ep.* 5 (*CCL* 8.315.161-168); Lucifer, *Ep.* 8 (*CCL* 8.319); *De regibus apostaticis* 5.46; Jerome, *Dialogus contra Luciferianos* 21, 27 (*PL* 23.175, 182); *Chronicle* 239[i] Helm.

[43] The echo of Lucifer's complaint that Constantius condemned Athanasius 'inauditum absentem' (*De Sancto Athanasio* 1.2.4/5, 2.4.2) is deliberate and unmistakeable.

[44] See the embarrassed discussion by Brennecke, *Hilarius* (1984), 242/3, n. 98, who argues that these statements 'wahrscheinlich zur nachträglichen Deutung dieses Exils durch Hilarius gehören'.

[45] The present article is a much expanded version of a brief communication delivered on 20 August 1991 at the Eleventh International Patristic Conference in Oxford: it had its origin several years earlier in discussions of the career of Hilary with Daniel Williams and Michael Klassen, and the final version has been greatly improved by detailed comments from Professor P. Smulders.

XVIII

THE CAPITULATION OF LIBERIUS
AND HILARY OF POITIERS

THE ARREST OF LIBERIUS, the bishop of Rome, by the *praefectus urbi* was an event conspicuous enough to be recorded by Ammianus Marcellinus, despite his evident determination to say as little as possible about the internal affairs of the Christian church during the reign of Constantius (15.7.6–10). Ammianus notes that, when Leontius was instructed to arrest Liberius and send him to the imperial court, he was only able to remove him from the city with difficulty and at night, because the whole population was so passionately devoted to him (*metu populi, qui eius amore flagrabat*). The passage, which immediately follows the arrest of Peter Valvomeres (15.7.4–5), so memorably discussed by Erich Auerbach,[1] deserves a full analysis for its extremely one-sided and tendentious presentation of Athanasius of Alexandria, whose condemnation and deposition Liberius refused to endorse.[2] The present article, however, confines itself to the problem of the date of this central event in the ecclesiastical politics of the 350s, for which Ammianus happens to provide the best evidence, and to the relevance of the correct date to the lost work of Hilary of Poitiers against Ursacius and Valens, which survives in fragments.[3]

The following frequently cited works are referred to hereafter by author's name alone: T. D. Barnes, *Athanasius and Constantius. Theology and Politics in the Constantinian Empire* (Cambridge, Mass. 1993); H. C. Brennecke, *Hilarius von Poitiers und die Bischofsopposition gegen Konstantius II. Untersuchungen zur dritten Phase des arianischen Streites (337–361)* (Berlin and New York 1984, Patristische Texte und Studien 26); A. Chastagnol, *Les Fastes de la Préfecture de Rome au Bas-Empire* (Paris 1962); L. Duchesne, "Libère et Fortunatien," *MEFR* 28 (1908) 31–78; A. L. Feder, *Studien zu Hilarius von Poitiers 1*, *SBWien* Phil.-hist. Kl. 162.4 (1909; publ. 1910) = Feder (1909); id., *Studien zu Hilarius von Poitiers 2*, *SBWien* Phil.-hist. Kl. 166.5 (1910) = Feder (1910); R. P. C. Hanson, *The Search for the Christian Doctrine of God. The Arian Controversy 318–381* (Edinburgh 1988); O. Seeck, *Regesten der Kaiser und Päpste für die Jahre 311 bis 476 n. Chr. Vorarbeit zu einer Prosopographie der christlichen Kaiserzeit* (Stuttgart 1919).

[1] E. Auerbach, *Mimesis. The Representation of Reality in Western Literature*, tr. W. R. Trask (Princeton 1953) chapter 3. His interpretation has recently been re-evaluated by J. F. Matthews, "Peter Valvomeres, Re-Arrested," *Homo Viator. Classical Essays for John Bramble* (Bristol and Oak Park 1987) 277–284.

[2] For the most recent discussion, see J. Matthews, *The Roman Empire of Ammianus* (Baltimore 1989) 421, 441.

[3] *Clavis Patrum Latinorum*[2] (Steenbrugge 1961) no. 436: the individual documents are listed as nos. 437–459. An English translation is forthcoming in the series *Translated Texts for Historians* (Liverpool).

THE HISTORICAL CONTEXT

Liberius had been consecrated bishop of Rome in the spring of 352.[4] He avoided attending either the Council of Arles in the winter of 353/4 or the Council of Milan in the summer of 355, both of which were summoned by Constantius so that western bishops might ratify and subscribe to the decisions taken by the predominantly eastern Council of Sirmium in 351.[5] When Liberius subsequently refused the emperor's request to endorse the synodical letter of the Council of Milan, he was arrested by Leontius, taken to the imperial court at Milan, and, when he persisted in his obduracy, sent into exile at Beroea in Thrace. After two years of exile, Liberius finally capitulated to Constantius' demands and was allowed to return to Rome (Athanasius, *Apol. c. Ar.* 89.3; *Hist. Ar.* 41.2; Theodoretus, *HE* 2.17.1). The *Liber pontificalis* certifies the day on which he re-entered Rome after his exile as 2 August (37.6, p. 208 Duchesne), but neither the year of his exile nor the year of his return is directly and explicitly stated by any reliable ancient source. Although modern ecclesiastical historians have usually preferred 355 to 356 as the year of Liberius' arrest, several scholars have recently claimed with a large measure of assurance that the later date of 356 is established by prosopography.[6] For André Chastagnol's standard fasti of the urban prefecture in the fourth century prolong the tenure of Leontius' predecessor into June 356,[7] and the full-scale study of Ammianus as a historian of the Roman Empire in the fourth century by John Matthews assumes without discussion that Leontius did not become prefect until 356.[8] Hence Liberius (it seems) cannot have been arrested by Leontius before the summer of 356, from which it follows that he did not capitulate to the demands of the emperor Constantius until 358.[9] But is the standard chronology of Leontius' prefecture correct?

THE PREFECTURE OF LEONTIUS

Leontius' predecessor, Memmius Vitrasius Orfitus, had became *praefectus urbi* on 8 December 353 (*Chron. min.* 1.67), and his tenure of the office

---

[4]The precise date was probably 17 May: see L. Duchesne, *Liber pontificalis* 1 (Paris 1883) cxl.

[5]On these three councils, see now Barnes chapter 13.

[6]C. Piétri, *Roma Christiana: Recherches sur l'église de Rome, son organisation, sa politique, son idéologie, de Miltiade à Sixte III (311–440)* (Rome 1976, BEFAR 224) 246–247; Brennecke 266; n. 99; Hanson 340, 358–360.

[7]Chastagnol 139–147.

[8]Matthews (above, n. 2) 24, 417–418, 421, 441. In the index, however, Leontius is "*praefectus urbi* 355–6" (592).

[9]The theory advanced by H.-G. Opitz, *Athanasius Werke* 2 (Berlin-Leipzig, 1934–1941), in his note on 167.19–20, that Liberius was exiled in 355 and allowed to return to Rome in 358, can be dismissed out of hand: it entails the improbable corollary that Liberius' contemporary Athanasius was wrong in stating that his exile lasted two years rather than three (*Apol. c. Ar.* 89.3: διετίαν ἔμεινεν ἐν τῇ μετοικίᾳ).

ıs firmly attested by moderately abundant evidence until 6 July 355 (*CTh* 14.3.2). But the only evidence that Orfitus continued to serve as prefect into 356 is a fragment in the Theodosian Code addressed to him with what is clearly an incomplete subscription: *pp. [i.e., proposita] in foro Traiani Constantio Aug. VIII et Iuliano Caes. conss.* (*CTh* 9.17.3). The date of 13 June 356 for this imperial constitution results from two modern hypotheses: first, that the fragment comes from a constitution which originally accompanied the document addressed *ad populum* which follows it in the Theodosian Code and which was, according to the manuscripts, issued at Milan on 13 June 357 (*CTh* 9.17.4 = *CJ* 9.19.4); second, that the date of the latter document should be emended to 13 June 356 on the grounds that Constantius was not in Milan in June 357.[10] But the month in the latter subscription could just as easily be emended as the year, and the emendation "dat. id. Ian." for "dat. id. Iun." (which gives an emended date of 13 January 357) commends itself on palaeographical grounds, since it is known that Constantius spent the winter of 356/7 in Milan.[11] Moreover, there is no compelling reason for holding that the two fragments were in fact issued on the same day at all. The constitution addressed to Orfitus and published in Rome in the consular year 356 may have been issued at Milan in the preceding summer, but only posted in the forum of Trajan after the lapse of several months, perhaps after Orfitus had ceased to be prefect of the city any more—such a phenomenon would not be unparalleled in the Theodosian Code or in reality.[12] Alternatively, the consular date assigned by the compilers of the Theodosian Code may be erroneous and the constitution may really have been issued in 354, when Constantius was consul for the seventh time and Gallus for the third: confusion between imperial

[10] Seeck 202. Seeck believed that "nothing hinders the assumption that [Orfitus] was still in office in 356" (45).

[11] Seeck 202–203, cf. T. Mommsen, ad loc.: *aut in mense erratum est aut restituendus consulatus a. 356.* PLRE 1. 652 adopts the date of 13 January 357 for both constitutions: they then provide the earliest attestation of Orfitus' second urban prefecture, which is otherwise securely documented from late April 357 (Ammianus 16.10.4) to 25 March 359 (*CTh* 14.6.1).

[12] The normal lapse of time between the issuing of an imperial constitution in Milan and its publication in Rome was obviously much shorter: see R. Duncan-Jones, *Structure and Scale in the Roman Economy* (Cambridge 1990) 17–21. But one delay of several years between issue and publication is firmly attested and another seems probable. (1) Julian issued his *constitutio de postulando* (published by B. Bischoff and D. Nörr, *Eine unbekannte Konstitution Kaiser Julians* [c. *Iuliani de postulando*], AbhMünchen Phil.-hist. Kl. 58 [1963] 7) to the newly appointed *praefectus urbi* Apronianus in Antioch on 17 January 363, but it was not read in the prefect's court in Rome until the consular year 371. (2) *CTh* 3.5.6, which was published at Hispalis in Spain in April 336, may have been issued at Constantinople as long before as April 332: see T. D. Barnes, *The New Empire of Diocletian and Constantine* (Cambridge, Mass. 1982) 145, n. 17.

consulates is notoriously frequent in the Code.[13] Whatever the explanation, it would be imprudent to prolong Orfitus' prefecture into 356 on the strength of a single imperial constitution with an incomplete, inconsistent, or problematical subscription.

On other grounds entirely, it seems probable that Flavius Leontius replaced Orfitus in 355 rather than the following year. The correspondence of Libanius reveals that the prefecture of Rome was offered to Anatolius, a native of Berytus, in the winter of 354/5 (*Ep.* 311, 391, 423).[14] That implies that Orfitus' tenure was already drawing to a close, and it is not at all plausible to argue that Anatolius' refusal led Constantius to prolong Orfitus in office for almost another year.[15] The emperor had good reason to replace the Roman aristocrat Orfitus by an easterner who was more beholden to him—and Leontius could be relied upon to enforce with enthusiasm an ecclesiastical policy which was proving to be unpopular in the West, for he shared Constantius' theological views and had been among the official witnesses who certified the accuracy of the minutes of the interrogation of Photinus by Basil of Ancyra at Sirmium in 351 (Epiphanius *Pan.* 71.1.5).[16]

Ammianus Marcellinus places his notice of the urban prefecture of Leontius before the proclamation of Julian as Caesar on 6 November 355 (15.7–8). It is hard to see why he should have placed it here if Leontius did not in fact become *praefectus urbi* until some eight or nine months after Julian was proclaimed Caesar.[17] But, if Leontius became *praefectus urbi* in the summer or autumn of 355,[18] he could have arrested Liberius in either 355 or 356. Moreover, the fact that Ammianus has chosen to place his notice of the conspicuous events of Leontius' prefecture before 6 November 355, *prima facie* implies that he thought that they occurred in the summer or autumn of 355—a date which is strongly preferable on all other criteria too.

THE ARREST OF LIBERIUS

On general historical grounds, Liberius' arrest should be an immediate consequence of his encouragement of resistance to Constantius at the Council of Milan.[19] Moreover, the specific evidence of ecclesiastical sources points unambiguously to 355 as the date of his arrest and 357 as the year of his return to Rome. First, Hilary of Poitiers puts the arrest of Liberius

---

[13]Seeck 23–66; R. S. Bagnall, Alan Cameron, S. R. Schwartz, and K. A. Worp, *Consuls of the Later Roman Empire* (Atlanta 1987) 72–76.

[14]For Anatolius' origin, Eunapius *Vit. phil.* 10.6.1–2; Libanius *Ep.* 339, 438.

[15]As Chastagnol 143.

[16]On the career of Leontius, see Chastagnol 147–149.

[17]For Ammianus' care in such matters, see T. D. Barnes, "Structure and Chronology in Ammianus, Book 14," *HSCP* 92 (1989) 413–422.

[18]As is correctly inferred from Ammianus in *PLRE* 1. 503, 1054.

[19]Barnes chapter 13.

between the Council of Milan and his own condemnation at the Council of Baeterrae, i.e., between the summer of 355 and the late spring of 356 (*In Const.* 11).[20] Second, both Theodoretus and a document composed in Rome ca 370[21] explicitly connect his return with Constantius' visit to Rome in the spring of 357. According to Theodoretus, the bishop returned from exile as a result of a demonstration during the emperor's visit to Rome, in which the crowd in the circus cried out "One God, one Christ, one bishop" (*HE* 2.17). Theodoretus (it is true) might be discounted as a witness for events in Rome, especially since he asserts that, when Liberius returned, his replacement Felix withdrew to become a bishop elsewhere—which appears to be totally false.[22] But the account of *quae gesta sunt inter Liberium et Felicem episcopos* which stands as the first document in the so-called *Collectio Avellana* is another matter:

post annos duos venit Romam Constantius imperator; pro Liberio rogatur a populo. qui mox annuens ait "habetis Liberium, qui, qualis a vobis profectus est, melior revertetur." hoc autem de consensu eius, quo manus perfidiae dederat, indicabat. tertio anno redit Liberius, cui obviam cum gaudio populus Romanus exivit.   (*CSEL* 35.2.3–8)

After two years the emperor Constantius came to Rome, and was petitioned by the people on behalf of Liberius. He duly assented <to the request> and said: "You have Liberius, who will come back a better man than he was when he departed from you." He alluded in this way to his [sc. Liberius'] compliance, in having set his hands to treachery. Liberius returned in the third year, and the people of Rome went out to meet him with joy.

This passage clearly puts Liberius' return "in the third year" after his arrest and shortly after the visit of Constantius to Rome (29 April–28 May 357), and thus implies that he was arrested in 355 and returned in the summer of 357.

The date of Liberius' return is obviously relevant to identifying what document it was which he subscribed in order to secure his release from exile. A narrative fragment from Hilary states that Liberius subscribed his name to the "perfidy of Sirmium" (*CSEL* 65.170.3). Hence it has recently been inferred that he accepted "the second Sirmian formula of summer 357."[23] But it is not certain that the words *perfidia apud Sirmium descripta* are Hilary's own rather than an addition or comment of the compiler of the collection or a later editor. For in the letter which immediately precedes

---

[20] For discussion of this significant passage, see "Hilary of Poitiers on his Exile," *VigChr* 46 (1992) 129–140.

[21] *Clavis*[2] (above, n. 3) no. 1570.

[22] On his career, see still T. Mommsen, "Die römischen Bischöfe Liberius und Felix II.," *Deutsche Zeitschrift für Geschichtswissenschaft* NF 1 (1896–97) 167–179, reprinted in his *Gesammelte Schriften* 6 (Berlin 1910) 570–581.

[23] Brennecke 292–297.

the narrative fragment, Liberius writes to priests and bishops in the East and describes the document which he subscribed in the following terms:

> *nam ut verius sciatis me veram fidem per hanc epistulam meam proloqui, dominus et frater meus communis Demofilus quia dignatus est pro sua benivolentia fidem vestram et catholicam exponere, quae Sirmio a pluribus fratribus et coepiscopis nostris tractata, exposita et suscepta est ab omnibus, qui in praesenti fuerunt, hanc ego libenti animo suscepi, in nullo contradixi, consensum accommodavi, hanc sequor, haec a me tenetur.*   (CSEL 65.169.6–12)

So that you may more truly know through this letter of mine that I proclaim the true faith, since my lord and brother in communion Demophilus has out of his benevolence kindly explained your catholic creed, which was discussed by many of our brothers and fellow bishops at Sirmium, then formally put forward and received by all who were present, I <too> have received this <creed> with an eager heart, I have not contradicted it in any particular, I have given my full assent, I follow it, I hold fast to it.[24]

Since the "blasphemy" of 357 was not a creed propounded or adopted by the eastern bishops as a body,[25] it does not fit Liberius' description of the document that he accepted. Moreover, if Liberius returned to Rome on 2 August 357, then it is chronologically impossible for him to have subscribed to the "blasphemy of Sirmium" before he was released from exile at Beroea (no later than mid-July, even if he travelled post haste to Rome). Furthermore, the list of names which Hilary quoted as responsible for the creed which Demophilus, the bishop of Sirmium, presented to Liberius clearly belongs to 351:

> *perfidiam autem apud Sirmium descriptam, quam dicit Liberius catholicam, a Demofilo sibi expositam, hi sunt, qui conscripserunt: Narcissus, Theodorus, Basilius, Eudoxius, Demofilus, Cecropius, Silvanus, Ursacius, Valens, Euagrius, Hireneus, Exuperantius, Terentianus, Bassus, Gaudentius, Macedonius, Marcus, Acacius, Iulius, Surinus, Simplicius et Iunior.*   (CSEL 65.170)

The second name provides the decisive argument: Theodorus of Heraclea was dead by 355 (Theodoretus *HE* 2.16.11). The document to which Liberius set his hand was, therefore, the synodical letter of the Council of Sirmium in 351, which had previously been endorsed by the Councils of Arles and Milan, and in doing so he fulfilled the demand made of him by Constantius in 355.[26]

---

[24]The manuscript of this passage has been heavily interpolated by a scribe who could not stomach the idea that a bishop of Rome accepted an "Arian" creed: see Feder (1909) 123 ff.

[25]As Hilary, *Syn.* 8 (*PL* 10.485), makes clear.

[26]Duchesne 46–48; Feder (1910) 101–103.

THE DATE OF HILARY'S SO-CALLED *OPUS HISTORICUM*

Jerome reports that Hilary of Poitiers wrote a *Liber adversus Valentem et Ursacium, historiam Ariminensis et Seleucensis synodi continens* (*De viris illustribus* 100). It was presumably a work which combined historical and theological polemic and quoted documents on a lavish scale like Athanasius' *Defence Against the Arians*, and hence must be the ultimate source of the collection of extracts preserved in a ninth-century manuscript in Paris (Bibliothèque de l'Arsenal 483 fols 76^r–113^v), which have no title, only a subscription which states *explicit sci hilarii ex opere historico*.[27] The extracts were first printed in 1598 from derivative manuscripts by Nicole le Fèvre (Nicolaus Faber) and republished by Coustant in the Maurist edition of Hilary as *Fragmenta ex opere historico* (whence *PL* 10.627–721). Alfred Feder was the first editor to use the early manuscript which is the extant archetype of all the others: he edited the collection critically in 1916 as *Collectanea Antiariana Parisina* (*CSEL* 65.43–177). The documents included among these fragments are listed below with Feder's numbering and pagination and a statement of the date of each. All the documents are letters unless it is specified otherwise; the numbering is discontinuous because this summary excludes the narrative fragments which connect the documents and which Feder included in his continuous numeration.[28]

SERIES A

I (43–46)	Council at Paris to eastern bishops	360
II (46–47)	Eusebius of Vercellae to Gregory, bishop of Iliberris	360/1
III (47–48)	Creed of Germinius, bishop of Sirmium	366
IV.1 (48–67)	The eastern bishops at Serdica to certain named western bishops	343
IV.2 (68–73)	Creed of the eastern bishops at Serdica Also preserved: (1) by Hilary, *Syn.* 34, (2) in Cod. Ver. LX (58), fols 78^v–79^v, (3) in Paris, ms Syriaques 62, fols 185–186[29]	343
IV.3 (74–78)	Subscriptions to the preceding letter and creed	343

[27] The collection itself was probably compiled from Hilary as early as the fifth century: see Feder (1910) 113–133.

[28] On the other versions which exist of some of the documents, see Feder's prolegomena to his edition, *CSEL* 65 (1916) xxxix ff.

[29] The two latter versions are edited in C. H. Turner, *Ecclesiae Occidentalis Monumenta Iuris Antiquissima* 1 (Oxford, 1899–1939) 638–640; H. Schulthess, *Die syrischen Kanones des Synoden von Nicaea bis Chalcedon*, AbhGött Phil.-hist. Kl. NF 10.2 (1908) 167–168.

263   LIBERIUS AND HILARY OF POITIERS

V.1 (78–85)   The pro-Nicene bishops at Ariminum to Con-   359
                   stantius (Quoted in Greek by Athanasius,
                   Syn. 10)
V.3 (85–86)   Minute of the adoption of a creed at Nike in 10 October 359
                   Thrace
VI (87–88)   The anti-Nicene bishops at Ariminum to   359
                   Constantius
VII (89–93)   Liberius to Constantius   353/4
VIII (93–94)   Constantius to the Council of Ariminum   359
IX.1 (95–96)   Creed of the pro-Nicene bishops at Ariminum   359
                   (Also extant in Ms. Bodl. e Mus. 101, fol. 62ᵛ)
IX.3 (96–97)   Condemnation of the anti-Nicene leaders at   20 July 359
                   Ariminum

                            SERIES B

II.1 (103–126)   The western bishops at Serdica to all the   343
                   churches
                   This letter survives in three other versions:
                   (1) Cod. Ver. LX (58), fols 81ʳ–88ʳ: appar-
                       ently a Latin retroversion from a Greek
                       translation of the original;
                   (2) Athanasius *Apol. c. Ar.* 44–49: with a
                       list of signatories, including more than
                       200 who subscribed their names after
                       343;
                   (3) Theodoretus *HE* 2.8.1–54.
                   Hilary's text is close to Athanasius' (2), while
                   versions (1) and (3) not only agree closely
                   in wording, but also include a theological
                   statement which both Athanasius and Hilary
                   omit.[30]
II.2 (126–130)   The western bishops at Serdica to Julius   343
II.3 (131)   Names of the Arian leaders deposed by the   343
                   council, appended to the preceding letter
II.4 (131–139)   List of the original subscriptions to the same 343
                   letter
II.6 (143–144)   Ursacius and Valens to Julius   347
II.8 (145)   Ursacius and Valens to Athanasius   347
II.10 (150)   The Nicene creed   325
III.1 (155)   Liberius to the bishops of the East   357
IV.1 (156–157)   Liberius to the bishops of Italy   362/3
IV.2 (158–159)   Bishops of Italy to the bishops of Illyricum 363
V (159–160)   Valens and others to Germinius   366

---

[30] On its probable origin, see now M. Tetz, "*Ante omnia de sancta fide et de integritate veritatis.* Glaubensfragen auf der Synode von Serdica," *ZNTW* 76 (1985) 243–269.

VI (160–164)   Germinius to Rufianus and others   366
VII.2 (164–166)   Liberius to Eusebius, Dionysius, and Lucifer 355
VII.4 (166)   Liberius to Caecilianus of Spoletium (excerpt) 353/4
VII.6 (167)   Liberius to Ossius (excerpt)   353/4
VII.8 (168–170)   Liberius to the eastern bishops   357
VII.10 (170–172) Liberius to Ursacius, Valens and Germinius   357
VII.11 (172–173) Liberius to Vincentius of Capua   357
VIII.1 (174–175) Envoys from the Council of Seleucia to the   359
                  envoys from the Council of Ariminum

APPENDIX (181–184)[31]
The western bishops at Serdica to Constantius 343

Many of these documents are not preserved elsewhere. Among those which survive only because Hilary quoted them in his lost work are the synodical letter of the eastern bishops at Serdica (A IV.1) and nine letters of Liberius, the authenticity of some of which used to be challenged (A VII; B III.1; IV.1; VII.2, 4, 6, 8, 10, 11). The principal (or rather, the only) objection to the letters was a priori and invalid, viz., that, if genuine, they indicated that a bishop of Rome not only condemned Athanasius but also subscribed to a creed later considered heretical—an action which some scholars found hard to reconcile with their acceptance of the dogma of papal infallibility.[32] Yet there is nothing in the letters themselves that tells against Liberius' authorship and much, on the contrary, that speaks strongly for it, especially the precise historical allusions to events whose significance was soon forgotten or misrepresented (e.g., Liberius' reference to the Council of Milan of 345 in A VII).[33]

On the other hand, the date of Liberius' exile, and hence of the letters announcing his volte face (B III.1; B VII.8, 10, 11), is very relevant to the date of the first edition of Hilary's lost work. The common view has been that Hilary composed the first edition or first version of the work either in 356, perhaps even before his exile, or at latest in early 357, and hence

---

[31]For the identification of this letter and the narrative fragment which follows it (184–187), see A. Wilmart, "L'Ad Constantium liber primus de S. Hilaire de Poitiers et les Fragments historiques," Revue bénédictine 24 (1907) 149–179, 291–317; Feder (1909) 133–151. These two pieces have an entirely different textual tradition from the Collectanea Antiariana Parisina and had previously been published in the standard editions of Hilary as Ad Constantium Augustum liber primus (PL 10.557–564, from Coustant).

[32]H. M. Gwatkin, Studies of Arianism² (Cambridge 1900) 194, acidly remarked: "Believers in papal infallibility may hesitate, but the historian cannot." For a brief survey of the controversy, Brennecke 271–274. The decisive blows in favour of the authenticity the letters were struck by Duchesne (31–78) and Feder ([1909] 153–183). But the letters are still occasionally rejected, as by P.-P. Joannou, Die Ostkirche und die Cathedra Petri im 4. Jahrhundert (Stuttgart 1972) 126–127.

[33]Barnes chapter 10.

that he cannot have included in it the letters of Liberius, but must have added them later when he revised and expanded the work.[34] But if Liberius returned to Rome on 2 August 357 (rather than 358), then he capitulated before the "blasphemy of Sirmium." If it was this event which provoked Hilary to compose the lost work (as seems probable),[35] then there is no obstacle to holding both that Hilary composed the first version of his *liber adversus Ursacium et Valentem* in the winter of 357/8,[36] and that this first edition or first book included all but one of the nine letters of Liberius.

[34]B. Marx, "Zwei Zeugen für die Herkunft der Fragmente I und II des sog. *Opus historicum s.* Hilarii. Ein Beitrag zur Lösung des Fragmentenproblems," *Theologische Quartalschrift* 88 (1906) 390–406; Wilmart (above, n. 31) 291–317; Feder (1909) 151–153; C. F. A. Borchardt, *Hilary of Poitiers' Role in the Arian Struggle* (The Hague 1966) 31–37; C. Kannengiesser, *Dictionnaire de Spiritualité* 7 (1969) 474–475; J. Doignon, "L'*Elogium* d'Athanase dans les fragments de l'*Opus Historicum* d'Hilaire de Poitiers antérieurs à l'exil," in C. Kannengiesser (ed.), *Politique et théologie chez Athanase d'Alexandrie. Actes du Colloque de Chantilly 23–25 septembre 1973* (Paris 1974, Théologie historique 27) 337–348; Hanson 469–470; J. Doignon, *Handbuch der lateinischen Literatur der Antike* 5 (Munich 1989) 470–473.

[35]See Brennecke 301–312.

[36]As argued by D. H. Williams, "A Reassessment of the Early Career and Exile of Hilary of Poitiers," *JEH* 42 (1991) 202–217.

XIX

THE DATE OF THE COUNCIL OF GANGRA

THE decisions of the council of bishops which met at Gangra in Paphlagonia during the middle decades of the fourth century acquired an importance which the bishops who attended could scarcely have foreseen. Perhaps by chance, their synodical letter to the bishops of Armenia, which includes twenty canons laying down rules related to problems of ecclesiastical discipline, for which they blame the teaching of Eustathius of Sebasteia, was included in a collection of synodical decisions which formed the nucleus of all later collections of canon law.[1] Hence the letter and canons of the Council of Gangra survive in full in several Latin versions and Georgian as well as in Greek, while the canons alone survive also in Syriac, Armenian, Arabic, Ethiopic, and Old Church Slavonic.[2] The Syriac translation of the canons offers a date, but it does so inconsistently, to both the consular year 343 and year 390 of the era of Antioch, i.e. 1 October 341/2.[3] The correct date has long been a matter of controversy: the present brief note will argue that, even if the precise date is undiscoverable, a correct appreciation of the import of the best evidence points to an approximate date different from those most favoured in modern scholarship.

Tillemont provided the first significant discussion of the date of the council: he argued for 340,[4] and an identical or closely similar date has subsequently been argued anew or adopted by the weighty names of H. M. Gwatkin, F. Loofs, C. H. Turner, E. Schwartz, and J. Gribomont.[5] At the other extreme, H. R. Reynolds identified the

---

[1] E. Schwartz, 'Die Kanonessammlungen der alten Kirche', *Zeitschrift der Savigny—Stiftung*, Kan. Abt. xxv (1936), pp. 1–114, reprinted in his *Gesammelte Schriften*, iv (Berlin, 1960), pp. 159–275. Schwartz explained the inclusion of the canons of Gangra together with those of 'Reichssynoden' on the grounds that Eusebius of Nicomedia presided (p. 31 = 190).

If the Council of Gangra is correctly dated *c*.355, as argued below, then Schwartz's theory that this original 'Corpus canonum' was compiled at Antioch in the 370s and is thus 'ein Produkt der antiochenischen, von Euzoius . . . geleiteten Reichskirche' (p. 41 = 200) may require some modification.

[2] *CPG* iv (Turnhout, 1980), nos. 8553 and 8554.

[3] F. Schulthess, 'Die syrischen Kanones der Synoden von Nicaea bis Chalcedon', *Abh. Göttingen*, NF, x. 2 (1908), p. 63, cf. G. Downey, *A History of Antioch in Syria* (Princeton, 1961), p. 157.

[4] *Mémoires pour servir à l'histoire ecclésiastique des six premiers siècles*, ix (Paris, 1703), pp. 650–2.

[5] H. M. Gwatkin, *Studies of Arianism*[2] (Cambridge, 1900), pp. 189–92 (the first edition was published in 1882); F. Loofs, *Eustathius von Sebaste und die Chronologie*

122

bishop who presided at Gangra as Eusebius of Samosata and proposed the date of 372 or 373,[6] while R. Ceillier argued that the council met in 379 or 380, after the death of Basil of Caesarea, or at the very least after 376.[7] Moreover, P. J. Fedwick has recently contended that, since the problems to which the council addressed itself seem to be reflected only in the later ascetical writings of Basil of Caesarea, it can most plausibly be lodged in the middle or late 360s.[8] The most prudent course, therefore, might seem to be to abandon any search for precision and, with M. Simonetti, to pronounce the date uncertain.[9] But the evidence of Sozomenus merits reassessment: it need not necessarily (as is usually assumed) imply a date no later than 341, but it does establish a *terminus ante quem* of 360.

Sozomenus gives a long account of the deposition of many bishops by the Council of Constantinople in the early months of 360 (*HE* iv. 24–5). He states the charges against each of the accused separately, succinctly, and in detail. Those against Eustathius comprised the following counts:

1. When he was a priest, he was condemned and excluded from prayers by his father Eulalius, the bishop of Caesarea in Cappadocia;

2. He was excommunicated by a council at Neocaesarea in Pontus and deposed by Eusebius, the bishop of Constantinople, after being condemned over some transactions entrusted to him;

3. He was deprived of his episcopal status by those who met at Gangra for teaching, acting, and believing improperly;

4. He was convicted of perjury at the Council of Antioch;

5. He attempted to overturn the decision of the bishops who met at

---

der Basilius-Briefe. Eine patristische Studie (Halle, 1898), pp. 79–90; C. H. Turner, EOMIA ii. 2 (Oxford, 1913), p. 146; Schwartz, op. cit., pp. 18 and 31(= pp. 176 and 190); J. Gribomont, Studia Patristica ii (TU lxiv, 1957), p. 401, reprinted in his Saint Basile. Évangile et Église, i (Spiritualité orientale, xxxvi, 1984), p. 27.

G. Bardy, Dictionnaire de droit canonique, v (1953), cols. 935–8, implied dissent by declining to proffer a precise date ('vers le milieu du ive s.'). But a date close to 340 subsequently re-established itself as the communis opinio: see A. Bigelmair, Lexicon für Theologie und Kirche, iv (1960), col. 514; Dictionnaire d'histoire et de géographie ecclésiastiques, xix (1981), col. 1103; W. D. Hauschild, Theologische Realenzyklopädie, x (1982), p. 547. However, P. Brown, The Body and Society. Men, Women and Sexual Rununciation in Early Christianity (New York, 1988), pp. 288/9, assumes a date in the early 350s.

[6] H. R. Reynolds, Dictionary of Christian Biography, ii (London, 1890), pp. 370/1.

[7] R. Ceillier, Histoire générale des auteurs sacrés et ecclésiastiques, iv (Paris, 1733), pp. 734–6.

[8] P. J. Fedwick, Basil of Caearaea: Christian, Humanist, Ascetic, i (Toronto, 1981), p. 14 n. 87. He concludes by observing that 'a date in the 370s is also possible'. A date between 362 and 370 had been advocated by the Ballerini brothers, Leonis Opera, iii (Venice, 1757), pp. xxiv–xxv, reprinted in PL lvi, cols. 33–5.

[9] M. Simonetti, La crisi ariana nel iv secolo (Rome, 1975), p. 411 n. 35.

Melitene and, though guilty of many charges, presumed to sit as judge and called the others heterodox.[10]

Sozomenus here names three councils of bishops besides Gangra that condemned Eustathius. The council at Neocaesarea appears to be otherwise unknown. The council of Antioch to which Sozomenus refers need not be either the Dedication-Council of 341,[11] or any other known council—though it could well be the council which met at Antioch under Eudoxius in 358 (Sozomenus, *HE* iv. 12. 5–7). The council of Melitene alone is independently datable: it probably belongs to 358 or 359 (Sozomenus, *HE* iv. 24. 16, 25. 1, cf. Basil, *Ep.* cclxiii. 5).

Sozomenus is clearly drawing on a documentary source, presumably the collection of synodical decisions compiled by Sabinus of Heraclea.[12] But if he is summarizing (even at second hand) a documentary record of the proceedings of the Council of Constantinople in 360, then he ought not to be mistaken in reporting that the bishops at that council appealed to the decisions of the Council of Gangra—which entails that the council occurred before 360. On the other hand, Sozomenus' summary of the charges against Eustathius in 360 provides no more than a *terminus ante quem* of 358 or 359. Eustathius had a long career: he had been a pupil of Arius, allegedly in Alexandria and hence before *c*.320 (Basil, *Ep.* cclxiii. 3), and Eusebius,who deposed him when bishop of Constantinople, occupied that see from autumn 337 to late 341. But, if the council of Antioch that condemned Eustathius is not the known council of 341, then there is no good reason, on the evidence of Sozomenus, to put the Council of Gangra close to 340 rather than in the 350s.

What of the discordant testimony? Socrates also refers to the Council of Gangra in the context of the same council of Constantinople, and he summarizes the contents of its synodical letter and canons (*HE* ii. 43. 1–7). But he twice states that the Council of Gangra occurred later. Does Socrates deserve preference as the earlier writer? Not on this occasion at least, since, even if he too has consulted a documentary record of the proceedings of the Council of Constantinople, he is more interested in summarizing the letter and canons of the Council of Gangra itself. Sozomenus' straightforward summary

---

[10] Basil, *Ep.* cclxiii. 3, gives a slightly different summary of Eustathius' career, but he confirms that Eusebius expelled him from Constantinople (2) and that the council of 360 appealed to the earlier deposition at Melitene (5). Significantly, Basil puts Eustathius' election as bishop after his expulsion from Constantinople.

[11] Hence G. C. Hansen's separate entry in his index to the edition of Sozomenus by J. Bidez, which he completed (*GCS* L, 1960), p. 436.

[12] G. Schoo, *Die Quellen des Kirchenhistorikers Sozomenos* (Berlin, 1911), pp. 129 and 144.

124

should be the more reliable report. The precise dates in the Syriac translation appear to be secondary: since they do not occur in the Greek or Latin versions and one of them uses the local era of Antioch, they too are more likely to be the product of later guesswork than to transmit original and authentic information.

The heading of the letter unfortunately fails to supply sees for the thirteen bishops who met at Gangra. Nevertheless, it has long been recognized that three of the signatories can be identified securely with Paphlagonian bishops who attended the Council of Serdica in 343, viz. Proaeresius of Sinope, Philetus of Juliopolis, and Bithynicus of Zela.[13] It seems probable, therefore, that all thirteen bishops come from the province of Paphlagonia and hence that the Eusebius who presided was bishop of the metropolis of the province, i.e. of Gangra itself.[14] On the other hand, the coincidence of three names of the thirteen or so who attended with three in the list of eastern bishops at the Council of Serdica provides no strong argument in favour of a date very close to 343. In the light of the available evidence, it may be suggested that the Council of Gangra probably met close to the year 355.

The surviving text of the synodical letter of the Council of Gangra does not depose Eustathius from his see, as the bishops at Constantinople in 360 alleged. Perhaps that was a deliberate misrepresentation. If the Council of Gangra was a local gathering of Paphlagonian bishops, they had no obvious jurisdiction over a bishop whose see lay in another province. Perforce, therefore, they contented themselves with writing to the bishops of Armenia to complain about Eustathius and pointedly refrained from describing him as a bishop. The Council of Gangra may have been one of the twice-annual provincial councils which the Council of Nicaea instructed to foregather both between Easter and Ascension and in the autumn of each year.[15]

---

[13] *CSEL* lxv, pp. 75. 14, 76. 3, and 75. 23.

[14] Gangra was the metropolis of the Diocletianic province of Paphlagonia: no authentic bishop seems to be indubitably attested before Basilides in 375/6, cf. R. Janin and D. Stiernon, *Dictionnaire d'histoire et de géographie ecclésiastiques*, xix (1981), cols. 1093 ff.—though they assume that Eusebius of Caesarea presided at the Council of Gangra, and hence that Hypatius, whose name stands second in the list of bishops attending, may have been the bishop of Gangra *c.*340.

[15] Canon 5. I am much indebted to Paul Fedwick and Leigh Gibson for discussion of the varied problems posed by the Council of Gangra.

XX

ANGEL OF LIGHT OR MYSTIC INITIATE? THE PROBLEM OF THE *LIFE OF ANTONY**

THE Greek version of the *Life of Antony* traditionally attributed to Athanasius is a 'classic of western spirituality', which had an enormous influence on monastic practice and monastic thought for many centuries both in the Byzantine Empire and, in translation, throughout medieval Europe.[1] More recently, the Greek *Life* has attracted a vast scholarly literature as 'the most important document of early monasticism',[2] while eminent scholars have hailed it as the best thing that Athanasius ever wrote.[3] Unfortunately, it now seems certain (at least to the present writer) that the Greek version of the *Life of Antony* is neither an original composition nor from the pen of Athanasius.

Challenges had been made against the traditional ascription of the *Life* to Athanasius on historical grounds (most firmly and confidently by H. Weingarten more than a century ago),[4] but they were not able to withstand criticism of their arguments and premisses.[5] It is a recent study of the Syriac version which places obstacles in the way of accepting Athanasius as the author of the original *Life of Antony* which appear to be insuperable. The Syriac version of the *Life* survives in two recensions (long and short) and in no fewer than fourteen manuscripts. A text was published as long

---

* For advice and much helpful criticism of an earlier draft I am grateful to Sebastian Brock, Gianfranco Fiaccadori, Kathy Gaca, John Rist, Maurice Wiles, and, above all, Susan Harvey, who first persuaded me to take Draguet's arguments seriously. The translations are all my own; those from the Syriac *Life* have been checked against Draguet's French and Wallis Budge's English versions.

[1] See R. C. Gregg, *The Life of Antony and the Letter to Marcellinus* (*The Classics of Western Spirituality*, xvi, 1980), pp. 1 ff.

[2] J. Quasten, *Patrology*, iii (1960), p. 39, cf. L. von Hertling, 'Studi storici antoniani negli ultimi trent' anni', *Antonius Magnus Eremita* (*Studia Anselmiana*, xxxviii, 1956), 13–34.

[3] E. Schwartz, *Gött. Gel. Nach.* (1911), p. 485 n. 4 = *Ges. Schr.* iii (1959), p. 286 n. 3; K. Holl, *Neue Jahrbücher für das klassische Altertum*, xxix (1912), p. 425 n. 1 = *Gesammelte Aufsätze zur Kirchengeschichte*, ii (1928), p. 267 n. 2.

[4] H. Weingarten, *ZKG* i (1887), 10 ff.; *Ursprung des Mönchtums im nachconstantinischen Alter* (1877). These conclusions were accepted and refined by H. M. Gwatkin, *Studies of Arianism* (1882), pp. 98 ff. (repeated in the second edition of 1900, pp. 102 ff.).

[5] For a full scrutiny of Weingarten's arguments, and refutation of many of them, see A. Eichhorn, *Athanasii de vita ascetica testimonia collecta* (Diss. Halle, 1886), esp. pp. 10 ff., 35 ff. Subsequently, Weingarten's main premiss (the late development of monasticism) was shattered by the work of scholars such as K. Heussi, *Der Ursprung des Mönchtums* (1936), esp. pp. 69 ff. Hence a scholar as alert and critical as J. Gribomont was recently able to assert confidently that 'questa tesi troppo scettica non ha più appoggio' (*Dizionario degli istituti di perfezione*, i (1974), col. 700).

354

ago as 1895 by Paul Bedjan, though without a translation,[6] and nine years later E. A. Wallis Budge published a text and English translation of the version of the *Life* which Ḥenān-Īshō incorporated in his 'paradise of the fathers' in the later seventh century.[7] Yet it was only the recent publication, in 1980, of a proper critical edition accompanied by a literal French translation and a substantial introduction by René Draguet which identified and described the linguistic nature of the original *Life* lying behind the Syriac translation.[8] Since Draguet's edition has not been reviewed at all widely in academic journals, and has not so far gained entry to *L'Année Philologique* under the rubrics of Athanasius, Monastica, or Vitae, there is an obvious need both to publicize and to evaluate his hypothesis about the origin of the *Life of Antony*—all the more so since a recent bibliographical survey of work on Athanasius between 1974 and 1984 dismisses Draguet's conclusions out of hand with the apparently judicious, but in fact totally uninformative, verdict that 'serious reservations must be expressed about the highly speculative "discussion" of this text by the late Professor Draguet'.[9] Ideally, of course, a critic of Draguet's work needs to be fluent in Greek, Syriac, and Coptic. But few scholars possess outstanding expertise in all of these three languages, and it is arguable that progress now depends less on the linguistic expertise of Draguet's critics than on scholars' willingness to rethink a familiar problem and to discard cherished beliefs when they become untenable. The present writer has read a large amount of Greek, but only a small amount of Syriac and has no knowledge whatever of Coptic. He is prepared, however, to follow evidence and argument wherever they may lead.

In 1894 Friedrich Schulthess wrote a dissertation on the Syriac version of the *Life of Antony*, in which he described three manuscripts, provided a text and German translation of the first fifteen chapters, and compared the Greek and Syriac versions as a whole. In this discussion Schulthess left open the question of who wrote

---

[6] P. Bedjan, *Acta Martyrum et Sanctorum*, v (1895), 1–121.

[7] E. A. W. Budge, *The Book of Paradise* (*Lady Meux Manuscript*, no. 6, 1904), i. 1–108 (translation), ii. 1–93 (text). The translation 'printed for private circulation only' is more widely accessible in Budge's later *The Paradise of the Holy Fathers*, i (1907), 3–76.

[8] R. Draguet, *La Vie primitive de S. Antoine conservée en syriaque*, CSCO ccccxvii = Scriptores Syri clxxxiii (1980) (text); CSCO ccccxviii = Scriptores Syri clxxxiv (1980) (translation).

[9] C. Kannengiesser, 'The Athanasian Decade 1974–84: A Bibliographical Report', *Theological Studies*, xlvi (1985), 524–41, at p. 529. The insulting quotation-marks around 'discussion' are Kannengiesser's.

the *Life* in the hope that full publication of the Syriac text and further study would provide elucidation, though he also reported a suggestion of his teacher, Theodor Nöldeke, that the Syriac *Life* was not translated from the extant Greek, but represented a more primitive recension.[10] That suggestion provoked the ire of Eduard Schwartz,[11] and was subsequently dismissed by Gérard Garitte as pure fantasy.[12] However, when Draguet came to edit the Syriac *Life of Antony* for the Louvain *Corpus Scriptorum Christianorum Orientalium*, he brought to the task a knowledge of the peculiar nature of certain recensions of the Syriac translation of the *Lausiac History*, which he had already edited in the same series.[13] In both Syriac texts Draguet detected a large number of varied linguistic oddities which seemed to him either only explicable or at least most plausibly explicable as Copticisms. Hence the introduction to his translation of the Syriac *Life of Antony* comprises three main sections: first, a proof that the short recension is an abbreviation of the long recension, not an independent or more primitive version; secondly, an analysis of some thirty-one different types of Copticism in well over three hundred passages of the Syriac *Life*; and thirdly, an adumbration of the corollaries of the linguistic nature of the text which the Syriac translator had before him.[14]

Draguet argues that the Syriac translation presupposes an original text different from the Greek *Life of Antony* in two crucial respects. First, individual passages often diverge in the two versions

---

[10] F. Schulthess, *Probe einer syrischen Version der Vita St. Antonii* (Diss. Strassburg, publ. Leipzig, 1894), pp. 14–25.

Since Schulthess's dissertation is not widely accessible, let me quote the two passages where he adumbrates a thesis close to that argued here. His comparison of the Greek and Syriac versions begins with the claim 'dass der uns vorliegende griechische Text nicht die ursprüngliche zu sein braucht, sondern dass die Vita Antonii des Athanasius oder Pseudo-Athanasius schon sehr früh in zwei, vielleicht auch mehreren, z.T. stark abweichenden Gestalten existiert hat' (p. 14). And it concludes: 'Aus mehreren Stellen wird es wahrscheinlich, dass die uns erhaltene vita [i.e. the Greek life] eine Überarbeitung der echten, in Aegypten verfassten, vita für den Gebrauch der Nichtägypter ist. Diese Vermutung, die mir Herr Prof. Nöldeke als solche mitteilte, kann sich auf eine Anzahl von Stellen stützen, die im griechischen Texte entweder gemildert oder sonstwie geändert oder geradezu weggelassen sind' (p. 25).

[11] E. Schwartz, *Gött. Gel. Nach.* (1904), p. 338 n. 1 = *Ges. Schr.* iii (1959), p. 7 n. 1: 'Nur die platteste Tendenzkritik kann an der Echtheit dieses Werkes zweifeln.'

[12] G. Garitte, *Antonius Magnus Eremita* (1956), p. 9 n. 37: 'cette hypothèse ... est entièrement fantaisiste.... Il est heureux que (par suite sans doute de la rareté de son ouvrage) les conclusions de Schulthess n'aient guère eu d'écho.'

[13] See his discussion of 'Inspiration coptisante de R1 et R2' in *Les Formes syriaques de la matière de l'Histoire Lausiaque*, i: *Les recensions. Version des pièces liminaires et des ch. 1–19 (CSCO* cccxc = Scriptores Syri clxx, 1978), 22*–60*.

[14] *CSCO* ccccxviii (1980), 13*–24*; 25*–100*; 100*–112*.

356

in amplitude, verbal expression, and factual detail in such a way that the Greek appears to be a reworking of the text represented by the Syriac translation.[15] Secondly, the Syriac translation exhibits such frequent Copticisms that it must have been made, not from the extant Greek *Life*, but from a more primitive version with a different linguistic character, i.e. from a *Life of Antony* written in Copticizing Greek.[16] Hence Draguet deduces that Athanasius cannot be the author of the *Life of Antony*, since the primitive version whose existence is implied by the Syriac *Life* must be the work, not of someone as adept in writing Greek as Athanasius, but of a Hellenized Copt.[17]

This thesis, at least as Draguet himself formulated it, contains two obvious weak links. First, Draguet argued that the Syriac translation was produced in Persia in the fifth or sixth century. His argument is vulnerable in itself, and the conclusion entails a major historical implausibility. Draguet deduced the provenance of the translation from a single phrase of undoubtedly Nestorian inspiration, which could easily be a later interpolation into a pre-existing text.[18] And so late a date would require the belief that the postulated Copticizing Greek *Life* circulated for a century or more in competition with the extant version written in educated Greek without leaving any other discernible traces. Secondly, Draguet's stated reasons for postulating a Greek original of any sort behind the Syriac translation are inadequate and unconvincing: presumption, grammatical objects preceding verbs or standing first in a clause, and the occurrence of θεοφιλής transliterated (which need show no more than origin in a Greek and Coptic bilingual milieu).[19]

---

[15] *CSCO* ccccxviii (1980), 13*-15*.   [16] Ibid. 98*-100*.

[17] Ibid. 112*. He rejects the concept of 'Athanase écrivain copte' advocated by L. T. Lefort, *Le Muséon*, xlvi (1933), 1-33, and denies that Athanasius, who could presumably speak the language, ever wrote for publication in Coptic.

[18] R. Draguet, *CSCO* ccccxviii (1980), 104*, 112*, 72 (chap. 74 n. 4, where the first 'VS' is a misprint for 'VG'). The Syriac adds 'by combination with our humanity' when describing the Incarnation.

[19] Ibid. 25*. Since the point is important, it will be apposite to quote the whole of the paragraph which Draguet devotes to it:

Bien que VS n'ait certainement pas eu VG pour modèle, il traduisait quand même du grec. Que les anciennes versions syriaques soient faites d'après le grec le ferait déjà présumer. La présomption prend consistance par le parallélisme de plan, de matière, voire, mais dans une mesure notablement moindre, de correspondance verbale qui s'observe entre VS et VG. Des faits de style vont dans le même sens. Le plus tangible réside dans les prolepses du syriaque: souvent, en effet, VS loge en tête de phrase, contrairement au génie de la langue syriaque, des régimes directs que le grec, disposant du cas accusatif, peut mettre en prolepse sans nuire à la clarté. Qu'il suffise d'un exemple, au ch. 2: *Ces choses et de pareilles alors qu'il (les) considérait* (cfr VG ταῦτα δὲ ἐνθυμούμενος), d'autant plus démonstratif que les codd. KLMFO ont rétabli l'ordre syriaque normal en lisant: *alors qu'il considérait ces choses et de pareilles*

However, these two weak links can easily be removed by a minor modification of Draguet's thesis. The following threefold hypothesis incorporates what is valid in Draguet's arguments, but avoids these two implausibilities:

1. The *Life of Antony* was originally composed in Coptic by someone close to Antony for the benefit of the Pachomian communities in the Thebaid.

2. The Syriac *Life of Antony* is a reasonably faithful translation of this lost Coptic *Life* made not long after its composition for monastic readers in Syria or Mesopotamia.

3. The extant Greek *Life of Antony* is a reworking or redaction of the lost Coptic *Life* made in Alexandria, which subtly alters the emphases and sometimes the content of the original in order to make it more palatable or attractive to the urban culture of the Greco-Roman world.

Bold though it may seem, I submit that this hypothesis, or something closely similar to it, is necessary to explain the divergences which can be observed between the Syriac *Life of Antony* and all other known versions.

The linguistic argument has three stages. First, it must be shown that the phrases or expressions in question are alien to Syriac; secondly, that they do not occur in other Syriac translations from Greek originals themselves unaffected by possible Copticisms; and thirdly, that the phrases or expressions are of a type either peculiar to Coptic (the strongest case) or else common to Greek and Coptic (less decisive). Draguet has abundantly documented the linguistic oddness of the Syriac *Life of Antony* and shown that many of its peculiarities reflect Coptic rather than Greek.[20] For my part I can add that these linguistic features do not seem to occur in Syriac translations of Greek texts, with the significant exception of versions of the *Lausiac History*. The linguistic argument, therefore, seems extremely powerful in itself. What I believe makes Draguet's case, as modified here, conclusive is a series of non-linguistic arguments from individual passages.[21]

For brevity and ease of exposition, the following sigla will be employed:

(app. n. 37). Autre genre d'indice stylistique: au ch. 4, VS reproduit le mot grec et en donne ensuite l'explication: *or un chacun, de par ses hauts faits, l'appelait théophile, ce qui est interprété 'aimant Dieu'* (VG οὕτως αὐτὸν ὁρῶντες ἐκάλουν θεοφιλῆ).

[20] Ibid. 29* ff., discusses more than thirty different types of Copticism.

[21] For similar arguments, to those advanced below, see Draguet, op. cit. 15*/16* (on chap. 15); p. 25 n. 3 (on the varying treatment of Ezek. 3: 17).

358

VCo   the postulated Coptic original of VS

VS   the Syriac *Life*, edited by R. Draguet, *La Vie primitive de S. Antoine conservée en Syriaque* (*CSCO* ccccxvii = Scriptores Syri clxxxiii, 1980)

VG   the Greek *Life*, of which a proper critical edition is still lacking, so that the text employed is that printed in *PG* xxvi, cols. 837–976, reproducing B. de Montfaucon, *Sancti Patris Nostri Athanasii Opera* i.2 (Paris, 1698), pp. 793–866 (= *BHG*³ 140)

VLR   a very early Latin translation which survives in one manuscript and has been edited by G. Garitte, *Un témoin important de la vie de S. Antoine. La version inédite latine des Archives de S. Pierre à Rome* (Rome, 1939); H. Hoppenbrouwers, *La plus ancienne version latine de la vie de S. Antoine par S. Athanase. Étude de Critique Textuelle* (*Latinitas Christianorum Primaeva*, xiv, 1960), pp. 67–195; G. J. M. Bartelink, *Vita di Antonio* (*Vite dei Santi*, i, 1974), pp. 4–178

VLEv   the more elegant and less literal Latin version by Evagrius, printed in *PL* lxxiii, cols. 125–70 = *PG* xxvi, cols. 833–976 (= *BHL* 609)[22]

VSa   the existing Coptic translation of VG, published by G. Garitte, *S. Antonii vitae Versio sahidica* (*CSCO* cxvii = Scriptores Coptici, xiii, 1949, with a Latin translation in *CSCO* cxviii = Scriptores Coptici, xiv, 1949)[23]

Before individual passages are discussed, however, the explicit testimony to Athanasian authorship of these versions must be weighed. It is far less decisive than is normally believed.[24] The only manuscript of VLR begins 'incipit vita sancti Antonii monachi edita a sancto Hieronymo'. Of the fourteen manuscripts of VS described by Draguet, only nine attribute the *Life* to Athanasius, but most of these are late manuscripts which include the *Life* as part of the 'paradise' of Ḥenān-Ishō—and hence their ascription merely reflects the opinion of the seventh-century compiler. Of the three most ancient manuscripts of the long recension of VS, one attributes the *Life* to Jerome, while two leave it anonymous, among them BL, Add. 14646 of the sixth century. Similarly, of the three manuscripts of the short recension, two leave the *Life* anonymous.

---

[22] On Evagrius' translation, see G. J. M. Bartelink, *Revue bénédictine*, lxxxii (1972), 98 ff.

[23] I do not believe that the evidence of other versions inaccessible to me (such as Armenian, Georgian, Old Slavonic, and Ethiopic) is likely to invalidate the arguments presented here.

[24] As Draguet notes, op. cit. 103*–106*.

The fact that VLEv, VSa, and all the more than 160 manuscripts of VG ascribe the work to Athanasius merely reflects the standard belief in his authorship which can be documented as early as 380 in Gregory of Nazianzus (*Orat.* xxi. 5)[25] and in 392 in Jerome's *De viris illustribus* (87; 88; 125). It may be more significant that Augustine, writing in Africa in the 390s and recalling a conversation a decade earlier, leaves the work anonymous. In Milan, the *Confessions* report, Ponticianus told Augustine about two *agentes in rebus* at Trier who were converted to the ascetic life when they found and read a codex 'in quo scripta erat vita Antonii' (viii. 6. 15). If Jerome was one of the *agentes in rebus*, as has been argued,[26] then the incident occurred *c.*370. Furthermore, when Jerome had occasion to refer to the *Life of Antony* in the preface to his *Vita Pauli* *c.*375, he recorded the existence of both a Greek and a Latin version, but refrained from naming the author:

de Antonio tam Graeco quam Romano stylo diligenter memoriae traditum est (*PL* xxiii, col. 18).

Admittedly, these two anonymous references do not exclude the possibility that both Jerome *c.*375 and Ponticianus when he was in Trier believed the *Life* to be by Athanasius. However, since works were often ascribed to Athanasius which he most certainly did not write,[27] the lack of unanimous attestation of his authorship raises a doubt about whether his name had always been attached to the *Life of Antony* from the very beginning.

In comparing individual passages of VS and VG, it is necessary to use VLR as a check, since VLR is a very early and very literal translation of VG (unlike VLEv, which often paraphrases, and VSa, which is not early). The following comparisons of VS and VG on specific details strongly confirm the hypothesis that both derive independently from a lost original.

[25] On the date of Gregory, *Orat.* xxi, see J. Mossay, *Grégoire de Nazianze, Discours 20–23* (*Sources chrétiennes*, cclxx, 1980), 99 ff.
    It is often alleged that the Syriac writer Ephrem, who died in 373, provides the earliest external attestation of Athanasius' authorship of the *Life* (PG xxvi, cols. 825/6, citing the passage later edited by S. E. Assemani, *Sancti Patris nostri Ephraemi Syri Opera Omnia, Graece et Latine*, i (Rome, 1732), 249). But the work in question (*CPG* no. 3932) was written long after Ephrem's death, cf. D. Hemminger-Iliadou, *Dictionnaire de Spiritualité*, iv (1960), col. 811.
[26] P. Courcelle, *Recherches sur les 'Confessions' de saint Augustin* (1950), pp. 181 ff. Courcelle's identification is accepted as probable by J. Matthews, *Western Aristocracies and Imperial Court A.D. 364–425* (1975), p. 50, but rejected as a 'brilliant but implausible guess' by J. N. D. Kelly, *Jerome. His Life, Writings and Controversies* (1975), p. 30.
[27] M. Geerard, *Clavis Patrum Graecorum*, ii (1974), nos. 2230–309 lists eighty Athanasian *spuria*.

360

1. Sailing on the Nile

The introductory letter in VG is, as Draguet noted,[28] less than half the length of the introductory letter in VS. Towards the end of both versions the author explains that he is writing in haste. According to VG,

After receiving your letter, I wished to send for some of the monks, those especially who were accustomed most often to visit him, so that I might learn more and write to you more fully. But, since the sailing season was drawing to a close and the letter-carrier was in a hurry for this reason, I have made haste to write to your piety what I myself know (for I have seen him often) and what I have been able to discover from the man who accompanied him for no short time and poured water on his hands.[29]

The recipients of the *Life* thus appear to be outside Egypt, and VLEv supplies the heading 'ad peregrinos fratres' (the manuscripts of VG have something closely similar). VS has two significant divergences. First, it explains the reason for haste more precisely: 'the time was short for[30] boats to travel from Egypt to the Thebaid and from there to here' (p. 5. 12–13). Secondly, it claims a more profound knowledge of Antony: the writer promises to report 'what I have come to know in my constant attendance upon him' (p. 5. 14–15: ܡܘܠܟܐ , ܗܘܣܪܟܒ). The preface in VS makes clear what is obscure in the text of VG, viz. that the *Life* was written in reply to a request for information from the Thebaid, i.e. presumably from the Pachomian monastic communities there. Schulthess drew attention to this divergence of VS and VG and justly observed that the former appears more likely to be the original.[31]

2. Emerging from the cave

Antony spent twenty years in a mountain of the outer desert close to the Nile (*Life* 13–14). VS states that 'he entered [his abode] and dwelt there as in a cave' (p. 30. 16), using a word (ܡܥܪܐ) which often denotes an animal's den. VG makes it a special sort of cave (ὥσπερ ἐν ἀδύτοις ἐγκαταδυόμενος). After twenty years, Antony emerged. According to VS,

when he came out like a man who rises from the depths of the earth, they saw his face as that of an *angel of light* (2 Cor. 11: 14) (VS, p. 34. 8–9).

---

[28] Op. cit. 16*.

[29] VS and VLR confirm the correctness of the reading παρὰ τοῦ ἀκολουθήσαντος ... καὶ ἐπιχέαντος, cf. M. Tetz, *ZNW* lxxiii (1982), 7 f.

[30] The correct reading ܡܒܢ ܪܐܝܪ is printed by Draguet in p. 5 n. 160. (This is clearly not the place to discuss the editorial principles employed in his edition.)

[31] Schulthess, op. cit. 17, 25.

The Greek *Life* presents a very different image of the emerging holy man:

Antony came forth like a mystic initiate full of the power of God from some sacred shrine (ὥσπερ ἔκ τινος ἀδύτου μεμυσταγωγημένος καὶ θεοφορούμενος).

Neither VS nor VG can here be a translation of the other: they present totally different images of Antony, one wholly Christian, the other as a mystic initiate.[32] It is not likely that VS has substituted its image for the rather pagan VG. VSa shows how the puzzled or embarrassed translator normally reacts: it simply omits the most suggestive words of its Greek exemplar to produce the innocuous 'tum egressus est Antonius, Deum in se ferens'. Moreover, another significant divergence occurs a few lines later. According to VS Antony was calm because 'reason had been made his pilot' (p. 34. 13-14). VG expands the explanation into 'ὡς ὑπὸ τοῦ λόγου κυβερνώμενος καὶ ἐν τῷ κατὰ φύσιν ἑστώς'.

In a celebrated study, Richard Reitzenstein argued that Athanasius modelled the *Life of Antony* on a lost life of Pythagoras also used by Porphyry in his extant life of the Greek sage.[33] The Greek passage discussed above was Reitzenstein's prime piece of evidence, allowed as cogent even by scholars who dismissed the other parallels which he adduced as inconclusive.[34] A.-J. Festugière subsequently claimed to strengthen Reitzenstein's case that Athanasius was using a pagan model by adducing Iamblichus' *Life of Pythagoras*.[35] But the undoubted similarities of content between VG and its presumed exemplars are outweighed by the fact that VS omits all that is characteristically Greek rather than Christian in a list of virtues:

τί οὐ μᾶλλον κτώμεθα, ἃ καὶ μεθ' ἑαυτῶν
ἆραι δυνάμεθα, ἅτινά ἐστι φρόνησις,
δικαιοσύνη, σωφροσύνη, ἀνδρεία, σύνεσις,
ἀγάπη, φιλοπτωχία, πίστις ἡ εἰς Χριστόν,
ἀοργησία, φιλοξενία; (VG 17)

Let us show eagerness, therefore, and amass it [i.e. what we can take from this world into the next], that is, the love of God, charity towards one another, belief in Christ, simplicity of mind, love towards strangers, patience of spirit (VS, p. 39. 1-3).

Such divergences are systematic, not haphazard. Either VS has

[32] J. Gribomont, *Dictionnaire de spiritualité*, x (1980), col. 1540: 'le héros . . ., dont la sagesse thaumaturgique imite et dépasse celle d'un Pythagore'.
[33] R. Reitzenstein, *Des Athanasius Werk über das Leben des Antonius* (*Sb.* Heidelberg, Phil.-hist. Klasse 1914, Abh. 8), esp. pp. 14 ff.
[34] Thus H. Dörries, 'Die Vita Antonii als Geschichtsquelle', *Wort und Stunde*, i (1966), 145-224 (reprinted from *Gött. Gel. Nach.* 1949, pp. 357-410), at pp. 186/7.
[35] A.-J. Festugière, *REG* l (1937), 489 ff.

362

successfully filtered out expressions which assimilate Antony to a pagan holy man or VG has introduced them into an exemplar where they were lacking.

3. *The desert a city*

After emerging from his retreat, Antony inspired so many to emulate his eremitical life that soon 'the desert was made a city by monks who left their places of origin and enrolled in the city of heaven' (*Life* 15). This famous sentence of VG has not only provided the title for an important study of early monasticism,[36] but also provoked a brilliant comparison with Heliodorus' *Aethiopica* 'for a similar deliberate sense of paradox surrounding a brigand's lair in the marshes'.[37] VS lacks the phrase which has fired the imagination of modern scholars:

By these words he persuaded many to renounce this world and its tire-someness, and to take refuge in a life of solitude. And from that time the life of the solitaries in the desert and the mountains began to multiply and increase in the manner of a tabernacle of the new world (p. 35. 7–9).

It is hard to see why any translator would have filtered out the striking image of a heavenly city in the desert—least of all a Syriac translator familiar with Syrian or Mesopotamian monasticism.

4. *Antony's escort*

Antony visited Alexandria in the summer of 338, doubtless at the pressing invitation of Athanasius and in order to bolster support for the embattled bishop, whose enemies outside Egypt were planning his deposition and removal from office (achieved in the spring of 339). Scholars from Montfaucon on have seen a sort of signature in an apparent reference to Athanasius himself:

When he was departing and we were escorting him, as we reached the city-gate, a woman shouted behind: 'Stay, man of God, etc.' (VG 71)[38]

But VS lacks the first-person verbs:

When he had finished all these things in Alexandria, he departed in order to go to the desert. And while the whole city accompanied him, as they reached the level of the gate of the city, a woman behind the people ran with great

---

[36] D. J. Chitty, *The Desert a City. An Introduction to the Study of Egyptian and Palestinian Monasticism under the Christian Empire* (1956).

[37] P. Brown, *The Cult of the Saints. Its Rise and Function in Latin Christianity* (1981), p. 134 n. 34. The text to the note observes 'how wholeheartedly Christians wished to patronize communities which had opted pointedly for the antithesis of settled urban life' (p. 8).

[38] *PG* xxvi, cols. 823–6, cf. E. Schwartz, *Ges. Schr.* iii (1959), p. 286 n. 3: 'gerade diese Kapitel [sc. 69–71] gehören zu den sichersten Beweisen für die Echtheit des Buches.' That claim is true only if the first-person verbs are original.

impetuosity and cried: 'Please wait a brief moment, man of God, etc.' (p. 117. 12–118. 3).

Why should any translator both expand VG and turn its 'we' into 'the whole city'? VSa dutifully reproduces both first-person verbs of VG. VLR and VLEv drop one, but VLR expands the adverb ὄπισθεν into 'depost nos'. In this passage, VS is not a translation of VG, but VG can be a redaction of the exemplar of VS by someone who did escort Antony to the city-gate of Alexandria in the summer of 338.

5. *A list of pagan dieties*

When some Greek philosophers came to Antony, he harangued them at length through an interpreter (*Life* 74–80). According to VG, Antony attacked the allegorization of traditional deities:

> εἴπατε δὲ καὶ ὑμεῖς ἡμῖν τὰ ὑμέτερα.
> τί δ᾽ ἂν εἴποιτε περὶ τῶν ἀλόγων ἢ ἀλογίαν καὶ
> ἀγριότητα; ἐὰν δέ, ὡς ἀκούω, θελήσητε λέγειν μυθικῶς
> λέγεσθαι ταῦτα παρ᾽ ὑμῖν, καὶ ἀλληγορεῖτε ἁρπαγὴν
> Κόρης εἰς τὴν γῆν, καὶ Ἡφαίστου χωλότητα εἰς τὸ
> πῦρ, καὶ Ἥραν εἰς τὸν ἀέρα, καὶ Ἀπόλλωνα εἰς
> τὸν ἥλιον, καὶ Ἄρτεμιν μὲν εἰς τὴν σελήνην, τὸν
> δὲ Ποσειδῶνα εἰς τὴν θάλασσαν—οὐδὲν ἧττον αὐτὸν
> οὐ θεὸν σέβεσθε, ἀλλὰ τῇ κτίσει λατρεύετε παρὰ τον
> τὰ πάντα κτίσαντα θεόν (VG 76).

The corresponding passage in VS has a significantly different content:

Describe your literature for us and explain to us what is in it: which are the animals that are worshipped, which are the reptiles that are called by the names of gods, if not [objects of] ridicule and mockery. But, according to your way of thinking, if a man devoid of understanding comes to you, you wrap up[39] each one of these things in rational language and you expound everything which is improbable so that it will be believed as true by those who lack understanding. You give names to the sky and the earth, to the sun and moon, to the air and water, to light and the sea, and you name the rest of creatures and you call them gods in order by them to entice men away from the one God creator of all (p. 123. 10–124. 1).

Although the general point made in the two passages may be identical, the precise object of their polemic differs. VG is concerned with the systematic allegorization of traditional cults in

---

[39] Both reading and translation are difficult. I translate the reading which Draguet prints (ܚܣܡܝܢ), but as he notes (p. 123 n. 8), the variant ܚܡܣܢܝܢ is closer to VG and perhaps preferable. Budge, op. cit. i (1907), 62, accepts the latter and translates 'ye liken each one of them [unto gods]'.

364

contemporary pagan thought, while VS attacks the divinization of animals and natural phenomena. Schulthess commented that, whereas VS alludes to Egyptian animal-worship, 'the redaction intended for non-Egyptians' substitutes the worship of Greek deities.[40]

6. A Letter of Constantine

The repute of Antony reached the emperors, who wrote to him as to a father (*Life* 81). VG names the emperors as Constantine and his sons Constantius and Constans the Augusti—which implies imperial letters both before Constantine died on 22 May 337 and after his sons became Augusti on 9 September 337. VS omits the title of Augusti for the sons of Constantine, so that it may allude to a single imperial letter, from Constantine as Augustus and his sons as Caesars. If that is indeed so, then VS falls into line with what Sozomenus reports, viz. that Antony wrote to Constantine after the Council of Tyre and the emperor replied (*HE* ii. 31. 2/3). A letter written by Constantine between 335 and 337 would have been sent in both his name and the name of the four Caesars in the imperial college, but a writer in the 350s would naturally omit the two Caesars of that imperial college who had become unpersons (viz. Dalmatius in 337 and Constantinus in 340). This divergence between VS and VG may thus not be a trivial one: external considerations indicate that VS correctly reports the heading of a single imperial letter where VG multiplies it through misunderstanding imperial protocol.

7. Arian persecution

The *Life* reports a prophecy of Antony which came true after two years, when the Arians pillaged the churches (82). VS is clear and consistent, since the context as well as the content point to the events of 339, when pagan sacrifice on Christian altars is alleged to have occurred in Alexandria (cf. Athanasius, *Ep. enc.* 3. 5).[41] VG introduces a problem by offering 'ἡ νῦν ἔφοδος τῶν Ἀρειανῶν' where VS has merely 'this commotion from the Arians' (p. 132. 8). 'The present attack' can only refer to the events of 356—which is impossible in the context of the *Life*. Similarly, a few lines later, the present reference in the clause ἃ νῦν οἱ Ἀρειανοὶ ἀλόγως πράττουσιν ὡς τὰ κτήνη has no equivalent in the somewhat different parallel passage in VS. In both passages, the version in VG seems to be clearly secondary to that in VS.

[40] Schulthess, op. cit. 19, 25.
[41] R. Reitzenstein, op. cit., p. 28 n. 1. Athanasius makes no similar allegation for 356/7 (cf. *De Fuga* 6. 7 ff.; *Hist. Ar.* 48. 1 ff.).

The comparison of individual passages thus shows a pattern of divergence between VS and VG which can, in theory, be explained in three ways, viz.

(A) the translator who produced VS had before him VG or something which resembled it closely, but instead of reproducing its content faithfully he revised it deliberately and systematically;

(B) VS and VG are based on a common source which differed substantially from both of them;

(C) VS reproduces, with reasonable accuracy, a lost Coptic original which the Greek translator systematically revised to produce VG.

Hypothesis (A) represents the traditional view, recently reasserted against Draguet by Martin Tetz,[42] but it requires the improbable postulate that the Syriac translator both filtered out Greek elements and introduced Egyptian ones, and it is incompatible with Draguet's analysis of the linguistic character of VS. A choice between hypotheses (B) and (C) is less clear-cut, since they both entail the postulate of a lost original whose precise lineaments are *ex hypothesi* unknown.[43] Nevertheless, both Draguet's linguistic characterization of VS and the comparison of individual passages where VS appears to be prior to or more primitive than VG tell in favour of the third hypothesis, which can be depicted schematically as follows:[44]

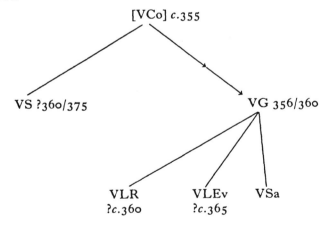

[VCo] *c*.355

VS ?360/375   VG 356/360

VLR   VLEv   VSa
?*c*.360   ?*c*.365

[42] M. Tetz, *ZNW* lxxiii (1982), pp. 1/2 n. 3.

[43] It should be observed that fourth- and fifth-century Syriac translations from Greek tend to be very free, close literal translation being characteristic of the seventh century: see S. P. Brock, 'Towards a History of Syriac Translation Technique', *III°* *Symposium Syriacum 1980* (*Orientalia Christiana Analecta*, ccxxi, 1983), 1-14.

[44] The dates require justification. (*a*) The traditional date of 356 for Antony's

366

The postulate of direct translation from Coptic into Syriac is something which may seem unacceptable because it is (to the best of my knowledge) unparalleled. Such an objection is mitigated by at least two facts. It was Arabs (ܣܪ̈ܩܝܐ : Σαρακηνοί in VG 49/50) who led Antony to his retreat in the inner mountain, and direct contact between Syriac and Coptic cultures is attested by the fact that the Manichaean psalms were translated directly from Syriac into Coptic.[45] Syriac-speaking Manichees brought Syriac texts with them to Egypt:[46] is it possible that Manichees were responsible for transmitting the *Life of Antony* to Syria and Mesopotamia?

Only a close and systematic textual comparison of VS and VG by scholars fluent in Syriac, Greek, and Coptic will provide a completely satisfactory proof of the thesis argued here. I lack the linguistic skills (and perhaps the patience) needed for the full study which I hope that others will undertake. The case at present rests on a combination of Draguet's linguistic arguments, external considerations, and the comparison of key passages, and could perhaps be disproved. Such a caveat, however, should not be allowed to become a deterrent to adumbrating some corollaries of the thesis advanced here.

If the thesis is correct, we have two versions of the *Life of Antony*, not one, and we can exploit their differences to explore the contrast between the Coptic milieu of the postulated lost Coptic original and the Alexandrian milieu of its Greek reworking. Tetz has recently argued that VG is a reworking by Athanasius, with systematic theological corrections, of a written account of Antony composed for him by Serapion, bishop of Thmuis, who was 'carus Antonii

death derives from Jerome, *Chronicle*, p. 240[b] Helm, and the assumption that Athanasius wrote the *Life* during a period of persecution (82), i.e. between 356 and 362. If this assumption is discarded, Jerome's exact date ought no longer to be pressed. The latest datable event in the *Life* seems to be the death of Valacius in 345/6 (86, cf. *PLRE* i. 625 f., 929), while Antony is last attested among the living in 352 or 353 by *Epistula Ammonis*, 29 (F. Halkin, *S. Pachomii Vitae Graecae* (*Subsidia Hagiographica*, xix, 1932), pp. 115/16, cf. pp. 31*f.). (*b*) The uniqueness of VS indicates an extremely early date. (*c*) VG is dated by its allusions to persecution by Arians in Alexandria (82). (*d*) VLR ought to be earlier than VLEv, which was presumably the version read by the *agentes in rebus* at Trier, perhaps as early as *c*.370.

[45] See T. Säve-Söderbergh, 'Some Remarks on Coptic Manichaean Poetry', *Coptic Studies in honor of W. E. Crum* (*Bulletin of the Byzantine Institute of America*, ii, 1950), 159–73. A Greek intermediary is postulated by C. R. C. Allberry, *A Manichaean Psalm-Book II* (*Manichean Manuscripts in the Chester Beatty Collection*, ii, 1938), p. xix; H. J. W. Drijvers, *Studies in Gnosticism and Hellenistic Religions presented to G. Quispel* (1981), p. 118.

[46] F. C. Burkitt, *The Religion of the Manichees* (1925), 111 ff. Although the Oxyrhynchus fragments are on papyrus, the rest are on vellum.

monachi' (Jerome, *De viris illustribus* 99).[47] It is significant that Tetz detects two strata in VG, but his identification of their authors should be rejected. The fact that VS speaks of 'my constant attendance' on Antony should locate the author of VCo close to the outer mountain, whereas Serapion's see was in the Nile delta. The Greek redactor or adapter was almost certainly not Athanasius himself. It need not be decisive that, of the four key words in the description of Antony's dwelling in and emergence from his cave (14–15), two do not occur in Athanasius' writings at all (viz. ἄδυτον and ἐγκαταδύω), while a third only occurs in the synodical letter of the Council of Alexandria in 338, which Athanasius wrote or at least drafted—where it bears a totally different sense.[48] But it is hard to believe that, if Athanasius had produced VG, he could so totally have effaced himself, or resisted the temptation to rewrite the passage which puts Athanasius and Serapion on the same level (*Life* 91). The redactor doubtless moved in Athanasian circles and the first-person verb in his account of Antony's departure from Alexandria implies that he was among those escorting the monk in 338, perhaps in the bishop's entourage, but nothing in the text of VG need point to Athanasius himself as the redactor.[49]

The hypothesis propounded here does not diminish the historical value of the *Life of Antony* for the study of early monasticism. On the contrary, it enhances it considerably. The Syriac *Life* becomes our primary evidence for Antony, rather than the apophthegmata attributed to Antony to which Heinrich Dörries assigned primacy in his classic study of the *Life of Antony* as a historical source (*PG* lxv, cols. 75–88).[50] The paternity and transmission of these sayings attributed to Antony are obscure, whereas the original *Life of Antony* which the Syriac translation reproduces comes from a man close to Antony—and one who spoke the hermit's own language.

It now becomes clear why no convincing analysis of the literary form of the *Life* as a whole in terms of Greek patterns of biography has yet been given. Such analyses have indeed been attempted, but they have not shown that the *Life* reproduces the formal features of

---

[47] M. Tetz, 'Athanasius und die Vita Antonii. Literarische und theologische Relationen', *ZNW* lxxiii (1982), 1–30.

[48] Athanasius, *Apol. c. Ar.* 17. 4: τὸν ἐν αὐτῷ μυσταγωγοῦντα, referring to Athanasius himself as a celebrant of the eucharist. The fourth key word (θεοφορῶ) occurs only in *Orat. c. Ar.* iii. 23, 41 (*PG* xxvi, cols. 372, 409). (For all these statistics, I rely on G. Müller, *Lexicon Athanasianum* (1952), cols. 22, 367, 651, 933.)

[49] In the light of Tetz's study I unreservedly withdraw my unfounded assertion that 'the long discourse put into Antony's mouth (16–43) is wholly Athanasius' own' (*Constantine and Eusebius* (1981), p. 370 n. 51). The question now is whether any part of VG has peculiarly Athanasian characteristics.

[50] H. Dörries, *Wort und Stunde*, i (1966), 147 ff.

the Greco-Roman biographical genre, only that it shares with some
earlier biographies themes or individual images which it need not
have borrowed from them.[51]

Above all, it is both interesting and significant that it was not the
historical Coptic hermit of the Egyptian *chora* who exerted a formative influence on western monasticism and Byzantine asceticism,
but an Alexandrian refurbishment more attuned to the spiritual
yearnings of an urban Mediterranean culture. Paul Peeters would
not have been surprised to learn that, though the Greek *Life of
Antony* provided the 'prototype of all Greek monks',[52] it produced
its image of Antony through a subtle transformation of 'le tréfonds
oriental de l'hagiographie byzantine'.

[51] See G. J. M. Bartelink, 'Die literarische Gattung der Vita Antonii. Struktur
und Motive', *Vig. Chr.* xxxvi (1982), 38–62, esp. 58–60. (The article reproduces a
lecture of 5 January 1981 and was written without awareness of Draguet's work.)
[52] K. Holl, *Preussische Jahrbücher*, xciv (1898), 408 = *Gesammelte Aufsätze*, ii
(1928), 271.

RELIGION AND SOCIETY IN THE AGE OF THEODOSIUS

The title "Religion and Society in the Age of Theodosius" deliberately evokes the title of a volume of essays by Peter Brown who, through his biography of Augustine and many other studies, has transformed our understanding of Augustine and the age in which he lived and has, for more than twenty years, inspired a generation of younger scholars and historians with enthusiasm for Late Antiquity.[1] My intention is to ask how Brown's work and that of others has altered our picture of the society in which Augustine grew to maturity, underwent conversion, and then discovered his vocation as a bishop and theologian. For during recent decades much has changed in the scholarly landscape against which we view Augustine of Hippo and his conversion.

Let me begin, as the present occasion perhaps demands, with an ancient after-dinner conversation. Macrobius' *Saturnalia* used to be almost universally regarded by modern scholars as first-hand evidence for paganism in the highest echelons of Roman society in the late fourth century. The *Saturnalia* shows pagan aristocrats and scholars discoursing learnedly on Roman religion and philosophy at the Saturnalia of 384, and it was assumed that Macrobius wrote the work not long after 384, that he belonged to the same cultural milieu as the protagonists in his dialogue, and that he could be used unguardedly as primary evidence to reconstruct that milieu.[2] In 1966, Alan Cameron proved that Macrobius was writing after 430, at a distance of half a century from the dramatic date of his *Saturnalia*.[3] It follows that his picture of the *saeculum Praetextati*, the age of Vettius Agorius Praetextatus, is an idealised, retrospective panegyric of a bygone age, not the depiction of a living ideal. The wider consequences of this redating are enormous: they compel a more differentiated approach to paganism in the late fourth century Rome—an approach evident in much recent work on the period, particularly that of John Matthews.[4]

I must confess a personal motive in choosing to tackle my topic as I have. My own work on Constantine and the Constantinian period has led me to a number of novel, even heterodox or idiosyncratic views. These include a conviction that the Roman Empire became Christian earlier, and in the fourth century became more thoroughly Christian than has normally been supposed by academic historians of the last hundred years.[5] Of late I have been endeavouring to apply my interpretation of the reign of Constantine to the career of Athanasius under his sons. I hope to show that there is little or nothing in the later fourth century which is not consonant with my picture of the age of Diocletian and Constantine. Unfortunately, the subject is so large that I must be highly selective. I shall of necessity say a great deal, perhaps too much, about the senatorial aristocracy and the imperial court (since our evidence for them is fuller and more explicit than for other segments of society), but I shall try to allow due weight to the immense local variety which existed within that fictitious legal unity, the Later Roman Empire.

In theory, the Roman Empire was an *indivisum patrimonium* with the same laws and government from Hadrian's Wall in Britain to the Euphrates, from the mouth of the Danube to the cataracts of the Nile. In fact, for almost all the fourth century, there were two quite separate Roman Empires, in East and West. Constantine came to power in 306 in Britain, Gaul and Spain. In 312 he added Italy and Africa, in 316/7 most of the Balkans and Greece. It was only in 324 that he conquered Asia Minor and the East, and it was only there that he had the political opportunity to make the sweeping changes in established religion which Eusebius of Caesarea describes. From 324 onwards, therefore, the religious situation in East and West was very different. In the West, Constantine had come to power as a champion of religious tolerance and hence, despite his conversion in 312, he was committed to allowing pagans equal freedom of worship with Christians. From 312 he began to bestow endowments, favours and privileges on the Christian church and its clergy, but it was politically unwise, probably impossible, to attempt to repress long established non-Christian ceremonies. And the same picture, I believe, obtained for the territories which Constantine conquered in 316/7, including Greece—where a still unpublished inscription shows the praetorian prefects in 342 reaffirming the privileges of the priest of Apollo at Delphi.

In 324, however, Constantine conquered the East in a war which he fought as a Christian crusade, and in the immediate aftermath of that war he had the opportunity to carry through a religious reformation. I believe that he used it.[6] First, those who had supported Licinius' persecution of the Christians were killed, presumably most or all of them lynched by the relatives and friends of their victims. Second, all the ill-effects of Licinius' policies were undone, and Constantine restored confiscated Christian property without compensation to the subsequent owners. Third, pagans were forbidden to consult oracles, erect new cult-statues or to sacrifice at all, and.Constantine renewed the prohibition when protests were made. He allowed pagans to retain their temples and shrines as places of prayer, but the sacrifices which were an integral part of pagan worship were now illegal. Finally, commissioners toured the eastern provinces confiscating all the precious metals to be found in temples and shrines—not just dedications, but doors, ceilings and even cult-statues.

Imperial policy was clear. But enforcement was uneven and erratic. Constantine destroyed a few cult-centres which were notorious, for moral or propaganda reasons. In general, however, local conditions determined whether pagan temples continued to exist unmolested or were pillaged and destroyed. An excellent article has recently documented the role of eastern bishops such as Mark of Arethusa in this long process of sporadic suppression throughout the fourth and early fifth centuries.[7]

Such was the situation in the East. What of the West? I am inclined to think that Constantine's prohibition of pagan sacrifice was not merely not enforced, but probably not even promulgated in the West. I would see the reiteration of the prohibition by Constans in 341 in a constitution addressed to the *vicarius Italiae* as not only the first attempt seriously to enforce the prohibition in Italy, but also probably the first formal proclamation of Constantine's policy there.[8] Of course, Constantine never expressly restricted the application of his prohibition of 324/5 to the East; he simply extended the familiar practice of enforcing universally binding legislation in only part of the Roman Empire. (The clearest examples of this are Diocletian's price edict of 301 and his fourth persecuting edict of early 304, neither of which was ever promulgated in the West.) Moreover, the diatribes of Firmicus Maternus in his *De errore profanarum religionum*, written in 343, make it clear that temple treasures had not been confiscated in the West.[9] It has been customary to play Firmicus Maternus against Eusebius in order to convict the latter of lying or exaggeration;[10] I prefer to accept both witnesses as basically truthful in reporting what each of them knew. The discrepancy is striking testimony to the real, and in some areas enormous, differences between East and West.

Between the death of Constantine in 337 and the death of Theodosius in 395, the Roman Empire had a single emperor and single administration for a total of approximately seven years out of fifty-eight, viz.

| 354/5 | between the deposition of Gallus and the proclamation of Julian as Caesar |

361–364   between the death of Constantius and the proclamation
of Valens as Augustus

388–391, 394/5   while Theodosius was in the West after defeating Magnus Maximus and Eugenius (Valentinian II during the earlier period and Arcadius, who was left in Constantinople in 394, were young and totally without political independence or authority of their own.)

I emphasise this fact because, despite his Spanish origin, Theodosius was primarily an eastern emperor—and his religious policies reflect the difference between East and West. In the East, he could be aggressive towards the practice of paganism; in the West, it was still politically unwise gratuitously to offend the religious sentiments of prominent pagans in the Roman aristocracy.

The reign of Theodosius marks an important stage in the Christianisation of the Roman Empire. When Constantine assumed the title of Augustus long before his conversion, he automatically took the title *pontifex maximus* and regarded himself, *qua* emperor, as head of the college of *pontifices* and in charge of traditional Roman cults.[11] Constantine did not drop the title in 312, and his Christian successors also took the title of *pontifex maximus*—until Theodosius. It has now been demonstrated that Theodosius was the first emperor to renounce the title and that he declined to accept it at his accession in January 379.[12] Eastern pagans knew what was likely to follow. Nicomachus Flavianus the younger might be appointed proconsul of Asia, as he was for 383/4; the sophist Himerius might greet Flavianus rapturously as he travelled through Greece; and the *consularis* of Crete might conspicuously honour pagan as well as Christian Roman aristocrats.[13] But when Maternus Cynegius toured the East as praetorian prefect between 384 and 388, he went on a rampage against pagan shrines wherever the opportunity offered.[14] Theodosius not only reiterated the prohibition of pagan sacrifice, which had been rescinded by Julian and probably not reinstated by Jovian, Valentinian or Valens, but withdrew imperial protection from temples and similar buildings.[15] That was not entirely an innovation: although Constantine and Constans had forbidden their destruction, Constantius ordered temples to be closed and access to them prevented—thereby disproving an ancient and modern *canard*, frequently repeated, that Arians were softer on paganism than catholics.[16] Theodosius in 391/2 forbade anyone to enter temples or shrines, and set out to enforce the prohibition by laying down precise penalties. At the same time he officially encouraged the destruction of pagan cult-centres, most conspicuously the Serapeum in Alexandria.

Within the church, Theodosius took an equally strong line. In 380 he defined "catholic" not in neutral or platitudinous terms, but as denoting Christians whose beliefs coincided with those of Damasus, the bishop of Rome, and

Peter, the bishop of Alexandria: he stigmatised all who refused to accept the Nicene creed as heretics and forbade them to own churches, or even to meet for worship inside cities. It is perhaps anachronistic to complain that Theodosius was the "first of the Spanish Inquisitors."[17] But it is important to stress that his personal piety, and that of the Gauls and Spaniards who accompanied him to Constantinople and staffed the highest positions in his administration, created a welcoming framework for the development of asceticism, the cult of the saints and the pursuit of relics.[18]

In the reign of Constantine, the true cross could be discovered by the bishop of Jerusalem. In the reign of Theodosius, it had to be an empress—though those who manufactured the familiar legend in the late 380s could not agree whether to attribute the discovery to Helena, the mother of Constantine, or to "Protonice," a wife of the emperor Claudius unknown to history.[19]

The precise religious situation in the East varied in accordance with local factors. In a backward area like Greece, pagan rites and rituals proved very tenacious.[20] On the other hand, in the prosperous villages of the hinterland of Antioch, Christianity already permeated peasant society and created fertile ground for the growth of the holy men so lovingly brought to life by Theodoret and Peter Brown.[21] And of course there were pagan intellectual centres in Athens and Asia Minor, which we know relatively well and which have attracted much recent attention.[22] But the variations cannot mask the fact that the eastern Roman Empire integrated the Christian church into its social, political and economic fabric earlier and more effectively than the West. That is probably due largely to its more urbanised structure. But there was also a cultural barrier. Since the middle of the second century, it had been possible for Greek writers like Justin, Clement, Origen and Eusebius to expound Christianity in terms easily understandable to non-Christians through the medium of Middle Platonism.[23] Somehow, it seems to me, there was no similar common intellectual currency among those who thought in Latin until Augustine developed his theological language, initially on the basis of Marius Victorinus' translations of some treatises by Plotinus.[24] The dependence of Ambrose on Philo, Origen and Athanasius' ascetical writings indicates the lack of a living Latin tradition of philosophical theology.[25] But here I stray into territory that belongs to others. Let me turn now to the political and social framework of the western empire between 379 and 395. It is complicated.[26]

When Valentinian died suddenly in November 375, he left two sons: Gratian, aged sixteen and an Augustus since 367, and Valentinian, a boy of four whom the generals at once proclaimed Augustus. After an obscure period of political intrigue with several executions of high officials, including the general Theodosius, Gratian established some sort of ascendancy with an administration led by his elderly tutor Ausonius. In 378, however, came the disaster of Adrianople in which Valens perished. Gratian recalled the younger Theodosius, who became Augustus of the East in January 379, either on Gratian's initiative or, more probably, because Gratian accepted a proclamation by the troops under Theodosius' command.

Relations between Theodosius and the sons of Valentinian were never very warm, not even, I suspect, after Theodosius fell in love with and married Galla, the sister of Valentinian II. The order to execute his father at Carthage in the winter of 375/6 had been issued in the names of Gratian and Valentinian II—and Magnus Maximus, who supplanted Gratian as ruler of Britain, Gaul and Spain in 383, was a relative of Theodosius. Theodosius recognised Maximus as a legitimate emperor and colleague. We cannot avoid asking ourselves what Theodosius' policy would have been in 387 if he had not been a widower and if Justina had not possessed an attractive daughter to ensnare him. Would he have rescued and restored the Arian Valentinian II, whose name authorised his father's death-warrant, at the price of war against a good catholic kinsman? I personally doubt it very much. Consequently, I am tempted to explain Theodosius' lenient treatment of Maximus' noble supporters in Rome, like Symmachus, less by a need to conciliate a politically powerful pagan party in the aristocracy than by a sincere recognition that, since Maximus was not a normal usurper, their support of him was not as criminal as it seemed in retrospect after his defeat. It is a pity that we do not have the panegyric which Symmachus delivered before Maximus: I suspect that it was very flattering to Theodosius.

The political background impinges vitally on the religious policies of the western emperors from 379 to 395. I should like to consider them in an order which is not quite chronological: first Maximus, then Gratian and Valentinian, then Theodosius, and finally Eugenius, who was proclaimed Augustus in Gaul in August 392 and defeated by Theodosius in September 394.

Maximus in many ways exemplifies the predicament of the usurper who, whatever his personal predilections, must seek political support wherever he can find it. When Maximus invaded Italy in 387, he tried to conciliate pagans without offending Christians by offering private subsidies to replace the public ones recently suspended, and he made the grave political mistake of ordering a Jewish synagogue in Rome which had been burnt down in a riot to be rebuilt. However, the most famous episode associated with Maximus' name arose from his need to satisfy the catholic bishops of Gaul by showing that he would not tolerate what they perceived as a heretical challenge to their authority. The execution of Priscillian of Avila is not the first execution of a Christian for heresy, nor is it the first execution of a bishop by the secular authorities for an ecclesiastical offence. Although the case of Priscillian is complicated and controversial, it seems clear that he was a layman condemned for magic and probably also immorality.[26]

The sources for the career of Priscillian are unsatisfactory: mainly the eleven tractates, some by Priscillian himself, discovered by Schepss at Würzburg in 1885, and Sulpicius Severus, whose main concerns seem to be to defend and magnify Martin of Tours, and to belittle and calumniate the episcopal enemies of Priscillian, in each case as a means of attacking the prosperous and spiritually flabby bishops of Gaul with whom he was at odds.[28] Given the state of the evidence, it is difficult, though not impossible, to unravel the course of events. The crucial point is that Priscillian was a layman.[29] A synod at Saragossa in 380 condemned his teaching, which had Gnostic affinities, and his ascetical practices. In the following year, the two bishops who had supported him consecrated him bishop of Avila, but the consecration was clearly invalid: the Council of Nicaea had made the consent of three bishops, including the metropolitan bishop of the province, a necessary condition for a valid consecration and had implicitly provided that provincial councils of bishops decide disputed cases. His opponents, therefore, held that Priscillian was not a bishop and never had been—and by normal criteria they were correct. Priscillian and his supporters then sought support in Italy and with some success at the court of Gratian. Magnus Maximus, however, convened a council of bishops to try the case at Bordeaux in 384/5: there Priscillian made the ultimately fatal mistake of appealing to the emperor, and his appeal was allowed by the council precisely because he was a layman not a bishop. Finally, despite the opposition of Martin, Priscillian was tried at Trier by the praetorian prefect of Maximus and executed together with some of his supporters. The ill-feeling which this provoked in certain quarters has unfortunately misled many modern scholars: even the normally judicious Henry Chadwick depicts Priscillian throughout as a bishop and brushes aside any doubt with the assertion that it is improbable that the Nicene rulings about the consecration of bishops were understood to be force in Spain.[30]

The case of Priscillian tells us a great deal about Christianity in Spain and Gaul, but it is not the striking precedent which some have seen. In the context of the 380s the real innovation came from Gratian, under the influence of Theodosius. In 382, he ordered the altar of Victory to be removed from the senate-house in Rome, and public subsidies for ancient Roman cults to be discontinued. Constantius had removed the altar when he visited Rome in 357; Julian had restored it; Valentinian made no change in the *status quo*. In 382, Gratian acted and when the Senate sent an embassy to protest, he renounced the title of *pontifex maximus* too. The rest of the story of the altar of Victory is familiar and need not be repeated.[31] The altar became a symbol and Ambrose won a symbolic victory in 384 when, after Gratian's death, he persuaded

Valentinian II to deny a formal request for the restoration of the altar from the *praefectus urbi* Symmachus representing the Roman Senate. One issue perhaps deserves consideration here. Both Symmachus and Ambrose claimed to have the majority of the Senate on their side. How can that be? I suspect that Ambrose was thinking of the whole senatorial class, whereas Symmachus refers only to the majority at a particular meeting. It would be bad method to discount Ambrose, then to take Symmachus as evidence that the Roman Senate was still predominantly pagan in 384. Our evidence consistently gives us only a minimum for estimating the number of Christian senators, not an accurate count. This point needs emphasis because the two are often confused. For example, when it was recently and convincingly argued that the first Christian *consul ordinarius* was Ovinius Gallicanus, consul in 317, that was subsequently construed as proving how few Christians there were in the Roman aristocracy under Constantine.[32] But the earlier article never addressed that question, and so far as I can see, the majority of non-imperial consuls between 317 and 337 were probably Christians.[33] When the emperor Julian accused Constantine of making barbarians consuls, he did not mean Germans, as Ammianus Marcellinus thought: he meant non-Hellenes, i.e., Christians.[34]

No biography of Ambrose of Augustine will omit the struggle between the bishop of Milan and Justina over whether Arians should be allowed a church in the city in which to worship.[35] In the present context, therefore, I can content myself with singling out two aspects of the struggle for comment. First, it is extremely misleading to talk of "the persecution of Justina." Ambrose, like Athanasius in Alexandria, was determined that the Arians should have no church for worship. If the term "persecution" is to be used at all, the Arians were the victims. Second, although the Arian Auxentius held the see of Milan from 355 to 374, the sentiment of the Christian populace of the city was probably solidly catholic by the 380s. Ambrose would not have been able to win by using techniques of passive resistance if there had been serious opposition to him in the city. The Arians who needed a church were primarily Gothic troops—as in Constantinople in 400 when the inhabitants slaughtered the followers of Gainas. We already see signs of the socio-religious differentiation which was to prevent the development of the barbarian kingdoms of the fifth century into enduring states: the Gothic and Germanic invaders, the Franks excepted, had a different religion from the existing population and remained socially distinct. At the end of the fourth century, it is not surprising that Arianism was strongest in Pannonia, that is, in an area where the population contained a high proportion of "barbarians."

Valentinian fled to Theodosius when Maximus invaded Italy in 387. Acceptance of Nicene Christianity was a condition of his restoration. Theodosius defeated Maximus in 388, then resided in Italy until 391 with the intention of organising the government of the West under his hegemony on a permanent basis. In Milan he confronted Ambrose, who won two symbolic victories over the emperor.[36] First, in 388, he compelled Theodosius to rescind an imperial order that the Christians of Callinicus on the Euphrates rebuild a Jewish synagogue and a conventicle of the Valentinians which they had burned down under the leadership of their bishop. Second, in 390, he compelled Theodosius to perform penance after he ordered a punitive massacre in Thessalonica, where the people had murdered a barbarian general. In both cases, Ambrose exerted moral pressure of a type only possible because Theodosius was a baptised Christian. He had been baptised in 380 when ill. He was not the first emperor to be a baptised Christian: that distinction belongs to Constans (or possibly to his older brother Constantinus).[37] But Theodosius was the first Christian emperor who was forced publicly to confront the dilemma which Constantine and Constantius had avoided by postponing baptism: can a Christian rule without committing serious sin? Constantine clearly did not think so: when he received the catechumen's robe, he laid aside his imperial insignia. Augustine moves in a different world, where bishops often act as judges and magistrates—and are perhaps present when witnesses are tortured. Before he left Milan in 391, Theodosius shattered any impression which he might have given of sympathy towards paganism: he banned all sacrifices, public and private, and prohibited access to temples.[38]

Theodosius' arrangements for the government of the West did not last long after he returned to the East. Within a year Valentinian II was dead, either murdered or, more probably, by suicide, and the general Arbogast had put up Eugenius as emperor of the West. The revolt of Eugenius has received an enormous amount of modern attention as the last pagan revival in the West, and the issues of interpretation which it raises are so important that they deserve a careful analysis. I should like to concentrate here on what seem to me to be the two basic problems, which lie at each end of a spectrum. At the highest level of generality, the nature of late Roman paganism is in dispute; at the most specific level, the date and target of the anonymous poem normally known as the *Carmen contra paganos*. Let me take the general issue first.

Two approaches must, I think, be rejected outright. First, the cynical view that Symmachus and his friends had no real religious opinions, only social prejudices and a financial stake in official subsidies for the traditional cults.[39] Their snobbery and financial interests cannot be denied, but they can hardly be the whole story. It was too easy in the 380s to join the bandwagon, and prosper by being a Christian. When Praetextatus said "Make me bishop of Rome and I will become a Christian," he was voicing a jocular criticism of Damasus' behaviour, not revealing his deepest convictions. However, when Symmachus proclaimed that "Not by a single route can one penetrate so great a mystery," he was voicing a view widely espoused by pagans confronting intolerant Christianity—and which may derive from Porphyry. Secondly, we should reject the view that paganism was no more than old-fashioned antiquarianism with no political overtones at all, or at least, to quote the proponent of this view, that after 384 "the very slight tendency toward organised resistance and action which [Praetextatus] represented among the pagan aristocracy disappeared."[40] Despite the eloquence with which this view has been argued, I believe that there is too much evidence for pagan support of Eugenius to explain away. Moreover, the plausible suggestion has recently been made that Prudentius wrote the first book of his *Contra Symmachum*, not in 402/3 when he wrote Book Two, but in 394/5, immediately after the Battle of the Frigidus.[41] The poem depicts Theodosius as converting the Roman Senate after his defeat of Eugenius.

If we discard these two approaches, we can see three main, and successive, interpretations. First, the view which D.N. Robinson stated in 1915, and to which Herbert Bloch gave classic expression: that there were two pagan parties in the Roman aristocracy of the late fourth century, viz. the traditionalists, led by Symmachus, who were concerned to preserve the traditional cults of ancient Rome (Vesta, Jupiter, the Altar of Victory), and the orientalists, led by Praetextatus and then the elder Flavianus, whose religious emotion was attached to oriental cults and practices like the taurobolium and the cults of Cybele, Isis and similar deities.[42] This view was subjected to searching scrutiny by John Matthews in a long study of the religion of Symmachus. His argument is complex, but its conclusion can be summarised as follows: first, the nature of Symmachus' letters is such that we could not expect him to say much, if anything, about Oriental cults, whatever his personal beliefs were; second, the epigraphical and other evidence which attests the devotion of other aristocrats to Oriental cults is of a type which we lack for Symmachus himself; therefore, third, for all that we know, Symmachus may have been a *tauroboliatus* himself.[43] Matthews' view is carefully formulated with a keen eye for the precise value and import of evidence, and with a proper emphasis on the cultural context. However, much of the same evidence has been marshalled into a significantly different pattern by Lelia Cracco Ruggini. She adopts a very political interpretation of late Roman paganism, in this siding with Bloch against Matthews.

Ruggini argues that the death of Praetextatus in 384 deprived Roman pagans of their leader and began an ebb-tide for their cause, and that the cause itself changed significantly: whereas the generation of Praetextatus had practised every sort of cult, with a predilection for the Oriental and exotic, the generation of Flavianus and Symmachus, though only a few years younger, was exclusively Roman and traditional in its religious loyalties.[44] I have to confess that that sort of argument has an innate appeal for anyone who reflects on the differences between the two generations of students that came of age in the late 1960s and early 1980s. But the strength of Ruggini's case, and the impetus to her conclusions, come from a consideration of the date of the *Carmen contra paganos*—the very specific problem so germane to any overall interpretation of Roman paganism.

The so-called *Carmen contra paganos* is a poem of one hundred and twenty-three hexameters transmitted anonymously in a sixth century manuscript of Prudentius (Paris, Bibliothèque Nationale, Fonds Latin 8084). The poem has been edited several times, and is now translated into English.[45] It attacks a prominent Roman pagan aristocrat who has recently died at the age of sixty. Ruggini revives the suggestion made in 1868 by the despised Robinson Ellis that the target of the poem was Vettius Agorius Praetextatus.[46] This suggestion was eclipsed in 1870 by Mommsen's identification of the prefect and consul whom the poem lampoons as Nicomachus Flavianus the Elder, consul in 394.[47] So strong indeed was the influence of Mommsen's authority that when John Matthews in 1970 published an article entitled "The Historical Setting of the *Carmen contra paganos*," he considered and decisively rejected G. Manganaro's proposal to identify the prefect as the *praefectus urbi* in 408/9, but never even mentioned the claims of Praetextatus.[48] And I must add a *mea culpa*: twice in recent years I have accepted Matthews' conclusions and built on them.[49] Let me now announce a repentance, perhaps even a conversion. Since this is not the context in which to assess all the details of an often obscure text, let me make five central points. First, the man attacked in the *Carmen contra paganos* is described as both prefect and consul: that rules out all identifications except two, viz. Praetextatus, who died as praetorian prefect of Italy, Illyricum and Africa in late December 384 a few days before he was due to take up the *fasces* as ordinary consul on 1 January 385, and Flavianus, who served Eugenius as praetorian prefect in Italy and ordinary consul in 394. Second, what is said about the prefect's death is difficult to square with Flavianus' suicide, and I no longer think that any of the other personal details necessarily favour Flavianus over Praetextatus. Third, a point made by Ruggini: the *Carmen* has no obvious or detectable allusion to the political and military *débacle* of 394, whereas anyone ridiculing or satirising the dead Flavianus would surely have made that a central part of his indictment. Fourth, a medieval catalogue from the Benedictine Abbey of Lobbes describes a poem which can hardly be anything other than the *Carmen contra paganos* as "Damasi episcopi versus de Praetextato praefecto urbis."[50] Damasus was too competent a versifier to have written the halting hexameters of the *Carmen*, but the identification of its target as Praetextatus must be taken seriously. Fifth, and last, a strong *prima facie* case has now been made for believing that Proba's introduction to her Virgilian cento retelling Biblical stories uses and adapts a phrase from *Carmen contra paganos*. If this is so, then for reasons to do with the textual transmission of Proba's cento, the *Carmen* must have been written some years before 395, i.e., before the death of Flavianus.[51]

I must apologise for being so technical in a general exposition. But the problem of attribution has wide ramifications. I have already commented on the change of perspective which Alan Cameron's redating of Macrobius' *Saturnalia* brought about. A similar change comes with redating the *Carmen contra paganos*. To change the metaphor, we have a somewhat different matrix into which to fit the rest of our evidence. Overall, I think, pagans in the reign of Theodosius were less powerful than the traditional view held, but more embittered. Peter Brown has emphasised the peaceful aspects of the "Christianisation of the Roman aristocracy."[52] I do not wish to deny those aspects which he emphasises, but he seems to me to downplay the religious tensions and even hostility between Christians and pagans which surfaced not infrequently. The issue of how important paganism was still remains to be settled. Roman historians have sometimes discounted too heavily the religious significance which Augustine around 413 read into the Battle of the Frigidus; we come closer, I think, to the spirit of the reign of Theodosius when we read Robert Markus on the triumphal phase of Augustine's thinking about history. Under the impact of contemporary events, Augustine briefly accepted a providential view of history as leading towards the victorious Christianity of the reign of Theodosius.[53] The later Augustine reacted strongly against such optimism. Therein lay both his genius and his originality: everyone else, pagan and Christian alike, saw God's hand actively assisting the course of history to ensure the success of his true worshippers. Hence the pagan argument, formulated by Eunapius in the East, but also perhaps perceptible in Ammianus, that the disaster of Adrianople in 378 was the consequence of the conversion of the Roman Empire to Christianity. Christians replied, at lease in part, by stressing the piety and the victories of Theodosius.

An adequate discussion of religion and society in the reign of Theodosius would require a book rather than a lecture. With a broad canvas, I could begin to develop the theme of local variations. For it is obvious, to take only cities associated with Augustine, that Thagaste was not like Carthage, Rome was not like Milan, nor Ostia Hippo—any more than Calgary is like Edmonton. As it is, I must leave that theme largely unexplored, and conclude with something which I, as a Roman historian, tend to take for granted. It is not only our approach to religion and society which has changed in the last generation, it is our approach to the Later Roman Empire as a whole.

An earlier generation approached the fourth century in a censorious spirit:

The administration of justice in the least civilized kingdom of modern Europe seems ideal in comparison with the system which obtained during the fourth century in the Roman Empire.

Thus the Roman world was already in decay. The population was steadily dwindling. Hundreds of thousands of acres formerly cultivated had returned to waste. The middle class, crushed by overwhelming financial burdens and degraded by the caste-system to a condition resembling serfdom, was ruined and fast disappearing. The bureaucracy, from top to bottom, was incorrigibly corrupt. The army, packed with barbarians, was in a state of chaos. Justice was in abeyance; political freedom was non-existent. In short, the fabric of the Empire, though still imposing in appearance, was rotten to the core. A series of shocks from without could hardly fail to bring about a complete and final and irremediable collapse.[54]

That is Homes Dudden setting the stage for Ambrose's career as a bishop of Milan from 374 to 397. He was writing in the early 1930s—a man with a secure well-paid job in the great depression.

After the Second World War, a more positive note begins to be sounded. Let me quote (in translation) the concluding lines of André Piganiol's *L'empire chrétien*, published in 1947 and reflecting the spirit of a renascent France:

It is false to say that Rome was decadent. Pillaged, disfigured by the barbarian invaders of the third century, she was rebuilding her ruins. At the same time was being accomplished, at the cost of a grave crisis, a work of internal transformation: there was forming a new conception of the imperial power, that of Byzantium, a new conception of truth and beauty, that of the Middle Ages, a new conception of collective and joint labour in the service of social ends. All the ills from which the empire suffered, stifling taxation, the ruin of fortunes and social classes, have their origin not in this fertile work of transformation, but in the perpetual warfare carried on by the unorganised bands of these Germans who, on the frontiers of the empire, had succeeded in living for centuries without becoming civilised.

It is too easy to pretend that when the barbarians arrived in the Empire "everything was dead, it was a worn out body, a corpse stretched out in its own blood," or even that the Roman Empire of the West was not destroyed by a brutal blow, but just fell asleep.

Roman civilisation did not die of its own accord. It was assassinated.[55]

There speaks the spirit of the French Resistance. Yet most who now write about the age of Theodosius accept Piganiol's principal assertion that Augustine grew to manhood in a society which was changing, alive, vibrant. That perception inevitably affects the way all of us think about Augustine himself and his conversion.

NOTES

The present paper is a superficially revised and lightly annotated version of the lecture delivered in Calgary on Halloween 1986, and prepared for publication in the following year. I am most grateful to the organisers, Hugo Meynell and Shadia Drury for inviting me to participate in a most successful colloquium—and for persuading me to venture in print some assertions which I probably could not prove to the satisfaction of my academic peers.

1. See especially *Augustine of Hippo. A Biography* (London 1967); *The World of Late Antiquity* (London 1971); *Religion and Society in the Age of Saint Augustine* (London 1972); *Society and the Holy in Late Antiquity* (Berkeley and Los Angeles 1982).

2. e.g., S. Dill, *Roman Society in the Last Century of the Western Empire,* 2nd ed. (London 1899) 92 ff., 154 ff., dating the work to "the first quarter of the fifth century."

3. Alan Cameron, "The Date and Identity of Macrobius," *Journal of Roman Studies* 56 (1966): 25–38.

4. See J. Matthews, *Western Aristocracies and Imperial Court A.D. 364–425* (Oxford 1975), 1 ff., 370 ff.

5. *Constantine and Eusebius* (Cambridge, MA., 1981), 191 ff., 210 ff., 245 ff. For a fuller statement of the thesis, see "The Constantinian Reformation," *The Crake Lectures 1984.* (Sackville, N.B., 1986), 39–57. The principal evidence is provided by Eusebius, *Life of Constantine* 2, 19–60, 3, 54–59; *Panegyric of Constantine*, 8.1 ff. In formulating the thesis around 1980 I drew a conscious analogy in my own mind with the situation in Iran immediately after the fall of the Shah.

7. G. Fowden, "Bishops and Temples in the Eastern Roman Empire A.D. 320–435," *Journal of Theological Studies*, N.S. 29 (1978): 53–78.

8. *Theodosian Code*, trans. C. Pharr (Princeton 1952), 472 (16.10.2).

9. Firmicus Maternus, *De err. prof. rel.* 16.4, 28.6 ff. For an English translation of the relevant passages, see C.A. Forbes, *Firmicus Maternus: The Error of the Pagan Religions (Ancient Christian Writers* 37, 1970), 77 f., 110 ff. I have argued for the precise date of 343 in *American Journal of Ancient History* 3 (1978): 75, n. 100.

10. For a recent example of the traditional disparagement of Eusebius, see H.A. Drake, *In Praise of Constantine: A Historical Study and New Translation of Eusebius' Tricennial Orations* (Berkeley 1976), 65, 150. In his defence on this issue, "Constantine's Prohibition of Pagan Sacrifice," *American Journal of Philology* 105 (1984): 69–72.

11. On this aspect of an emperor's function, F. Millar, *The Emperor in the Roman World (31 B.C.-A.D. 337)* (London 1977), 355 ff.

12. Alan Cameron, "Gratian's Repudiation of the Pontifical Robe," *Journal of Roman Studies* 58 (1968): 96–102.

13. See now "Himerius and the Fourth Century," *Classical Philology* 82 (1987): 206–225.

14. J.F. Matthews, "A Pious Supporter of Theodosius I: Maternus Cynegius and his Family," *Journal of Theological Studies* 18 (1967): 438–446.

15. *Theodosian Code* 16.10. 3–12; 16.1.2. The interpretation of Theodosius' policy offered by N.Q. King, *The Emperor Theodosius and the Establishment of Christianity* (London 1961), 71 ff. is unfortunately unsatisfactory.

16. Stated in its most extreme form by H.M. Gwatkin, *Studies of Arianism,* 2nd ed. (London 1900), 273: "Arianism was an illogical compromise. It went too far for heathenism, not far enough for Christianity."

17. H. Trevor-Roper, *The Rise of Christian Europe* (London 1965), 36.

18. J.F. Matthews, *Western Aristocracies* (1975), 131 ff.; E.D. Hunt, *Holy Land Pilgrimage in the Later Roman Empire A.D. 312–460* (Oxford 1982), 135 ff., 155 ff.

19. Constantine's letter to Macarius alludes to the discovery of the cross *(Life of Constantine* 3.30.1) and wood from the cross soon found its way to remote areas of North Africa: see Yvette Duval, *Local Sanctorum Africae* 1 (Rome 1982), nos. 157, 167. On "Helena-History and legend" see E.D. Hunt, *Pilgrimage* (1982), 28 ff. However, Hunt builds too much on the silence of Eusebius, which must be regarded as deliberate rather than probative. I am inclined to explain Eusebius' silence by his detestation of

Macarius, the bishop of Jerusalem; for a more complicated explanation in terms of his attitude towards Constantine, see H.A. Drake, "Eusebius on the True Cross," *Journal of Ecclesiastical History* 36 (1985): 1–22.

20. T.E. Gregory, "The survival of paganism in Christian Greece," *American Journal of Philology* 107 (1986): 229–242.

21. Theodoret's *History of the Monks (Philotheos historia)* has been edited critically with a French translation by P. Canivet and A. Leroy-Molinghen, *Théodoret de Cyr: Histoire des Moines de Syrie (Sources chrétiennes* 234, 1977; 235, 1979): this text is now excellently translated into English by R.M. Price, *Cistercian Studies Series* 88 (Kalamazoo 1985). On the historical background, see G. Tchalencko, *Villages antiques de la Syrie du Nord* (Paris 1953-1958); P. Brown, "The Rise and Function of the Holy Man in Late Antiquity," *Journal of Roman Studies* 61 (1971): 80–101, reprinted in *Society and the Holy* (1982): 103–152.

22. For a conspectus, see G. Fowden, "The Pagan Holy Man in Late Antique Society," *Journal of Hellenic Studies* 102 (1982): 33–59, esp. 40–48.

23. H. Chadwick, *Early Christian Thought and the Classical Tradition* (Oxford 1966); T.D. Barnes, *Constantine and Eusebius* (1981), 86 ff., 181 ff.

24. See the still important paper by P. Henry, "The *Adversus Arium* of Marius Victorinus, the first systematic Exposition of the Doctrine of the Trinity," *Journal of Theological Studies* N.S. 1 (1950): 42–55.

25. A systematic modern exploration of this important topic seems to be lacking: for a bibliography of work before 1930 and a summary of its results, see F. Homes Dudden, *The Life and Times of St. Ambrose* (Oxford 1935), 113 f.; on Ambrose's use of Philo, H. Savon, *Saint Ambroise devant l' exégèse de Philon le Juif* 1 (Paris 1977); "Saint Ambroise et saint Jérome, lecteurs de Philon," *Aufstieg und Niedergang der Römischen Welt* II. 21. 1 (1984), 731–759. G. Nauroy, "La structure du *De Isaac vel anima* et la cohérence de l'allégorèse d'Ambroise de Milan," *Revue des études latines* 63 (1985): 210–236, rightly stresses Ambrose's originality and creativity as a biblical exegete, while incidentally confirming that the texts and hermeneutical traditions on which he draws are exclusively Greek.

26. The following exposition owes much to my pupil John Vanderspoel, whose thesis *Themistius and the Imperial Court* (Diss. Toronto 1989), Ch. 7, suggests some significant modifications in standard narratives of Theodosius' reign, such as that offered by J.F. Matthews, *Western Aristocracies* (1975), 55 ff., 173 ff., 223 ff.

27. The affair of Priscillian has been discussed many times: one of the best introductions is by A.R. Birley, "Magnus Maximus and the Persecution of Heresy," *Bulletin of the John Rylands Library* 66 (1982/3): 13–43.

28. On these two sources of information, see respectively, H. Chadwick, *Priscillian of Avila* (Oxford 1976), 57 ff; C. Stancliffe, *St. Martin and his Hagiographer. History and Miracle in Sulpicius Severus* (Oxford 1983), 278 ff.

29. Best demonstrated (in German) by K.M. Girardet, "Trier 385. Der Prozess gegen die Priszillianer," *Chiron* 4 (1974): 577–608.

30. H. Chadwick, *Priscillian* (1976) 111 ff. (the trial and its political context), 33 f. (the validity of Priscillian's consecration).

31. The main sources are collected and translated by B. Croke and J. Harries, *Religious Conflict in Fourth-Century Rome* (Sydney 1982), 30 ff.

32. E.J. Champlin, "Saint Gallicanus (consul 317)," *Phoenix* 36 (1982): 71–76, cf. Averil Cameron, *Journal of Roman Studies* 73 (1983): 185.

33. Between 317 and 337 there are twenty-nine *consules ordinarii* other than emperors, among whom I count seven certain and seven probable Christians, three certain and two probable pagans, and ten men whose religious adherence is uncertain: see "Christians and Pagans in the Reign of Constantius" *Entretiens Hardt* 34 (1989), 301–337.

34. Ammianus Marcellinus 21.10.8, cf. *Constantine and Eusebius* (1981), 403, n. 3.

35. F.H. Dudden, *St. Ambrose* (1935), 270 ff.; P. Brown, *Augustine* (1967), 81 f.

36. For a sensible account of these two episodes, F.H. Dudden, *St. Ambrose* (1935), 371 ff.; on their symbolic significance, G.W. Bowersock, "From Emperor to Bishop: The Self-conscious Transformation of Political Power in the Fourth Century A.D.," *Classical Philology* 81 (1986): 298–307.

37. Athanasius, *De Fuga* 7, implies that Constans had been baptised long before 350: there seems to be no explicit evidence.

38. *Theodosian Code* 16.10.10.

39. Voiced in English by J.A. McGeachy, *Q. Aurelius Symmachus and the Senatorial Aristocracy of the West* (Chicago 1942), and, more recently, in French by F. Paschoud, "Réflexions sur l'idéal religieux de Symmaque," *Historia* 14 (1965): 215–235.

40. J.J. O'Donnell, "The Demise of Paganism," *Traditio* 35 (1979): 45–88.

41. J. Harries, "Prudentius and Theodosius," *Latomus* 43 (1984): 69–84. It is not necessary to believe, however, that Symmachus ever published or circulated Book One separately.

42. D.N. Robinson, "An Analysis of the Pagan Revival of the Late Fourth Century, with Especial Reference to Symmachus," *Transactions of the American Philological Association* 46 (1915): 87–101; H. Bloch, "A New Document of the Last Pagan Revival in the West, 393–394 A.D.," *Harvard Theological Review* 38 (1945): 199–244; "The Pagan Revival in the West at the End of the Fourth Century, in A.D. Momigliano, *The Conflict between Paganism and Christianity in the Fourth Century* (Oxford 1963), 193–218. The view was by no means novel in 1915: see S. Dill, *Roman Society* (1899), 74 f.

43. J.F. Matthews, "Symmachus and the Oriental Cults," *Journal of Roman Studies* 63 (1973): 175–195.

44. L. Cracco Ruggini, "Il paganesimo romano tra religione e politica (384–394 D.C.): per una reinterpretazione del "Carmen contra paganos,"" *Memorie dell' Accademia Nazionale dei Lincei*, Classe di Scienze Morali, storiche e filologiche, Serie VIII 23 (1979), 3–141.

45. B. Croke and J. Harries, *Religious Conflict* (1982), 80–83. The most recent edition is by D.R. Shackleton Bailey, *Anthologia Latina* I.1 (Leipzig: Teubner, 1982), 17–23; the two most important earlier editions are by M. Haupt, *Hermes* 4 (1870): 354–358 (an edition often misattributed to T. Mommsen despite his clear statement: "ipsum carmen Hauptius sic constituit") and A. Riese, *Anthologia Latina* I.1 (Leipzig: Teubner, 1894): 20–25.

46. R. Ellis, "On a recently discovered Latin poem of the Fourth Century," *Journal of Philology* 1.2 (1868): 66–80.

47. T. Mommsen, "Carmen Codicis Parisini 8084," *Hermes* 4 (1870): 350–363, reprinted in his *Gesammelte Schriften* 7 (Berlin 1909): 485–498. Flavianus had already been identified as the target of the poem by C. Morel, "Recherches sur un poème latin du IVe siècle," *Revue archéologique*, N.S. 17 (1868): 451–459; 18 (1868): 44–55.

48. J.F. Matthews, *Historia* 19 (1970): 464–479.

49. *Revue de l'Université de Ottawa* 52 (1982): 69, n. 37; *Phoenix* 37 (1983): 257.

50. F. Dolbeau, "Damase, le *Carmen contra paganos* et Hériger de Lobbes," *Revue des études augustiniennes* 27 (1981): 38–43.

51. D.R. Shanzer, "The date and identity of the centonist Proba," *Revue des études augustiniennes* 32 (1986): 232–248.

52. P. Brown, *Religion and Society* (1972), 161 ff., 183 ff.

53. R.A. Markus, *Saeculum: History and Society in the Theology of Saint Augustine* (Cambridge 1970), 22 ff.

54. F.H. Dudden, *St. Ambrose* (1935), 106.

55. A. Piganiol, *L'Empire chrétien* (Paris 1947), 421–422.

XXII

AUGUSTINE, SYMMACHUS, AND AMBROSE

After teaching rhetoric in Carthage for several years, Augustine left Africa in 383, at the age of twenty-nine, and went to Rome. There he lodged with a Manichaean "hearer" and made the acquaintance of other Manichees in the city. He began to teach rhetoric in Rome and had completed the school year 383/4 when an imperial order came that the *praefectus urbi* Symmachus send someone to Milan to hold the official chair of rhetoric in that city. Augustine offered himself as a candidate through his Manichaean friends: Symmachus tested his skills in impromptu declamation and chose him. Augustine then went to Milan – and to Ambrose.[1]

The next three years (384-387) were the most momentous in the whole of Augustine's life and have been much studied from many different perspectives.[2] The present brief paper does not set out to describe yet again the turbulent political background to the conversion of Augustine, to investigate its precise intellectual context, or to follow Augustine's mental, moral, and spiritual development. It merely examines one aspect of the relationship between the young African rhetor, the *praefectus urbi* at Rome, and the bishop of Milan – for it is not always realized that Symmachus and Ambrose may have been first cousins.

The father of Ambrose the bishop was Ambrosius, praetorian prefect in Gaul at the time of his son's birth, i.e., in 339.[3] Since Ambrosius died soon after his son was born, it is an attractive conjecture that he perished in 340 when, as praetorian prefect of the emperor Constantinus, he would have accompanied his imperial master on his ill-fated invasion of Italy.[4] On the prevailing contemporary definition of *nobilis* as the descendant of prefects and consuls, therefore, Ambrose was a man of noble birth.[5] But his father was not the first holder of high office in the family. Ambrose observes that his sister Marcellina must have been inspired to her life of virginity by her ancestor Soteris, who endured martyrdom without flinching.[6] Presumably, Soteris was tortured and executed in the Diocletianic persecution.[7] Moreover, what Ambrose says about Soteris in his *Exhortatio Virginitatis* assumes that his forbears attained nobility through office-holding before the fourth century: "*nobilis virgo maiorum prosapia consulatus et praefecturas parentum sacra posthabuit fide, et immolare iussa non acquievit.*"[8]

These implied consuls and prefects of the third century cannot be identified with any confidence. Consideration should go, however, to the Marcellinus who was ordinary consul with Aurelian in 275. Nothing else is known for certain about him, but the consul has been attractively identified both with the Marcellinus whom Aurelian left in charge of the eastern frontier in 272 and also with the Aurelius Marcellinus attested as *dux ducenarius* at Verona in 265.[9] If the double identification is correct, then this Marcellinus made his family both senatorial and noble.

Ambrose discloses, though only on one occasion in his voluminous writings, that he was related to Symmachus. In the funeral lament for his brother he refers to Satyrus's insistence on coming to Milan despite the danger of a barbarian invasion: "*cum a viro nobili revocareris, Symmacho tuo parente, quod ardere bello Italia diceretur, quod in periculum tenderes, quod in hostem incurreres, respondisti hanc ipsam tibi causam esse veniendi, ne nostro deesses periculo, ut consortem te fraterni discriminis exhiberes.*"[10] In Ambrose's mouth, the term *tuus parens* used of another should imply kinship, not merely benevolent protection by an older friend, as the bare *parens* or the phrase *parens meus* so often does in writers of the late fourth century.[11] Ambrose and Satyrus, therefore, were related to the noble Symmachus. But to which Symmachus, the orator or his father? In theory, the Symmachus whom Ambrose names here could be either L. Aurelius Avianius Symmachus, *praefectus urbi* in 364-365, or his son Q. Aurelius Symmachus, who was *praefectus urbi* in 384-385, and modern scholars have espoused both identifications.[12] But there is a decisive argument in favour of the son. The elder Symmachus (it is attested) died as consul designate in late 376.[13] On the other hand, Ambrose refers to a barbarian peril beginning in the autumn before the winter during which Satyrus died, and it has now been proved beyond reasonable doubt that the winter in question is that of 377-378.[14] It follows that the Symmachus who communicated with Satyrus in the autumn of 377 must have been the younger Symmachus.

The relationship between Symmachus and Ambrose also surfaces in a letter of Symmachus to his brother Celsinus Titianus, which describes Satyrus as their *frater communis*.[15] Even though Symmachus uses the terms *frater noster* and *frater meus* somewhat freely, the explanation may be that Ambrose and Symmachus were first cousins. The grandfather of the orator Symmachus was Aurelius Valerius Tullianus Symmachus, ordinary consul in 330. He has sometimes been identified as one of the barbarians whom Constantine advanced to the consulate according to the emperor Julian.[16] That is doubly mistaken. First, Julian did not mean "barbarian" in the literal, racial sense, even though Ammianus interpreted him thus and criticized him for inconsistency in appointing the barbarian general Nevitta consul in 362. By "barbarian" Julian meant non-Hellene, i.e., Christian, and quite a few Christians can be identified among the consuls whom Constantine appointed.[17] Second, it seems probable that the Symmachi of the fourth century descended from a senatorial family of the third, among whose members was the Chrysaorius to whom Porphyry dedicated his *Isagoge* and who had an ancestor called Symmachus.[18] The consul of 330 had been proconsul of Achaea in 319,[19] and was born, therefore, no later than 290. His son, the father of Symmachus, was born c. 310, Symmachus himself c. 335.

Like Symmachus, Ambrose possessed the *nomen* Aurelius:[20] he may have derived it from his mother, who could be a daughter of the consul of 330, and thus the aunt of Symmachus. The praetorian prefect Ambrosius may, therefore, have been the son-in-law of the consul of 330, so that his son was a cousin of Symmachus. But if prosopography allows Symmachus and Ambrose to be cousins, by the same token it fails to provide positive confirmation for the precise inference drawn from Ambrose's speech and Symmachus's letter.

What then of the attested relations of the two men with each other? Their confrontation in 384 over the Altar of Victory was conducted with great elegance and a politeness on both sides which may seem surprising in the circumstances. Yet it is not remarkable for two aristocrats to treat each other with courtesy, especially if they were in fact cousins. The eight letters of Symmachus to Ambrose which survive have a cool and distant tone, a formality verging on the querulous. They do not bespeak any sort of warm friendship between the two men.[21] On the other hand, the

10

letters appear to presuppose some tie of kinship or amity, since Symmachus writes as one who expects his addressee to accede to the requests made, even if they need to be repeated – though he never states precisely or alludes plainly to the nature of the obligation on which he obviously feels entitled to call.

All the eight letters of Symmachus to Ambrose are requests to help someone, and in one case Symmachus virtually warns Ambrose to avoid exercising his episcopal jurisdiction in a matter affecting one of the writer's clients. The circumstances of the majority of the letters remain somewhat obscure. But two request Ambrose to intervene at court on behalf of former magistrates. One of the men was Magnillus, who is attested as *vicarius* of Africa in 391, but was detained there after he left office for an investigation into his official conduct.[22] It would be worth knowing the precise date and with what emperor or high official Symmachus hoped Ambrose to intercede for Magnillus's return. It should be one of the legitimate emperors rather than the usurping regime of Eugenius in 392-394.

The other former magistrate was Marcianus, who was being dunned for repayment of the salary (*annonarum pretia*) which he had received under a usurper (*invidia tyrannici temporis involuti*).[23] It is hard to avoid identifying this Marcianus with the Marcianus whom the unnamed prefect of the anonymous *Carmen contra paganos* appointed proconsul. The letter has usually been dated to 394-395 and used to document Symmachus's political influence at court after the usurpation of Eugenius.[24] However, the date of 394-395 for the *Carmen contra paganos* seems now to have been disproved.[25] The poem is to be lodged, rather, in the later 380s, with Vettius Agorius Praetextatus (who died in December 384) as the prefect denounced. Marcianus could be the proconsul of Africa for 384-385 or else a proconsul of Campania.[26] More important, he was embroiled in the usurpation, not of Eugenius, but of Maximus, a more serious and more ambiguous affair.[27] Theodosius recognized Maximus as a legitimate emperor in 383 and was very slow to disown him – indeed there is much to be said for the discredited view that it was only after his interview with Valentinian, Justina, and Galla in 387 that he turned against his fellow catholic and kinsman. If that is so, then Symmachus's panegyric of Maximus on 1 January 387 need not have been, at the time, an act of open hostility or disobedience towards Theodosius. In 388 Theodosius took a lenient view of the conduct of men like Symmachus between 383 and 387: he had excused many magistrates of that period from repaying the proceeds of their employment under the tyrant before Symmachus wrote to Ambrose on behalf of Marcianus. Such clemency, it can be argued, does not so much attest the political power of the pagan nobility at Rome as reflect the real political ambiguities of the years which Augustine spent in Italy.

It has often been asserted that "Augustine went to Milan as the protégé of Symmachus" or that he "came to Milan under the highest pagan patronage ... to reap the rich rewards of a now established career" with a commendation to Bauto, who was "the most powerful man in the Empire," or, even more extravagantly, "the effective ruler of the Empire."[28] On Augustine's own showing, he had no prior acquaintance with Symmachus before the *praefectus urbi* chose him after testing him in an impromptu declamation. Would it be naïve or cynical to suggest that Symmachus chose Augustine precisely because he was not a protégé? In late 384, after the affair of the Altar of Victory and in an ambiguous political situation, Symmachus may have wished to preserve his distance from the court of Valentinian at Milan. Augustine's chair in Milan is sometimes presented as a "vital post," whose occupant "would have found himself, in many ways, a 'Minister of Propaganda.'"[29] That is a false perspective. In 384 Augustine was a bright young man from the provinces who had lived on the fringe of aristocratic society in Rome: he came to Milan with ambitions, but to a very modest place at the outer fringe of the imperial court. It was his conversion which brought Augustine rapid social mobility in a Christian society.

NOTES

1. *Conf.* 5.13.23.

2. Among classic modern treatments, note P. Courcelle, *Recherches sur les Confessions de Saint Augustin* (Paris: E. de Boccard, 1950), 78 ff.; *Les Confessions de Saint Augustin dans la tradition littéraire* (Paris: Etudes Augustiniennes, 1963), 17ff.; P. Brown, *Augustine of Hippo: A Biography* (London: Faber and Faber, 1967), 79ff.; R.J. O'Connell, *St. Augustine's Early Theory of Man, A.D. 386-391* (Cambridge, Mass.: Belknap Press of Harvard University Press, 1968).

3. Paulinus, *Vita Ambrosii* 2.3, cf. Ambrose, *Epp.* 59, the date of which was established by J.-R. Palanque, *Saint Ambrose et l'Empire Romain* (Paris: E. de Boccard, 1933), 480-82, 542-43.

12

4. *PLRE* I (1971), 51; T.D. Barnes, *Phoenix* 34 (1980), 161 n.5.

5. T.D. Barnes, "Who were the Nobility of the Later Roman Empire?" *Phoenix* 28 (1974), 444-49.

6. *De virginibus* 3.7.38 (*PL* 16.244): *qui enim fieri posset, ut sancta Soteris tibi non esset mentis auctor, cui auctor est generis?*

7. *PLRE* 1.850.

8. *Exhort. Virg.* 12.82 (*PL* 16.376).

9. Respectively, Zosimus 1.60-61 and *ILS* 544, cf. A. Stein, *PIR*^{2} A 1546; *PLRE* 1.544, 545, 549; *PIR*^{2} M 178.

10. *De excessu fratris* 1.32 (*CSEL* 73.227-28).

11. O. Faller, *CSEL* 73 (1955) 227. Symmachus's letters to Ambrose alone furnish several examples of the looser use of familial terms with *meus: fratres mei Dorotheus et Septimius* (3.32), *frater meus Marcianus* (33), *frater meus Magnillus* (34), *filius meus Caecilianus* (36). S. Roda, "Simmaco nel gioco politico del suo tempo," *Studia et Documenta Historiae et Iuris* 39 (1973) 53-114, at 68-69, denies kinship and uses the evidence adduced here as proof of a deep and longlasting friendship between Symmachus and the two brothers Satyrus and Ambrose.

12. F.H. Dudden, *The Life and Times of St. Ambrose* (Oxford: Clarendon Press, 1935), 176-77 (father); *PLRE* 1.886-87 (son).

13. Symmachus, *Orat.* 4; *ILS* 1257 (Rome), cf. A. Chastagnol, *Les fastes de la préfecture de Rome au Bas Empire* (Paris: Nouvelles Editions Latines, 1962), 163.

14. O. Faller, "Situation und Abfassungszeit der Reden des hl. Ambrosius auf den Tod seines Bruders Satyrus," *Wiener Studien* 44 (1924-25), 86-102; *CSEL* 73 (1955), 81*-89* – tying the allusion to and correctly dating Ammianus Marcellinus 31.10.1-5.

15. Symmachus, *Ep.* 1.63.

16. Ammianus 21.10.8, 12.25, cf. E.A. Thompson, *The Historical Work of Ammianus Marcellinus* (Cambridge: Cambridge University Press, 1947), 80.

17. T.D. Barnes, "Christians and Pagans in the Reign of Constantius," *L'Église et l'empire au IVe siècle* (*Entretiens sur l'Antiquité classique*) 34 (1989), 301-37.

18. Elias, *In Porphyrii Isagogen*, praef. 15, cf. T.D. Barnes, *The New Empire of Diocletian and Constantine* (Cambridge, Mass.: Harvard University Press, 1982), 103-4.

19. G. Polara, "Il nonno di Simmaco," *Parola del Passato* 29 (1974), 261-66.

20. *ILCV* 1800 (the manuscript report of an inscription from the church of St. Nazarius in Milan).

21. Symmachus, *Ep.* 3.30-37, cf. J.F. Matthews, *Colloque genevois sur Symmache* (Paris: Société d'édition Les Belles Lettres, 1986), 173-74. For a different assessment (and the details known about all the men named in these letters), see M. Forlin Patrucco and S. Roda, "Le lettere di simmaco ad Ambrogio. Vent'anni di rapporti amichevoli," *Ambrosius Episcopus* 2 (Milan: Universita Cattolica del Sacro Cuore, 1976), 284-97.

22. *CTh* 10.17.3 (19 June 391); Symmachus, *Ep.* 3.34; 9.122.

23. Symmachus, *Ep.* 3.33.

24. *Carmen contra paganos* 56, cf. S. Roda, "Simmaco" 112; J.F. Matthews, *Western Aristocracies and Imperial Court, A.D. 364-425* (Oxford: Clarendon Press, 1975), 245, 266.

25. D.R. Shanzer, "The Date and Identity of the Centonist Proba," *REAug* 32 (1986), 232-48.

26. The names of all the proconsuls of Africa between 363 and 386 appear to be known except for that of the proconsul of 384-385: see T.D. Barnes, "Proconsuls of Africa, 337-392," *Phoenix* 39 (1985), 144-53, 273-74. The rank of the governor of Campania was raised from *consularis* to proconsul in 378, and two proconsuls are attested before 382, but it is not known precisely when the governors again became *consulares* (*PLRE* 1.678, 152, 1093). It is not plausible to suppose that Praetextatus could secure the appointment of Marcianus as proconsul of Achaea – which was under the control of Theodosius.

27. For what follows, see the essay "Religion and Politics in the Age of Theodosius," in *Grace, Politics and Desire: Essays on Augustine*, ed. H.A. Meynell (Calgary: University of Calgary Press, 1990), 157-75.

28. P. Brown, *Augustine* (1967), 70; J.J. O'Meara, *The Young Augustine* (London: Longman, Green and Company, 1954), 115, 127.

29. P. Brown, *Augustine* (1967), 69.

XXIII

THE CONVERSION OF THE ROMAN ARISTOCRACY IN PRUDENTIUS' *CONTRA SYMMACHUM*

Prudentius' description of the mass conversion of the Roman Senate at the behest of the emperor Theodosius (*Contra Symmachum* 1.506–607) has often been adduced and exploited by modern historians of the late fourth century.[1] Paradoxically, however, it seems that this familiar passage has rarely (if ever) been analysed carefully as a whole.[2] The present article has three aims. First, it will consider precisely who the individuals are to whom Prudentius alludes in lines 552–565; second, it will suggest that line 551 probably did not stand in the passage as Prudentius originally wrote it; third, it will ask why the poet has included precisely those men named or alluded to in lines 552–565, and explore the corollaries that this selection has for the genesis and composition of the *Contra Symmachum* as a whole.

I

After the speech in which the victorious Theodosius addresses Rome (415–505), Prudentius turns to its salutary effects. Instructed by such edicts, the city abandoned its old errors in order to follow Christ: this service to Rome by a Christian emperor, the poet proclaims, far surpassed the benefits which her Republican saviours such as Marius and Cicero had conferred on her, since Theodosius has ensured eternal youth and eternal vigour for the city (506–543). Prudentius then turns to the effect of the speech on the Senate. He first describes the Senate's reaction in general terms

---

The following works will be cited by author's name alone, or in abbreviated form:
A. Chastagnol, *Les Fastes de la préfecture de Rome au Bas-Empire* (Paris 1962); M. C. Eagan, tr. and ed., *Prudentius: The Poems* 2 (Washington, D.C. 1965, *Fathers of the Church* 52); M. Lavarenne, ed., *Prudence* 3[2] (Paris 1963, Budé edition); W. Taegert, ed., *Claudius Claudianus: Panegyricus dictus Olybrio et Probino consulibus* (Munich 1988, Zetemata 85); H. J. Thomson, tr. and ed., *Prudentius* 1 (London 1949, Loeb edition); A. H. M. Jones, J. R. Martindale, and J. Morris, *The Prosopography of the Later Roman Empire* 1 (Cambridge 1971) = *PLRE* 1.

[1] E.g., O. Seeck, *Symmachus* (1883, *Monumenta Germaniae Historica* Auct. Ant. 6.1) xciv, civ; S. Dill, *Roman Society in the Last Century of the Western Empire*[2] (London 1899) 23; E. Stein (J.-R. Palanque, tr. and rev.), *Histoire du Bas-Empire* 1[2] (Paris 1959) 217; Alan Cameron, *Claudian: Poetry and Propaganda at the Court of Honorius* (Oxford 1970) 230; C. Pietri, *Roma Christiana* (Rome 1976, BEFAR 224) 429, 438–439. On the other hand, the passage seems not to be cited at all in S. Mazzarino, "La conversione del senato," *Antico, tardoantico ed erà costantiniana* 1 (Bari 1974) 378–397—who argues that the "decisive period" for the conversion of the Senate fell between 395 and 409.

[2] Not even in the recent and lengthy article of A. Baldini, "Il *Contra Symmachum* di Prudenzio e la conversione del senato," *RivStorAnt* 17–18 (1987–1988) 115–157.

under the same two aspects of renouncing the old religion and embracing the new. The old Catos exchanged their togas and pontifical insignia for the white robes of catechumens, and the Senate of Evander, leaving only a few on the Tarpeian rock, rushed into the shrines of the Nazarenes and to the baptismal fonts of the Apostles:

545 *exultare patres videas, pulcherrima mundi*
lumina, conciliumque senum gestire Catonum
candidiore toga niveum pietatis amictum
sumere, et exuvias deponere pontificales.
iamque ruit, paucis Tarpeia in rupe relictis,
ad sincera virum penetralia Nazareorum
550 *atque ad apostolicos Euandria curia fontes.*

The following line (551: *Amniadum suboles et pignora clara Proborum*) refers to the youthful brothers who became ordinary consuls together in 395. Since we believe that this line is intrusive to its context, we shall discuss it separately below (Section II) and, for the present, analyse the passage without it. If line 551 is removed, Prudentius' general description of the conversion of the Roman aristocracy (i.e., lines 544–550) avoids specific examples, and *enim* in line 552 marks the transition from general to particular.[3] When selecting his particular examples, Prudentius adopts a procedure which Tertullian had frequently employed: he focuses his attention first on the earliest aristocratic conversion (552–553), then on contemporary aristocrats who were prominent Christians (554–565).

552 *fertur enim ante alios generosus Anicius urbis*
inlustrasse caput: sic se Roma inclyta iactat.

Who was the noble Anicius who was the first Christian in the Roman Senate?[4] Hardly the great Petronius Probus himself, as Peter Brown assumed without argument in his immensely influential article on the conversion of the Roman aristocracy.[5] The *generosus Anicius* of Prudentius is usually identified as Sex. Anicius Paulinus, consul in 325, whose Christian

---

[3] For this common use of *enim* as "introducing a particular instance in support of a general assertion," see *OLD* 608, s.v. 3 d; cf. M. Leumann, J. B. Hoffmann, and A. Szantyr, *Lateinische Grammatik* 2^2 (Munich 1965) 507–509.
   Professor J. N. Grant points out that, with or without line 551, *enim* involves a slight logical incoherence because Prudentius jumps from Theodosius' speech, whose clearly indicated dramatic date is autumn 394, and its general consequences (415–550) to a series of specific conversions which occurred well before 394 (552–565). We believe that this tends to corroborate the hypothesis advanced below in Section III that Prudentius here incorporates a passage originally drafted in the mid-380s.
[4] For *caput urbis* = the senate-house, cf. Cic. *Mil.* 90.
[5] P. Brown, "Aspects of the Christianization of the Roman Aristocracy," *JRS* 51 (1961) 1–11, reprinted in *Religion and Society in the Age of Saint Augustine* (London 1972) 161–182, at 9 = 177: "the late baptism of the *doyen* of Roman society, Petronius Probus, celebrated in a grandiose epitaph, and acclaimed by Christian writers as the

religious sympathies appear to be confirmed by an inscription lauding him as *benignus* and *sanctus* (*CIL* VI 1681).[6] But Prudentius' stress on *ante alios* should point to a date significantly earlier than the 320s. Some years ago, E. J. Champlin convincingly demonstrated that the consul Gallicanus who donated silver objects and lands producing over 800 solidi a year to the church of Saints Peter and Paul and John the Baptist at Ostia, while Constantine was emperor and Silvester bishop of Rome (*Liber Pontificalis* 34.29 [Duchesne p. 184]), was the aristocratic Ovinius Gallicanus, ordinary consul in 317.[7] Moreover, it seems probable that some of the ordinary consuls between Gallicanus in 317 and Anicius Paulinus in 325 were also Christians.[8] Hence the noble Anicius who became a Christian *ante alios* ought rather to be the Anicius Faustus who held the consulate under Diocletian in 298 and served as *praefectus urbi* in 299/300.[9]

An altar from Rome is also relevant. The inscription on the front of the altar is now erased so badly as to be completely illegible, but according to a Renaissance antiquarian it once bore a dedication to Hercules Invictus by M. Iun(ius) Caesonius Nicomachus Anicius Faustus Paulinus as *praetor urbanus*, while the side still bears the consular date of 20 September 321 (*ILS* 3409). The name and the date appear to imply that the dedicand must be a son of the consul of 322.[10] But good technical reasons have been adduced for disjoining the date on the side of the altar from the dedication on the front and for dating the latter to the late third century.[11] If that is correct, then the praetor should be the consul of 298—whose explicitly attested much briefer nomenclature is no bar to the identification.[12] Hence it may be suggested that the oral tradition on which Prudentius implies that he draws (*fertur ... : sic se Roma inclyta iactat*) preserves the memory of

---

'first' conversion among the Roman aristocracy." The translation by M. C. Eagan (133), appears to identify "great Anicius" with the "heir of the blood and name of Olybrius."

[6] Chastagnol 85. The case is developed more fully by D. M. Novak, "Constantine and the Senate: An Early Phase of the Christianization of the Roman Aristocracy," *Ancient Society* 10 (1979) 271–310, at 291–297; "Anicianae domus culmen, nobilitatis culmen," *Klio* 62 (1980) 473–493, at 491.

[7] E. J. Champlin, "Saint Gallicanus (Consul 317)," *Phoenix* 36 (1982) 71–76.

[8] T. D. Barnes, "Christians and Pagans in the Reign of Constantius," *L'Église et l'empire au IVe siècle* (Vandoeuvres-Geneva 1989, *Entretiens sur l'antiquité classique* 34, Fondation Hardt) 301–337, classifies Severus (*cos.* 323) as a certain Christian and Petronius Probianus (*cos.* 322) as a probable Christian.

[9] On his career, see briefly *PIR²* A 601; *PLRE* 1.329.

[10] *PLRE* 1.681; T. D. Barnes, *The New Empire of Diocletian and Constantine* (Cambridge, Mass. 1982) 120–121.

[11] Chastagnol 32; cf. G. Barbieri, *L'Albo senatorio da Settimio Severo a Carino* (Rome 1952) 640 (addenda to no. 1802). The former argues from the similar dedication to Hercules by a group of four praetors (*CIL* VI 314).

[12] D. M. Novak, "The Early History of the Anician Family," *Studies in Latin Literature and Roman Literature* (Brussels 1979, Collection Latomus 164) 119–165, at 164–165.

an episode, whether historical or legendary, which has otherwise left no trace in our lamentably incomplete evidence for the reign of Diocletian—a public declaration of his conversion by a consul and *praefectus urbi* who embraced Christianity shortly before the "Great Persecution."

Not everyone in Prudentius' day would have conceded the Anician claim to the first conversion among the Roman aristocracy: a pair of metrical inscriptions probably composed in the late fourth century once stood on the Via Salaria praising one Liberalis as a *patricio clarus de semine consul* who earned the crown of martyrdom (*ILCV* 56–57, from a seventh-century manuscript). The date of Liberalis' consulate and martyrdom are unknown: recent scholarly opinion prefers the third century, but admits the reign of Diocletian as a possibility.[13]

As a postscript to this discussion, it may be observed that, if Anicius Faustus the consul of 298 became a Christian before 303, this creates a presumption that the Anicii who were ordinary consuls under Constantine in 322, 325, and 334 were probably also Christians.[14]

> quin et Olybriaci generisque et nominis heres,
> 555   adiectus fastis, palmata insignis abolla,
> martyris ante fores Bruti submittere fasces
> ambit, et Ausoniam Christo inclinare securem.

The identity of the heir of the Olybrian name and race admits of no doubt whatever. He is Q. Clodius Hermogenianus Olybrius, *praefectus urbi* in 369/70, praetorian prefect of Illyricum and briefly of the East in 378, and ordinary consul in 379, who was still alive in 384 (Symmachus *Relat.* 28) but died before his young grandsons became consuls on 1 January 395 (Claudian *Cons. Olyb. et Prob.* 30).[15] Prudentius refers explicitly and directly to Olybrius' ordinary consulate: he was "added to the fasti" and lowered "the *fasces* of Brutus" (the legendary consul of 509 B.C.) before the doors of a martyr's shrine. The poet may also refer to Olybrius' urban and praetorian prefectures. The "western axe" which Olybrius made bow to Christ and the cloak decorated with a pattern of palm-leaves can certainly allude to the attributes and the dress of a consul,[16] but the axe could also symbolise the capital jurisdiction of a praetorian prefect and the *abolla*

---

[13] See A. Degrassi, *I fasti consolari dell'Impero Romano dal 30 avanti Cristo al 613 dopo Cristo* (Rome 1952) 128; *PIR*² L 163; W. Eck, "Das Eindringen des Christentums in den Senatorenstand bis zu Konstantin d. Gr.," *Chiron* 1 (1971) 381–406, at 389; T. D. Barnes, "More Missing Names (A.D. 260–395)," *Phoenix* 27 (1973) 135–155, at 145.

[14] Barnes (above, n. 8) 316–317 classifies Anicius Julianus (*cos.* 322), Anicius Paulinus (*cos.* 325), and Anicius Paulinus (*cos.* 334) as consuls whose religious sympathies are not known for certain.

[15] For a full discussion of Olybrius' career, see Chastagnol 178–184.

[16] Lavarenne 207. Thomson (392–393) translates "enjoyed the glory of the palm-figured robe" and sees an allusion to the *toga palmata* of a consul.

54

could be the cloak of a *praefectus urbi*. The cloak of the prefect is well attested,[17] but the word *abolla* is quite rare, and Prudentius perhaps took it from Juvenal's fourth satire where the *praefectus urbi* Pegasus hurries to Domitian *rapta abolla* (4.77).[18]

> non Paulinorum, non Bassorum dubitavit
> prompta fides dare se Christo, stirpemque superbam
> 560   gentis patriciae venturo attollere saeclo.

Who are these Paulini and Bassi who did not hesitate to give themselves to Christ? Several scholars (including one of the present writers) have thought that Prudentius alludes to Meropius Pontius Paulinus, better known as Paulinus of Nola, who governed Campania in 381, withdrew from political life shortly thereafter, and finally settled into an ascetic existence at Nola in 395.[19] But the context renders this identification most improbable. Paulinus of Nola was a Gallic aristocrat from an established and wealthy family of Bordeaux.[20] The Paulinus and Bassus of Prudentius' poem are blue-blooded aristocrats of the Roman metropolis, "the arrogant stock of a patrician race," not noble provincials, however cultured and wealthy. Hence the Paulinus to whom the poet alludes is surely Anicius Paulinus, *praefectus urbi* in 380.[21] As for Prudentius' Bassi, there are three prominent men with that name known from the late fourth century: Anicius Auchenius Bassus, *praefectus urbi* in 382/3,[22] L. Valerius Septimius Bassus, *praefectus urbi* between 379 and 383 (*ILS* 782), and Tarracius Bassus, *praefectus urbi* not long after 374, perhaps precisely in 375/6.[23] Prudentius could in theory be alluding to all three of these Bassi, but in fact probably alludes only to the first two.[24]

---

[17] A. Chastagnol, *La Préfecture urbaine à Rome sous le Bas-Empire* (Paris 1960) 197–198.

[18] E. Courtney, *A Commentary on the Satires of Juvenal* (London 1980) 215, glosses *abolla* as "a double cloak" and explains that "Pegasus probably wears it because of the cold."

[19] T. D. Barnes, "The Historical Setting of Prudentius' *Contra Symmachum*," *AJP* 97 (1976) 373–386, at 379, n. 17; cf., e.g., *PLRE* 1.683.

[20] On him, see especially J. F. Matthews, *Western Aristocracies and Imperial Court A.D. 364–425* (Oxford 1975) 151 ff.

[21] As argued by Chastagnol (207).

[22] On Bassus' career, see *PLRE* 1.152–154.

[23] Amm. Marc. 28.1.27; *ILS* 6072; cf. Chastagnol 195–196.

[24] Chastagnol (195) deduces that Tarracius Bassus must have been a pagan because he was accused in the early 370s of using magic to help a charioteer to win (Amm. Marc. 28.1.27). The inference is not peremptory—and does not formally exclude the possibility that this Bassus too had embraced Christianity before his prefecture. Nevertheless, what Ammianus reports renders him an unlikely exemplar for Prudentius to praise in this context.

561   *iam quid plebicolas percurram carmine Gracchos,*
iure potestatis fultos et in arce senatus
praecipuos, simulacra deum iussisse revelli,
cumque suis pariter lictoribus omnipotenti
565   *suppliciter Christo se consecrasse regendos?*

As with Olybrius (554–557), Prudentius makes his allusion so specific that none can doubt either the man or the precise event to which he refers. During his urban prefecture, the *praefectus urbi* Gracchus, who is attested in office in the winter of 376/7 (*CTh* 2.2.1, 9.35.3), destroyed a shrine of Mithras and was baptised as a Christian (Jerome *Ep.* 107.2). It seems probable that Gracchus' full name was Furius Maecius Gracchus,[25] and hence that he was a descendant of M. Maecius Memmius Furius Baburius Caecilianus Placidus, ordinary consul in 343 and a member of a family whose consular status goes back at least as far as the middle of the third century.[26]

II

So far we have deliberately omitted any substantive discussion of line 551 or of why we believe that it is intrusive to its context. Our objections arise from a combination of linguistic and prosopographical arguments. Line 551 (*Amniadum suboles et pignora clara Proborum*) refers solely and precisely to the young brothers Olybrius and Probinus who assumed the *fasces* as ordinary consuls on 1 January 395, and thus strikes a jarring note in a context where all the other allusions are to men who held high office at Rome in the late 370s and early 380s. It is also problematical in itself.

What does the line mean? The two phrases *Amniadum suboles* and *pignora clara Proborum* must be taken in apposition to *Euandria curia* in the preceding line. In itself, that is linguistically both natural and unobjectionable. Hence the standard translations duly render "Evander's Senate, the descendants of the family of Annius and the illustrious children of the Probi," "the Evandrian Senate, sons of Annius and children of the Probi," and "la curie d'Évandre, la race des Amniades et les illustres enfants de Probus."[27]

---

[25]So Chastagnol (198–200), adducing *ILS* 5717 (Tibur).

[26]R. Syme, *Ammianus and the Historia Augusta* (Oxford 1968) 162–163; *PIR*² M 460.

[27]Respectively, Thomson (393), Eagan (133), and Lavarenne (154). Thomson prints *Anniadum* in the text, even though the form *Amniadum* not only has far stronger manuscript attestation, but is also confirmed as correct by contemporary inscriptions. The critical editions of J. Bergman (*Aurelii Prudentii Clementis Carmina* [Vienna 1926, *Corpus scriptorum ecclesiasticorum latinorum* 61]), Lavarenne, and M. P. Cunningham (*Aurelii Prudentii Clementis Carmina* [Brepols 1966, *Corpus Christianorum: series latina* 126]) all correctly print *Amniadum*.

56

The problem arises from the fact that both phrases refer to the same pair of blue-blooded aristocrats, and thus can hardly refer to the Senate as a whole. As it stands, the text represents the ancient equivalent of equating "the House of Lords" with "the family of the Duke of Devonshire." Provincial though he was, Prudentius cannot have been so ignorant or insensitive as to equate the the Roman Senate as a whole with the noblest Christian family of the city. Nor is it likely that the difficulty can be overcome by taking the line as intended to illustrate what precedes—as meaning "all the aristocracy, even Olybrius and Probinus." Prudentius carefully marks both the transition to individual Christians in line 552 (*fertur enim ante alios*) and the later transition back from individuals to the rest of the Senate:

> 566   *sescentas numerare domos de sanguine prisco*
> *nobilium licet.*

Line 551 (we hold) is socially tactless and interrupts its context. It is also relevant that it appears to be modelled on two phrases in Claudian's panegyric on Olybrius and Probinus, which he recited in Rome on 1 January 395.

The name Amniades occurs for the first time in Latin literature in Claudian's poem (*Cons. Olyb. et Prob.* 9), in the plural and apparently meaning "the race of Amnii." It seems probable that Claudian coined the noun *Amniades* himself,[28] just as elsewhere he coins both *Honoriades* to designate the male heir to be produced by the union of Honorius and Maria (*Nupt. Hon. et Mar.* 341) and the feminine *Honorias* in the sense of "daughter of Honorius' (*Carm. min.* 30.131). Names formed by adding the Greek suffix –ades to a Roman nomen or cognomen are not common in Latin, but the practice of inventing them, dictated by metrical considerations, goes back to the origins of Latin poetry.[29] It seems that it was Ennius who coined *Scipiades* (- ˘ ˘ -) as a synonym for Scipio, since the ordinary form of the name would not fit into dactylic hexameters with the prosody normal at that period (*viz.* - ˘ -):[30] both Lucretius (3.1034) and Virgil (*G.* 2.170; *Aen.* 6.843) use the plural *Scipiadae* with the meaning "Scipios," while Lucilius uses the singular *Publius Cornelius Scipiadas* (fr. 1139 Marx, the model for Horace *Satires* 2.1.17, 72), with dative *Scipiadae* (fr. 394). Similarly, and presumably on the model of Ennius, Lucretius coined *Memmiades* to use in the dative case instead of the unmetrical *Memmio* (1.26), and Valerius Flaccus

---

[28] Taegert 89: "vielleicht—wie wohl auch *Honoriades* (nupt. Hon 341)—Claudians eigene Prägung, die bei Prud. c. Symm. 1,551 wiederkehrt."

[29] See especially L. Müller, *De re metrica poetarum Latinorum praeter Plautum et Terentium*[2] (St. Petersburg and Leipzig 1894) 490–492; E. Norden, ed., *P. Vergilius Maro Aeneis Buch VI*[4] (Darmstadt 1957) 333 (on *Aen.* 6.842-843); E. Courtney (above, n. 18) 147–148 (on Juvenal 2.154); Taegert 89.

[30] Except of course with correption of the final vowel, as in Ennius *Varia* 3 Vahlen[3] = *Scipio*, fr. 7 Warmington: *Scipio invicte*.

has *Caspiadae* (nominative plural) for Caspii (6.107), while an inscription in elegiacs from Naples styles Appius Claudius Julianus, who was consul for the second time in 224, *progenies Claudius Appiadum* (*ILS* 1184 = *CLE* 888). In all these cases, unlike the frequent *Aeneadae* (= Romans), the suffix -*ades* has no patronymic force whatever. Claudian's normal usage, therefore, differs from that of the classical Latin poets who provided his inspiration in that, as a Greek speaker, he retained the patronymic force of the suffix, except for *Amniadae* and *Scipiades* (= Scipio) which he uses no less than seven times, twice in a passage clearly intended to depict himself by implication as the Ennius of Stilico (*Cons. Stil.* 3, pr. 1, 21, contrasting *maior* with *noster Scipiades*, i.e., Stilico).[31] Linguistic criteria, therefore, indicate that the first half of line 551 reflects the coinage of the noun *Amniadae* by Claudian in a poem recited in Rome on 1 January 395.

The phrase *Amniadum suboles* also deserves prosopographical comment. Fourth century references both to the *gens Amnia* and to individual Amnii are surprisingly rare.[32] Ausonius praises Sex. Claudius Petronius Probus, four times praetorian prefect and ordinary consul in 371, as *stirpis novator Amniae* (*Ep.* 16.2.32) for marrying and producing offspring by Anicia Faltonia Proba, who was honoured by her sons a generation later as *Amnios Pincios Aniciosque decorans* and the daughter, wife, and mother of consuls (*ILS* 1269). As for individuals, the only bearers of the name Amnius specifically attested in the fourth century are Amnius Anicius Julianus, consul in 322, his son Amnius Manius Caesonius Nicomachus Anicius Paulinus, consul in 334 (*ILS* 1220),[33] and possibly their close relative Sex. Anicius Paulinus, consul in 325.[34] Since Ausonius reveals that the *stirps Amnia* was saved from extinction by Petronius Probus when he married Anicia Faltonia Proba ca 370 (*Ep.* 16.2.31–35), the phrase *Amniadum suboles* had a very precise reference ca 400— to the issue of that marriage, viz. a son born in the early 370s who died young, Anicius Hermogenianus Olybrius and Anicius Probinus, the consuls of 395, Anicius Probus, consul in 406, and probably a sister Anicia Proba.[35]

---

[31] Also *Cons. Olyb. et Prob.* 149; *In Eutr.* 1.455; *Cons. Stil.* 1.381, 2.384; *Goth.* 141; *Carm. min.* 30.42. In addition, note *Heliades* (feminine plural) = "daughters of the sun" and *Thyestiades* = Aegisthus (*VI Cons. Hon.* 164,113).

[32] For a list, see *TLL* 1.1939.

[33] *PLRE* 1.473–474, 679. Symmachus' brief poem on the consul of 322 styles him *Amnius* (*Ep.* 1.2.5).

[34] In the fragmentary list of names belonging to the early fourth century published in *NSc* 16 (1917) 22 = *Bull. Comm.* 45 (1917) 225, cf. Barnes (above, n. 10) 121–122, the fifth name is preserved as "]n. Anicius P[aulinus]." There seems to be little doubt that he is Sex. Anicius Paulinus, consul in 325, but the name preceding Anicius can be restored as either [Am]n(ius) or [Iu]n(ius).

[35] *PLRE* 1.1144, Stemma 24; cf. *AJP* 111 (1990) 418–419. In the fifth century her epitaph describes Demetrias, the daughter of Olybrius the consul of 395 and Anicia

The second half of line 551 has the same parentage as the first. Claudian salutes the consuls of 395 as *pignora cara Probi* (*Cons. Olyb. et Prob.* 143). That was surely the inspiration for *pignora clara Proborum* in the *Contra Symmachum* (which means, not "the illustrious children of the Probi," but "the illustrious children of Probus and Proba"). Line 551 is thus a pastiche of two phrases modelled on the poem which Claudian delivered in Rome on 1 January 395, both of which describe the children of Petronius Probus.

On these grounds, which we realise that most scholars will probably not consider conclusive, we propose to delete line 551 as an interpolation by an early reader who had also read Claudian's poem and missed an allusion in Prudentius to the leading members of the *gens Anicia* ca 400.[36] The feebleness of the line renders it unlikely, in our view, that it was Prudentius himself who added it in 402/3 while revising an earlier draft of the passage. It is no obstacle to this hypothesis that the line appears in all the manuscripts of the *Contra Symmachum* that preserve the passage. Unfortunately, the only two pre-Carolingian manuscripts of Prudentius are lacking here: the sixth-century Puteanus (Paris, BN lat. 8084) does not contain the *Contra Symmachum* at all, and the seventh-century Ambrosianus (D 36 sup.) omits 1.337–560 and 2.85–1132. Admittedly, the line stands even in the Durham manuscript (Dunelmensis B 4.9) which originally omitted a passage of five lines which has been interpolated into Book Two (2.423–427: added by a later hand in the margin).[37] But the Durham manuscript is no earlier than the tenth century, and our hypothesis posits that line 551 was interpolated early enough to establish itself as part of the paradosis in every branch of the manuscript tradition before the eighth century. For, if Prudentius did not write it himself, it must have been interpolated in the fifth century by someone who knew about the children of Petronius Probus.[38]

III

If the preceding arguments are correct, then Prudentius' account of the conversion of the Roman Senate refers precisely and exclusively to the following late fourth-century aristocrats:

Juliana, as Am[nia virgo] (*ILCV* 1765, cf. J. R. Martindale, *Prosopography of the Later Roman Empire* 2 [Cambridge 1980] 351–352).

[36] The type of interpolation which we posit is similar to that recently discussed by R. J. Tarrant, "The Reader as Author: Collaborative Interpolation in Latin Poetry," in J. N. Grant, ed., *Editing Greek and Latin Texts* (New York 1989) 121–162.

[37] C. Gnilka, "Zwei Textprobleme bei Prudentius," *Philologus* 109 (1965) 246–258.

[38] For several certain interpolations in Claudian (most of which appear to be very early and all of which are disallowed by the recent Teubner editor), see C. Gnilka, "Beobachtungen zum Claudiantext," in C. Gnilka and W. Schetter, eds., *Studien zur Literatur der Spätantike* (Bonn 1975) 45–90—where a brief appendix surveys "das Interpolationenproblem bei Prudentius" (86–90). Recently, and with the encouragement of Gnilka, Taegert (111–116) has convincingly diagnosed another substantial interpolation in Claudian, viz. *Cons. Olyb. et Prob.* 48–54.

554–557 Q. Clodius Hermogenianus Olybrius, *cos.* 379
558–560 Anicius Paulinus, Anicius Auchenius Bassus, and L. Valerius Septimius Bassus, who were all *praefecti urbis* between 379 and 383
561–565 (Furius Maecius) Gracchus, prefect of the city in 376/7

Why has Prudentius chosen precisely these individuals? What do they all
have in common? Perhaps all the men named belonged to the family of the
Anicii, the leading Christian aristocratic family of Rome. Anicius Paulinus
and Anicius Bassus are clearly Anicii born, and Olybrius married Turrania
Anicia Juliana (*ILS* 1271), while marriage alliances with the *gens Anicia* for
both Gracchus and Septimius Bassus could easily be postulated.[39] Alternatively, and perhaps more plausibly, all the men whom Prudentius mentions
may have been prominent signatories of the *libellus* which Damasus sent
to Ambrose in 382 protesting that the majority of the Senate supported
Gratian's removal of the altar of Victory from the senate-house (Ambrose
Ep. 17.10). More important, once line 551 is removed, all of Prudentius'
references to contemporary aristocrats cluster around men who were prominent between 376 and 383. That is very relevant to the genesis and composition of the *Contra Symmachum*—a problem which has of late attracted a
certain amount of scholarly attention.

The assumption, long prevalent in discussions of the *Contra Symmachum*, that the two books were conceived and composed as a unity,
has been replaced by a growing awareness that various internal features of
the poem indicate that its final version incorporates passages which must
have been drafted some years earlier and rewritten only in part. To be
sure, the unity of the poem still finds determined defenders.[40] But such
a view is difficult to reconcile with the fact that the first book focuses
on Theodosius, while the second addresses his sons and openly alludes to
the battle of Pollentia on Easter Day 402.[41] Moreover, the fact that Symmachus himself is not mentioned until towards the very end of the first book

---

[39] It may be relevant that Gracchus was related to Laeta, the daughter of the pagan
Publilius Ceionius Caecina Albinus (Jerome *Ep.* 107.2). Otherwise the collateral ties of
both men appear to be totally obscure.

[40] So recently S. Döpp, "Prudentius' *Contra Symmachum* eine Einheit?," *Vigiliae
Christianae* 40 (1986) 66–82. A. Baldini (above, n. 2) 145, characterises the poem as
"frutto di concezione unitaria tradotta in continuità di composizione nel tempo."

[41] J. B. Hall, "Pollentia, Verona, and the Chronology of Alaric's First Invasion of
Italy," *Philologus* 132 (1988) 245–257, has recently argued that both the battle of
Pollentia and the battle of Verona occurred in 403. Surprisingly, he does not discuss (or
even explicitly refer to) the central argument advanced by Barnes (above, n. 19) 375–376,
for dating the two battles to the spring and summer of successive years, viz. that Stilico
visited Rome between them: Claudian *Goth.* pr. 1–6; *VI Cons. Hon.* 122–126, cf. M. Balz-
ert, *Die Komposition des claudianischen Gothenkriegesgedichts c. 26* (Hildesheim 1974,
Spudasmata 23) 18 ff.; G. Garuti, *Cl. Claudiani de bello Gothico* (Bologna 1979) 94 ff.
  The chronology proposed in 1976 (it may be noted) was not new: although most
Roman historians had dated both battles to 402 (Cameron [above, n. 1] 180–187), most
students of Prudentius dated Pollentia to the spring of 402, Verona to the summer of

(1.622 ff.) presents a further serious difficulty for any hypothesis of unitary composition.

Since G. Zappacosta first suggested that Book 1 was written to attack Nicomachus Flavianus in 394,[42] there have been three acute, significant and divergent discussions of its date of composition. J.-P. Callu argued that most of Book 1 was composed as early as 391.[43] But in order to do so, he was compelled to claim that when Prudentius styles Theodosius *gemini bis victor caede tyranni* (1.410), he refers only to his victory over Magnus Maximus and his son Victor in 388, not to his two victories over Maximus in 388 and Eugenius in 394. That is not at all plausible. Maximus did indeed proclaim his infant son Flavius Victor Augustus ca 384 and Victor was duly put to death after his father's defeat. But the speech which Pacatus delivered before Theodosius in Rome in 389 makes it clear that the propaganda of the victorious emperor did not celebrate the outcome of the campaign of 388 as a triumph over two usurpers: the existence of Victor was simply ignored altogether.[44] J. Harries subsequently (and independently of Callu) argued that Prudentius wrote and published Book 1, more or less as it stands, between the defeat of Eugenius in September 394 and the death of Theodosius on 17 January 395.[45] But F. Solmsen long ago pointed out that the end of Theodosius' speech appears to reflect a change of imperial policy towards statues in pagan temples which occurred in 399[46]—from which it follows that the relevant lines (501–505) were written several years later than 394. Most recently, D. R. Shanzer has noted that line 385 appears to echo Claudian's panegyric on the consulate of Manlius Theodorus delivered

---

the following year: see A. Kurfess, *RE* 23 (1957) 1043; I. Lana, *Due capitoli prudenziani* (Rome 1962) 2, n. 3; F. Solmsen, "The Powers of Darkness in Prudentius' 'Contra Symmachum': A Study of His Poetic Imagination," *Vigiliae Christianae* 19 (1965) 237–257, at 238. The chronology adopted by most Roman historians, which puts both battles in 402, is now restated against Hall by M. Cesa and H. Sivan, "Alarico in Italia: Pollenza e Verona," *Historia* 39 (1990) 361–374.

[42] G. Zappacosta, "De Prudentii Libro I Contra Symmachum," *Latinitas* 15 (1967) 202–218.

[43] J.-P. Callu, "Date et genèse du premier livre de Prudence *Contre Symmaque*," *REL* 59 (1981) 235–259.

[44] Note especially *Pan. Lat.* 2 (12). 45.4: *tu ipsius victoriae victor ita omnem cum armis iram deposuisti ut ceciderit nemo post bellum, certe nemo post Maximum*. In fact, Maximus had left his son in Gaul: after his death at Aquileia Theodosius sent Arbogast to Gaul, who put Victor to death at Vienne (Zosimus 4.47.1; Orosius *Hist. adv. pag.* 7.34.10; *Chr. min.* 1.245, 298, 462; 2.62, cf. Renatus Profuturus Frigeridus, as quoted by Gregory of Tours *HE* 2.8).

[45] J. Harries, "Prudentius and Theodosius," *Latomus* 43 (1984) 69–84.

[46] F. Solmsen, "The Conclusion of Theodosius' Oration in Prudentius *Contra Symmachum*," *Philologus* 109 (1965) 310–313. Observe, however, that A.-M. Palmer, *Prudentius on the Martyrs* (Oxford 1989) 260, takes lines 501–505 to refer to *CTh* 16.10.8, issued in 382.

in Milan on 1 January 399 and that "only a complicated hypothesis fits the contradictions apparent in the *Libri contra orationem Symmachi*."[47] Specifically, Shanzer proposes that Book 1 itself may represent a conflation of two original drafts—"a standard invective against pagan gods combined with a panegyrical treatment of Theodosius' anti-pagan legislation." On the other hand, it may be presumed that those parts of Book 1 which cannot have been composed before 399 (379–407, 501–505) were added when Prudentius revised and rewrote the whole poem in 402/3.

If line 551 were integral to its context, if Prudentius had written it at the same time as the lines adjacent to it, and if the basic analysis of the first book of the *Contra Symmachum* argued by Harries and Shanzer were accepted, then it would follow that the poet composed his description of the conversion of the Roman aristocracy in Rome after he heard Claudian recite his panegyric on Olybrius and Probinus on 1 January 395 but before he learned of the death of the emperor Theodosius on 17 January. We have argued that the line is a later addition, conceivably by Prudentius himself but more probably interpolated by a later hand. If we are correct, then the line cannot be used to date the original composition of the draft of the passage which Prudentius incorporated into the finished poem in 402/3. On the contrary, if the line is deleted, it becomes possible to accept the *prima facie* implication of the identity of the individuals to whom Prudentius alludes in lines 552–565, *viz.* that Prudentius originally drafted his description of the conversion of the Roman aristocracy to Christianity in or shortly after 384. If that inference is correct, then it in turn opens up the possibility that Prudentius may originally have composed a first version of what now stands as the second book of the *Contra Symmachum* in or shortly after 384.[48]

[47] D. R. Shanzer, "The Date and Composition of Prudentius's *Contra Orationem Symmachi libri*," *RFIC* 117 (1989) 442–462.

[48] This article had its origin in a seminar paper prepared by R. W. Westall for T. D. Barnes. It was the latter who first suggested that line 551 may be interpolated, but we have worked together in elaborating this initial hypothesis. We are grateful to Professor Shanzer both for allowing us to see a copy of her recent paper in advance of its publication and for her comments on our penultimate draft.

Aspects of the Background of
the City of God*

In the opening sentence of the *City of God*, Augustine described its composition as "a large and difficult task". In preparing this lecture I have been constantly aware that the completed masterpiece is indeed both large and difficult, and I hope that what I have to say will not be unworthy either of my subject or of the occasion. The theme of the Vanier lectures in 1980 is "Roman Africa and its Contribution to Western Civilisation". When the Department of Classical Studies at Ottawa last organised the Vanier lectures (in 1970/1), the theme was "Classical Values and the Modern World". My subject today in a sense links the two series of lectures. Augustine wrote the *City of God* in Roman Africa, he explored the relationship between classical values and his own time, and the milieu in which he lived already possessed many features of the modern world. I shall not attempt to expound the *City of God* in its full complexity and richness of thought. Rather, as a Roman historian, I shall try to contribute to a better understanding of the background, both historical and intellectual, against which Augustine wrote.

*
*   *

The *City of God* comprises twenty-two books, whose careful structure Augustine himself describes. The first ten books are primarily apologetical, devoted mainly to the refutation of opposing viewpoints while the last twelve contain Augustine's positive message. The first five books attack the opinions of those who believe that worship of the traditional gods of the Greco-Roman world is necessary to ensure success and prosperity in this life, and hence that the prohibition of traditional

---

* I am most grateful to Professor J. J. O'Donnell for detailed comments on the first draft of the lecture.

paganism has caused disasters such as the sack of Rome in 410. The second five books address themselves to the view that, while mankind is fated to endure temporal ills, nevertheless the worship of the pagan gods will guarantee a happy and immortal existence hereafter. The subsequent twelve books comprise three groups of four books each: the first four describe the origin of the two cities, the one of God, the other of this world, the second four their progress (or rather pilgrimage) through the course of human history, and the last four their allotted ends.[1]

When the work was complete, Augustine wrote from Hippo and instructed Firmus, his literary agent in Carthage, to divide it either into two large codices of ten and twelve books or into five smaller codices, of which two were to contain five books each, three four books each. Firmus was then to allow one or two chosen Christians of Carthage to copy out the text, and they in turn would make their copies available to all who wished to read the work, both Christians desirous of instruction and pagans who might by reading it be liberated from the bonds of superstition. Further, Augustine sent Firmus a list of contents to stand before the work, whose function must have been to serve as an index to guide any who wished to consult the work on a specific point.[2] The size of the *City of God*, its careful organisation and the signposting of its arguments inevitably recall Eusebius' great apologetical work of a century earlier, the *Preparation for the Gospel* and the *Proof of the Gospel* in a total of thirty-five books.[3] Like Eusebius, whose apologetical writings he did not know, Augustine spent many years elaborating views which he had long held into a vast and systematic evaluation of human history and Greco-Roman culture.

Augustine began the *City of God* in 412, probably publishing Book One in the summer or autumn of that year.[4] Books Two and Three followed before September 413, and the first three books circulated together, provoking a pagan to essay a riposte, which he was, however, too timid to publish.[5] Augustine then appears to have interrupted composition for more than a year after Marcellinus, to whom he dedicated Books One to Three, was executed for treason (14 September 413).[6]

---

[1] *Retr.*, 2.69 (*CSEL*, 36.180 f.); *Ep. ad Firmum*, published by B. LAMBOT, *Revue bénédictine*, 51 (1939), pp. 209 ff. (both conveniently reprinted in *CCL*, 47, i-iv). Also *CD*, 6. pr. 1; *Epp.*, 184A, cf. B. LACROIX, *Mediaeval and Renaissance Studies*, 4 (1958), pp. 163 ff.

[2] *Ep. ad Firmum*, cf. H. I. MARROU, *Vig.Chr.*, 3 (1949), pp. 117 ff.; *Mélanges J. de Ghellinck*, 1 (Gembloux, 1951), pp. 235 ff.

[3] On which, see now *Constantine and Eusebius* (Harvard, 1981), Chapter X.

[4] O. PERLER, *Les voyages de Saint Augustin* (Paris, 1969), p. 459. Augustine probably added the preface to Book One, and perhaps the last chapter (36), in 413 after completing Books Two and Three, cf. J. LAMOTTE, *Augustiniana*, 11 (1961), pp. 439 ff.

[5] *Epp.*, 155.1.2, cf. 152.3; 154.2 (Macedonius to Augustine); *CD*, 5.26.75 ff.

[6] *Epp.*, 151.6; OROSIUS, *Hist. adv. pag.*, 7.42.14, 17. Marcellinus appears to have been condemned to death and executed as a result of Donatist intrigues or pressure, in revenge for his conduct of the Conference of Carthage in 411, cf. M. MOREAU, *Le dos-*

66

Books Four and Five were added to the first three by the spring of 415,[7] and Six to Ten followed rapidly: whether or not Six and then Seven and Eight were published separately (as Augustine seems to imply),[8] Orosius reveals that the whole of the first ten books had been given to the world by 417.[9] Neither internal hints nor external evidence appears to establish seriatim publication of Books Eleven to Twenty-two: it may be that Augustine published them all together, perhaps not long after 422.[10] Be that as it may, when Augustine sat down in 426 or 427 to survey his enormous literary production, the complete *City of God* was in circulation.[11]

Augustine did not invent the idea of interpreting history in terms of two cities.[12] In the New Testament, Paul contrasts contemporary Jerusalem which observes the Jewish law and the Jerusalem above, which is free and the mother of us all, while the author of Revelation contrasts Jerusalem, the heavenly city, with the whore Babylon, which represents Rome.[13] Closer to Augustine, the Donatist writer Tyconius, in his commentary on Revelation, had already developed the antithesis into the classic formulation of "two cities" or "two peoples", one of God, the

---

sier Marcellinus dans la Correspondance de saint Augustin (Paris, 1973), pp. 131 ff. The Donatists sought thereby to have the verdict of the Conference set aside (*CTh*, 15.5.55). The charge will have been treason: Marcellinus was presumably implicated in the revolt of Heraclianus in the winter of 412/3 (on which, see S. I. OOST, *CP*, 61 (1966), pp. 236 ff. — through the fragment of a chronicle published by B. BISCHOFF and W. KÖHLER, *Medieval Studies in memory of A. Kingsley Porter*, 1 (Cambridge, Mass., 1939), pp. 125 ff. = *Studi Romagnoli*, 3 (1952), pp. 1 ff., states that Heraclianus was executed on 7 March 413).

[7] *Epp.*, 169. Rutilius Namatianus, writing in 418 and describing a journey from Rome to Gaul in late 417, appears to know Books One to Five (possibly also Six), cf. A. DUFOURCQ, *Rev. d'hist. et de litt. rel.*, 10 (1905), pp. 488 ff.; J. LAMOTTE, *op. cit.*, pp. 466 ff.; A. CAMERON, *JRS*, 57 (1967), pp. 31 ff.

[8] *CD* 7.1.8 f.; 9.1/2; 10.1.6 ff.

[9] OROSIUS, *Hist. adv. pag.*, 1. pr. 11.

[10] The relationship between these books and Augustine's writings against the Pelagians deserves full examination — and may indicate a more precise chronology.

[11] *Retr.*, 2.69. The composition of the *Retractationes* is described in *Epp.*, 224.2. The calculation in *CD*, 18.54.64 ff., where the period from 399 to date is reckoned as *per triginta ferme annos*, favours completion somewhat after 422.

[12] The Christian background has often been discussed, cf. R. A. MARKUS, *Saeculum: History and Society in the Theology of Saint Augustine* (Cambridge, 1970), pp. 45 ff.; 105 ff. Possible pagan antecedents of the antithesis between the *Civitas Dei* and the *civitas terrena* require more investigation than they have so far received. John Rist has drawn my attention to two striking formulations of the Cynic (and later Stoic) idea that the wise man is a citizen of the universe but not of his native city (on the origin of the idea, cf. H. C. BALDRY, *The Unity of Mankind in Greek Thought* (Cambridge, 1965), pp. 108 ff.). Marcus Aurelius expresses the underlying contrast as being between "dear city of Cecrops" and "dear city of Zeus" (4.23, quoting ARISTOPHANES, frag. 110 Kock). And Seneca uses the language of two societies: *duas res publicas animo complectamur, alteram magnam et vere publicam qua di et homines continentur,... alteram cui nos adscripsit condicio nascendi* (*De Otio*, 4.1).

[13] Gal., 4.21 ff.; Rev., 16.9 ff.; 20.8 ff.

other of this world.[14] In Augustine's own writings the theme appears in a clear, explicit and unmistakeable form in the catachetical manual which he sent to the priest Deogratias in Carthage in 400 or shortly thereafter:

> Two cities, one of the wicked, the other of the holy, are led on their way from the beginning of the human race to the end of the world, at present mixed together physically though separate in will, but to be separated physically too at the day of judgement.

The one city is the Babylon of Revelation, its citizens all who love worldly pomp and temporal power; the other is Jerusalem, and its citizens, who renounce the devil and his angels, can be found both on earth and in heaven.[15] The theme of the two cities (it is clear) had already become Augustine's chosen or personal way of presenting the history of salvation.[16] It recurs in several works which Augustine wrote at about the same time, and it became a constant refrain in sermons which he delivered on the Psalms in the years following 410.[17]

In his detailed commentary on the biblical account of creation, and probably writing c. 411, Augustine announced a work which is identical with the last twelve books of the *City of God*:

> These two loves, of which one is holy, the other unclean, one social, the other private, one devoted to the common good for the sake of the society above, the other diverting even common property to private control for the sake of proud domination... have founded and distinguished among mankind two cities under the admirable and ineffable providence of God, who governs and orders all that he creates, one society of the just, the other of the wicked. In this world the two exist commingled temporarily, until they are separated at the last judgement, and the one, joined to the good angels, gains eternal life in their king, while the other, joined to the bad angels, is sent to eternal fire with their king. But of these two cities I shall perhaps speak more fully elsewhere, if the Lord wills.[18]

Augustine would have written a *City of God* even if Alaric had not sacked Rome. Yet the *City of God* which he did write has been deeply influenced, in both form and content, by the historical circumstances of its composition.[19] The Carthaginian audience for which Augustine wrote included loyal Catholics, Donatist sympathisers, overt and secret followers of Pelagius, and pagans who rejected the claims of Christianity.[20] The precise milieu must be reconstructed largely from Augustine's hints and from indirect evidence — and it is problematical. In order to understand

---

14 G. B. LADNER, *The Idea of Reform* (Harvard, 1959), pp. 262 f.

15 *De catechizandis rudibus*, 13.31; 20.36; 21.37; 24.45.

16 A. LAURAS and H. RONDET, *Études Augustiniennes* (Paris 1953), pp. 99 ff.

17 A. LAURAS and H. RONDET, *op. cit.*, pp. 108 ff.; 114 ff. As examples of the theme close to 400 they cite *Contra Faustum*, 12.36 (*PL*, 42.273); *Contra Ep. Parmeniani*, 2.4.8 f. (*CSEL*, 52.53 f.); *Enarr. in Ps. 36*, 3.4 (*CCL*, 38.370 f.).

18 *De genesi ad litteram*, 11.15 (*CSEL*, 28.348).

19 J. J. O'DONNELL, *Augustinian Studies*, 10(1979), pp. 75 ff.

20 On the intellectual ambience in Carthage, see above all P. BROWN, *Augustine of Hippo. A Biography* (London, 1967), pp. 287 ff.

Augustine properly, we need to know not only the sources and motivation of his own arguments, but the strength of the positions which he attacks.[21]

* * *

Christianity became the official religion of the Roman Empire thirty years before Augustine was born, when Constantine, having defeated the last of the persecutors, first forbade pagans to perform traditional rite of sacrifice, to erect new cult statues or to consult oracles, then con fiscated temple treasures.[22] Constantine refrained, however, from any serious attempt to enforce these measures in the western provinces of the Empire: there the "Great Persecution" was too brief and too partial to create the political conditions which permitted a frontal assault on pagan religion in the East.[23] The emperor Constans reiterated his father's prohibition of sacrifice in a constitution addressed to the *vicarius* of Italy in 341, perhaps with little immediate effect.[24] For Firmicus Maternus subsequently denounced the continuance of sacrifice and urged Constans to seize temple treasures.[25] Nothing came of the request: when Constantius visited Rome in 357, he supplemented the ancient priesthoods and thus implicitly confirmed the endowments and privileges of Rome's tradi tional cults.[26] The rule of the apostate Julian then intervened, and his Christian successors Jovian and Valentinian responded to Julian's harass ment of the church with a policy of toleration for pagan practices.[27] The reign of Theodosius, however, brought a decisive change. Sacrifice was again prohibited — and the ban was enforced.[28] In both East and West cults were suppressed, sometimes swiftly and easily, in other place only with difficulty and ruthless violence.[29] The process began early in Theodosius' reign in the East, but in the West, especially in Africa, the decisive stages came after Theodosius' death. In 399, the imperial com missioners Gaudentius and Jovius arrived in Carthage, and on 18 April they desecrated pagan shrines and destroyed cult statues.[30] The bishop

---

[21] On the problems of understanding paganism in the late fourth and fifth centu ries (and the concept itself), see recently J.J. O'DONNELL, *Traditio*, 35 (1979), pp. 45 ff From what follows it will be obvious that I dissent from some of the views there expressed.

[22] EUSEBIUS, *VC*, 2.43 ff.; *Triac.*, 8.1 ff.

[23] For this interpretation of Constantine's policies, see *Constantine and Eusebius* (Harvard, 1981), Chapter XIV.

[24] *CTh*, 16.10.2, cf. *ILS*, 1228 (Calama).

[25] *De err. prof. rel.*, 16.2 ff.; 20.7; 28.6 ff.

[26] SYMMACHUS, *Rel.*, 3.7.

[27] On the religious policies of Julian, Jovian and Valentinian, see A. PIGANIOL *L'Empire chrétien* (Paris, 1947), pp. 134 ff.; 147 ff.; 190 ff.

[28] *CTh*, 16.10.7 ff., cf. G. FOWDEN, *JTs*, n. s. 29 (1978), pp. 53 ff.

[29] See, e.g., J.F. MATTHEWS, *Western Aristocracies and Imperial Court A.D 364-425* (Oxford, 1975), pp. 140 ff., on the "rampage against paganism" conducted by Cynegius Maternus as praetorian prefect of the East from 384 to 388.

[30] *CD*, 18.54.65 ff.

Aurelius, the friend of Augustine, gratefully converted the temple of Caelestis into a Christian church.[31]

Political events impinged upon both imperial policy and pagan resistance. Shortly before his death in 383, the emperor Gratian (probably under the influence of his colleague Theodosius) repudiated the title of *pontifex maximus*, stopped public subsidies for the official cults at Rome and the salaries of Vestal virgins, and ordered that the altar of Victory be removed from the senate house.[32] In 384, Symmachus came to Milan and presented Valentinian II with a petition for the restoration of the altar and the traditional subsidies: he did not need to remind the emperor explicitly that the usurper Maximus had killed his brother Gratian in the interval.[33] Valentinian denied the petition. The Roman Senate renewed its request to Theodosius himself when he was in Italy between 389 and 391, conciliating pagans and appointing them to high office, lest, in their disaffection, they support another usurper.[34] Two more requests came in 392. An embassy of priests of the ancient Roman brotherhoods petitioned Valentinian immediately before his death, but in vain.[35] The usurper Eugenius, approached in his turn, did not feel strong enough to deny the request completely: after an initial refusal, he allowed the altar to be restored, and he gave private subsidies to the Roman cults.[36] Thus conciliated, a party in the Roman aristocracy attempted to turn the usurpation of the Christian Eugenius into a pagan revival. Nicomachus Flavianus, as praetorian prefect and consul, ostentatiously celebrated ancient festivals at Rome in the spring of 394.[37] Moreover, when the usurper's

[31] QUODVULTDEUS, *De prom. et praed. Dei*, 3.44.

[32] ZOSIMUS, 4.36, cf. A. CAMERON, *JRS*, 58 (1968), pp. 96 ff.

[33] Observe, however, the clear hint in *Rel.*, 3.19: *eum religionum statum petimus, qui divo parenti numinis vestri servavit imperium, qui fortunato principi legitimos suffecit heredes*.

[34] AMBROSE, *Epp.*, 57.4. On Theodosius' actions in Italy, see A. LIPPOLD, *RE*, Supp. 13 (1973), 881 ff.; J. F. MATTHEWS, *op. cit.*, pp. 225 ff.

[35] AMBROSE, *Epp.*, 57.5; *De obitu Valentiniani*, 19 f.; 52.

[36] AMBROSE, *Epp.*, 57.6; PAULINUS, *Vita Ambrosii*, 26 f., cf. J. ZIEGLER, "Zur religiösen Haltung der Gegenkaiser im 4. Jh. n. Chr.", *Frankfurter Althistorische Studien*, 4 (1970), pp. 85 ff.

[37] *Carmen contra paganos*, edited by M. HAUPT, in T. MOMMSEN, *Ges.Schr.*, 7 (Berlin, 1909), pp. 489-493; cf. J. F. MATTHEWS, *Historia*, 19 (1970), pp. 464 ff. J. J. O'DONNELL, *Phoenix*, 32 (1978), pp. 140 ff., has recently denied that the target of the poem is Flavianus. But the poem specifies several precise details which fit Flavianus far better than the alternative candidates proposed, viz. L. Aurelius Avianius Symmachus, *praefectus urbi* in 364/5; Vettius Agorius Praetextatus, *praefectus urbi* in 367/8 and praetorian prefect in 384; and Gabinius Barbarus Pompeianus, *praefectus urbi* in 408/9. First, the man attacked was both *praefectus* (25, 28) and consul (112: in the context, *te consule* appears not to be prospective). Second, he was aged sixty at the time of the activities described (67). Third, he was *parvo donatus sepulchro* (111): whereas Flavianus died in disgrace (cf. *ILS*, 2948, of 431), the dead Symmachus was honoured with statues in both Rome and Constantinople (*ILS*, 1257), while the tomb of Praetextatus was unusually grandiose (*ILS*, 1259). Moreover, the Marcianus whom the prefect and consul installed as proconsul (86) can attractively be identified as the Marcianus about whom Symmachus wrote to Ambrose c. 395 (*Epp.*, 3.33, cf. J. F. MATTHEWS, *op. cit.*, (1970), pp. 476 f.).

army met Theodosius at the River Frigidus in September 394 at least part of it fought under a pagan banner: statues of Jupiter and Hercules were displayed in the disappointed hope that they would ensure weather which aided the rebels.[38]

Victorious over this "army of unbelievers", Theodosius spared his political opponents who survived the war and encouraged them to become Christians.[39] Yet even after 394 pagans did not abandon all hope of restoring their ancient cults. When Alaric invaded Italy in the winter of 401/2, the now elderly Symmachus again journeyed from Rome to Milan, apparently in order to request Honorius to restore the altar of Victory to the senate house, though again in vain.[40] When Alaric besieged Rome for the first time in the winter of 408/9, the *praefectus urbi* was Gabinius Barbarus Pompeianus, a man of notorious pagan sympathies.[41] According to a historian of the early fifth century, Pompeianus was approached by some Etruscan *haruspices*, who claimed to have saved the city of Narnia: with the connivance of the bishop of Rome, the Senate ascended the Capitol and witnessed the *haruspices* perform their ancestral divination, but did not dare to perform the traditional sacrifice which alone would have averted the peril.[42] In these desperate years, even the imperial government acknowledged a need to conciliate pagans and heretics by relaxing legislation against them: by a significant coincidence Honorius ended the policy of toleration once and for all on the day after Alaric entered Rome.[43]

Some pagans had bitterly resented the establishment of Christianity from the start. Their protests were of no avail, for both Constantine and the supporters of his policies could appeal to the emperor's success in every sphere as manifest proof that he acted at God's behest — an argument convincing on traditional assumptions shared by Christians and pagans alike.[44] But what if a Christian emperor failed spectacularly? If Christian success permitted an inference to the truth of Christianity, then Christian failure must allow pagans to develop a historical apologetic of

---

[38] RUFINUS, *HE* 11.33; AUGUSTINE, *CD*, 5.26.22 ff., cf. W. JOBST, *Sb. Wien*, Phil.-hist. Klasse, 335 (1978), 34.

[39] *CD*, 5.26.38 ff., cf. AMBROSE, *De obitu Theodosii*, 10 (*exercitus infidelium*).

[40] SYMMACHUS, *Epp.*, 4.9; 5.94-96; 7.13, 14; PRUDENTIUS, *C. Symm.*, 2.5 ff., cf. *AJP*, 97 (1976), pp. 380 ff.

[41] *Vita Melaniae*, 19 (ed. D. GORCE, *SC*, 90 (1962), pp. 166), cf. A. CHASTAGNOL, *Les Fastes de la Préfecture de Rome au Bas-Empire* (Paris, 1962), 265 f. *PLRE*, 2.897 takes ZOSIMUS, 5.41.2 to describe Pompeianus as a Christian. That is not necessarily the correct interpretation of the phrase "τὴν κρατοῦσαν κοτὰ νοῦν ἐλόμβονε δόξαν."

[42] ZOSIMUS, 5.41; SOZOMENUS, *HE*, 9.6.3. Their source is clearly Olympiodorus, cf. J. F. MATTHEWS, *JRS*, 60 (1970), pp. 80 ff.

[43] *CTh*, 16.5.51 = 56, cf. A. C. DE VEER, *Rev. ét. byz.*, (1966), pp. 189 ff.

[44] EUSEBIUS, *VC*, 2.48 ff. (Constantine c. 325); *Triac.*, 7.1 ff.; *VC*, 1.3 ff.

their own.[45] The disastrous defeat of Valens at Hadrianople in 378 enabled disgruntled pagans to argue that Christianity was ruining the Roman Empire.[46] Hadrianople was immediately compared to Cannae. The Christian Vegetius invited Theodosius to recreate the Roman army which had defeated Hannibal,[47] while the pagan Ammianus gloomily and circumspectly lamented the passing of the old Roman ways and ethos.[48] Subsequent disasters drew forth similar debates and facile opinions. When Alaric entered Italy in late 401 pagans blamed Christianity; when he was defeated at Pollentia, Claudian claimed that the victory surpassed Marius' triumph over the Cimbri and Teutones, Prudentius that it was Christ's handiwork.[49] When Radagaisus invaded Italy in 405/6, pagans in Carthage began to assert that he could not be defeated by men who refused to sacrifice to their gods; when his army was massacred, Christians immediately attributed his defeat to the intervention of their God.[50] When Alaric captured Rome, pagans had a ready explanation, specific as well as general. Stilicho betrayed the city by destroying the Sibylline books which had rendered it inviolable over many centuries.[51] And the Goths were admitted by Proba, a noble matron of the Anicii, the most distinguished Christian family in Rome.[52]

In Africa, paganism was by no means dead.[53] When the statue of Hercules at Sufetula (Sbeïtla) was overturned (probably in 399), a pagan mob killed sixty Christians and the local senate demanded that the church make good the damage.[54] At Calama in 408, pagans organised a religious procession, which was illegal, and subsequently rioted and looted Christian property.[55] These two incidents, known only because they appear in Augustine's correspondence, need not have been isolated episodes. Coun-

---

[45]   On the concept, J. STRAUB, *Heidnische Geschichtsapologetik in der christlichen Spätantike* (Bonn, 1963); *Regeneratio Imperii. Aufsätze über Roms Kaisertum und Reich im Spiegel der heidnischen und christlichen Publizistik* (Darmstadt, 1972), pp. 195 ff.

[46]   Eunapius probably published the first edition of his violently anti-Christian history c. 380, cf. *CP*, 71 (1976), 265 ff.; *The Sources of the Historia Augusta (Collection Latomus* 155, 1978), pp. 114 ff.

[47]   VEGETIUS, 1.28, cf. *Phoenix*, 33 (1979), pp. 254 ff.

[48]   P.-M. CAMUS, *Ammien Marcellin. Témoin des courants culturels et religieux à la fin du IV* siècle (Paris, 1967), pp. 103 ff.

[49]   CLAUDIAN, *Get.*, 635 ff.; PRUDENTIUS, *C. Symm.*, 2.708 ff., cf. *AJP*, 97 (1976), pp. 383 ff.

[50]   *CD*, 5.23.

[51]   RUTILIUS NAMATIANUS, *Red.* 2.41 ff., cf. L. VARÁDY, *Acta Antiqua*, 16 (1968), pp. 413 ff.

[52]   PROCOPIUS, *Bella*, 3.2.27 — only a rumour, but probably deriving ultimately from Olympiodorus. Anicia Faltonia Proba was the widow of Petronius Probus, consul in 371, and mother of the consuls of 395 (*PLRE*, 1.732 f.). Jerome confirms that she was on good terms with the Goths who pillaged Rome (*Epp.*, 130.7). She came to Africa shortly afterwards (AUGUSTINE, *Epp.*, 130; 131).

[53]   F. VAN DER MEER, *Augustine the Bishop*, translated by B. BATTERSHAW and G. R. LAMB (London, 1961), pp. 29 ff.

[54]   *Epp.*, 50.

[55]   *Epp.*, 91.8 ff.

cils which met at Carthage in 407 and 408 sent embassies to the imperial court at Ravenna to protest at the conduct of pagans and heretics: their complaints included the murder of bishops.[56]

*

*   *

While Theodosius still reigned, and for some time after, Augustine shared the optimism of his contemporaries and regarded the triumph of Christianity as the culmination of human history.[57] But by 410 he had come to question conventional assumptions. When Alaric sacked Rome Augustine responded without hesitation. In a sermon entitled "On the Fall of the City", he instinctively stressed themes which would permeate the *City of God*: the sack was not an utter disaster; everything earthly and human must perish, so that no pagan god can protect Rome for ever; yet even Christian Rome is earthly and perishable, for God sends or permits worldly disasters in order to encourage mankind to contemplate the eternal.[58] Other sermons of 410 and 411 adopt very similar arguments,[59] and Augustine was preparing to embark on his detailed elaboration of the theme of the two cities, when events in Carthage diverted him — and gave the *City of God* its bipartite form.

Many aristocrats fled Rome in order to escape the Goths.[60] Some went as far as Palestine, while others merely retreated into the Italian countryside, and others again came to Africa.[61] Among those who arrived in Carthage (where they insisted on continuing their customary aristocratic style of life) was Rufius Antonius Agrypnius Volusianus, a member of the prominent family of the Ceionii and a former proconsul of Africa.[62] Volusianus was a pagan, but not implacably hostile to Christianity: his sister and niece were Christians, notable for their charity and asceticism and he eventually died a Christian.[63] Augustine wrote to Volusianus in

---

[56] *Reg. Eccl. Carth. Excerpta*, 106, 107 (*CCL*, 259.219).

[57] R. A. MARKUS, *op. cit.*, 22 ff. Markus places the decisive shift in Augustine' attitude towards the *tempora Christiana* c. 410 (35 ff.): on the evidence which he presents, it could be as early as 403 — i.e. contemporary with Alaric's first invasion of Italy.

[58] *De excidio urbis Romae sermo* (*CCL*, 46.249-262).

[59] O. ZWIERLEIN, *ZPE*, 32 (1978), 45 ff. (on *Sermones*, 81, 105 and 296).

[60] E. DEMOUGEOT, *De l'unité à la division de l'Empire romain* (Paris, 1948), 481 ff. P. COURCELLE, *Histoire littéraire des grandes invasions germaniques*³ (Paris, 1964), pp. 60 ff.

[61] JEROME, *Comm. in Ez.*, 7 pr. (*PL*, 25.199 = *CCL*, 75.277), exclaimed hyperbolically that Bethlehem had been turned into a hotel. For Africa, the decisive event was not the capture of Rome, but Alaric's march to the Strait of Messina in the autumn of 410, which drove Roman refugees out of southern Italy. Even Sicily no longer seemed a safe haven (cf. *Vita Melaniae*, 19).

[62] On whom, A. CHASTAGNOL, *REA*, 58 (1956) pp. 241 ff.; *op. cit.* (1962) pp. 276 ff. Augustine complains that refugees from Rome continue to frequent theatres and go mad over actors (*CD*, 1.32/33), to whom they give enormous presents (3.19.34 ff.).

[63] *Vita Melaniae*, 50 ff. For Volusianus' sister Albina and her daughter Melania the Younger, *PLRE*, 1.33; 593.

the summer of 411 urging him to read the Bible. Volusianus replied politely and tactfully: he offered himself as a willing pupil, but reported a salon conversation in which a speaker shocked everyone by ridiculing the Incarnation as a philosophical absurdity which demeaned the dignity of the divine ruler of the universe.[64] Volusianus appealed to Augustine for an answer. Augustine will not have missed the artifice in the aristocrat's letter. Volusianus and his doubts were known to Flavius Marcellinus, who had recently presided over the Conference of Carthage between Catholics and Donatists (June 411).[65] Marcellinus too may have had philosophical reservations about certain Christian doctrines: at all events, he urged Augustine to answer Volusianus, and also to explain to sceptics how Christ differed from magicians like Apuleius and Apollonius.[66] Augustine replied with two lengthy epistles, one to Volusianus and one to Marcellinus, and returned to Hippo.[67] From there he wrote again to Marcellinus in or around November 411, in terms which show that the *City of God* in its present form was not yet contemplated.[68] Soon, however, Augustine began the enormous task. He dedicated the first three books to Marcellinus,[69] and he designed his arguments primarily to fit the situation in Carthage.

Augustine identifies his adversaries with care and precision. They are not merely worshippers of false gods or demons who "prefer their own gods to the founder of the City of God", they are pagan Roman refugees of noble birth — "the offspring of men like Regulus and Scaevola, Scipio and Fabricius".[70] Many of them escaped from Rome when it was taken by seeking sanctuary in Christian churches or by disguising themselves as Christian priests.[71] Once safe in Carthage, they began to mock and ridicule, to blame Christianity for recent disasters, to play on the fears of humble and simple folk, to stir up mobs against the Christians — in brief, "to alienate weaker and less skilful minds from that city in which alone life is eternally happy".[72]

Augustine devotes the first book largely to comforting unhappy Christians distressed at the sack of Rome and its attendant sufferings. To

---

[64] *Epp.*, 132; 135.

[65] On his career and character, M. MOREAU, *op. cit.*, pp. 137 ff. It is tempting to postulate Marcellinus as the model of the good and truly happy man described in *CD*, 4.3.14 ff.

[66] *Epp.*, 136.

[67] *Epp.*, 137; 138.

[68] *Epp.*, 139, cf. M. MOREAU, *op. cit.* pp. 49 ff. She assumes that Apringius, the brother of Marcellinus, was proconsul of Africa until 28 February 412 (*ib.*, 28; 78): although his successor is indeed first attested on 29 February 412 (*CTh*, 6.29.9; 8.4.23; 11.1.32; 11.7.19-21; 12.6.31), Apringius may have left office some time earlier.

[69] *CD*, 1. pr. 7 f.; 2.1.25 f.

[70] *CD*, 1. pr. 7; 2.29.1 ff. On the adversaries envisaged by Augustine, see esp. J. LAMOTTE, *op. cit.*, pp. 446 ff.

[71] *CD*, 1.1; 3.31.9 f.

[72] *CD*, 2.3; 3.17.38 ff.

be sure, he never forgets that his audience includes (or may include) sympathetic pagans — those enemies of the City of God who may yet become suitable enough citizens if they correct the error of their impiety.[73] But he wishes to do more than merely to reply to pagans: he desires to bring consolation to Christians.[74] For consolation was needed. Some of the Christians to whom Augustine addressed himself had lost their wealth or relatives. The Goths had raped married women, virgins, even nuns, they had tortured, they had carried off Christians into captivity, they had killed, and they had left the dead unburied, to be eaten by dogs.[75] Augustine needed to reassure respectable Christian women (and to convince those who mocked them) that their chastity had not been irrevocably destroyed by rape.[76]

The first book of the *City of God* often reads as if Augustine were responding to a sudden panic in Carthage. He becomes more systematic as he proceeds (though with one significant exception, at the end of Book Five). Books Two and Three controvert the pagan thesis that, whereas sacrifice to the gods brings success and prosperity, the recent prohibition of sacrifice has caused unparalleled disaster.[77] Augustine has no difficulty in showing that there is no correlation between pagan religiosity and its alleged benefits: he documents and discusses the moral and material ills which afflicted Rome before the advent of Christ.[78] The next two books offer an assessment of the place of the Roman Empire in God's overall scheme. It is God (Augustine argues), not the pagan gods, not fate, who controls all kingdoms and has allowed the Roman Empire to grow and to prosper. His purpose may be inscrutable, but it must be just: he desires men to discover the non-terrestrial nature of true felicity. In the closing chapters of Book Five, Augustine takes issue with and rejects the conventional contemporary belief that God grant worldly success to all truly Christian emperors.[79] Augustine refuses to call a Christian emperor happy if he merely reigns long, dies peacefully leaving his sons as heirs, and defeats his enemies in war.[80] Against a Constantine, he sets a Jovian and a Gratian.[81] As for Theodosius, it is only his services

[73] *CD*, 1.1.2 f. On the structure and content of Book One, T. ORLANDI, *Studi classici e orientali*, 14 (1965), pp. 120 ff.

[74] *CD*, 1.16.7 f.; 28.2 f.; 29.1 f., cf. 4.2.45 ff.

[75] *CD*, 1.7-17.

[76] *CD*, 1.18 ff., esp. 18.1: *at enim, ne vel aliena polluat libido, metuitur*; 29.6 f.: *illi vero, qui probitati eius insultant*. Augustine unmistakeably implies that some Christians committed suicide, either to avoid indignity in 410, or, like Lucretia, from shame at what they had suffered (17.1 ff.; 22.1 f.; 22.26 f.; 28.1 f.). The disproportionately large space which he devotes to suicide (17-28) indicates that it was a live issue among the émigrés at Carthage.

[77] Stated in its most extreme form at *CD*, 1.36.1 ff.; 3.18.59 ff.

[78] Yet he refused to descend to the level of "mere writers of history" (*CD*, 3.18.11 ff.).

[79] *CD*, 5.24-26, cf. Y. M. DUVAL, *Recherches augustiniennes*, 4 (1966), pp. 135 ff.; P. COURCELLE, *REA* 71 (1969), pp. 100 ff.

[80] *CD*, 5.24.1 ff.

[81] *CD*, 5.25.17 ff.

to true religion which Augustine deems truly praiseworthy: he was more pleased to be a member of the church than to be ruler of the world. A Roman emperor may earn eternal happiness by championing the church, but the power of his throne is "nothing but a passing mist".[82]

Augustine's discussion of the Christian emperors of the fourth century has been dismissed as one of "the most shoddy passages" in the *City of God*, a "sketchy and superficial panegyric".[83] The verdict is unjust. Augustine is not providing a "mirror of a Christian prince" nor writing panegyric; he is rejecting an interpretation of the fourth century known to and accepted by his readers. Rufinus translated Eusebius' *Ecclesiastical History*, adding a continuation down to 395 largely taken from Gelasius of Caesarea, at the request of Chromatius of Aquileia, during Alaric's first invasion of Italy (401-403). His avowed purpose was to make men forget their present ills by contemplating past glories, and Rufinus presented his work as a medicine or palliative for sick and distressed minds.[84] Augustine takes Rufinus' *Ecclesiastical History*, summarises Rufinus' interpretation of the fourth century, and rejects it.[85] He has deliberately placed his own, far less optimistic evaluation of the Christian Empire as the climax of the first five books of the *City of God* — where it fits imperfectly into its immediate context. Orosius' *Historiae adversus paganos* shows how difficult Augustine's readers in Carthage found it to credit his very explicit rejection of the prevailing assumption that right belief in God ensures felicity on earth.[86]

*

*   *

The second five books of the *City of God* take issue with those who believe that the gods of the nations should be worshipped for the sake of life after death.[87] The argument again exhibits a deliberate progression. Books Six and Seven are directed against Varro, or rather, against

---

[82] *CD*, 5.26.43 ff., esp. 59 f.: *ex isto temporali vapore cuiuslibet culminis et sublimitatis humanae*.

[83] P. BROWN, *Trends in Medieval Political Thought*, edited by B. SMALLEY (Oxford, 1965), 8 = *Augustine. A Collection of Critical Essays*, edited by R. A. MARKUS (New York, 1972), 319 ; 332 n. 28.

[84] *PG*, 12.583 ff. = *CCL*, 20.285 f.

[85] On Augustine's knowledge of Eusebius (only the *History* in Rufinus' translation, the *Chronicle* and *Onomasticon* in Jerome's, and possibly a Latin version of the Gospel Canons), B. ALTANER, *BZ*, 44 (1951), pp. 1 ff. On his rejection of Eusebius' and Rufinus' interpretation of history, T. E. MOMMSEN, *Medieval and Renaissance Studies* (Ithaca, 1959), pp. 265 ff. ; R. A. MARKUS, *op. cit.*, pp. 45 ff. ; 157 ff. ; G. F. CHESNUT, *Our Common History as Christians. Essays in Honor of A. C. Outler* (New York, 1975), pp. 69 ff.

[86] T. E. MOMMSEN, *op. cit.*, pp. 325 ff. James O'Donnell has plausibly suggested to me that Augustine wrote 5.21-26 at the same time as Books One to Three, but at once earmarked it as the conclusion of the first part of the whole work.

[87] *CD*, 1.36.13 ff. ; 6.1.1. ff.

contemporary readers of Varro who appeal to his authority on religious matters.[88] Towards such, Augustine is condescending, sometimes downright rude, for again he divides pagan readers into two classes: there are those whose stupidity and obstinacy render them immune to rational argument, but there are also many who can put aside longstanding error and weigh matters carefully.[89] It is surely for the benefit of the latter that Augustine adopts an attitude of polite deference towards Varro himself, whom he constantly compliments as an acute and learned man.[90] On the religious issue, however, politeness never blunts Augustine's firmness. In Book Six, he examines Varro's three types of theology or religion (mythical, physical and civic) and concludes that none offers any hope of eternal life.[91] In Book Seven, he deals similarly with Varro's select gods (Janus, Jupiter, Saturn and the like): he argues that Varro was justified in interpreting gods as the manifestations of physical objects or properties, but mistaken in investing the world with divine qualities which belong to God, the creator of everything both inanimate and sentient.[92]

The exordium of Book Eight marks an ascent to a higher realm of discourse. Augustine turns to the philosophers who approach the truth more closely than Varro — that is, the Platonists, who concede that there is a god who watches over human affairs, yet insist on the worship of a plurality of gods rather than of the one unchanging God alone.[93] Augustine situates Plato and Platonists within the Greek philosophical tradition and summarises the content of Platonism, stressing its similarities to Christian theology. As he candidly confesses,

> This is the reason why we prefer the Platonists to the rest: while other philosophers have wasted their talents and studies on searching for the causes of things and the right way to learn and to live, they have attained knowledge of God and have discovered where is the cause of the organised universe, and the light whereby truth is perceived, and the spring from which we can drink true happiness.[94]

Augustine states that his Christian readers will be surprised to be told that Plato agrees with so much of "our religion".[95] His pagan readers needed to be convinced by lengthy argumentation.

Augustine names four prominent Platonists of recent date who held, with Plato, that sacrifices should be made to many gods: they are Plotinus, Iamblichus, Porphyry and the African Apuleius.[96] Iamblichus appears to

---

[88] *CD*, 7.22.13 ff.
[89] *CD*, 6. pr. 7 ff., cf. 7. pr. 5 ff.: *ingenia celeriora atque meliora, quibus ad hanc rem superiores libri satis superque sufficiunt.*
[90] *CD*, 6.2.1 ff. ; 7.9.6 f. ; 7.28.1 f.
[91] *CD*, 6.12.1 ff.
[92] *CD*, 7.29.
[93] *CD*, 8.1.17 ff.
[94] *CD*, 8.10.46 ff.
[95] *CD*, 8.11.1 ff., cf. 10.1 f.
[96] *CD*, 8.12.25 ff.

be here on reputation alone: Augustine nowhere quotes him, there is nothing in the text which reflects specifically Iamblichean ideas, and no other Latin writer in the West shows clear knowledge of Iamblichus before Martianus Capella, who was probably writing towards 475.[97] But Plotinus, Porphyry and Apuleius are all quoted and their opinions discussed. Augustine had long been familiar with some of Plotinus' writings — not the collected edition made by Porphyry in 300/1 (the *Enneads*), but those treatises which Marius Victorinus had translated into Latin.[98] Augustine discovered these "few books of Plotinus" in Milan, and they both played a crucial role in his conversion and provided the matrix within which he initially formulated his Christian theology.[99] Porphyry never influenced Augustine in the same way.[100] Indeed, it has not yet been demonstrated that Augustine had read any Porphyry before he wrote *De consensu Evangelistarum* c. 400.[101] Hence it was in Africa, and as he learnt to read Greek with some fluency himself, that Augustine became acquainted with Porphyry's writings. The *City of God* quotes his *Philosophy from Oracles*, *On the Return of the Soul*, the *Letter to Anebo* and probably *On Images*.[102] These works, therefore, circulated in Africa, and at least *Philosophy from Oracles* had been translated into Latin.[103] A still more obvious reflection of the African background is the attention which Augustine pays to Apuleius, including the *Asclepius* which partially derived its authority from its accidental association with his name.[104] It is clear that the coterie of Volusianus took a lively interest in Apuleius, whom they revered as both philosopher and magician.[105]

---

[97]   On Martianus' indebtedness to Iamblichus, R. TURCAN, *REA*, 36 (1958), pp. 237 ff. ; on his date, D. SHANZER, *Beiträge zur Geschichte der deutschen Sprache und Literatur*, 104 (1982), p. 111. I am totally unconvinced by the argument of J.-C. Frédouille, *Recherches augustiniennes* 5 (1968), pp. 7 ff., that *CD*, 22.2.1 has been influenced by IAMBLICHUS, *De Mysteriis*, 1.13.

[98]   As demonstrated by P. HENRY, *Plotin et l'occident* (Louvain, 1934), pp. 63 ff.

[99]   R. J. O'CONNELL, *St. Augustine's Early Theory of Man, A.D. 386-391* (Harvard, 1968), pp. 1 ff. On the correct reading in *De beata vita* 1.4 (*CSEL*, 63.92: *lectis autem Plotini paucissimis libris*), P. HENRY, *op. cit.*, pp. 82 ff.

[100]   For discussion of Augustine's knowledge of Porphyry, W. THEILER, "Porphyrios und Augustin, "*Schriften der Königsberger Gelehrten Gesellschaft*, Geisteswissenschaftliche Klasse 10.1 (1933): P. COURCELLE, *Les lettres grecques en Occident de Macrobe à Cassiodore*² (Paris, 1948), pp. 159 ff. ; J. J. O'MEARA, *Recherches augustiniennes*, 7 (1969), pp. 121 ff. ; P. HADOT, *Porphyre et Victorinus*, 1 (Paris, 1969), pp. 475 ff.

[101]   R. J. O'CONNELL, *op. cit.*, pp. 20 ff. Furthermore, the echoes of Porphyry in this work may reflect a partial revision c. 412.

[102]   For a list of the quotations, W. HOFFMANN, *CSEL*, 40.722. J. J. O'MEARA, *Porphyry's Philosophy from Oracles in Augustine* (Paris, 1959), tried to identify that work with *On the Return of the Soul*: he was thoroughly refuted by P. HADOT, *Rev. ét. aug.*, 6 (1960), pp. 205 ff.

[103]   *CD*, 19.23.1 ff. Augustine shows no direct acquaintance with either *Against the Christians* or *On Abstinence*.

[104]   *CD*, 8.23-26.

[105]   *Epp.*, 136.1 (Marcellinus). H. HAGENDAHL, *Augustine and the Latin Classics*, 1 (Göteborg, 1967), pp. 17 ff., notes only one reference by Augustine to Apuleius outside the *City of God* and *Epp.*, 137/8. Significantly, Augustine is there reporting and refuting anti-Christian polemic deriving from Porphyry (*Epp.*, 102.32).

78

Augustine recognised the potency of this combination. He discusses Plotinus, Porphyry and Apuleius with his eye constantly on potential readers who prize Plato and cherish him "with whatever sort of love of wisdom or a curiosity for skills which Plato ought not to have learnt."[106] He uses arguments derived from Plato to attack the demonology of Apuleius, he appeals to Porphyry against theurgy, and he stresses, wherever possible, his essential agreement with Plotinus on fundamentals.[107] Above all, it is on Platonic principles that Augustine rests his crucial argument that Christ is the only possible mediator between God and man.[108] The Incarnation, so far from being philosophically repugnant, as the Roman aristocrat Volusianus believed, is necessary in order to link the divine and the human realms.

*
* *

The intellectual background of the first ten books of the *City of God* may receive some illumination from three pagan writers who were active in Africa in the early fifth century. Favonius Eulogius composed a partial commentary on the Dream of Scipio in Cicero's *De re publica*, which he dedicated to the senator Superius, *consularis* of Byzacena.[109] Eulogius was a pupil of Augustine in Carthage (i.e. between 376 and 383) and subsequently rhetor of the city.[110] The date of his work is unclear, but it is tempting to assign it to a period c. 402 or c. 409 when overt pagans held high office: Superius might, for example, have governed Byzacena while Volusianus was proconsul of Africa.[111] Eulogius' product is inconsequential, and perhaps incomplete, for it discusses only two topics, viz. the properties of the numbers one to nine (which explain why Scipio died at the age of fifty-six), and the music of the spheres. The fabulist Avienus glorified the Roman past directly, by putting improving episodes from Virgil into iambic fables.[112] Macrobius,

---

[106] *CD*, 10.29.23 ff.
[107] *CD*, 8.14 ff.; 10.9 ff.; 10.2.1 f.: *sed non est nobis cum his excellentioribus philosophis in hac quaestione conflictus*.
[108] *CD*, 9.15 f.
[109] Edited by R.-E. van Weddingen, *Collection Latomus*, 27 (1957). On textual problems, cf. M. Sicherl, *Abh. Mainz*, Geistes- und Sozialwissenschaftliche Klasse, 1959 Nr. 10, pp. 667 ff.
[110] *De cura pro mortuis gerenda*, 11.13 (*CSEL*, 41.642).
[111] R.-E. van Weddingen, *op. cit.*, pp. 7, dates the work between 390 and 410; *PLRE*, 1.294 between 388 and 426 (since Macrobius, *Sat.*, 2.4.11 may criticise Eulogius, *Disputatio*, 22.1). Volusianus' proconsulate must fall shortly before 410 (A. Chastagnol, *op. cit.* (1962), pp. 276 ff.).
[112] Servius, on *Aeneid*, 10.272. Avienus appears to have written his *Fables* after Macrobius' *Commentary* but before his *Saturnalia*, cf. A. Cameron, *CQ*, n.s., 17 (1967) pp. 385 ff.

who makes him participate as a young man in his *Saturnalia*, set in 383 or 384, reveals that Avienus was an African.[113]

Whether Augustine knew the arithmology of Eulogius or the verse of Avienus probably matters little. With Macrobius, however, there is substantial common ground, whether or not either had read the other. Macrobius published his *Saturnalia* in Italy, probably in 431 or thereabouts.[114] The introduction discloses that the author hails from another country.[115] On various criteria, it seems that his native land should be Africa.[116] From that it follows that Macrobius acquired his intellectual baggage in Africa, and that he probably composed his *Commentary on the Dream of Scipio* in Africa.[117] Macrobius corresponds to the pagan audience envisaged in the *City of God* in details large and small. He idealises Rome's ancient past, he reveres Virgil as a pagan Bible, he has read deeply in Varro, and he takes his philosophical ideas from Porphyry, repeating his authorities with almost parrot-like fidelity.[118] Significantly, both Macrobius and Augustine name the philosopher and antiquarian Cornelius Labeo, a shadowy figure of uncertain date, but clearly known in Carthage in the fifth century.[119] Macrobius' *Commentary* quotes with approbation and expounds a passage of Cicero which resonates through the whole of the *City of God*:

> All those who have saved, aided or enlarged the commonwealth have a definite place marked off in the heavens where they may enjoy a blessed existence for ever. Nothing that occurs on earth, indeed, is more gratifying to that Supreme God who rules the whole universe than the establishment of associations and federations of men bound together by principles of justice, which are called commonwealths. The governors and protectors of these proceed from here and return hither after death.[120]

Augustine systematically denies pagan opinions which appealed to the authority of these words of Cicero. The *City of God* sets itself up in deliberate antithesis to Cicero's *De re publica*: according to the definitions which Cicero put into the mouth of Scipio, so Augustine contends, there never was a Roman *res publica*.[121] Conversely, Macrobius' *Saturnalia*,

---

   113   MACROBIUS, *Sat.*, 7.3.24: *vester Apuleius.*
   114   A. CAMERON, *JRS*, 56 (1966), 25 ff.
   115   *Sat.*, pr. 11: *nisi sicubi nos, sub alio ortos caelo, Latinae linguae vena non adiuvet.*
   116   L. JAN, in his edition, 1 (Leipzig, 1848), pp. vii ff.; K. MRAS, *Sb. Berlin*, Phil.-hist. Klasse, 1933, pp. 280 ff.
   117   For proof that the *Commentary* is the earlier work, G. WISSOWA, *De Macrobii Saturnaliorum fontibus capita tria* (Diss. Breslau, 1880), pp. 12 ff.
   118   On the culture of Macrobius, see now the enormous study of J. FLAMANT, *Macrobe et le Néo-platonisme latin, à la fin du IVe siècle* (Leiden, 1977). For his sources, W. H. STAHL, *Macrobius: Commentary on the Dream of Scipio* (New York, 1952), pp. 23 ff.; E. TÜRK, *Macrobius und die Quellen seiner Saturnalien. Eine Untersuchung über die Bildungsbestrebungen im Symmachuskreis* (Diss. Freiburg, 1961).
   119   For whom, see now P. MASTANDREA, *Un neoplatonico latino: Cornelio Labeone (Testimonianze e frammenti)* (Leiden, 1979).
   120   *Comm.*, 1.8.1 (trans. Stahl).
   121   *CD*, 19.21.

80

which takes Cicero's *De re publica* as a literary model, can be read as a reaffirmation of pagan culture and ideals against Augustine's wholesale denigration.

*
*   *

Augustine himself, and still more the index of his works drawn up by Possidius, have been responsible for a serious misunderstanding of the nature of the *City of God*, which is perpetuated by editors and translators who entitle the work "Concerning the City of God against the Pagans".[122] It is less a defence of Christianity against pagans than a protreptic addressed to them. Augustine constantly asserts that the best philosophers accept the central propositions of Christian theology. Both Plato and Porphyry are partly right: if only they had been able to discuss their disagreements, they might well have become Christians! And the central Christian doctrine of the Resurrection of the Body combines three great truths of which Plato, Porphyry and Varro each saw one: at the end of time, holy souls will return to bodies, they will return to where there is no evil, and they will return to the same bodies as before.[123]

Augustine assumes, as Plato had, that a human society mirrors the individual man writ large.[124] Just as the *Confessions* had charted the odyssey of a soul,[125] so the *City of God* charts the odyssey of human society — from God through time to God. In terms which reflect an African background, Augustine invites pagans to join the Christian church, the *civitas Dei*, on its pilgrimage through the world.

---

[122] So MIGNE (*PL*, 41.13 f.) and H. BETTENSON (Penguin, 1972). Possidius' index does not use that title, but includes *De civitate dei libri viginti duo* among Augustine's works *contra paganos* (ed. A. WILMART, *Miscellanea Agostiniana*, 2 (Rome, 1931), pp. 161 ff.).

[123] For the final statement of the theme, *CD*, 22.26-28.

[124] *CD*, 4.3.15 ff., cf. PLATO, *Rep.*, 368 d.

[125] R. J. O'CONNELL, *St. Augustine's Confessions. The Odyssey of Soul* (Harvard, 1969).

ADDENDA AND CORRIGENDA

The following supplements and corrections are deliberately brief and selective. They do not in any way to attempt to bring up to date the twenty two papers reproduced. I have deliberately refrained from giving cross-references from earlier to later papers in the volume which discuss the same problems, since the relevant passages can be located through the index and the list of contents. Similarly, I have added references to *Athanasius and Constantius. Theology and Politics in the Constantinian Empire* (Cambridge, Mass., 1993) only where it seemed indispensable in the interest of brevity.

STUDY I

The general issue of the public visibility of early Christians is well discussed by L.M. White, *Building God's House in the Roman World. Architectural Adaptation among Pagans, Jews and Christians* (Baltimore and London, 1990), 102–148.

Pages 238–241: For Celsus, Porphyry and Julian, reference should be made to the texts collected, translated and discussed in M. Stern, *Greek and Latin Writers on Jews and Judaism* (Jerusalem, 1974, 1980).

Page 239: I have now restated the case for dating Porphyry's polemic later than 300: 'Scholarship or Propaganda? Porphyry *Against the Christians* and its Historical Setting,' *Bulletin of the Institute of Classical Studies* (forthcoming).

STUDY II

On the the rain and the lightning 'miracles', which were separate episodes, see A.R. Birley, *Marcus Aurelius. A Biography*[2] (London, 1987), 171–174, 251–253.

STUDY III

For a more extreme thesis, which makes Constantine a Christian before 312, see J. Szidat, 'Konstantin 312 n. Chr. Eine Wende in seiner religiösen Überzeugung oder die Möglichkeit, diese öffentlich erkennen zu lassen und aus ihr heraus Politik zu machen?', *Gymnasium* 92 (1985), 514–525; T.G. Elliott, 'Constantine's Conversion: Do We Really Need It?, *Phoenix* 41 (1987), 420–438. Baynes's view is restated and amplified by R. Lane Fox, *Pagans and Christians* (Harmondsworth, 1986), 612–627, cf. 775, to whom I allude on pages 376 and 389.

Pages 383/4: On Lactantius, see now the edition of *On the Deaths of the Persecutors* with translation and commentary by J.L. Creed (Oxford, 1985).

STUDY V

Page 45: A date after 312 for the Council of Elvira is argued by Lane Fox, *Pagans* (1986), 664–667.

STUDY VI

Page 135: The preface to the *Itinerarium Alexandri* is edited and discussed by J.-P.Callu,'La préface à l'*Itinéraire d'Alexandre*', *De Terullien aux Mozarabes. Mélanges offerts à J.Fontaine* 1 (Paris, 1992), 429–443. Robin Lane Fox has kindly shown me the draft of an unpublished paper which not only identifies the author as Julius Valerius (as argued by Callu) but also with Polemius the consul of 338.

STUDY X

On Ulfila, see now the translation of the letter of Auxentius and the relevant passage of Philostorgius in P. Heather and J. Matthews, *The Goths in the Fourth Century* (Liverpool, 1991), 133–153 ('Life and Work of Ulfila'). They note (144 n.21) that the only other ancient evidence for Sadagolthina is an unpublished inscription reported by S. Salaville, 'Un ancien bourg de Cappadoce: Sadagolthina', *Echos d' Orient* 15 (1912), 61–63.

STUDY XIV

In answer to this article, J. Arce published a riposte, 'Constantius II Sarmaticus and Persicus: A Reply,' *ZPE* 57 (1984), 225–229. Since the issues in dispute seemed clear enough, I forbore to prolong the controversy, even though my own views have remained unchanged: see now *Athanasius* (1993), 219, 224, 310–311 n.4.

Pages 233/4: I am persuaded by W. Portmann,'Die 59. Rede des Libanios und das Datum der Schlacht von Singara', *Byzantinische Zeitschrift* 82 (1989), 1–18, that the nocturnal battle of Singara should be dated to 344 (not 348) and that Libanius delivered his panegyric of Constantius and Constans in the academic year 344/5 (not 348/9). In *Athanasius* (1993), 315–316 n.49, I have argued that Libanius was compelled to deliver the speech by the praetorian prefect Philippus when he came to deport Paul from Constantinople in the autumn of 344.

STUDY XVI

Pages 210/1: Since W. Portmann, *Byzantinische Zeitschrift* 82 (1989), 1–18, has now shown that Libanius delivered *Orat.* 59 in 344/5, his five years in Nicomedia could be 343–348 rather than 344–349.

Pages 212–220: The proconsuls of Achaea are discussed by R. von Haehling, *Die Religionszugehörigkeit der hohen Amtsträger des Römischen Reiches seit Con-*

stantins I. Alleinherrschaft bis zum Ende der Theodosianischen Dynastie (Bonn, 1978), 157–169, who makes the explicit assumption that Himerius began to teach in Athens c. 340 and hence dates Cervonius' proconsulate 'um 340', that of Hermogenes between 353 and 358.

Page 214: On the career of Musonius (2), see F. Paschoud, 'Eunapiana,' *Bonner Historia-Augusta-Colloquium 1982/1983* (1985), 239–303, at 266/7, who argues that *Suda* M 1306 (3.416 Adler) = Eunapius frag. 45.1 Müller (not included as a fragment by Blockley) implies that he had been *rationalis* of the *res privata* or *largitiones* before 362.

Pages 217/8: The discussion of *Orat.* 46. 10 should have made some reference to Alan Cameron, '*Pap. Ant.* III 115 and the Iambic Prologue in Late Greek Poetry', *CQ*, N.S. 20 (1970), 119–129, esp. 126/7. It should be noted, however, that the ὕπατε Ῥοῦφε invoked in an epigram at Tegea (*IG* 5.2.153) appears to be a local magnate rather than the proconsul: Groag, *Reichsbeamte* (1946), 58, connected the epigram with Alaric's invasion of Greece in 395/6 and deduced that the imperial reward to which it later alludes was an honorary consulate.

J.W. Leopold, 'Himerius and the Panathenaea,' *Ancient World* 12 (1985), 121–127, argues from *Orat.* 47 that the festival was rescheduled to coincide with the arrival of Basilius as proconsul.

Page 221: Goulet's chronology for Eunapius' sojourn in Athens was refuted by T.M. Banchich, 'On Goulet's Chronology of Eunapius' Life and Works', *JHS* 107 (1987), 164–167, and his arrival in Athens is now persuasively dated to autumn 361 by C.W. Fornara, 'Eunapius' *Epidemia* in Athens', *CQ*, N. S. 39 (1989), 517–523.

STUDY XX

Quite independently of my article, J. Herrin, *The Formation of Christendom* (Princeton, 1987), 60n, 66, postulated an original *Life of Antony* 'probably composed in Coptic by a monk in Antony's monastery', although she attributed the Greek version to Athanasius. My denial of Athanasius' authorship was initially accepted more widely than I had expected: the discussion of the *Life* in P. Brown, *The Body and Society. Men, Women and Sexual Renunciation in Early Christianity* (New York, 1988), 213–216, 223–226, pointedly refrains from repeating its traditional ascription and commends both Draguet and myself (213 n.1). But strong arguments have been marshalled against the priority of the Syriac version by L. Abramowski, 'Vertritt die syrische Fassung die ursprüngliche Gestalt der Vita Antonii? Eine Auseinandersetzung mit der These Draguets,' *Mélanges A. Guillaumont* (*Cahiers d'Orientalisme* 20 [Geneva, 1988]), 47–56; R. Lorenz, 'Die griechische Vita Antonii des Athanasius und ihre syrische Fassung,' *ZKG* 100 (1989) 77–84. The traditional attribution to Athanasius is reasserted by A. Louth, 'St. Athanasius and the Greek *Life of Antony*,' *JTS*, N. S. 39 (1988), 504–509; S. Rubenson, *The Letters of St. Antony. Origenist*

Theology, Monastic Tradition and the Making of a Saint (Lund, 1990), 126–144, and appears to be regaining ground: P. Brown, *Power and Persuasion in Late Antiquity. Towards a Christian Empire* (Madison, 1992), 72 n.5, now states that 'Many arguments still support the traditional ascription of the *Life of Anthony* to Athanasius'.

I remain convinced that the Greek *Life* was not written by Athanasius, for the reasons given in my review of Rubenson in *JTS*, N. S. 42 (1991), 723–732. Moreover, the earliest external reference to the *Life* seems to me to confirm my scepticism: in his *Letter to the Monks* of 362 Serapion the bishop of Thmuis and a close associate of Athanasius appeals to a series of exemplars of holiness, among them Antony 'whose life is preserved among you in writing' (*PG* 40.940: ἐξ ὑμῶν ἀββᾶ Ἀντώνιος δι' ἀκρότατον βίον γενόμενος οὗ καὶ ὁ βίος ἔγγραπτος παρ' ὑμῖν διασώζεται). No mention here of Athanasius' authorship: on the contrary, an implication that the *Life* belongs to a monastic milieu.

STUDY XXI

Pages 161, 171/2 n.19: On the finding of the cross, see now P.W.L. Walker, *Holy City, Holy Places? Christian Attitudes to Jerusalem and the Holy Land in the Fourth Century* (Oxford, 1990), 235–281; S. Borgehammar, *How the Holy Cross was Found. From Event to Medieval Legend* (Bibliotheca Theologiae Practicae/ Kyrkovetenskapliga studier 47, 1991); J.W. Drijvers, *Helena Augusta. The Mother of Constantine the Great and the Legend of Her Finding of the True Cross* (Brill's Studies in Intellectual History 27, 1992), with my review of Borgehammar and Drijvers in the *Journal of Ecclesiastical History* 44 (1993), 292–297.

INDEX

This index concentrates on the names of ancient men and women and ancient writers and sources: some geographical names are included, and a number of modern scholars whose views are explicitly assessed. The names in the lists of consuls and prefects of the period 317–361 in VII are not entered in the index unless there is a substantive discussion of their family connexions or careers, though mentions of these men elsewhere in the volume are of course registered.

Abaris: XVI 214
Abinnaeus, commander of troops in
    Egypt: XV *passim*
Abraham: XI 111
Abydenos: XI 109
Acacius, bishop of Caesarea: V 48; XII 1
Acacius, *comes*: XI 121 n.60
Achilles: VIII 336
Aconius Catullinus, cos. 349: XIII 256
Actium, battle of: III 378
Acts of John: II 473
Adrianople, battle of: I 241; XXI 168;
    XXIV 71
Aedesius: VIII 335
Aelius Aristides: I 235, 242 n.19; XVI 208n
Aegeae: VIII 325n, 326; IX 650
Aeneas: X 544
Aetius, theologian: VIII 335
Agamemnon: VIII 336
Alaric: XXIV 67, 70, 71, 72n, 75
Alcibiades: XVI 219
Alexander, bishop of Alexandria: XI 106,
    111
Alexander, bishop of Constantinople: X
    544
Alexander, of Abonuteichos: I 234
Alexander, the Great: VI 135; XI 104;
    years of: VI 128–130, 133–134
Alexander, praised by Himerius: XVI 216
Alexander, proconsul of Constantinople:
    XVI 210, 216
Alexander Polyhistor: XI 109
Alexandria: VIII 326–327; XVII 131
Ambrose: XXI 161, 163–165, 172 n.25;
    XXII *passim*; XXIII 59
Ambrosius, praetorian prefect: XIII 251,
    253; XXII 7
Ameinias, rhetor: XVI 210

Amida: VI 132n; XIV 235
Ammianus Marcellinus: I 241; XIII 249,
    255–256, 259–260; XVI 214, 217n;
    XVII 134; XVIII 256–259; XXI 164,
    168; XXII 9; XXIV 71
Amniades: XXIII 55–57
Ampelius: XVI 214, 215–216
Anastasia: XI 104
Anatolius, praetorian prefect (343/4–346):
    XIII 258; XVI 216
Anatolius, praetorian prefect (357–360):
    XIII 259; XVI 216; XVIII 259
Andreas Lopadiota: XVI 207
Andrew, apostle: II 473
Anicetus, praetorian prefect: XIII 257
Anicia Faltonia Proba: XXIV 71
Anicii: XXIII 51–59; XXIV 71
Anicius Bassus: XVI 224
Anicius Claudius: XVI 225
Anicius Faustus, cos. 298: XXIII 52–53
Anicius Paulinus, *praefectus urbi* (380):
    XVI 225
Anicius Paulinus, Sex., cos. 325: VII 3;
    XXIII 51–52, 53n, 57n
Annius Tiberianus, praetorian prefect:
    XIII 250, 251; XVIII 258 n.
Antioch: the episcopal election of 328 at:
    XI 111–112, 123 n.86; XII 6, 10
Antinous: II 473
Antoninus Verus: II 474
Antonius Marcellinus, cos. 341: XIII 251,
    255
Antonius Primus: III 377
Antony, hermit: XV 374; XX 364;
    authorship of his *Life*: XI 110;
    XX *passim*
Anullinus, proconsul of Africa (303–305):
    III 378; IX 640

Anullinus, proconsul of Africa (312–313):
    IX 646, 648; XV 374
Aphaca: VIII 325; IX 650
Aphrahat: VI; XIV 234
Aphrodite: VIII 325
Apis bull: XVI 223
Apollinaris, second century writer: II 474
Apollonius, of Tyana: I 240; IX 650; XI
    103; XXIV 73
Apphianus, martyr: IX 641
Appius Claudius Julianus, cos. II 223:
    XXIII 57
Apringius, proconsul of Africa: XXIV 73
Apronianus, *praefectus urbi* (363–364):
    XVIII 258n
Apuleius: I 233; XXIV 73, 76, 77
Arbogast: XXI 165; XXIII 60n
Arcadius, praised by Himerius: XVI 216
Arce, J.: XIV 231–235
Aristophanes: XXIV 66
Aristotle: VIII 330
Arians: XX 364; XXI 160, 164
Arius: X 544; XI 105, 106, 111, 115; XII 6,
    10
Arles: XVI 208; Council of (353/4):
    XVII 129, 131, 133, 136
Armenia: VI 131, 132, 135, 136; IX 635,
    649; XIV 230, 232
Arnobius: VIII 331
Arrian: I 235
Arsaces, king of Armenia: VI 135;
    XIV 230
Artemidorus: I 232
Artemius, *dux Aegypti*: VIII 327
Arycanda: IX 642
Asclepiodotus, *consularis* of Crete:
    XVI 224–225; XXI 160
Asclepius: VII 4; VIII 326
Asclepius: XXIV 77
Athanasius: VI 135; VII 2; VIII 332;
    XI 101, 102; XII 2; XIII 254–255;
    XV 374; XVII 131, 133, 136, 137, 140
    n.43; XVIII 256, 257, 262, 263;
    XXI 161, 164; and the *Life of Antony*:
    XX *passim*
Athenagoras: I 234
Athenaeus, praised by Himerius: XVI 215
Athens: XVI *passim*; XXI 161
Augustine: III 391; XIII 253n; XXI 157,
    168–169; XXII *passim*; XXIV *passim*;
    and the *Life of Antony*: XX 359
Augustus: III 378; IX 647; X 544
Aurelius, bishop of Carthage: XXIV 69
Aurelius Heron, deacon: XV 373
Aurelius Sakaon: XV 369

Auxentius, bishop of Durostorum:
    X 541–544
Auxentius, bishop of Milan: XXI 164
Aurelian, emperor (270–275): V 43;
    IX 635
Ausonius: XXI 161
Avienus: XXIV 78–79

Babylon: III 380; VI 132; XXIV 66–67
Baeterrae: Council of: XVII *passim*;
    XVIII 260
Basil, bishop of Caesarea: XVI 212;
    XIX 122–123
Basilius, praised by Himerius:
    XVI 217–218
Bassianus: XI 104
Bassus, men of that name in Prudentius:
    XXIII 54
Batiffol, P.: XI 97, 98; XII 1
Baynes, N. H.: III 376, 381; V 42, 48, 51,
    56 n.61; XI 97, 98; XII 1–2
Belaeus: VIII 328
Bemarchius: VIII 333–334
Bethlehem: XXIV 72n
Bible: I 238, 240; III 472–473; V 44;
    XXIV 66, 73
Bithynicus, bishop of Zela: XIX 124
Blemmyes: X 544; XI 115; XV 369–370
Bloch, H.: XXI 166
Bostra: VIII 328
Brennecke, H. C.: XVII 129–130, 138 n.7,
    140 n.44
Brown, P. R. L.: VII 1n; XI 114; XX add.;
    XXI 157, 161, 168; XXIII 51;
    XXIV 75
Bruttius Praesens: I 235
Bruun, P.: XI 96–97
Brutus, legendary consul: XXIII 53
Burckhardt, J.: V 41–42, 46, VIII 324;
    XI 121 n.70

Caecilianus, bishop of Carthage: IX 648;
    XV 374
Caesarea, in Cappadocia: VIII 327
Calama: XXIV 71
Calcidius: III 389
Callinicus: XXI 165
Calliopius, *consularis*: XVI 216, 221
Callu, J.-P.: XXIII 60
Cameron, Alan: VII 1n; XXI 157, 168
Cameron, Averil: XI 102, 114, 115–116,
    119 n.34; XXI 164
Cannae: XXIV 71
Carmen contra paganos: XXI 167–168;
    XXII 10; XXIV 69n

Carnuntum: emperors meet at (308): III 375–376; VIII 329; IX 644
Carthage: I 236, 237; XXIV
Cassius Dio: I 232; XI 109, 110
Cassius Longinus: XI 109
Ceionius Rufius Volusianus, C.: XIII 256
Celsinus Titianus: XXII 9
Celsus: I 238–239
Cervonius, proconsul of Achaea: XVI 216
Chadwick, H.: XI 94, 97; XVII 129; XXI 163
Chrestus, bishop of Syracuse: IX 648
Chromatius, bishop of Aquileia: XXIV 75
Chrysanthius: VIII 335
Chrysaorius, probable ancestor of Symmachus: XXII 9
Cicero: XXIII 50; XXIV 78–80
Cirta: I 236
Claudian: XXIII 56–57, 58, 60–61; XXIV 71
Claudius Mamertinus, cos. 363: XIII 249
Clement, of Alexandria: I 236; V 43; XXI 161
Cluvius Rufus: XI 110, 120 n.53
Codex Justinianus: IV 71–72
Colbassa: IX 642
Collectio Avellana: XVIII 260
Constans, emperor (333–350): IV 71; VIII 323, 331–332; XI 99; XII 7n, 9; XIV 230; XVI 208n, 215; XXI 159, 160, 165, 173 n.37; XXIV 68; praetorian prefects of: XIII 249–252, 255, 256–259
Constantia, wife of Orfitus: VII 10
Constantine: I 240–241; III *passim*; IV *passim*; V *passim*; VII *passim*; IX 636, 638, 642–653; XI; XIV 229, 231–235; XV 369–370, 374; XVI 219; XX 158–160, 165; XXII 9; XXIV 74; age and early career: V 40–41; VI 132; favours Christians before 312: III 379–380; V 47, 50; conversion: III 375–387; V 41–43, 51; *Speech to the Assembly of the Saints*: III 387–391; XI 96, 108, 113, 116 n.5; religious policies after 324: IV *passim*; V 49–52; VI 130–136; VIII 322–335; X 542, 544–545; XI 105, 111; XII 8–9; XXIV 68; letter to Shapur: VI 131–132; XI 100, 107, 112–113; praetorian prefects of: XIII 249–251; and Antony: XX 364
Constantinople: XI 115; XVI 206, 207, 219, 221–222

Constantinus, emperor (317–340): VI 135; XI 99; XII 7n; XIV 230, 231–232; XXI 165; praetorian prefects of: XIII 250, 251, 253
Constantius, emperor (293–306): III 373–374; V 50; IX 640; XI 99; XI 104, 119 n.42; XIV 232n; XVI 207; XVII *passim*
Constantius, emperor (324–361): I 240–241; VI 133, 135–136; VIII 325–337; XI 99; XII 7n; XIV *passim*; XV 369–372; XVI 209; XVIII 257–261; XXI 160, 165; praetorian prefects of: XIII *passim*; visit to Rome: VIII 332–333; XVIII 260; XXI 163; XXIV 68
Cornelius Labeo: XXIV 79
Cracco Ruggini, L.: XXI 166–167
Crake, J. E. A.: V 39, 53 n.2
Crepereius Madalianus: IV 71; VIII 331; XII 9; XXI 159
Crispinus, friend of Libanius: VIII 330; XII 9
Crispus, Caesar (317–326): II 471; V 46–47; IX 635, 649; XI 115
Ctesiphon: VI 129; IX 635
Cynics: I 235, 242 n.19
Cynegius, praetorian prefect: XVI 225; XXI 160; XXIV 68n
Cyprian: I 237; V 45
Cyril, of Alexandria: I 240
Cyrillus, deacon and martyr: VIII 326
Cyrus: IX 651; XI 104

Dacia: X 544; XIV 231
Dalmatius, Caesar (335–337): VI 133; XI 96, 99; XI 115; XIII 250–251; XIV 229, 231–232
Damasus: I 231; XXI 160–161, 165; XXIII 59
Daniel: I 239; VI 133–134
Decimius Germinianus: XIII 257
Decius: I 237; XVII 133
Delphi: XIII 252; XXI 158
Demetrias: XXIII 57–58n
Demophilus, bishop of Sirmium: XVIII 261
Deogratias, priest: XXIV 67
Dexippus: XI 109
Didascalia Apostolorum: V 43–44, 54–55 nn.34–39
Dio, historian: I 232; XI 109, 110
Dio Chrysostom: I 232

Diocletian: I 239–240; III 373–374;
VIII 329; IX 635–636, 638–640;
XII 7n; XIII 249n; XXI 159; XXII 8;
XXIII 53
Diodorus Siculus: XI 109
Dionysius, bishop of Alexandria: II 473;
V 44
Dionysius, bishop of Milan:
XVII 130–131, 134–135
Dionysus: XVI 217
Domitian: XXIII 54
Domitianus, praetorian prefect: XIII 256
Domitius Leontius, cos. 344: XIII 252,
253–254
Domitius Zenophilus, cos. 333: VII 4;
XIII 249n
Donatists: VII 4; IX 648; XI 106;
XXIV 65–66n, 67
Draguet, R.: XX 353–357, 360, 365
Drake, H. A.: IV 70–72; XII 8; XXI 171
n.10
Dudden, F. H.: XXI 169

'Edict of Milan': III 379n; IX 645
Egypt: VIII 331
Eleusis: mysteries of: VIII 330, 336
Eleusius, bishop of Cyzicus: VIII 326
Elliott, T. G.: XII 6n, 9–10
Elvira: canons of the Council of: V 45, 55
nn.42–48; VIII 325
Ennius: XXIII 56
Ephesus: VIII 335
Epictetus: I 235
Epicureans: I 234
Epiphanius: VII 2
Errington, R. M.: XII 8–9
Eudoxius, bishop of Antioch: XIX 123
Eugenius: XXI 166; XXII 10; XXIII 60;
XXIV 69
Euhemerus: VIII 336
Eunapius: I 241; V 40; VI 132n; VIII 325n;
XIII 249; XVI 208n, 220–221, 225,
add.; XXI 168; XXIV 71n
Eusebius, bishop of Caesarea: I 237–238;
IX passim; XXI 161, 171–172 n.19; on
Constantine: III 384–385; V 40, 41–42,
47–50; VI 131; VIII 323, 325; IX 643,
646–653; X 544; XI; XXI 159;
Martyrs of Palestine: I 237;
II 470–471; IX 637, 639, 641, 653n;
XI 110; Ecclesiastical History:
II passim; III 384; IX 642–643,
647–648, 650, 653n5; XI 106, 107,
113–114; XXIV 75; Chronicle: II 472;
IX 650; XI 109; Defence of Origen:

II 474; Life of Constantine:
III 384–387; IV passim; VI 131 n.;
VIII 323–324, 329; IX 637–638,
649–650; XI passim; XII passim;
Panegyric on Constantine: IV 71; V 53
n.7; IX 637, 652–653, 657 n.61; XI 96,
101–102; XII 6; Commentary on
Isaiah: V 51; IX 638, 651–653,
656–657 nn.56–60; XI 113; Theophany:
IX 650; XII 6; Treatise on the Church
of the Holy Sepulchre: XI 96, 101–102;
works against Marcellus of Ancyra:
XI 102; Preparation for the Gospel:
XI 108–109; XXIV 65
Eusebius, bishop of Nicomedia and
Constantinople: X 542; XIX passim
Eusebius, bishop of Vercellae:
XVII 130–131
Eusebius, philosopher: VIII 335
Eustathius, bishop of Antioch: XI 115
Eustathius, bishop of Sebasteia: XIX passim
Eustathius, praefectus praetorio et urbis:
XIII 258
Eutropius: XI 119 n.42
Euzoius: XI 115; XII 6
Evagrius, praetorian prefect: XIII 249n
Expositio totius mundi et gentium: VIII
330–331

Fabius Rusticus: XI 110
Fabius Titianus, cos. 337: XIII 252, 256
Favonius Eulogius: XXIV 78, 79
Feder, A.: XVII 129, 138 n.5;
XVIII 262–264
Feissel, D.: XIII 250
Felix, bishop of Rome: XVIII 260
Felix, praetorian prefect: XIII 250;
XVI 217
Festugière, A.-J.: XX 361
Festus: XIV 234
Fiey, J. M.: VI 127–128
Firmicus Maternus: V 50; VIII 331–332;
XXI 159, 171 n.9; XXIV 68
Firmilianus, governor of Palestine: IX 641
Firmus, friend of Augustine: XXIV 65
Flacillus, bishop of Antioch: XI 102
Flavianus, proconsul of Asia (383/4):
XVI 208, 213–214, 224–225; XXI 160
Flavius Abinnaeus: XV passim
Flavius Ablabius, cos. 331: XIII 249n,
250–251
Flavius Amantius, cos. 345: VII 5
Flavius Bonosus, cos. 345: VII 5
Flavius Domitius Leontius, cos. 344:
XIII 252, 253–254

Flavius Eugenius, *ex praefecto praetorio*: XIII 253n
Flavius Felicianus, priest of Apollo at Delphi: XIII 252
Flavius Florentius, cos. 361: XIII 257, 259
Flavius Hypatius, cos. 359: XVI 225
Flavius Julius Sallustius, cos. 344: VII 5
Flavius Lollianus, cos. 355: VII 6–7; XIII 259
Flavius Marcellinus: XXIV 65–66, 73
Flavius Nigrinianus, cos. 350: VII 5
Flavius Philippus, cos. 348: VIII 334; XIII 251, 254–255; XIV add.; XVI 211
Flavius Romulus, cos. 343: VII 5
Flavius Sallustius, cos. 363: XIII 257
Flavius Taurus, cos. 361: VIII 332; XIII 258
Florus, *praeses* of Numidia (303): III 378; IX 640
Franchi de' Cavalieri, P.: XII 11
Frigidus, battle of: XXI 166, 168; XXIV 70
Fronto: I 233–234, 236
Fructuosus, martyr: I 237
Furius Maecius Gracchus: XXIII 55, 59
Furius Placidus, cos. 343: XIII 252, 255, 257; XXIII 55

Gabinius Barbarus Pompeianus: XXI 167; XXIV 69n, 70
Galen: I 235–236
Galerius: III 373–375, 377, 389–390; VI 131; VIII 329; IX 635–636, 638–641, 643–645; XI 99; XII 7n; XVII 133; intensifies persecution in 305: V 47, 55 n.53; VI 134; IX 640
Galilaean, as sobriquet for Christians: I 235, 240–241
Galla, wife of Theodosius: XXI 162; XXII 10
Gallienus: IX 638
Gallus, Caesar (351–354): VIII 335; XIII 251, 255–256; XVI 209, 219
Gangra: Council of: XIX *passim*
Gaudentius, *comes*: XXIV 68
Gaza: VIII 326
Gelasius, of Caesarea: XXIV 75
Gennadius: VI 126n
George, bishop of Alexandria: VIII 326–327
Gibbon, Edward: I 241; VIII 324
Gorgonius, correspondent of Libanius: XVI 212
Gortyn: XVI 224–225

Goths: VI 131; X *passim*; XI 105; XXIV 71
Gracchus, *praefectus urbi*: XXIII 55, 59
Grant, R. M.: II 471–474; IX 655 n.38
Gratian, emperor (367–383): XXI 161–162, 163; XXIV 69, 74
Grégoire, H.: XI 96, 97
Gregory, bishop of Alexandria (339–345): XI 102; XV 374; XVII 131
Gregory, of Nazianzus: V 55 n.53; IX 640; XVI 212; XX 359

Habicht, C.: XI 96
Hadrian: IX 652
Haehling, R. von: VII 1–2
Hannibal: XXIV 71
Hannibalianus: VI 132
Harnack, A.: I 239
Harries, J.: XXIII 60, 61
Hegesippus: II 472 n.473
Heikel: I., XI 97
Helena, mother of Constantine: XI 100, 104; XII 5, 7n; XXI 161, 171 n.19
Heliodorus: XX 362
Heliopolis: VIII 325n, 326
Hellenism: VIII 326, 327
Helpidius, praetorian prefect: XIII 260
Hegesippus: II 472, 473
Heraclianus, rebel in Africa: XXIV 66n
Hercules: staues of: XXIV 70, 71
Hermogenes, praised by Himerius: VII 9; VIII 335; XVI 218–220, 222, 224
Hermogenes, general lynched in Constantinople: XVI 210
Hermogenes, *praefectus praetorio et urbis*: VII 8; XIII 258
Hermogenes, praetorian prefect (358–360): XIII 259
Herodian: XI 109
Herodotus: XI 109
Hierocles, anti-Christian writer: I 240; II 472n
Hilarius, deacon: XVII 137
Hilary, bishop of Poitiers: XVII *passim*; XVIII 256, 260–265
Himerius: VIII 337; XI 115, 122 n.81; XVI *passim*; XXI 160
Historia Augusta: I 231
Honoratus: XIII 257; XVI 213
Honorius, emperor (393–423): XXIII 56; XXIV 70
Horace: XXIII 56
Hormizd, brother of Shapur: VI 131n
Hypatius, bishop: XIX 124n

Iamblichus: VIII 334–335; XVI 218n; XX 361; XXIV 76–77
Iberia: VI 132
Ibycus: XVI 206
Ilium: VIII 336
Innocentius, bishop of Rome: XXIV 70
Itinerarium Alexandri: VI 135; XV 370
Irenaeus: II 473
Isaiah: IX 651–653
Isocrates: XII 3; XVI 216

Jacob, bishop of Nisibis: VI 126, 133n
James, apostle: II 472
Jerome: VI 133; IX 651, 655 n.24; X 541; XVII 134, 138 n.10; XX 358–359; XXIII 55
Jerusalem: II 472; IX 651–652
Jesus: I 231, 233, 234–235, 240–241; V 44; IX 651–652; non-canonical saying of: VI 134
Jews: I 237, 238; VI 127; IX 651–652; XI 115, 122 n.79; XXI 162, 165
John, evangelist: II 473
John, the Lydian: XIII 251
Jones, A. H. M.: III 384, 386; V 42, 49, 51; XI 96
Josephus: XI 110, 120 n.53
Jovian, emperor (363–364): XXI 160; XXIV 68, 74
Jovius, *comes*: XXIV 68
Jovius, *quaestor sacri palatii*: XVI 219–220
Julia Mammaea: I 236; V 43
Julian, emperor (360–363): I 240–241; VIII 325–327, 335–337; XI 122 n.81; XIV 231, 233; XVI 206, 207, 209, 212, 216, 221–223; XVII 130, 136; XXI 160, 163, 164; XXII 9; XXIV 68
Julianus, correspondent of Iamblichus: VIII 334–335
Julianus, cos. 325: VII 6; VIII 334
Julius Africanus: XI 109
Julius Valerius: VI 135
Junius Bassus, cos. 331: VII 3; XIII 249n
Jupiter: VII 6; XXI 166; XXIV 70, 76
Justin: I 238, 239; XXI 161
Justina: XXI 164; XXII 10
Juvenal: I 232; XXIII 54

Kee, A.: III 376; V 40, 53 n.7
Keil, B.: XVI 207–208

Labarum: III 385, 387; V 42; IX 646
Lactantius: III 379–384, 389; V 41, 46–47, 50; IX 635, 638, 642–644, 653 n.2, 655 nn.33–38

Laeta: XXIII 59
Lane Fox, R.: III 376, 389, add.; VI add.; VIII 322, 324, 325n; IX 656 n.42; XI 116–117 n.5
Leo, F.: XI 103–104
Leontius, *praefectus urbi*: XVII 134; XVIII 256, 257–259
Libanius: IV 71–72; VIII 324, 328–330, 334, 335; XI 119 n.42; XII 3n, 9; XIV 233; XVI 208n, 210–212, add.
Liber Pontificalis: IX 646; XVIII 257
Liberius, bishop of Rome: XVII 134; XVIII *passim*
Licinius: III 375–377; IV 68; V 42, 49, 50, 52, 57 n.79; VI 131; VIII 322–323, 333–335; IX 637, 642–649; XI 106–107, 123 n.86; XII 7; XV 370; XVI 219
Life of Antony: XI 110; XX *passim*
Limenius, cos. 349: VII 8; XIII 258; XVI 210
Lucian, of Antioch: III 380; V 41; IX 642; XVI 208n
Lucian, satirist: I 234–235; XVI 208n
Lucifer, bishop of Caralis: XVII 130–131, 137, 140 n.43
Lucilius: XXIII 56
Lucius Verus: II 473–474
Lucretia: XXIV 74n
Lucretius: XXIII 56
Lyon: martyrs of: I 234, 237; II 473–474

Macarius, bishop of Jerusalem: XI 111, 112, 120–121 n.59; XII 5; XXI 161, 171–172 n.19
Macarius, of Magnesia: I 239
Macrobius: XXI 157; XXIV 78–80
Maecilius Hilarianus, cos. 332: XIII 258
Maecius Memmius Furius Baburius Caecilianus Placidus, M.: XIII 252, 255, 257; XXIII 55
Magnentius: XIII 254–255, 257; XIV 235; XVI 211, 216
Magnillus: XXII 10
Magnus Maximus, emperor (383–388): XXI 162–163; XXII 10–11; XXIII 60; XXIV 69
Maiorinus, praetorian prefect: XIII 255
Mamre: oak of: XI 111
Mani: VI 136
Marcellina, sister of Ambrose: XXII 8
Marcellinus, *tribunus et notarius*: XXIV 65–66, 73
Marcellinus, possible ancestors of Ambrose named: XXII 8

Marcellus, bishop of Ancyra: IX 657 n.61;
X 544; XI 102, 115; XVII 133
Marcianus, magistrate under a usurper:
XXII 10–11
Marcus Aurelius: I 233–234, 235, 242 n.21;
II 473–474; XXIV 66n
Maria, bride of Honorius: XXIII 56
Marianus, *notarius*: XI 112, 113, 120 n.58,
121 n.64
Marianus and Jacobus, martyrs: I 237
Marcionites: XII 10
Marius: XXIII 50; XXIV 71
Marius Victorinus: XXI 161; XXIV 77
Mark, bishop of Arethusa: VIII 326, 328;
XXI 159
Markus, R. A.: XXI 168
Martial: I 232
Martianus Capella: XXIV 77
Martin, bishop of Tours: VIII 325; XI 110;
XXI 163
Maternus Cynegius: XVI 225; XXI 160;
XXIV 68n
Matthews, J. F.: XVIII 257; XXI 158, 166,
167
Maurice, J.: XI 97, 98
Maxentius: III 373–378, 380; V 42–43, 47;
IX 636, 640, 641, 644, 646; XI 106;
XII 7n
Maximian, emperor (285–305):
III 373–374, 378; IX 636, 640, 644;
XI 104; XII 7n
Maximinus, author: X 541–544
Maximinus, emperor (305–311): II 470;
III 374–375, 377, 380, 389–390;
IX 640–645, 647; XI 99; XII 7n;
XV 370
Maximus, philosopher: XVI 222
Maximus, *praefectus urbi* (361–363):
XVI 217, 218
Melas: rivers of that name:
XVI 222–223
Melitians: XI 100, 105
Melitene: council of bishops at:
XIX 122–123
Memmius Vitrasius Orfitus: VII 10;
XVIII 257–259
Memnon: colossus of: XVI 223
Menander: rhetorical handbooks attributed
to: XI 98, 104; XII 2–3
Metrodorus: VI 132
Milan: XXI 164; XXII 7, 11; alleged edict
of: III 379n; IX 645; Council of (345):
XVIII 264; Council of (355):
XVII *passim*; XVIII 257, 259–260
Miltiades, bishop of Rome: IX 648

Milvian Bridge, battle of: III 376–378,
382–387; V 42, 47, 51, 55 n.56; IX 646
Minucianus: XVI 222
Minucius Felix: I 236; V 45
Mithras: VIII 326, 329; XVI 221–222;
XXIII 55
Mitchell, S.: IX 655 nn.30, 31, 35
Momigliano, A.: XI 114
Mommsen, T.: XXI 167, 174 n.45
Montanists: XII 10; XVII 132, 133
Montanus and Lucius, martyrs: I 237
Montius Magnus: XIII 251, 255
Moses: XI 104
Mucianus, i.e., Licinius Mucianus, cos.
III 72: III 377
Musonius, proconsul of Achaea: XVI 214,
220
Musonius, *vicarius*: XVI 214, 220, 221
Musonius Rufus: XVI 222

Naissus: XI 104
Napoleon: V 42
Narnia: XXIV 70
Narses, Persian prince: VI 132; XIV 235
Nebridius, praetorian prefect: XIII 257
Nebuchadnezzar: IX 651
Nepotianus, usurper in Rome (350):
XIII 257
Nero: I 231, 233; XI 109–110, 120 n.53;
XVII 132–133
Nestorius, hierophant at Eleusis: VIII 336
Nestorius, prefect of Egypt: XV 372
Nestorius Timonianus: XIII 250
Nevitta, cos. 362: XXII 9
Nicagoras, of Athens: XVI 222
Nicaea: Council of: XI 100, 105–106, 111;
XII 10; application of its canons:
XVII 135; XIX 124; XXI 163
Nicomachus Flavianus, cos. 394:
XXI 166–168, 174 n.47; XXIV 69
Nicomachus Flavianus, proconsul of Asia
(383/4): XVI 208, 213–214, 224–225;
XXI 160
Nicomedia: IX 642, 646; XVI 210–212
Nile: XVI 223
Nisibis: VI 133, 135
Novatianists: XII 10
Nunechius, praetorian prefect: XIII 255
Numenius: III 390
Nymphidianus: XVI 220

Octavian: III 378
Olybrius, cos. 379: XXIII 53, 59
Olybrius, cos. 395: XXIII 55–57, 61
Olympiodorus: XXIV 70n, 71n

Opitz, H.-G.: XVIII 257n
Oribasius: VIII 336
Origen: I 236, 237–239; II 474; V 43;
    IX 651; XXI 161
Origo Constantini Imperatoris: III 375;
    V 54 n.21
Orion, friend of Libanius: VIII 328–329
Ossius, bishop of Corduba: III 389; V 45,
    55 n.47; XI 120 n.58
Otacilia Severa: I 236
Ovinius Gallicanus, cos. 317: XXI 164;
    XXIII 52

Pachomius: XV 370
Pamphilus: XI 106
Panegyrici Latini: III 382; V 40, 42, 53
    n.12
Papa, Persian *catholicos*: VI 127
Papias: II 472, 473
Papius Pacatianus, L., cos 332: XIII 249n,
    250–251
Pasquali, Giorgio: IV 69; V 48, 56 n.1;
    XI 97–102, 110, 115–116; XII 1–2
Passover: V 44
Paul, apostle: III 391; XXIV 66
Paul, bishop of Constantinople: X 542;
    XIII 254; XIV add.; XVI 210
Paul, of Samosata: V 43; IX 635
Paulianists: XII 10
Paulinus, biographer of Ambrose: XIII 251
Paulinus, bishop of Trier: XVII 130–133,
    134
Paulinus: men of that name in Prudentius:
    XXIII 54, 59
Paulinus, of Nola: XXIII 54
Peeters, P.: XX 368
Pegasius, bishop of Ilium: VIII 336
Pegasus, *praefectus urbi*: XXIII 54
Pelagius: XXIV 67
Peregrinus: I 234–235
Pergamum: VIII 335
Persia: VI *passim*; XIV 230, 233–235
Peter, bishop of Alexandria: IX 642;
    XXI 160–161
Peter Valvomeres: XVIII 256
Petronius Probianus, cos. 322: VII 3
Petronius Probus, cos. 371: VII 1n;
    XVI 225; XXIII 51, 57; his children:
    XXIII 55–58
Phalaris: XVI 218n
Phasganius, uncle of Libanius: VIII 329
Philagrius, prefect of Egypt: XVII 131
Philetus, bishop of Juliopolis: XIX 124
Philip, emperor (244–249): I 236;
    VI 133–134

Philippus, Asiarch: I 237
Philippus, praetorian prefect: VIII 334;
    XIII 251, 254–255; XIV add.;
    XVI 211
Philo: XI 119 n.36; XXI 161
Philo, of Byblos: I 239; XI 109
Philostorgius: X 541–544
Philostratus: XI 103
Phlegon, of Tralles: XI 109
Photinus, bishop of Sirmium: XVII 133;
    XVIII 259
Photius: XVI 206–207, 212–220
Piazza Armerina: VII 6n
Piganiol, A.: XXI 169
Plato: I 238; III 389, 390; V 48; XI 108;
    XXIV 76, 78, 80
Platonism: I 238; XI 108; XXI 161;
    XXIV 76–78
Pliny: I 232–233
Pliny, the Elder: XI 110
Plocianus, praised by Himerius: XVI 220
Plotinus: I 240; XXI 161; XXIV 76–78
Plutarch: I 232; XVI 222
Pollentia: battle of: XXIII 59; XXIV 71
Polybius: XI 109; XII 3
Polycarp: I 237
Pompeianus, *praefectus urbi* (408/409):
    XXI 167; XXIV 69n, 70
Pompeianus, governor of Bithynia:
    XVI 211–212, 220
Ponticianus: XX 359
Pontius Pilate: I 233
Pontus: IX 649
Porfyrius, poet: VI 131
Porphyry: I 238–240, 243 n.32; VIII 330;
    XI 109; XVI 218n; XX 361; XXI 166;
    XXII 9; XXIV 76–78, 79, 80
Praetextatus, cos. des. 385: I 231; XVI 220,
    225; XXI 165–167; XXII 10, 13 n.26
Praxagoras, historian: VIII 333; XI 119
    n.42
Priscillian: XXI 162–163, 173 nn.27–30
Priscus, philosopher: VIII 336
Proaeresius, bishop of Sinope: XIX 124
Proaeresius, Christian rhetor: VIII 330;
    XVI 208, 221
Proba, alleged betrayer of Rome:
    XXIV 71
Proba, author of Virgilian cento:
    XXI 167–168
Probinus, cos. 395: XXIII 55–57, 61
Proculus, cos. 325: VII 5; VIII 334
'Protonice': XXI 161
Prudentius: IX 655 n.24; XXI 166;
    XXIII; XXIV 71

Publilius Optatianus Porfyrius: VI 131
Pythagoras: XVI 218–219; XX 361

*Quae gesta sunt inter Liberium et Felicem
episcopos*: XVIII 260
Quirinus, bishop of Siscia: IX 654 n.21,
655 n.24

Radagaisus: XXIV 71
Regulus: XXIV 73
Reitzenstein, R.: XX 361
Revelation: II 472–473
Rhodanius, bishop of Toulouse:
XVII 134–136, 139 nn.30–32
Rocher, A.: XVII 132, 139 n.10
Romanus, deacon and martyr: IX 639
Rome: church of: V 44; IX 646; XXIII 52;
sack of: XXIV 70–74
Rougé, J.: III 383–384
Rufinus, ecclesiastical historian: III 383;
XVII 134; XXIV 75
Rufinus, son of Himerius: XVI 222
Rufius Antonius Agrypnius Volusianus:
XXIV 72, 77, 78
Rutilius Namatianus: XXIV 66

Sabinus, bishop of Heraclea: XIX 123
Sabinus, praetorian prefect: IX 641
Sadagolthina: X 544, add.
Salutius Secundus, praetorian prefect:
XIII 249; XVI 216–217
Sappho: XVI 206
Sappo, *dux limitis Scythici*: XIV 230, 232
Sarmatians: VI 131; XI 105; XIV 230–231
Saturninus, bishop of Arles: XVII
130–131, 136, 140 n.40
Satyrus, brother of Ambrose: XXII 8–9
Scapula, proconsul of Africa (212/3): I 236;
V 43
Schrörs, H.: III 381
Schulthess, F.: XX 354–355, 360, 364
Scylacius: XVI 215
Seleucid era: VI 128–130, 133–134
Seleucia, on the Tigris, council of bishops
at: VI 127–128
Seneca: XXIV 66n
Septimius Acindynus, cos. 340: XIII 253
Septimius Severus: VI 133–134; IX 647
Serapion, bishop of Thmuis: XX 366–367,
add.
Serapis, cult of: VIII 325n, 331; XXI 160
Severus, cos. 323: VII 2–3
Severus, emperor (305–307): IX 636
Severus, praised by Himerius:
XVI 212–213, 222

Severus Alexander: I 231
Sextus, of Chaeronea: XVI 222
Shanzer, D. R.: XXIII 60–61
Shapur, king of Persia (?309–379):
VI 128–129, 131–136; receives letter
from Constantine: VI 131–132;
XI 100, 107, 112–113
Sibylline books: XXIV 71
Sibylline Oracles: III 389
Silius Italicus: III 387
Silvanus, *magister militum*: XIII 254
Simeon, bishop of Seleucia/Ctesiphon:
VI 129
Singara: battles near: XIV 234, add.
Sirmium: assemblies of bishops at:
XVII 136; XVIII 260–261;
'blasphemy' of: XVIII 261, 265
Smulders, P.: XVII 132, 137
Smyrna: I 237
Socrates: XVI 219
Socrates, ecclesiastical historian: VIII 326;
XIII 251, 254; XIX 123
Sol Invictus: V 50
Solmsen, F.: XXIII 60
Sopater: VIII 334, 335n
Sossianus Hierocles: I 240; II 472n
Soteris, martyr and relative of Ambrose:
XXII 8
Sozomenus: IV 71–72; VIII 327; XVII 134;
XIX 122–123; XX 364
Stilico: XXIV 71
Strategius Musonianus: XIII 259; XVI 211,
220
Suetonius: I 233; XI 103, 110
Sufetula: XXIV 71
Sulpicius Severus: XI 110; XVII 134;
XXI 163
Superius, *consularis* of Byzacena: XXIV 78
Symmachus, cos. 330: XXII 9
Symmachus, *praefectus urbi* (364/5):
XXII 8
Symmachus, *praefectus urbi* (384/5):
XXI 162, 164, 165–167; XXII; XXIII
59–61; XXIV 69, 70
Syrianus, *dux*: XVII 131

Tacitus: I 233; XI 110; XVII 133
Tartiglia, L.: XII 11
Taurus, praetorian prefect: VIII 332;
XIII 258
Tertullian: I 236, 237; II 474; V 43, 54
n.35; VIII 331; XXIII 51
Tetz, M.: XX 365, 366–367
Thalassius, praetorian prefect: XIII 251,
255–256

Themistius: VIII 330, 334, 337
Theodoretus, ecclesiastical historian:
    XVIII 260; XXI 161, 172 n.21
Theodorus, bishop of Heraclea:
    XVIII 261
Theodosian Code: IV 71–72; XI 122 nn.78,
    79; XVIII 258–259
Theodosius, emperor (379–395): X 542;
    XXI passim; XXIII 50–51, 59–61;
    XXIV 68–70, 72, 74–75
Theodosius, father of the emperor:
    XXI 162
Theodulus, friend of Libanius: VIII 329n
Theophanes: XIV 235
Theotecnus: IX 647
Thessalonica: XXI 165
Thucydides: XI 109
Titus, emperor: II 472
Trajan: I 232–233; VI 132, 135; X 544
Trier: XVI 208
Tyconius: XXIV 66–67
Tyre: IX 642, 648

Ulfila: X passim
Ulpius Limenius, cos. 349: VII 8; XIII 258;
    XVI 210
Ursacius, bishop of Singidunum:
    XVII 130, 136; XVIII 262–264
Ursacius, praised by Himerius: XVI 214

Valacius, dux et comes in Egypt:
    XV 371–373, 374
Valens, bishop of Mursa: XVII 130, 136;
    XVIII 262–264
Valens, emperor (364–378): VIII 335;
    XVI 220; XXI 160; XXIV 71
Valentinian, emperor (364–375): XXI 160,
    161, 163; XXIV 68
Valentinian, emperor (375–392): XXI 162,
    164, 165; XXII 10, 11; XXIV 69
Valentinians: XII 10; XXI 165
Valerian, emperor: I 237; VI 131

Valerius, comes: VII 6n
Valerius Felix: XIII 250; XVI 217
Valerius Florus, praeses of Numidia (303):
    III 378; IX 640
Valerius Maximus: different men with
    these names: VII 4, 10; XIII 249n;
    XVI 217–218
Valerius Proculus, cos. 325: VII 5;
    VIII 334
Valerius Proculus, cos. 340: VII 6, 10;
    XI 122 n.76; XIV 229–230
Valerius Severus: XVI 224–225
Varro: XXIV 76, 79, 80
Vegetius: XXIV 71
Verona: battle of: XXIII 59–60n
Vespasian: IX 652
Vesta: XXII 166
Vetranio: XVI 211
Vettius Agorius Praetextatus: I 231;
    XVI 220, 225; XXI 165–167; XXII 10,
    13 n.26
Vettius Probianus: XVI 225
Victor, son of Magnus Maximus: XXIII 60
Victory, altar of: VIII 332–333;
    XXI 163–164, 166; XXII 9; XXIII 59;
    XXIV 69, 70
Virgil: III 389, 390; X 544; XXIII 56;
    XXIV 79
Volusianus, coorespondent of Augustine:
    XXIV 72–73, 77, 78
Vulcacius Rufinus, cos. 347: VII 6;
    XIII 256, 257, 259

Wilamowitz-Moellendorf, U. von:
    XI 102–103; XII 3
Winkelmann, F.: XI 96–98; XII 2, 11

Xenophon: XI 104, 109; XII 3

Zeno, bishop of Verona: XII 8–9
Zosimus: I 241; V 40, 54 n.21; XIII 249;
    XXIV 70